Ruth Royce

Historical Sketch of the State Normal School at San José, California

With a catalogue of its graduates and a record of their work for twenty-seven years

Ruth Royce

Historical Sketch of the State Normal School at San José, California
With a catalogue of its graduates and a record of their work for twenty-seven years

ISBN/EAN: 9783337096892

Printed in Europe, USA, Canada, Australia, Japan

Cover: Foto ©ninafisch / pixelio.de

More available books at **www.hansebooks.com**

HISTORICAL SKETCH

OF THE

STATE NORMAL SCHOOL

AT

SAN JOSÉ, CALIFORNIA,

WITH A

CATALOGUE OF ITS GRADUATES AND A RECORD OF THEIR WORK FOR TWENTY-SEVEN YEARS.

SACRAMENTO.
STATE OFFICE : : : : : : J. D. YOUNG, SUPT. STATE PRINTING.
1889.

First Normal School Building, San José, Cal. Burned February 10, 1880.

Present Normal School Building, San José, Cal. Erected 1880-81.

TABLE OF CONTENTS.

	PAGE.
Preface	5
Introduction	7
Historical Sketch, with Reminiscences by Graduates	9
Statistical Tables	102
Members of the Boards of Trustees	106
Biographical Sketches of Principals	108
List of Teachers	123
Alphabetical List of Graduates	130
Holders of Elementary Diplomas	145
Graduates' Record	148
Prospectus for 1889-90	283

such a history required more time than was given in the circular, and the sketch was, therefore, retained here. It was thought, following the lead of some of the older schools, that the history might be issued at the expiration of the first twenty-five years of the School's existence, but the large number of graduates, scattered over so large a State, made it impossible to collect, in so short a time, any accurate record of their work. For six years past information has been gradually, yet diligently, collected, and even now the work is not complete. It is, however, thought best no longer to delay the publication.

Few who read these pages will appreciate the amount of labor expended in collecting and arranging the facts herein contained. In the catalogues of the school for the past five years, in circulars, and personal letters, information has been sought in all directions. To most of the circulars and letters courteous responses have been received, and thanks are due to many for their lively interest in the history and their willing contributions to it.

It is now presented, containing all the attainable information, from reliable sources, and it is sincerely hoped that the work will prove satisfactory. If the good that results from the publication is at all commensurate with the labor that has been bestowed upon it, it will prove indeed valuable as a contribution to the educational history of California.

It is but just to state, that almost the entire labor of collecting, arranging, preparing statistical tables, in short of editing the work, has been done by Miss Ruth Royce, a graduate of the school, and if the history proves at all valuable, the credit belongs to her.

With sincere and ardent hopes for the highest prosperity of the Normal School at San José, I for the last time sign myself,

      Sincerely,

        CHAS. H. ALLEN, Principal.

SAN JOSÉ, June 30, **1889.**

INTRODUCTION.

In an address before the California State Teachers' Institute, in May, 1863, Mr. Samuel I. C. Swezey* gave the following eloquent account of the founding of the first Normal School in the United States:

> On the third day of July, eighteen hundred and thirty-nine, the first American Normal School was opened, at Lexington, Massachusetts. The place and the time were fittingly chosen. The *place* was where the opening battle of the Revolution was fought, when it first became clear that freedom was to be secured for this great land where we dwell, and that henceforth the people were to be trusted with power for evermore. It was fitting that there, also, should first be formally commenced the special preparation of teachers for the work of teaching humbly and teaching well in the public schools of the State which that battle ground had proven worthy to be free. It was a fitting *time* for the commencement of such a work—the day before the anniversary of American Independence—shadowing forth, with a wisdom greater than the founders of that Normal School designed, the great fact that before a people can hope to be fully free, before they are worthy of the exalted privilege of ruling themselves, they must be taught aright. The *Third* of July must ever come before the *Fourth*.

At the time that the first State Normal School in California was opened, July, 1862, but eight out of the thirty-four States belonging to the Union had established State Normal Schools. These schools numbered fourteen in all, distributed, in order of the date of opening, as follows: Massachusetts, four, New York, two, Pennsylvania, three, Connecticut, one, Michigan, one, New Jersey, one, Illinois, one, and Minnesota, one. Besides these, Philadelphia, Boston, and St. Louis each had a flourishing City Normal School.

It is a matter of some educational interest, though perhaps only as a curiosity, that as early as 1836 there existed in California a school dignified by the title of "Normal School." Of this insti-

---

*Mr. Swezey was a graduate of the State Normal School at Albany, New York, class of 1850. He taught several years, was prominent in educational interests in California, and was for four years a Trustee of the California State Normal School.

tution, **Mr. Henry L.** Oak, Librarian of the **Bancroft Historical Library,** furnishes the following sketch:

Among the colonists who came to California from the City of Mexico in 1834, were half a dozen **teachers.** There was **need** enough for their services here at the time, but no opportunity whatever **to earn a** livelihood by their profession. Therefore, **most** of them, **like many** of other professions in the colony, soon **left the country.** Some remained, however, **one of** the number being **now a prominent** citizen of **Southern** California. **Another, José** Mariano **Romero,** attempted to found an educational establishment at the Capital, Monterey, giving it the somewhat absurd title of "Normal School." He obtained a few pupils, and even went so far as to publish a text-book, a little treatise on orthoëpy, or "orthology," dedicated to the "Alumni" of his institution. The title is as follows: *Catecismo de Ortologéa. Dedicado á los Alumnos de la Escuela Normal de Monterey por su Director, José Mariano Romero. Monterey, 1836. Imprenta del C. Agust V. Zamorano. 18 mo.** This work **is** preserved among the treasures of the Bancroft Library **in San** Francisco. **Don** José failed to achieve success; and, becoming implicated **in** a revolution, **was** soon banished from California. But the first Normal School and the first text-book merit prominent notice in **the educational annals of** our country.

*Catechism of Orthoepy. Dedicated to the Alumni of the Normal School in Monterey, by its President, José Mariano Romero. Monterey, 1836. Printing office of August V. Zamorano.

HISTORICAL SKETCH.

ORIGIN OF THE SCHOOL

The necessity for the establishment of a State Normal School in California was first urged by a few gentlemen of San Francisco, who were prominent in forwarding the educational interests of the State during its early history. Among the most active of these, were State Superintendent Andrew J. Moulder, his successor, Mr. John Swett, and City Superintendent Henry B. Janes.

By the earnest efforts of these gentlemen, a City Normal School was established in San Francisco in 1857, with George W. Minns as Principal, and John Swett, Ellis H. Holmes, and Thomas S. Myrick assistants. This was known as the "Minns' Evening Normal School." The sessions of the school were held weekly, on Monday evenings, and the attendance of city teachers was made compulsory. Superintendent Janes, in his reports of 1857 and 1858, reported favorably on the success and efficiency of the City Normal School. This school was continued until 1862, its graduates numbering fifty-four.

In his annual school report of 1859, State Superintendent Moulder recommended the establishment of a State Normal School, and in 1860 repeated the recommendation, but both of the succeeding Legislatures adjourned without action. Mr. Moulder writes: "When I appealed personally to the members of the Legislature at that early day, to pass the law organizing the school, not a few of them admitted that they did not know what a Normal School was. It was several years after I recommended the measure before legislators could be educated up to a knowledge and appreciation of the value of such an institution."

During the session of the first California State Teachers' Institute, held in San Francisco in May, 1861, a committee, consisting of Henry B. Janes, Geo. W. Minns, and Ellis H. Holmes, was appointed to examine and report upon the subject of Normal Schools. In conformity with their instructions, they addressed the following communication to the State Superintendent:

Hon. A. J. MOULDER, *Superintendent of Public Instruction:*

SIR: The undersigned were appointed a committee upon a State Normal School by the recent Educational Convention.

In part performance of the duty thus devolved upon us, we desire, through you, to present to the next Legislature some considerations favoring the establishment of such a school, and respectfully solicit your coöperation with us. In so doing, we are actuated by the opinion that such a measure would do much to advance the educational interests of this State, and that while it is deferred, our public school system will fail to secure to us the greatest benefits of education, or the largest return for the money expended in its support.

In a Normal School the principles of teaching are considered both as a science and an art. Its subjects are the powers, capacities, and laws of growth of the mind; the order, as to time, in which the different faculties are to be addressed and developed; the best modes of their development; the special adaptation of each school study to the particular necessities and faculties of the juvenile mind; the laws of bodily health as to ventilation, posture, school calisthenics and gymnastics; and the moral natures of children. It also considers the best methods of school organization, classification, programmes of daily exercises, and modes of teaching, as exemplified in the best systems and best schools in the world; and the knowledge so acquired is practically applied in the model or experimental school (a necessary part of a Normal School) in the presence of competent and experienced teachers.

This statement of the objects of such a school, forces the mind to the conclusion that a teacher thus educated and trained, thus taught how to teach, must be incomparably superior to one who lacks such advantages. The possession of knowledge is one thing, ability to teach is another and a far different thing. The most limited observer is aware that a very learned man may profoundly understand a subject himself, and yet fail egregiously in elucidating it to others. The profession of a teacher imperatively demands a special school for instruction in its appropriate science and methods.

How to teach and **what to teach** are classes of knowledge equal in importance to the teacher, and absolutely necessary to the proper progress of the scholar. Both *must* be acquired somehow. It may well be asked why this should be reserved for the common school-room; why the time of the school and the public money should be squandered by empirics rather than husbanded by adepts.

No one would intrust a steam engine to a man who was acquainted with that machine only through books. The danger and folly of thus risking life, time, and money in educating an engineer would not be questioned; universal opinion would force him to an apprenticeship under a competent master. Is there less of folly or danger in intrusting the mysterious and subtle mechanism of the mind to teachers unlearned in the practical duties of their profession? Such is the principle insisted on in all the common occupations of life. The gardener, for instance, we should all insist, must have a practical acquaintance with the nature of different soils, the habits of different plants, the best modes of cultivating and training them, and the soil and position suitable for each. In his case, no amount of book knowledge would compensate for his want of such practical knowledge. So of the farmer and the mechanic; the State fosters and endows societies which constantly reward their best practical skill.

Are not the best methods of performing the highest social duty, the intellectual, moral, and physical training of our children, equally worthy of the attention of the State?

Horace Mann, widely and justly celebrated as an eminent educator, expressed his amazement "that a parent will often intrust the education of his children to a person of whose experience and qualifications he knows nothing, when he would not allow him to mend a watch without first ascertaining that he possessed the requisite practical skill."

Such then being the design of a Normal School, to afford to those who design to become teachers that previous training which, **for** any other business, **is** deemed indispensable, we need not say more **of** its importance to California, than to call **attention to the** fact, that the large number of our citizens, male and female, who are looking to the profession of teaching as an employment for life, compete at a great disadvantage with **those** who come hither educated in the Normal Schools of **other States. Our citizens should not be** longer subjected to such **disadvantages.**

The report then goes on to mention the number **and efficiency of Normal** Schools in Europe and in the Eastern States, **with the cost of** supporting some of the most prominent, and closes **with the following paragraph:**

The amounts stated as the annual **expense of** these schools in other States, are referred to here as showing the **estimation in** which they are held, but do not constitute a criterion **for** judging **the amount necessary** to the establish**ment of** such a school here. We believe a **sum much less than either of those** named, will suffice to **secure** its **opening, upon** a **plan sufficiently extended to** meet the present **wants of our citizens.**

Hoping that these **views may meet your approval, we remain, sir,**
Very **respectfully, your obedient servants,**

HENRY B. JANES,
GEORGE W. MINNS,
ELLIS H. HOLMES,
Committee on State Normal Schools.

SAN FRANCISCO, January 2, 1862.

This communication was embodied **by Superintendent Moulder** in his report to the Legislature of 1862, and **earnestly commended** by him to their consideration, with the statement **that an appropriation of $5,000** would be sufficient to establish the school and put it in **successful** operation.

The result of these combined efforts of the **State** Superintendent and the **Teachers' Institute, was** an Act passed by the Legislature **May 2, 1862,** providing for the establishment of a State Normal School, **and appropriating** $3,000 for its support for five months. The following **is a copy of** the Act:

SECTION 1. The Board of Education of the State of California, together with the Superintendent of Common Schools in the Cities of San Francisco, Sacramento, and Marysville, are hereby constituted (*ex officio*) a Board of **Trustees for the** Normal School of the State of California, as hereinafter provided.

SEC. 2. **Such** Board of Trustees shall be known and designated as "The Board of Trustees **of** the State Normal School," and they shall have power to establish and maintain, in the City of San Francisco, or at such other place as the Legislature may hereafter direct, a Normal School, for the free instruction in the theory and practice of teaching of such citizens of this State as may desire to engage as teachers in the public schools thereof; to prescribe a course of study for such Normal School, and the text-books to be used therein; to examine, employ, and fix the salaries of teachers therein; to hold stated examinations of the pupils attending such Normal School, and to award diplomas and certificates, as hereinafter provided; to arrange and effect all the details necessary to carry out the purposes of this Act.

SEC. 3. The said Board of Trustees shall, on or before the first day of June, A. D. eighteen hundred and sixty-two, arrange for the opening of such Normal School, and may, in their discretion, adopt the Normal School now existing in the City of San Francisco, and may also agree with the Board of Education of said city for the establishment of an Experimental School, to be connected with such Normal School; also, for the use of buildings, furniture, apparatus, etc., necessary for the same; provided, that the sessions of such Normal and Experimental School shall be held in the day time, at least once each day for five days of each week, during five months of each year.

SEC. 4. Females, of fifteen years or over, or any male of the age of eighteen years or over, shall be entitled to admission, as pupils in such Normal and Experimental School, upon declaring, in writing, to the Superintendent of Public Instruction, his or her intention to engage permanently in teaching in the common schools of this State; provided, that all persons applying for admission as pupils may be instructed in said school for such rates of tuition as the Board of Trustees may determine.

SEC. 5. The seats in such Normal School shall be apportioned among the applicants therefor from the different counties of this State, as near as may be, in proportion to the representation of such counties in the State Legislature.

SEC. 6. The Superintendent of Public Instruction shall visit the said school at least once in each month, and, at the end of each annual session thereof, the Trustees shall examine such applicants as are pupils of the Normal School, regarding their proficiency in the studies of the course, and especially in their knowledge of the practice of teaching and school government, and shall grant diplomas to such only as give satisfactory evidence of their qualification in both the studies of the course and in the practice of teaching and school government. Certificates of qualification may be issued to those who have pursued only a practical course of study, specifying the grade of schools which they are qualified to teach; and such diplomas and certificates shall entitle the person to whom they are awarded to teach in any common school in this State, of the grade specified therein, for the term of two years from its date, without further examination by the State or County Board of Examination.

SEC. 7 The Trustees shall hold a meeting on the opening and closing day of each annual session of such Normal School, and as much oftener as they may deem necessary for the public interest.

SEC. 8. The sum of three thousand dollars is hereby appropriated for the purposes of this Act, payable out of the General Fund; and the Controller of State is hereby authorized and required to draw his warrant for that sum, in favor of the Board of Trustees of the State Normal School, to be expended by them solely for the purposes of this Act; and they shall report annually, on or before the tenth day of January of each year, to the State Legislature, all their expenditures; also, the number of pupils attending such Normal School, their name, age, and residence, and the number of diplomas and certificates of qualification granted, and to whom; provided, that no expense incurred by said

Board, under this Act, exceeding said sum of **three thousand dollars, shall be a** charge against the State.

SEC. 9. This Act shall take effect from and after its passage; and all laws and parts of laws inconsistent with the provisions of this Act are hereby repealed.

SUCCEEDING HISTORY.

1862-63.

(July 21, 1862—May 14, 1863.)

In pursuance of the Act passed May 2, 1862, the Board of Trustees held their first meeting May 23, 1862, at the office of the Governor, in Sacramento, and organized by electing Governor Stanford Chairman, and Superintendent Tait Secretary. There were present at this meeting, Governor Leland Stanford, Surveyor-General J. F. Houghton, State **Superintendent A. J. Moulder, City Superintendent George Tait of San Francisco, and City Superintendent G. Taylor of Sacramento.**

The Board accepted the offer of the San Francisco Board of Education tendering to the Normal School **the** use of a vacant room in the High School building, together with apparatus. The Benicia Board of Education offered the use of the old State House, but the offer could not be accepted, as the Act established **the** school at San Francisco. It was decided to publish in one newspaper of San Francisco, Sacramento, and **Marysville, respectively, the** intention of the Board to open the Normal **School on the third Monday in** July, and applicants were notified **to file their names with the** Secretary of the Board at least **three days before the** opening of the school. A large attendance seems **to have been anticipated,** and there was much discussion as to the proper apportionment of seats, "all desiring," as the minutes of the meeting record, "to secure to each county in the State its proportionate privileges in the **school, and at the same time** to afford sufficient advantages to the greater **number of** persons who will undoubtedly seek admission to the school **from** our large cities." The number of pupils to be admitted during the first **term** was finally limited to sixty; "*provided*, that at least one **pupil** shall be admitted from each county." The examination was advertised to be held **Friday, July 18, 1862, in San Francisco,** at the rooms of the Board of Education, then located in the Odd Fellows' Building, on Montgomery Street. The rate of tuition for those not entitled to gratuitous admission was fixed at $5 per month.

At a subsequent meeting, Ahira Holmes, of San Francisco, was elected Principal.

The expectation that a large number would apply for admission was not realized. Up to the day appointed, only one application was registered, and on the eighteenth day of July but five applicants presented themselves. These, with one additional, formed the first class organized, consisting of one gentleman and five ladies, whose names are worthy of mention here as the "pioneers" of the school: Frank G. Randle, San Francisco; Nellie Hart, San Francisco; P. Augusta Fink, San Francisco; Emily L. Hill, San Francisco; Ellen Grant, Nevada County; Ellen S. Baldwin, Contra Costa County. Four of these remained in the school and graduated. Miss Grant and Miss Baldwin are still teaching in the San Francisco schools; Miss Hart, now Mrs. Ramsdell, is teaching in Alameda; Miss Fink taught twelve years in San Francisco, then married, and is now Mrs. T. C. White, of Fresno; Mr. Randle is now in the office of the Southern Pacific Railroad Company in Stockton; of Miss Hill nothing has been learned.

On Monday, July 21, 1862, the school was organized in a room on the ground floor of the High School building on Powell Street. Fortunately the early history of the school is preserved in the form of a diary kept by Principal Holmes during the three years of his administration. From this diary the following record of the opening day is taken:

At the opening exercises of the school there were present Hon. A. J. Moulder, Superintendent of Public Instruction, and Dr. G. Taylor, of Sacramento, the former of whom made remarks to the class relative to the objects and designs of the institution and their duties as pupils. Remarks were also made by the Principal, regarding the course of study and the rules and regulations of the school. In this manner was planted the feeble germ of the State Normal School in California.

The number of students increased, until, by the close of the term, the school numbered thirty-one, only three of whom were gentlemen. There seems to have been some disappointment to the organizers of the school in the qualifications of many of the students admitted. "A considerable number," it is recorded, " are found exceedingly deficient in knowledge of the rudiments of the common school branches, as well as in the mental discipline and intellectual vigor necessary to pursuing the studies of the course to advantage. They have been admitted on probation in accordance with the suggestions of the Normal School Board." Another difficulty frequently mentioned is the irregular attendance of pupils, "which is a source of discouragement to the Principal, and greatly detrimental to their progress and improvement."

The declaration required by the Trustees at admission was as follows:

> We, the subscribers, do hereby declare that it is our intention to engage permanently in teaching in the common schools of this State, and that it is our object in resorting to this school to prepare ourselves for the discharge of this important duty; and we moreover pledge ourselves to remain at least one term in the school, and to observe faithfully all the regulations of the institution so long as we continue members thereof.

It differs from the form now in use, principally in declaring the intention to engage in teaching *permanently*, and in giving a pledge to remain in the school for a definite time. Two pupils attending during the first term declined to sign this declaration, and were therefore required to pay tuition.

For the first three months there was no model class, and the advanced pupils were "occasionally required to conduct the exercises in geography, arithmetic," etc.

October 31.—A Model Class was organized to-day in connection with the Normal School, located on Fourth Street near Mission, and placed under the charge of Miss H. M. Clark, formerly a teacher in the Model Department of the Normal School in Toronto. About thirty pupils have been received into the class, selected from the different Primaries of the city. These pupils are all girls, averaging about seven years of age.

November 12.—The Normal School was to-day removed to the old Music Hall, over the room occupied by the Model School. Although the room is more spacious than the one in which the sessions of the school have hitherto been held, it is in every way unsuitable for school purposes, being without facilities for ventilation, located on a noisy thoroughfare, and in close proximity to the street, and having windows only on one side. It is often almost impossible to hear the pupils distinctly when conducting class exercises, so great is the confusion produced by the sounds from the street.

November 20.—A Grammar Department of the Model School has also been formed, consisting principally of pupils from some of the City Grammar Schools, and Miss Clark has been appointed to conduct it. The Primary Department has been placed in charge of Miss K. Sullivan, formerly a teacher in one of the Chicago Primary Schools. The Model Grammar Department consists at present of only eighteen pupils. The members of the first division of the Normal School will be detailed to teach in both classes of the Model School.

December 21.—The first semi-annual examination of the Normal School took place to-day. The Superintendent of Public Instruction, A. J. Moulder, several of the public school teachers of the city, and some of the friends of the pupils were present. The examination was exclusively oral, and the exercises were interspersed with calisthenics and vocal music. None of the pupils were found qualified to graduate.

The Act establishing the school provided for but one session of five months, but as there was a balance of the appropriation still on hand, sufficient for the expenses of the school for two months, the Board decided to open a second session, and trust to the liberality of the Legislature to carry it through. The school was therefore reopened January 12, 1863, and in answer to an appeal from the Board, the Legislature granted an additional appropriation of twelve hundred dollars, enabling the Board to continue the session until May fourteenth. During the term, three special teachers were employed—Mr. Elliott in music, Mr. Burgess in drawing, and Mdlle. Paròt in calisthenics. Dr. Henry Gibbons gave, gratuitously, a series of lectures on botany. More time was spent in the Model Class, and students were sometimes detailed to act as substitutes in the San Francisco public schools.

The principal event of the term was the **Third California** State **Teachers'** Institute, **held in** Platt's Hall during **the week** beginning **May 4, 1863. The Board of Trustees ordered that** the school be adjourned **for the week, to** attend **the Institute. Accordingly,** the names of **the students of** the Normal School **appear on the** register as members of the Institute. At the request of the Board **and of the managers of the** Institute, the teachers of the Model **School appeared with their** classes, and gave exercises in **language, spelling, oral instruction,** etc., which are spoken of in **the report of proceedings in very** high **terms.** A calisthenic drill **given by a class from the** Normal School is thus **described:**

> Mdlle. Paròt, their instructress, a graduate of Dr. Dio Lewis' famous Institute at Boston, appeared at the head in calisthenic uniform, and ordered the class through a series of half a dozen different exercises, performed to music on the piano. First, wooden dumb-bells were handled, then rings, then little bags containing Indian corn were circulated with wonderful celerity in three or four different ways, and finally broom-sticks were brought into requisition, in a semi-military performance, with most graceful effect. Miss Paròt's class obtained the unqualified approbation of the audience.

It was at this Institute that Professor S. I. C. Swezey delivered **the able address on** State Normal Schools, from which the quotation at the opening of this sketch is taken. At **the close of his address, he spoke of** the California Normal School **as follows:**

> In our adopted State the experiment of sustaining a Normal School is about to close its first year. The difficulties have been very great; but one difficulty, which was perhaps the most dreaded, has been entirely removed. It was feared that where other employments afford so great inducements for active minds, there would be no students for a Normal School. But even now the number is estimated by the score, and not by the unit. The year has demonstrated

that even here, in the land of gold, there are young men and women who are willing to give themselves for the benefit of the race, and who, after full knowledge of the conditions, have accepted them all, and entered this institution with full purpose to prepare well for the teacher's work. As soon as the organization is completed, and there is a chance to do for these students what they need to have done, who can doubt that earnest-hearted men and women will be added greatly to this noble few, and the influences already at work will continue increasing in power for good until the number of students shall go by fifties, if not by hundreds, instead of by scores, as now. The teachers have done well. Too few in number to accomplish the half of what their hearts longed to accomplish, they have labored on in hope, and have brought to this institute some hints of the success which the Normal methods are yet to make general throughout the State. Three teachers, with so many Normal and Model pupils, in such rooms as they have used, with such apparatus as was theirs—in fact, no apparatus at all—have had full work in simple instruction, and could not possibly have done towards the strictly professional training what ought to be done. But they have cleared the way; have been the pioneers in this especial work, which we hope yet to see carried on in a building and with conveniences as worthy as those of our Society of California Pioneers. The Legislature and the people are willing to do their part. The $3,000 given for the first year became $6,000 for the coming year; and if the experiment succeeds, as the teachers of the State have the power to make it, this last sum may be doubled after a time, when a faculty may be secured numerous enough to do all parts of the normal work well, both for the classes who will throng the rooms and for the outside work among the teachers in their various fields. * * * All the arguments that support the establishment of these institutions in other States, have equal force in this new land and in this early time. Other States have, indeed, waited for their maturity in years before they thought of a Normal School. This State, in fact, is as mature as if the fathers had lived here before the sons who are working now, and has its needs as sharply defined. Most pressing of these needs is—not a University, important and desirable as that is acknowledged to be—but a place where teachers of the public schools can be trained as such, for laying the foundation of the work which the University will eventually complete and perfect.

Among the resolutions, adopted by the Institute at the close of the session, was the following:

WHEREAS, We believe the State Normal School to be one of the necessities of our State, and that its efficiency for the end designed is our only hope of continued or increased support from the State; and, whereas, we believe it has not thus far received a proper encouragement from teachers;

Resolved, That it is the imperative duty of all teachers and school officers to use their efforts to secure the maximum attendance allowed by law from every county of the State.

As provided by the law the annual examination was held during the closing week of the school. From the diary is taken this account of the first graduating day:

May 14, 1863.—This being the closing day of the term, and the written examinations having been completed, an oral examination of the pupils was conducted by the Examining Committee, Messrs. Swett, Tait, and Swezey, assisted by the Principal, Dr. Gibbons, and others. Exercises were conducted in most of the studies of the course, and some of the members of the First Division were required to conduct exercises in the Model School, before the committee, as a test of their skill in imparting instruction. The exercises were quite satisfactory, and most of the pupils acquitted themselves in such a manner as to merit special commendation. Many teachers and friends of the pupils were present.

After the examination of the manuscripts of the pupils was completed, it was decided by the committee and Principal that four of those in attendance during the year were entitled to receive diplomas, namely: the Misses **Bertha** Comstock, P. Augusta Fink, Nellie Hart, and Louisa A. Mails.

It appears from a later report, that as no form of diploma had yet been adopted by the Board, a certificate was issued to these four students, stating that they were entitled to receive diplomas whenever a form was adopted and engraved.

Thus closed the first year's work of the first California State Normal School.

The total number in attendance during the year was fifty, distributed among twelve counties as follows: Alameda, 2; Butte, 1; Contra Costa, 1; El Dorado, 1; Marin, 1; Napa, 1; Nevada, 1; Sacramento, 1; San Francisco, 37; San Joaquin, 1; Santa Clara, 1; Solano, 2.

In his annual report, the Principal speaks with regret of the small number in attendance from the mining and agricultural counties, but adds that "a considerable number of those registered from San Francisco must be considered as residents of other sections of the State," as they were living in San Francisco but temporarily, to enjoy its educational advantages.

He speaks again of the great difficulties encountered through irregular attendance, and the deficiency of the pupils in the elementary branches, and expresses a hope that the time may come when those only will be admitted who are well advanced in all the studies taught in the grammar schools. He reports:

The following branches have been taught in the school during the year Practical and mental arithmetic, physical and descriptive geography, English grammar and analysis, rhetoric, composition, reading, penmanship, algebra, plane geometry, physiology, natural philosophy, vocal music, calisthenics, and the theory and practice of teaching.

The direct instruction on the science or methods of teaching which has been given to the class, has been principally of an incidental nature, and in connection with the ordinary class drills. The more advanced pupils have been required to conduct class exercises in the Model Department, under the supervision of one of the teachers, and have done the same in the Normal School also, at every favorable opportunity. I have also conducted all the exercises of the school with special reference to the cultivation of the pupils' power of verbal expression; and have taken every available opportunity to call the attention of the classes to the best methods of teaching the various branches.

EXTRACTS FROM A LETTER OF REMINISCENCES OF THIS YEAR, BY MRS. AUGUSTA FINK WHITE, CLASS OF MAY, 1863.

We first occupied one of the rooms of the High School building, and to its teachers we are indebted for many acts of kindly interest. Professor G W. Minns, in particular, who gave us pleasant and profitable lectures and experiments in philosophy.

Our Principal was hard worked, having to teach all the solid branches.

Among the extra teachers, I remember Professor Elliott in music; always lively and pleasant, and always accompanied by his violin. Also Professor Burgess, in drawing. He must have taught the conjugation of the verb "love" successfully, as he selected a wife from our number. Mdlle. Paròt, in gymnastics, who *exercised us*, or we *exercised her*, poor soul, as she did not speak English very perfectly, and I fear we *sometimes* wished to misunderstand. Dr. Henry Gibbons often visited us, and gave us interesting "talks" on physiology and physical geography. The late Charles Swezey was a frequent visitor and firm friend and adviser of the class.

Four graduated at the end of the year, and composed the "First Class." Louisa Mails died soon after leaving school. She possessed ability, and I doubt not would have reflected credit upon the teachers and school had she engaged in teaching, but she passed on to a knowledge of a higher life. The remaining three taught, subsequently married, and are now fulfilling their missions as wives and mothers. My son asks me sometimes: "Mamma, why don't you teach now?" I wonder if, in the years to come, he will realize that the *best* and *truest* teaching is that dictated by "holy mother love."

The school was afterwards moved to San José. Of the results of its grand work, the gradual elevation of the schools throughout the State will bear evidence and prove the wisdom of its founders.

As I bring my reminiscences to a close, I feel grateful for the past, and proud of the future of our school. While "our class" may have been small, yet, like the rivulet in its tiny bed, as it unites with others, and at last becomes a mighty current, so may the "Normal" send out its representatives until its influence shall be as *broad* as truth itself.

1863-64.

(August 4, 1863—May 20, 1864.)

The California State Normal School began its second year, no longer an experiment, but an established State institution. Its first year of work had proved both the necessity for its existence, and its possibilities of usefulness. In April, 1863, the Legislature repealed the first Act, establishing the school, and approved a second Act, substantially the same, embodying it as a part of the State School Law. A few minor changes were made. The Superintendent of Marysville was omitted from the Board of Trustees, and the Governor was made *ex officio* Chairman. Applicants for admission were to be examined, and were not required to declare their intention to teach *permanently*, nor to remain any given length of time in the school. No provision was made, as in the former Act, for admitting, on tuition, those not intending to teach. The right to issue teachers' certificates was no longer given to the Board, but they were empowered to grant diplomas, entitling the holders to receive from the State Board of Examination a second grade certificate. The State Superintendent was to visit the school twice each term, instead of once a month, and was to embody in his annual report a full account of the proceedings and expenditures of the Board and of the condition of the school.

The appropriation for 1863-64 was made $6,000, double the original appropriation for the first year, and sufficient to continue the school two terms of five months each, from August 4, 1863, to May 20, 1864.

By October, 1863, the school had so increased in numbers that a second teacher was needed, and H. P. Carlton, a teacher in the San Francisco public schools, was appointed assistant. During the same month the school was removed to a building known as Assembly Hall, on the corner of Post and Kearny Streets. This building, though more commodious than the one formerly occupied, was little better fitted in other respects for Normal School work. It was close to a noisy street, the partitions were of thin boards, so that recitations disturbed classes in adjoining rooms, and some of the rooms were cold and damp. Considerable sickness among the pupils at this time is accounted for, in part, by unhealthful class rooms. Notwithstanding these drawbacks, the school grew and prospered. The Principal writes of being encouraged by greater studiousness in the pupils and increased interest in the work of the Model School. Visitors are frequently mentioned, among them several eastern teachers.

The primary grades of the Model School, numbering about one hundred and fifty, still occupied rooms in the Fourth Street building, under the charge of Miss Sullivan, and the grammar grades, numbering about fifty, in the Post Street building, under Miss Clark. Some fifteen of the most advanced pupils in the Model School were admitted to normal classes in October.

In January, 1864, the school was reorganized, and separated into Senior, Junior, and Sub-Junior Classes, and a regular course of study was prescribed by the Board, as follows:

SUB-JUNIOR CLASS.

Arithmetic, Grammar, Descriptive and Physical Geography with Map **Drawing**, History of United States, Penmanship, Drawing, Reading, Spelling, **Oral Exercises** from Charts, Elocution, Blackboard-writing and Drawing, **Vocal Music**, Calisthenics and Gymnastics, Elementary Instruction.

JUNIOR CLASS.

Arithmetic, Algebra, Grammar, Geography, **History United** States, Botany, Physiology, Reading, Definitions and Spelling, English **Com**position, Elocutionary **Exercises**, Elementary Instruction, Vocal Music, Calisthenics and Gymnastics.

SENIOR CLASS.

Arithmetic, Algebra, Geometry, Grammar, Rhetoric, **Geology, Natural** Philosophy, **General History**, Physiology, Botany, Physical Geography, **Bookkeeping, Select** Readings, Art of Teaching, Constitution of United **States, School Law of** California, Use of State School Registers, Forms, Blanks, **and Reports, Vocal** Music, Calisthenics and Gymnastics.

The division into three classes made another teacher necessary, and it was decided to appoint a lady. The position was filled during January by Miss Mary R. **Harris, a teacher from Boston.** Upon her resignation to take another position, she was succeeded by **Miss** Mary D. Bodwell, of **Buffalo,** New York. Dr. Gibbons continued to lecture at different times in the year on botany, physiology, and chemistry. Through the efforts of the Principal, donations of minerals and plants were received, forming the nucleus of a cabinet. By **March, the library** had grown **to one** thousand volumes, six **hundred being text-books, and the remainder** miscellaneous books and works of reference. Until **January, 1865,** pupils were supplied from the library with most of the **text-books** required. After that time they were expected **to furnish their own** text-books.

By the new regulations, each member of the Senior Class was required **to spend one** week in the Model School, **and to write a** full **report of the work done while** there. No pupil was graduated who **had not been a member of the** school for at least five months, and **teachers who had the** necessary scholarship, and wished to avail themselves **of the advantages of the** Model School training, were **invited to enter for a five** months' course. The Principal speaks frequently, however, of the *haste of pupils to graduate*, as a great hindrance to the best success of the school; as indeed it is even to the present day.

The daily sessions of the school were from 10 A. M. to 3:30 P. M., with an intermission at noon.

The highest attendance reached during the year was seventy. By the close of the second year, the entire attendance, from the first opening of the school, had been one hundred and twenty-six, representing nineteen different counties. Twelve of the number were gentlemen; twenty had engaged in teaching previous to entering.

The closing exercises of the year were held in Dashaway Hall, May 20, 1864, and are thus described:

> The school assembled at the usual hour in the morning. The exercises of the forenoon consisted of the reading of original essays and selections by members of the graduating class, original declamations by the young gentlemen, singing, under the direction of Mr. Elliot, and calisthenic exercises by all the pupils. In the afternoon similar exercises were held until three o'clock, at which time Dr. Bellows, President of the Sanitary Commission, addressed the school. His address was followed by one to the graduating class, from George W. Minns, of the San Francisco High School. The Principal of the school then delivered the diplomas to the graduating class, making a short address. The State Superintendent, Mr. Swett, then followed with remarks to the class, and delivered to them the State certificates to which they were entitled. The Rev. A. E. Kittridge then addressed the school in an eloquent and appropriate speech. The exercises were interspersed with vocal music and calisthenics.

Normal School graduates were already in demand. By the middle of June, nearly all of the nineteen members of the graduating class had secured positions, five of them in the San Francisco schools.

REMINISCENCES BY MARTIN V. ASHBROOK, CLASS OF MAY, 1864.

Your favor is at hand, requesting my salutation as an ancient to the modern Normal giant. Since my first acquaintance with the school, it has, indeed, grown from a pigmy to a giant. My introduction to the school was made in the fall of 1862. It was then held in a side room of the High School of San Francisco, on Powell Street. The room most resembled a hat room deprived of its racks and improvised with rickety seats.

The Normalites were intruders upon the domain of the High School pupils; hence had no rights they could call their own.

Ahira Holmes was Principal, Vice-Principal, Assistant, and Professor to all the twenty-five Normalites—that is, when they were in attendance. On semi-occasions, Mr. Holmes shed his many sided dignities and responsibilities, and allowed the Hope of the Golden West (us, the Normalites) to slip into side and back seats to hear Professor Minns give an illustrated lecture to his class in chemistry. In the beginning of 1863 we were moved to a tumble-down two-story wooden structure on Fourth Street, and to our great regret lost the lectures of Professor Minns, save only one which we went back to Powell Street to hear. The place we went to was worse than the room we left; for while it stood upon what can well be termed a *stable* foundation, it was shaky, and its outside stairs upon their two posts were shaky.

When vehicles went rumbling over their cobbled way we suspended class exercises; we had to, for the tremble, rattle, roar, and clatter drowned human voices. We had further misfortunes; there were neither maps, apparatus, nor books of reference in or about our school. We had one piece of furniture other than our seats and desks—a piano, hired by the pupils.

During the first term of 1863 the school waned and waxed. In waning it went down to about twenty, then ran up to about thirty pupils. It trembled in the balance. The pupils held council what to do—to forsake the institution in a body, or continue faithful to the end. The decision was to stay with the school, old house and all. We were faithful to the end. From that date the school has gone on to prosperity.

In perusing these hasty lines, allow me to pay my respects to my classmates, and say, you were heroines in meeting and overcoming obstacles almost insurmountable, and were worthy to represent the State in its forefront of intellectual battle; but understand that *vice versa* does not come in here; for at that time there were on the Pacific Coast few schools opening their portals to overgrown country louts. It was a sight to see a bearded youth carry school books. I *had* to go there or stay out of school.

I could tell many incidents of school teachers and classmates; but time and space admonish that a few incidents, and those mostly personal, must close this.

Thomas Starr King was expected to address our graduating class, but death rowed him over the dark river, and Rev. Drs. Kittridge and Bellows addressed us in old Dashaway Hall, and Hon. John Swett distributed our diplomas.

After graduation I took a small school on San Pablo Creek, and taught one year; from thence to Antioch for two years; thence to Walnut Creek one year, and from thence to Crescent City three years. So I was the pioneer Normal teacher in the counties of Contra Costa and Del Norte.

I never had school trouble and could have had each school longer, but preferred to change for higher grades and advanced wages.

I attributed my little success in teaching to my early realizing that what I had learned in the Normal School would only make a small and fragmentary volume, and what I did not know would make many volumes.

1864-65.

(July 11, 1864—May 31, 1865.)

Through the school year 1864-65 the records show a continued increase in attendance and in the efficiency of the school. The growing interest and confidence throughout the State in the Normal School work, is best shown by the fact that twenty-three counties were represented by the new students admitted during the year. The same number of teachers was employed in the Normal classes. Miss Bodwell, who resigned to take a position in the Girls' High School, was succeeded, in July, 1864, by Miss Eliza W. Houghton, a teacher from the High School, Providence, Rhode Island.

Miss Clark resigned her position as Principal of the Model School, and Miss Sullivan was elected Principal. In consequence of their being but one teacher to criticise the pupil teachers, the work of the Model School was not so efficient as formerly. An arrangement was made with the San Francisco Board of Education, by which four Normal students were detailed each week to teach, either as substitutes or assistants, in the city public schools, the Principals of the schools in which they taught being required to make a report of their work to the Principal of the Normal School. This arrangement did not prove altogether satisfactory, as these pupils had no special supervision or criticism. It made it possible, however, to increase the amount of practice, so that each member in the Senior Class spent about one fourth of the time in teaching.

A larger proportion of young men entered the school, and as a result, a lyceum was organized, holding literary exercises and debates on Friday afternoons.

Important additions were made to the cabinet, the principal being a collection of fine mineral specimens from D. C. Stone, Principal of the Marysville schools.

Two classes were graduated during the year: one in December, 1864, numbering nine; the other in June, 1865, numbering fourteen. Among the graduating exercises is given the administering of the Oath of Allegiance, which was then required, by legislative Act, of all teachers, before their certificates were issued.

REMINISCENCES BY AUGUSTA CAMERON BAINBRIDGE, CLASS OF JUNE, 1865.

When the State Normal School opened for the first session in the "Old Music Hall," on Fourth Street, in San Francisco, I was a pupil in the Model School, lower floor. What a glad day it was for us when we were invited up stairs to see the first class graduate! There were no white dresses, no immense audience, no show or display to attract our attention; but such earnest faces! A very strong sense of the real side of life came to us, as we listened to the exercises. Several good speeches were made by gentlemen present, picturing the future of the State Normal; but when John Swett addressed the class so seriously, and yet so cheerfully, and sent them on their mission with hope beaming brightly before them, a teacher's calling seemed the grandest on earth, and we longed the more intensely for the time to come when we could take our diplomas and join their band.

When the Model School disbanded, we all entered the State Normal, and a proud party of girls we were as we took up our march to the old Assembly Hall, on Post Street, near Kearny. The rooms were much more comfortable than those we had left, but the main assembly room, with blackboards on both sides, and its two tall windows, was our delight. We had patent desks, with chairs, and there were four rows. How neat and tasty it seemed! A fine piano, a good desk for the teacher, and a cabinet for minerals, curiosities, etc., and a fine, large globe were what I first noticed. Three classes were formed, Senior, Junior, and Sub-Junior. The school numbered about seventy-five in all. With one or two of my mates I entered the Junior Class, and found great delight in my studies.

The programme varied little save on Fridays. **After roll call—I can hear it yet**—singing by the school; reading of the scriptures by the Principal, and **the usual** opening remarks; a tap of the bell brought us all to our feet, the **Junior** Class to go to the front class-room, through the front hall, the Sub-Juniors to the back class-room through the back hall, and the Seniors to the front seats. At 10:40 o'clock we came to the assembly room for recess; then another tap, and another change. **At first it seemed disorderly, but,** as we became accustomed to the routine, and learned to **move quietly, we enjoyed it.**

Mr. A. Holmes, the Principal, was stern **and exact,** and though in many things he seemed hard, he did a good work **for us.** H. P. Carlton was kind and good, and **stirred up all that was noble in us, thus helping us to** see and love the better **side of everything.** Miss Houghton, with her pleasant, lady-like ways, **was a** pattern we loved to imitate.

Our arithmetic, algebra, philosophy, reading, and spelling we recited **to the Principal in the** main room. While physiology, history, **and grammar we recited** to Mr. Carlton. Our blackboard work in the assembly room **was often very extensive.** None of us will ever forget its trials **and its triumphs.** On Fridays Mr. Burgess came **to instruct us in penmanship and drawing.** Dr. Gibbons also gave us lectures on **physiology, using charts and other means of illustration.**

How proud **we were of our** Seniors! Julia Clayton's pretty ways; Jane Day, so precise; Annie Jewett, so bright and such **a good talker, and withal so kind to us "*Junes*;"** Jane Smith, so brisk and prompt; and Eva Solomon, who played and sang so well. That graduating **class of May, 1864, meant much to us. It** seemed sad to **lose them all;** and life began to be more earnest **when we had to stand in the front of the battle.**

Several new studies were added to our curriculum—ancient history, chemistry, **mental philosophy, bookkeeping, and natural history.** Mrs. Dr. Young **gave us** a very interesting series **of lectures on physiology,** and illustrated them with the manikin that the Board **had** just bought of her. Madam Parot gave us lessons in calisthenics, and was followed by Professor Robinson, and he by Professor Knowlton, who also added vocal culture. What good times we had with the wands, rings, dumb-bells, and **even free calisthenics! Miss Carrie Menges,** or Miss Carrie Field, or myself, **used to lead the school when Professor Knowlton** was not there. Carrie Menges was a **grand commander. She scolded us** roundly, and made us try again if we failed.

Our Lyceum, which met on Friday evenings, was our pride. Probably **we should smile** now at what we then thought were wonderful productions **of genius. We girls took** little part in the debates, but enjoyed music, essays, recitations, **and criticism.** Miss Youngberg wrote a few chronicles that were pronounced **excellent. Our paper was above** the average, we thought. Opinions were divided **as to whether W. R. Bradshaw** or H. E. McBride made the best President, **but both were good.**

The December **class of 1864 graduated out of our class.** I passed the examination and stood high, but barely **fifteen years could I** call my own; therefore Mr. John Swett advised **me to review, and** graduate with the next class.

We missed them very much, **but a few** new ones were added, and soon the usual order was restored, and we were as busy as bees. How we patronized the **Juniors,** and how we love to think of them now! Jennie Greer, who was **so kind, and** always ready to pay and sing for us, and who petted and nursed **us all when we** felt ill or disheartened. Mr. Loutitt, whom we would laugh at, but **could not outwit.** J. F. Kennedy, who would toss his head so independently **as he marched up to the blackboard** to give an explanation any of us might envy. Mary Hall, so earnest in her studies that a joke seemed mockery. Nettie Doud, whose merry laugh set every ringlet dancing. Lillie Gummer's sprightly ways, and Almira Flint's fair face.

In our own class Anna Gibbons, with **her** quiet Quaker ways, was the decided favorite; Florence Morgan, sweet and **pretty**; Mary Perkins, **our** baby, we **called her**; Fannie Nicols, whose quaint ways covered a kindly heart; **Cornelia Campbell, who used** to declare so earnestly that she "never would **marry, but would teach all** her life"—I can see them all **as** I write, and heartily **wish we could meet** again; for the saddest thought in **connection with our school life is, that** we, who were once so near, should so soon lose sight of each other and drift apart.

Our graduating day was **a** very bright one. The hall was filled with visitors. **Miss** Clark, our dear teacher at the Model, came and brought her pictures. I was very proud of the honor of being the first native Californian to graduate from the Normal, and not yet sixteen years of age. The law now in force, which prevents such "hot-house growth," is a good **one for** the school and for the State. After the essays, addresses, etc., our class conferred on me the privilege of presenting **the steel** engraving "Milton Dictating **his Last Poem**" to our teacher, **Mr. A. Holmes.** The Juniors presented H. P. Carlton with a copy of Webster's **Unabridged, and the** Sub-Juniors **also gave** Miss Houghton something nice.

I taught three years and a half in San **Francisco, and am** now teaching my fifteenth year in this county.

The onward march of the State Normal has been a source of great satisfaction to me; but those who see it now in its glory and pride have little idea of its earlier **struggles,** and all honor should be paid to its founders; particularly to Mr. **John** Swett, who labored for its welfare so untiringly.

1865-66.

(July 10, 1865—June 7, 1866.)

In June, 1865, Mr. George W. Minns, **Principal of** the Boys' High School, was elected Principal **of the** California State Normal School. H. P. Carlton was reëlected **first** assistant, and Miss E. W. Houghton, second **assistant.**

The school opened for the year, July 10, 1865, in Dashaway Hall, the Model School being for a time disbanded. After about six weeks it was transferred to the Lincoln School building, then just completed. In September it was again removed, this **time to** a primary school building between the Lincoln School **and** St. Ignatius College, the entrance **being on** Market Street. Here the Normal School found a **permanent** home during the remainder of its stay in **San Francisco, and though far from suitable** for Normal School purposes, **the** building **was a great improvement** upon those previously occupied. It had, at least, **the** advantage of a retired and comparatively quiet location.

A Training School of four classes was formed from classes in the city schools; Mrs. C. H. Stout was appointed by the City Board of Education as Principal, and Miss Helen M. Clark, assistant. As had been the custom in previous years, the salary of the Principal of the Training School was paid by the city, and the salary of the assistant by the State.

In January, 1866, Miss Clark resigned her position, and was succeeded by Mrs. John Swett.

During the year each member of the Senior Class spent four weeks in the Training School.

By a resolution of the Board of Trustees, no pupils were admitted to the normal classes from the San Francisco schools after June, 1865, until they had passed the examination for the High School.

Two classes were graduated, as in the year previous, a class of eleven, December 16, 1865, and a class of twenty-two, June 7, 1866.

In his annual report, Mr. Minns recommended that the long, written examination, customary at the close of each term, be held but once a year, and that there be but one class graduated during the year. He says:

> I have no doubt the Trustees will discourage the idea which some pupils appear to entertain, that they can learn all that is necessary for them to know to qualify them to become good teachers, in one term of the Normal School. Another objection to the present course is, that some actually enter the school merely to see how soon they can obtain a diploma, and only for the sake of the diploma; and not from a desire to learn systematically and thoroughly the different branches of their profession.

He urges the different counties of the State to contribute to the cabinet specimens in geology and natural history, and suggests that the school be made the medium of interchange of specimens among the different counties; also, that the Legislature make an appropriation for the purchase of apparatus.

EXTRACT FROM GOVERNOR LOW'S MESSAGE ON PUBLIC SCHOOLS, JANUARY, 1866.

> The Normal School has increased in usefulness during the last two years, and has fully demonstrated the fact that it is an indispensable auxiliary in the educational plan of the State.

EXTRACT FROM THE REPORT OF STATE SUPERINTENDENT SWETT, 1865.

> I take pleasure, in behalf of the Board of Trustees, in paying a merited tribute to the efficiency with which all the teachers of the Normal School have discharged their duties. Their positions are the highest and most responsible in the State. The Board of Trustees have paid them liberal salaries, have expected them to do their duty well, and have not been disappointed. The

school is rapidly gaining ground, and its influence is beginning to be felt on the common schools of the State. Many persons who have been engaged in teaching for years, enter the school to better fit themselves for their profession.

Most of the graduates who have gone out to teach, have proved themselves accomplished teachers. The Normal School is a part of the public school system of education, and every dollar expended in its support tends to elevate the character of the common schools.

At the close of the school year Mr. Minns asked for a leave of absence for five months to visit the East. The request was granted, and the following resolution was adopted by the Board:

Resolved, That the thanks of the Board of State Normal School Trustees be tendered to Mr. George W. Minns for the able manner in which he has discharged the duties of Principal of the State Normal School during the past year, and that the Secretary of the Board be instructed to present him with a general letter of introduction to eastern educators, expressive of their high appreciation of his educational services in this State during the past ten years.

Mr. H. P. Carlton was promoted to the principalship of the school for the next year, and Miss Houghton to the position of First Assistant. Mrs. C. R. Beale was elected to take the position made vacant by the promotion of Miss Houghton.

The graduating exercises, June 7, 1866, were held in Lincoln Hall, and occupied the whole day and evening, with intermissions. Essays were read by fourteen of the graduating class; sample exercises were given with classes from the Training School; and the whole was interspersed with music and calisthenics. Mr. Minns was presented with a handsome service of silver plate from his pupils, and a gold watch and chain from the teachers of San Francisco. In his closing entry on the school records, he says: "I desire to leave on record here an expression of my heartfelt thanks for the many kindnesses which I have received from all connected with the great cause of education. I can never forget my warm-hearted California friends."

REMINISCENCES OF THE YEAR. BY SILAS A. WHITE, CLASS OF JUNE, 1866.

Seventeen young women and five men were graduated in June, 1866. A more industrious class I have never known. Several had taught for years; Mr. Humphreys, Mr. Noah T. Flood, John A. Moore, and the writer of this had served an apprenticeship in the Eastern States. I had taught three years in this State. Every time I was employed to teach a new school I was obliged to submit to a reëxamination. I presume some of our classmates sympathized with the "old fellows" who had to go to school, because from the first day we were made welcome, and though well bearded, were not regarded as interlopers. John Swett, who was a Trustee of the school, had already systematized the school law and laid the foundation of the excellent system under which we are working to-day. Bernhard Marks was another earnest friend. They were constant and attentive visitors. In the infancy of the school, to be a Trustee implied labor, personal attention, and watchfulness. John Swett is the Horace Mann of this coast. The earnest class feeling and desire for self-improvement was engendered by him and fostered by our revered Principal, Geo. W. Minns. I never think of this good man without desiring to be like him.

We occupied four contiguous rooms, connected by folding doors, on the second floor of a miserable, old, wooden structure, back of the Lincoln School. It was reached by a narrow passage leading in from Market Street. We had a few antiquated charts, worn out maps, and a globe. I must not forget the old manikin, one half interest belonging to the city, the other half to the State. If we had but little to do with, in the way of apparatus, we used that little well. Our teachers, by zeal, ability, and personal interest in their pupils, more than made up the lack of accommodations and equipments. Henry P. Carlton (specialties, physiology and normal training) was indefatigable, and accurate in marking examination papers. Miss Houghton commanded our respect by her dignity and grace. Her specialties were English grammar, literature, and *belles-lettres*.

Mrs. Stout was Principal of the Model School. Her assistant was Mrs. John Swett, one of the kindest teachers and best women I have ever known. She was of invaluable service to me by criticism, suggestion, and encouragement. This Model or Training Department, down stairs, was to those who had experience, the most valuable adjunct of the State Normal school. I have taught in these city schools nearly twenty-three years. Had it not been for that able Faculty, the stimulus of my classmates, and the professional standing accorded to a graduate of the school, I should have ceased to teach. George W. Minns was a remarkable teacher, for his range of knowledge and his wonderful felicity in imparting it. In astronomy, botany, physical geography, or the higher mathematics, he seemed equally at home. He would hold us spellbound, entranced by the power of his thought and the magic of his words. Whether his topic was a picture of the magnificent *victoria regia*, or a date palm, or a rounded pebble from the seashore, he was always captivating, always instructive.

Almost the entire class have taught; many are teaching still. Some have died with the harness on; others will. God bless our teachers of "auld lang syne."

1866-67.

(July 5, 1866—June 3, 1867.)

By an Act approved in March, 1866, the State Board of Education was made to consist of the Governor, the State Superintendent of Public Instruction, the Principal of the State Normal School, the Superintendents of Schools of the City and County of San Francisco, Sacramento County, Santa Clara County, and San Joaquin County, and two professional teachers, nominated by the State Superintendent and elected by the Board.

By the same Act, the State Board of Education, except the Principal of the State Normal School, constituted the Board of Trustees of the State Normal School. The State Superintendent was made the Executive Agent and Secretary of the Board, with the same duties as in the former Act. The Board was empowered to appoint an Executive Committee to audit bills. Other rules governing the Board were made more specific than before. The age of admission to the school for males was changed to *seventeen*. It was made the duty of the Principal of the Normal School to attend Institutes; also, to make an annual report to the Board, including a catalogue of members of the school, which was to be printed, and copies furnished to all other Normal Schools in the United States. It was further provided that a biennial appropriation of $16,000 be made for the support of the Normal School.

On July 5, 1866, the school entered on its fifth year. The course of study was considerably modified. Some of the higher branches were omitted, allowing more time for professional work. The course required that in each class not less than half an hour each day must be devoted exclusively to instruction in methods of teaching and school government. Two pupils from the Senior Class and two from the Junior were detailed each week to teach, and two from the Sub-Junior Class each day to observe in the Training Schools. Reports were required from the teachers in charge, giving the standing of pupil teachers in the following points: Punctuality, neatness, thoroughness, energy, government, self-possession and manner, ability to interest pupils, teaching manners and morals, calisthenics, tact in teaching, carefulness.

No class was graduated at the middle of the year, and in place of the usual closing exercises in December, the pupils gave a literary entertainment, the proceeds of which were expended in additions to the library and cabinet. The *California Teacher* of that date comments as follows:

> The Normal School closed on the eleventh of December with a very pleasant elocutionary, literary, and calisthenic entertainment in Lincoln Hall. The readings by the young ladies were excellent, and give evidence of careful training by their teachers. The singing was good, and the calisthenic exercises were altogether the best we have ever seen. We commend the good taste of the pupils and teachers in dispensing with the clap-trap of theatrical imitations, and giving the audience what was infinitely better, a literary treat.

The Principal, in his report to the Board, says:

> This entertainment had an excellent effect upon the school, manifest through the entire following term. It was a trial of ability, and was successful. It removed, to a considerable degree, the impression that had hitherto existed, that the school was of an inferior grade, and occupied only a secondary position compared with others and with our High Schools. The exercises were spoken of by the press, without exception, as being of a superior order; and the classes,

particularly the class in calisthenics, were publicly complimented by the State Superintendent for their proficiency. These friendly notices developed confidence and self-reliance in the pupils, and made them hopeful for the future, and was altogether salutary.

The attendance was larger than in any previous year, reaching at one time one hundred and twenty-five, every seat being taken and many applicants rejected for want of room. This number was diminished toward the close of the year by the unusual demand upon the school to supply teachers. Over twenty from the different classes, some even from the Sub-Junior, left to take positions in various parts of the State, and, as shown by letters received by the Principal, gave "good satisfaction."

From the opening of the school, in July, 1862, up to the close of this year, there had been three hundred and eighty-five pupils admitted to the school, representing thirty-three counties of the State.

A class of thirty-one received their diplomas June 3, 1867. The percentages received by students in the studies of the Senior Class and in the Training School were recorded on the back of the diplomas.

1867-68.

(July 8, 1867—May 28, 1868.)

The resignation of Mr. Minns having been received, the Board of Trustees in July, 1867, elected Mr. George Tait Principal of the Normal School, and H. P. Carlton and Miss Houghton assistants. The Board adopted a resolution tendering their thanks to Mrs. Beale, whose services were now no longer needed, for the able and satisfactory manner in which she had discharged her duties as assistant teacher.

Mr. Tait was for four years City Superintendent of Schools in San Francisco, and was one of the earliest and warmest friends of the school. Both on account of his wide experience and personal fitness for the position, the appointment was considered a fortunate one for the school.

Mr. Tait did not, however, hold the position long. In February, 1868, he resigned to engage in real estate business, and Mr. Carlton was again made Principal for the remainder of the year. During this year again two classes were graduated—November 29, 1867, a class of ten; and May 28, 1868, a class of thirty-eight.

EXTRACT FROM THE REPORT OF STATE SUPERINTENDENT SWETT, 1867.

The design of the Normal School is to provide well trained teachers for the common schools of the State. More than nine tenths of the pupils since its organization have been young ladies who desired to fit themselves to engage in teaching City Primary Schools or ungraded Country Primary Schools.

It has been my object as the Executive Agent of the Board of Trustees, keeping these facts in view, to limit the course of study to the elementary branches; to require a large share of time to be devoted to practical work in the Training School, and to the study of the methods of teaching, and thus to graduate on a fair standard of scholarship as many teachers as possible, fitted to engage in Primary and Ungraded Schools.

Many of the young men and young women in the school have been struggling along to secure for themselves, and often for dependent parents, a livelihood by teaching. This has been an additional reason why the course of study has been kept down to a minimum.

The great demand in this State is for good teachers in the lower grade public schools, and it is in these schools that good teachers are most needed to make the system efficient.

Skill in teaching, with average scholarship in studies, for the common schools, is more desirable than the highest scholarship without a knowledge of the practical methods to be pursued in the school-room.

The revised school law provides that the graduates of the Normal School shall receive State certificates of a grade to be determined by the State Board of Examination. Under this provision certificates have been awarded to graduates according to ability and scholarship—some receiving diplomas, some first grade, and others second grade and third grade certificates.

Five members of the last graduating class had taught school from one to three years previous to entering the school; their standing was high, and they received State educational diplomas, which entitled them to teach as Principals of Grammar Schools. Six members of the class, whose standing was 80 per cent, received first grade certificates; eleven received second grade; and nine, whose standing was from 70 to 75 per cent, received only third grade certificates, which entitled them to teach only in Primary Schools.*

This seems to me to be a fair way of graduating pupils, according to ability and attainments. I am not aware that it is pursued in any other Normal School in the United States, but I feel confident it will be found the very best plan, even though it is without a precedent.

The percentage of a member of the graduating class is determined by taking into consideration the standing in recitation records during the term, the report of success in the Training School, and the result of the written examination at the close of the term.

WORK OF GRADUATES UP TO THE FALL OF 1867, AS GIVEN BY SUPERINTENDENT SWETT IN THE SAME REPORT.

Of the first graduating class, May, 1863, four young ladies, all engaged in teaching. Two of them, Miss Comstock and Miss Fink, are still teaching in the city schools. Miss Nellie Hart is married, and Miss Mails is dead.

Of the second class, 1864, nineteen members, all engaged in teaching. Five of the young ladies are married, and the rest are teaching. Miss Annie Jewett, Miss Lizzie Jewett, Miss Susie Carey, and Miss Jennie Smith have all distin-

---

*In July, 1867, the standard for graduation was fixed by the Board at not less than 80 per cent.

guished themselves as superior teachers in the various positions which they have filled. Mr. Ashbrook, the first young man who was graduated from the school, is engaged in teaching in Contra Costa County.

Of the third class, of nine members, all engaged in teaching, and all but two are still teaching. Mr. McBride has been for three years sub-master of the Washington Grammar School. Miss Carrie Field is head assistant of the Spring Valley Grammar School, and Miss Davis is a most successful primary teacher in the Fourth Street School.

The fourth class, June, 1865, numbered fourteen members, all of whom engaged in teaching. Nine of these are now teaching in San Francisco, one is married, and one has gone to Oregon.

Of the fifth class, eleven members, six are teaching in San Francisco. Mr. Louttit is teaching a grammar school at Brooklyn, and has distinguished himself as a most promising young teacher.

The sixth class, June, 1866, numbered twenty-two members, all of whom engaged in teaching. Fourteen of these are now teaching in San Francisco. Silas A. White is Principal of the Shotwell Street School, and Ervin D. Humphrey, Principal of the Mission Grammar School.

Of the seventh class, thirty-one, June, 1867, all engaged at once in teaching. Mr. Shipley engaged as teacher in the San Francisco Industrial School. Miss Heydenfeldt was employed in the Normal Training School, and the other members of the class are successfully engaged in teaching in different parts of the State.

Of the whole number of graduates, one hundred and ten, fifty-five are now teaching in San Francisco. All but thirteen are teaching, and have been teaching since their graduation.

REMINISCENCES BY HENRIETTA SLATER MCINTIRE, CLASS OF NOVEMBER, 1867.

Twenty years ago the California State Normal School was in its infancy; and although it had no commanding edifice, surrounded by spacious grounds to attract public gaze, yet it can look back with pride to its able corps of teachers, and the thorough normal training given to its pupils, which has been clearly proven by the marked success in the school-room of some of the graduates of that time.

Well do I remember the gateway on Market Street, San Francisco, with the arched sign, "State Normal School," over it, leading through a long passage-way, to a dingy, unpretentious, frame building, in the rear of the Lincoln Grammar School, the first floor being used for a Training School, under the able management of Mrs. Stout and Mrs. Swett, and the second story for the Normal School proper. Three class-rooms, connected by folding doors, together with a few small ante-rooms, were all the school could boast of. Apparatus, it had none, save a manikin, for the benefit of the physiology class, who found much to amuse, as well as instruct, in the dissection of this excellent representation of the human frame.

A favorite occupation of the pupils at recess was to look down into the yard of the Lincoln Grammar School, where hundreds of boys were marching, or going through with various evolutions with military precision.

During the two years, beginning with 1866, that it was my privilege to attend the Normal School, Henry P. Carlton and George Tait were successively Principals of the school, with Mrs. Beale and Miss E. W. Houghton, assistants.

Mr. Carlton's special fondness was for normal training and natural history, and his strenuous efforts to teach his pupils to think for themselves, and study nature as well as text-books, has been an incentive to many. Vagueness of ideas he abominated, and when a pupil rose to recite without having any definite conception of the subject under consideration, another was soon called upon.

The State Normal School was exceedingly fortunate in having Miss E. W. Houghton, a Mt. Holyoke graduate, for an instructor in arithmetic, botany, elocution, and vocal culture. The very embodiment of dignity, her simple presence commanded respect and attention, and no difficulty did she apparently ever experience in maintaining order. One look of hers was quite enough to cause any disorder to subside, and a word of rebuke was the keenest mortification to which a pupil could be subjected. Clear-cut in thought, finished in style, cultivated in manners, she was a most admirable teacher of those who were themselves to teach.

It was during this period that Hon. John Swett held the office of State Superintendent, and his warm interest in the State Normal School was shown by his frequent visits there, which were always hailed with delight by the pupils, whom he often addressed or examined in some study. We knew that if he happened in during class recitations we might expect some puzzling questions, quite out of the text-book order, which we always found of practical value.

While I was in the graduating class the Seniors conceived the idea of editing a paper, christened "The Acorn," of which I am the possessor of two copies—pleasant reminiscences of days gone by. From these I copy the following little poem by my classmate, C. D. McNaughton, now deceased:

Those Days Are Past.

Those days are past, and oft I track,
  With weary gaze their rapid flight,
Could I, on eagle's wings go back,
  Ah! quickly would I flee to-night.
But nothing beautiful can last—
Those bright and happy days are past.

Youth meets us once, and leaves us when
  We learn to love its fond embrace;
But once, and never comes again
  To cheer the heart's forsaken place.
How like the flowers around us cast—
They perish when their days are past.

In each bright scene we love to trace
  The joys and hopes we once have known,
And fancy in each youthful face
  An image that was once our own.
With time's malignant freezing blast,
That image and its days are past.

But after all why thus regret
  The ever buoyant flight of time?
Youth's follies let us all forget,
  And seek the sunlight of our prime.
Rich are the treasures round us cast,
And bright, though other days are past.

The parent bird, in search of food,
　Is joyous, as its growing young,
And noon calls sweetly from the brood
　The song the mother early sung.
The noon-tide joys are wedded fast
To those whose fleeting days are past.

In early life some settled grief
　Embitters oft the golden bowl,
But years remove with soft relief
　The burden clinging to the soul.
So perish all those griefs at last,
And pleasures come when they are past.

1868–69.

(July 1, 1868—May 21, 1869.)

In May, 1868, Dr. Wm. T. Lucky was elected Principal of the Normal School, H. P. Carlton Vice-Principal, and Miss E. W. Houghton and Mrs. Dorcas Clark assistants. Except for the occasional employment of an assistant or a special teacher for a short time, the faculty remained the same from this time until 1872. Dr. Lucky was a teacher of many years experience, chiefly in private institutions. At the time of his election, he was Principal of the Lincoln Grammar School in San Francisco.

As far as can be ascertained, during the remainder of the time that the school was located in San Francisco, the teachers in the Training School were paid by the city, though the work of the Training School was entirely under the supervision of the Trustees and teachers of the Normal School.

During this year, the form of diploma was adopted which has been in use ever since. The subject of a permanent location for the school now began to be agitated, and a committee was appointed by the Board of Trustees to consider the matter and report upon it. The claims of numerous places, most of them near the center of the State, were urgently presented, each by its residents and special friends. Oakland, Berkeley, Stockton, San José, San Francisco, Sacramento, Napa, Martinez, and many minor places were in turn recommended. State Superintendent Fitzgerald, Dr. Lucky, and others strongly favored San José, on account of its size—not so large as to present the disturbance and temptations of a city, and yet large enough to offer suitable boarding accommodations for students—its healthful climate, and its accessibility; also on the principle of an equitable distribution of State institutions. The question remained unsettled, however, until 1870.

At the beginning of Dr. Lucky's administration, the Sub-Junior, or " Entering Class " was dropped, and a regular two years' course adopted, consisting of Junior year and Senior year. Each year was divided into two divisions of five months each, as follows:

JUNIOR CLASS.—*Second Division*. Arithmetic, Grammar, Geography, **Reading, Moral** Lessons, Spelling. *First Division:* Arithmetic, Grammar, Rhetoric, **Physiology,** History, Vocal **Culture,** Bookkeeping, General Exercises, including Penmanship, Object-Lessons, Calisthenics, Methods of Teaching, School **Law,** Composition, and **Declamation.**

SENIOR CLASS.—*Second Division:* **Arithmetic** reviewed, Algebra, Grammar, Natural **Philosophy, Physiology, Rhetoric,** Natural **History.** *First Division:* Botany, **Physical Geography, Normal Training, Geometry,** English Literature, Bookkeeping, **General Exercises, same as in the Junior Year.**

EXTRACTS FROM A LETTER OF REMINISCENCES BY MARIETTA GOULD BUZZO, CLASS OF MAY, 1869.

Very little apparatus, and that little very **primitive, was furnished** us in those days. The great earthquake of October, 1868, demolished our largest and most valuable "aid to learning," the manikin, greatly to the disappointment of the physiology **class** (Senior), then under Professor Carlton's instruction. I do not think any **of us** have forgotten Professor Carlton's great delight when the class got very much wrought up *pro* and *con* over some question in physiology, **language, or methods,** and his quiet way of leaving us to settle the matter for ourselves, **if we could.** Nor, again, our hearty enjoyment of the recitations **conducted by Miss Houghton,** whose example of thorough preparation **for the exercise and womanly dignity** and decorum **was** ever esteemed a model **for our future emulation.**

The only excursions I remember, **of which there were many,** combining pleasure with profit in about equal proportions, **arranged for us** by Dr Lucky, were those to the Sugar Refinery, the Mission **Woolen Mills, the** Mint, to Sausalito, and one especially enjoyable, **to inspect a large China** steamer, the largest of that day. **Another memorable occasion was the cele**bration at the Mechanic's Pavilion of the completion **of the transcontinen**tal railway.

Our graduating exercises—to **us the** great **event** of the year—were held at Platt's Hall, where State Superintendent O P. Fitzgerald presented our coveted diplomas.

1869-70.

(July 1, 1869—March 10, 1870.)

The subject of the best times in the year for opening and closing the Normal School, has been in its past history, as it still is, an open question. For the first seven years, the school opened and closed at about the same time as the public schools in the cities. Many, however, of the schools throughout the State, especially in country districts, where a long winter vacation is unavoidable, open for the summer term in April or May. This made it seem, to some, desirable to send out the annual graduating class in time to take positions in these schools. It was therefore thought best to try the experiment; and in order to effect the change, the school year 1869–70 was shortened more than two months, and the class graduated in March. This plan was continued until 1877.

Miss Matilda Lewis, a graduate of the Oswego State Normal School of New York, became Principal of the Training School in 1869, and infused new life by putting into active operation the methods used in the Oswego school, making a specialty of object teaching. One episode of the year in connection with the work of the Training School, is given in the following account by one of the students specially interested:

Following the resignation of Mrs. Stout, Principal of the Training School, in 1869, came the introduction of teaching by the object system, by Miss Matilda Lewis, of the Oswego, New York, Normal Training School, who succeeded Mrs. Stout as Principal of the Training School. She found the school in a most unsatisfactory condition, on account of the insufficient number of regular teachers, the pupils having no regard for the authority of the young girls placed over them from week to week. The first request of Miss Lewis was for four young ladies to be placed as regular teachers in the Training Department, the pupil teachers to spend a week in the class-rooms as before, consulting with the regular senior teacher. This plan gave the children some one to look to as authority, and much valuable time previously devoted to reorganization of classes each week, was spent by both pupils and teachers in learning the new system of teaching from objects.

Miss Lewis, besides teaching by this system, gave regular lectures to the Senior Class illustrative of her methods, which were a most interesting and useful feature of the school work. The four pupils selected from the Senior Class were Emelie McNeil, Ada Oglesby, Sarah A. Rightmire, and Cornelia E. Greer. We remained in charge of the classes, under the direction of Miss Lewis, eight months, the pupils coming from the Normal School every week to teach with us. In March, 1870, the Normal School Class graduated, leaving us still in the Training School. In the meantime Miss Lewis went to the Legislature, and obtained diplomas for us. In May of the same year we passed examination in our class-rooms, with our pupils, before the Faculty, in methods of teaching all the primary branches, general government, etc., and were granted first grade State certificates and "Normal Training School diplomas," exactly like the diplomas of the March class, except for the addition of the word "Training."

Miss McNeil taught in one of the higher grades in a school in San Francisco for two and a half years, then married a gentleman by the name of Dwyer, and now resides in San Francisco.

Miss Oglesby taught in the San Francisco public schools eight years, then married (present name unknown), and resides in Kansas.

4

Miss Rightmire has been teaching constantly in San Francisco, and ranks high as the Principal of the Emerson Primary School.

I commenced teaching immediately after graduating, and taught successfully in Contra Costa County for three and a half years, at Pacheco. In 1872, I was granted an educational diploma (complimentary, the three years required by law before making application, not having expired). I taught continuously afterwards in San Mateo County till 1876, when I was married to William W. Cunningham of San Francisco, and now reside in Alameda.

CORNELIA E. CUNNINGHAM.

In March, 1870, the Legislature selected San José as the permanent location for the State Normal School, and enacted a law providing for the selection of a site, and the erection of a building. Some changes were made in the laws governing the school, the principal change being that the Board of Trustees were differently constituted. The following is a copy of the Act:

SECTION 1. There shall be established in the City of San José, County of Santa Clara, a school, to be called the California State Normal School, for the training and educating of teachers in the art of instructing and governing in the public schools of this State.

SEC. 2. The Governor of the State of California, the Superintendent of Public Instruction of the said State, and the Principal of the State Normal School are hereby appointed and created Trustees, with full power and authority to select a site for the permanent location of the State Normal School in the City of San José. Said Trustees shall, within thirty days after the passage of this Act, examine the sites offered by the City of San José for the location of the State Normal School buildings, and select therefrom a suitable location for said State Normal School buildings, and the site selected by them shall be and remain the permanent site for the State Normal School buildings.

SEC. 3. The Mayor and Common Council of the City of San José are hereby authorized, empowered, and directed, immediately after such site shall have been selected by said Trustees, to convey such site, by good and sufficient conveyance, to the Trustees of the State Normal School, who are hereby authorized and empowered to receive and hold the same and the title thereto in trust and for the use of said State Normal School; provided, that whenever the State Normal School shall be removed from said site selected, the same and the title thereto shall, immediately upon such removal, revert to said City of San José, and become the property thereof absolutely.

SEC. 4. The Governor, the State Superintendent of Public Instruction, and five others, to be appointed by the Governor, shall constitute the Board of Normal School Trustees. The appointed members, at the first meeting of the Board of Trustees, shall determine by lot their respective terms of office, which shall be for two, four, six, eight, and ten years.

SEC. 5. Said Board of Trustees shall have power, and are hereby authorized and required, to remove to said City of San José, County of Santa Clara, the State Normal School, now located in the City of San Francisco, and to continue the same for the gratuitous instruction of such persons residing in this State as may desire to prepare themselves to teach in the public schools of this State. They shall have power to expend all moneys appropriated or donated for building school rooms and boarding houses, and for furnishing the same, as well as all moneys for the current expenses of the school.

Sec. 6. The Board of Trustees shall have power to elect a Principal and all other teachers that may be deemed necessary; to fix the salaries of the same, and to prescribe their duties.

Sec. 7. It shall be the duty of the Board of Trustees to prescribe the course of study, and the time and standard of graduation, and to issue such certificates and diplomas as may, from time to time, be deemed suitable. These certificates and diplomas shall entitle the holders to teach in any county in this State for the time and in the grade specified in the certificate or diploma.

Sec. 8. The Board of Trustees shall prescribe the text-books, apparatus, and furniture, and provide the same, together with all necessary stationery, for the use of the pupils.

Sec. 9. Said Board shall, when deemed expedient, establish and maintain a training or model school, or schools, in which the pupils of the Normal School shall be required to instruct classes under the supervision and direction of experienced teachers.

Sec. 10. Said Board shall make rules for the government of the boarding house or houses; shall superintend the same, and make all necessary arrangements for conducting the same in the most economical manner that will make them self-sustaining.

Sec. 11. At each annual meeting the Board shall determine what number of pupils may be admitted into the school; and this number shall be apportioned among the counties of this State according to the number of representatives from said counties in the Legislature; *provided*, that teachers holding first or second grade certificates may be admitted from the State at large. The County Superintendents and the County Boards of Examination shall hold competitive examinations before the first of May in each year of all persons desiring to become pupils of the Normal School, which examinations shall be conducted in the same manner as examinations for third grade teachers' certificates. A list shall be made of the applicants thus examined, and they shall receive recommendation in the order of standing in the examination; *provided*, that Superintendents may discriminate in favor of those whose age and experience specially fit them to become normal pupils. After the expiration of the year, a new list must be prepared, and those not recommended must be reëxamined or forfeit their right to recommendation.

Sec. 12. To secure admission into the Junior class of the Normal School, the applicant, if a male, must be seventeen years of age, or if a female, sixteen years of age; to enter an advanced class the applicant must be proportionately older. Applicants must also present letters of recommendation from their County Superintendent, certifying to their good moral character, and their fitness to enter the Normal School. Before entering all applicants must sign the following declaration: "We hereby declare that our purpose in entering the California State Normal School is to fit ourselves for the profession of teaching, and that it is our intention to engage in teaching in the public schools of this State."

Sec. 13. Pupils from other States and Territories may be admitted to all privileges of the school on presenting letters of recommendation from the Executives or State School Superintendents thereof, and the payment of one hundred dollars. The money thus received shall be appropriated to the purchase of library and apparatus. Pupils from other States shall not be required to sign the declaration named in section twelve.

Sec. 14. The Superintendent of Public Instruction shall be the Executive Agent and Secretary of the Board of Trustees of the Normal School. He shall visit the school from time to time, inquire into its condition and management, enforce the rules and regulations made by the Board, require such reports as he deems proper from the teachers of the school and officers of the boarding house, and exercise a general supervision of the same. He shall, in connection with the Executive Committee appointed by the Board, expend all moneys appropriated for salaries and incidental expenses, and shall make a semi-annual statement, in writing to the Board, of all moneys received and expended.

SEC. 15. It shall be the duty of the Principal of the school to make a detailed annual report to the Board of Trustees, with a catalogue of the pupils, and such other particulars as the Board may require or he may think useful. It shall also be his duty, authorized by the Board, to attend County Institutes, and lecture before them on subjects relating to public schools and the profession of teaching.

SEC. 16. The Board of Trustees shall hold two regular meetings annually, at such time and place as may be determined; but special meetings may be called by the Secretary, by sending written notice to each member.

SEC. 17. The Board shall have power to make all rules and regulations necessary for discharging the duties named above.

SEC. 18. An annual *ad valorem* tax of two cents on each one hundred dollars' value of taxable property in this State is hereby levied, for the twenty-second and twenty-third fiscal years, and is directed to be collected in the same manner as other State taxes are collected; and the money raised by said tax shall be paid into the State Treasury, and said money and the money by this Act appropriated shall be known as the **State Normal School Building Fund**.

SEC. 19. Said State Normal School Trustees shall, from time to time, as the services herein provided for, or by them ordered and performed, and labor done or materials furnished for said State Normal School buildings, draw orders on the State Controller, specifically describing the services rendered, labor performed, or materials furnished, together with the amount, and to whom payable. Upon presentation of such orders, the State Controller shall draw his warrant on the State Treasurer, for the amounts thereof, payable out of said State Normal School Building Fund; and the State Treasurer is hereby authorized and directed to pay such warrants out of said fund. Said State Normal School Trustees and Controller each shall keep a correct register of the warrants or orders issued, the amount of each warrant, to whom ordered paid, and for what services or materials given; such registers shall be kept in their respective offices for public inspection.

SEC. 20. The sum of twenty-four thousand dollars is hereby appropriated, biennially, out of any moneys in the General fund not otherwise appropriated, which said appropriation shall be set apart at the commencement of each fiscal year, to support the California State Normal School; and the Controller is hereby directed to draw his warrants, from time to time, on the State Treasurer, payable out of said appropriation, and the unexhausted remainder, if any, of any appropriation for such claims or accounts as have been audited by the Board of Trustees of the Normal School, or the Executive Committee thereof, and the Board of Examiners; *provided*, that the bills for the salaries of regular teachers may be allowed by the Controller without the indorsement of the Board of Examiners; *provided*, also, that the aggregate of warrants drawn shall not exceed, in any one fiscal year, one half the appropriation herein made for such years, together with the remainder of unused appropriations, if any, of any previous fiscal year, or years; and whenever, at the close of any fiscal year, a balance remains to the credit of the California State Normal School Fund, such balance shall be carried forward and added to the appropriation for the succeeding year.

Sec. 21. All classes may be admitted into the Normal School, who **are admitted**, without restriction, into the public schools of the State.

Sec. 22. The provisions of this Act shall take effect from and after its passage; *provided*, that the removal of the school shall be made whenever the Board of Trustees decide that suitable accommodations have been prepared for the same.

Sec. 23. All Acts or parts of Acts passed by the Senate and Assembly of the State of California conflicting with the above are hereby repealed.

Reminiscences by Alberta Montgomery Ecker, Class of March, 1870.

The class of 1870 had its home in San Francisco, in the building now used by classes of the Lincoln Primary School.

Dr. Lucky was Principal. Prof. Henry P. Carlton, Miss E. W. Houghton, and Mrs. Dorcas Clark were assistants. Miss Houghton was in the East during the first term, and Miss Letitia Ryder taught in her place. Miss Lewis, of the Oswego Training School, superintended us while we taught in the Training Classes. Professor Carlton labored diligently to inspire us with a love for physiology and mental philosophy. Miss Houghton taught us elocution and rhetoric, and gave us such short lessons that we had no excuse for not getting them. Dr. Lucky instructed us in mathematics. His interest in his pupils ceased only with his life, and many can bear witness to his efforts in their behalf after they were engaged in teaching.

Our Principal's work is done, and he has been joined "over the river" by Leonora Carothers (Mrs. Barry Baldwin), Nellie Savage, Helen Stone, Jessie Wilson, Alice Snow (Mrs. George Pardee), Mrs. Tillotson, and Mary L. Greer. We weave a garland sacred to the memory of teacher and classmates; they shall be enshrined in our hearts till our life's drama has closed.

Rev. O. P. Fitzgerald was State Superintendent and made us frequent visits.

Our apparatus was limited, and our library small. We had access to the Mercantile and other city libraries, and were often addressed by talented speakers. We had a debate every Wednesday afternoon on a topic previously announced. Every pupil was required to express an opinion on the subject selected. We had special lessons in drawing and music.

The "Musical Festival," under the auspices of Madame Camilla Urso, was held in the spring of 1870. Many of our students were among the twelve hundred chorus singers. We remember also a very pleasant steamboat excursion taken by our school. We sailed around the bay, out to the Golden Gate, and made a visit to Alcatraz Island, where all points of interest were explained to us.

The subject of the removal of the Normal School from San Francisco had already been agitated. San José wished the new school. The Normal Trustees, the Faculty, and scholars, and members of the press went on a railroad excursion as guests of the City of San José. We were given a banquet at the Auzerais House, with the usual toasts and after-dinner speeches, and then visited the Convent, Court House, Washington Square, the site to be donated to the Normal School, and other points of interest. Probably the kind treatment given the excursionists helped San José in the decision that located the school.

The graduating exercises were held on the evening of March 10, 1870, two months earlier than usual, so that the graduates might obtain positions for the spring term. The exercises were held in Platt's Hall. Miss Belle Carruthers opened the exercises, after a prayer by Rev. Dr. Scott, with an essay on "The Artist's Implements." Miss Leonora Carothers followed with an essay on "The Shady Side of Teaching." The school sang "Hail Happy Day." Miss

Casey read an essay on "Mythology." The essay on "Localism," by Miss Garland, came next. Mr. Tillotson delivered an oration on "Teachers and Teaching." Miss Withrow read an essay on "Music and its Votaries," and afterwards gave a vocal solo "Ave Maria." Miss Montgomery followed with an essay on "The Seen and the Unseen." Miss Burrill's essay was entitled "Let In the Sunshine." Miss Allison read an essay on "Another Day," with valedictory addresses. The diplomas were delivered by Rev. O. P. Fitzgerald, after an appropriate address to the graduates. Dr. Lucky concluded with a brief farewell to his late pupils. After the Doxology and a benediction by Rev. Dr. Walker, the class of 1870 separated, never to meet again until we reach the "other side."

1870-71.

(June 1, 1870—March 11, 1871.)

The first meeting of the Board under the new law was held in Sacramento April 25, 1870. The appointed members drew lots, as provided by law, to determine the length of their terms of office, and the new Board was organized as follows: President, Governor H. H. Haight; Secretary (*ex officio*), Superintendent O. P. Fitzgerald; appointed members: Henry O. Weller, two years; Andrew J. Moulder, four years; C. T. Ryland, six years; James Denman, eight years; J. H. Braly, ten years. Of these, Mr. Moulder resigned in 1871, and was succeeded by Dr. B. Bryant; Mr. Braly resigned in 1873, and was succeeded by T. Ellard Beans; Mr. Ryland and Mr. Denman were reappointed at the expiration of their terms of office. An executive committee was appointed, and instructed to procure plans and initiate measures for the erection of a Normal School building.

In August the Board formally accepted from the City of San José, for the use of the Normal School, the property then known as Washington Square, containing over twenty-six acres. As provided for in the Act, the square was conveyed to them with the condition that whenever the State Normal School shall be removed from this site, the land shall revert to the City of San José.

The cornerstone of the first California State Normal School building was laid October 20, 1870, with imposing masonic ceremonies, conducted by the Grand Lodge of the State, assisted by Howard Chapter of Royal Arch Masons, and San José Encampment, No. 35, of I. O. O. F.

A large assembly was present, including the pupils and Faculty of the Normal School, from San Francisco, the public school children of San José, and many citizens. The address was delivered by State Superintendent O. P. Fitzgerald.

Address of Rev. O. P. Fitzgerald.

It was a joyful day for the Hebrew people when the moving tabernacle was superseded by the magnificent temple at Jerusalem. The moving tabernacle served its temporary purposes during the journey through the wilderness, but the permanent temple expressed the culmination of the national wealth, property, and glory. So this day may well celebrate the exodus of California from the transient condition of a new State, the change from its preparatory history to well organized society and established institutions, commercial, agricultural, literary, and religious. The cornerstone, which we lay to-day with the appropriate and impressive ceremonies of the "brethren of the mystic tie," is fitly celebrated by the parade of the military, the presence of the representatives of organized benevolence, the invocation of the blessings of God, the glad shouts of children, and the smile of beauty. The laying of this cornerstone is at once the register of our present attainment and the prophecy of our future progress. We have met to lay the cornerstone of the California State Normal School building in its permanent location on this magnificent square, in this beautiful valley, amid this hospitable and generous people; and it is a memorable and joyful day.

The occasion reminds us, fellow citizens, that we are passing from the old to the new; that we have closed one era in the life of our State, and are entering upon another. The day of reckless speculation, wild ventures, and transient expedients is gone. Farewell, California of the past! Farewell ox trains across the plains, canvas tents, board shanties, womanless houses, and hopeless bachelorhood! Hail the new California! Hail the great railway! Hail the opulent city, the thriving village, the well inclosed and beautiful farm, the comfortable and elegant mansion, the well built school house, the quiet and virtuous homes in which are realized all the blessings and delights of the one institution that has survived the fall! Pardon my enthusiasm. I am too much of a Californian to measure my words, or temper them to the rhetoric of a cold conventionality, when my pulses are quickened and my heart rejoicing in prospect of the consummation of a grand enterprise, which has for so many months excited my solicitude, aroused my hopes, and engaged my energies. The exuberance of my feelings is not lessened by the fact that I am surrounded here to-day by my old neighbors and friends, who have never allowed me to forget that this valley is my home. The laying of this cornerstone symbolizes the work which we of this generation are doing. We are laying the foundations of a new State. We are laying the foundations of an educational system. We must be careful to lay them properly, for the whole superstructure will conform to the character of its foundations.

The foundation plan of our system of popular education must be broad, embracing the principles of justice and right, giving equal privileges to all classes of citizens.

The foundation of our system must be strong, resting on right ideas clearly defined and firmly maintained.

The foundation of our system must be symmetrical. We want no patchwork or conglomerate of dissimilar elements or antagonistic principles. We must adopt a definite and consistent theory of education, and faithfully embody it in practice.

We must *begin at the beginning*. First in this structure is the concrete foundation harder than granite, capable of resisting the heaviest earthquake shocks, and incombustible by any heat short of the final fires of the last day. Then follows the brick work; after which the wooden framework, story by story; and last of all the cornices, capitals, and other ornamental and finishing touches, ending with the gilded or sculptured dome. So, in our system of education, we must begin at the beginning, not following the false fashion of giving our children a smattering of the "ologies" and teaching them to jabber bad French before they have learned to spell or cipher.

Above all, the *cornerstone* must be properly laid in its proper place. In practical architecture, every man understands the necessity for this. What is the cornerstone of a true system of popular education? I answer, a *pure morality*. Without this no system can stand. Leaving this out, there will be nothing to hold the different parts of a system of education in their proper relation toward each other. Using the untempered mortar of a false morality, it will dissolve upon its first contact with opposing elements, and the whole superstructure will sink into ruin. A pure morality must be based upon a recognition of God, submission to His will, and a sense of accountability to Him. A pure morality means a conscience enlightened by Divine truth, a nature molded, controlled, and directed by the Divine will. We owe it to our children and to all who shall come after us, to have this cornerstone fitly laid in our educational system.

Would it be straining the figure, or changing it too abruptly, to say that the State Normal School is itself the cornerstone of our public school system? The functions of the State Normal School are: To mold the type of the public school teachers, to inculcate the principle that shall guide and govern them in their work, and to suggest to them and drill them in the method they should follow in the school room. Upon its proper adjustment to the machinery of the system and the efficient performance of its proper functions will very greatly depend the success of the entire system. This being so, the laying of this cornerstone to-day becomes a very significant act, reminding us of the profound feeling of responsibility and the thorough conscientiousness which we should bring to bear in discharging our official duties in organizing and establishing this institution on a right foundation. Let, then, this noble structure rise upon its solid foundations. Let it rise in its beauty and grandeur, the mother institution of its class upon the Pacific Coast. Let it rise as a monument of the enterprise and far-reaching sagacity of an enlightened people. Let it rise here in this valley of surpassing beauty and fertility, in the very heart and center of California, where it will be accessible to all, and from which it shall radiate light and blessing all over the State, from the sunny crests of the Sierras to the orange groves of the south. This is the first State Normal School of California; others will be established in due time and in proper places.

The time is coming when California will contain two million inhabitants. This valley will then be a continuous garden, and the Alameda will be a willow-planted street running through one grand city, into which San José and Santa Clara will be merged. The three hundred miles of our "foothill" country will then rival the best vine-growing regions of Europe in the extent and value of its vineyards, and the density of its population. Should our provisions for popular education keep pace with our material development, additional normal schools will be demanded. At Los Angeles, on the north side of the Bay of San Francisco, at Napa, or at some other equally charming spot, in the San Joaquin and Sacramento Valleys, and "up north," will these intellectual light-houses be erected, leaving not a single spot in all our State unillumined by their beams. In view of the grand future thus hastily outlined, how great is the responsibility that rests upon us as the officers and guardians of this institution. We represent not only for the present, but for the future. We are now planting a tree whose growth coming generations will foster, and whose fruit they will gather. Let us do our work well, that those who come after us may follow our good example, and carry forward the great work which we shall transmit to them.

Mankind are learning more and more to appreciate the influence of natural surroundings in molding forms, features, and character. Without attempting here to give the philosophy of this fact, I accept it; and accepting it, let me ask, where could a better location be found for the State Normal School? Where will you find richer vegetation, brighter flowers, more fertile fields, more beautiful slopes, swelling hills, and towering mountains, than those that adorn and inclose this garden valley of the earth? Where can you look up to a bluer sky, or find breezes more balmy than those that float around us to-day? May the characters here developed be as symmetrical as the features of yonder landscape, as strong as yonder wall that beats back the surges of the vast Pacific, as pure as the silver waters that gush in their beauty from your artesian wells.

1871-72.

(June 14, 1871—March 14, 1872.)

The Normal School opened its first session in San José, June 14, 1871. Until the new building was ready for occupation, rooms for the use of the school were kindly furnished by the San José Board of Education; for the first few weeks in the High School building on Santa Clara Street; after that in the Reed Street building, then just completed. Dr. Lucky urged strongly the desirability of providing at once a boarding house for the young lady students, but the Board concluded that it was inexpedient, for the present, to undertake this, and boarding places were secured in private families. When the Political Code of California was established, in March, 1872, some slight changes were made in the laws relating to the Normal School. The age of admission was fixed at sixteen, for males as well as females. The faculty were no longer authorized to grant teachers' certificates to undergraduates, but graduates were given the right to teach in the public schools of the State, for the time and in the grade prescribed by their diplomas.

Extracts from the Report of Dr. Lucky, December, 1871.

Do Normal Graduates Teach?

The following facts in reference to the classes that have graduated since I have been connected with the school, will satisfactorily answer the above question:

There were twenty graduates in 1869, all of whom secured good situations in a few months.

Of the forty-four graduates in 1870, all except four are known to have commenced teaching. Twenty of the twenty-one graduates in 1871 have already entered upon their work. Thus it will be seen that only five in an aggregate of ninety-four are not teaching, and these are unemployed because of ill health or because they are unwilling to accept situations out of San Francisco.

Of the class of 1869, eight obtained situations in San Francisco, and twenty-one in fourteen different counties. Of the class of 1870, eleven obtained situations in San Francisco, and twenty-nine in fifteen different counties. Of the class of 1871, six are teaching in San Francisco, and fourteen in nine different counties.

The demand for Normal graduates is far greater than the supply All graduates can at once secure good situations, provided they are willing to go into the country.

The reason for the preference expressed for Normal School pupils, is the natural result of the uniform success of the teachers trained here. Very many complimentary and flattering reports have been received from County Superintendents and district trustees. The following is given as a specimen:

"The benefits of Normal instruction are especially seen in schools taught by teachers from our State Normal School at San José. The superior and systematized instruction and their well regulated government give the most complete satisfaction. They come forth from that school having well matured plans, and are prepared at once to enter on their great work."—[Mack Matthews, County Superintendent, Lake County.

During a period of nearly four years, I have heard no complaint of inability *to teach*, and I know of but three instances in which graduates, in their first schools, failed in government. These are *now* successful and popular teachers. All who attend the school are taught to believe there is a moral obligation resting upon them to become earnest teachers, in order that they may benefit the State that has so kindly assisted them.

REMINISCENCES BY CHARLES E. MARKHAM, CLASS OF MARCH, 1872.

You inform me that I am appointed to speak for the Class of '72. It is a pleasure to do so, for the task calls up a throng of happy memories. Perhaps, however, the duty should have fallen to other hands. Miss Rixon, for instance, would be more finished and picturesque; Miss Terry, more artless and pleasing; Miss Wagenseller, more piquant; Mr. Kennedy, more strong and original; Mr. Beal, more simple and direct. Miss Stephens could give us detail and delicate satire; Miss Hilton, grace and quiet beauty. And so, also, do the rest of the class come to me in memory, each with some special fitness for the work.

One pleasing feature of the school in the old time was the occasional excursion and half holiday. These were chiefly for the purpose of studying some piece of machinery or some process of manufacture. We young men, of course, had our literary and debating society. Then, too, there was our weekly afternoon institute for the discussion of school-room problems. Many visitors attended, and reporters were always present. Dr. Lucky presided, and all students joined in the debates. Many were the sallies of wit, many were the blows from Wisdom's logic fist, many were the ludicrous blunders, in that day of budding orators. Not a few of the students, however, were advanced in years, were even experienced teachers, and could speak to the point, and with precision. And, in this connection, it is pleasant to remember that several of the class have since reached distinction in educational work, as in the case of Mr. Thos. E. Kennedy, who is now Inspector of the San Francisco schools.

Another feature of our student life was Dr. Lucky's morning lecture on teaching. These lectures occupied five months in their delivery. He began the course by calling attention to the child entering the school for the first time, with its little fears and tremblings, and ended by pointing us to that higher school in heaven, where the Father and Mother truth unvail.

Ours was the first class graduated after the removal to San José. Dr. Lucky was Principal, Prof. H. P. Carlton, Vice-Principal, Miss Eliza W. Houghton, Mrs. Dorcas Clark, and others were assistants. Under Dr. Lucky the discipline was strict, yet kindly—the hand of iron in the glove of velvet. He was a man of impressive dignity, robust head and shoulders, countenance frank and open as the day, bold crag-like brows, and a smile that lighted up the face in a wonderful manner.

Professor Carlton had strong and pleasing traits of character. He strove to put off the pedagogue and to be a comrade, a fellow student. Nothing pleased him more than to have a pupil bring in matter outside of the text-book—something that showed independent investigation. To call out the shrill note of personality, to form habits of thought and study, to stir the spiritual forces—these were his aims. Of nervous temperament, he felt keenly, was terribly in earnest. He was himself impressed, and so he impressed others, with the mystery and pathos of life. His philosophy was a passionate idealism. His style of expression was bold and abrupt. His favorite quotation seemed to be that one from Kant: "Two things are sublime—conscience and the stars." He could recite *The Raven* with magical effect. Once he recited it before an assembly of teachers and students. The dim light of the lamps gave to him a half unearthly aspect. Figure tall and erect, face energetic and pale, hair thin and scattered, he himself seemed an apparition from "the tempest and the night's plutonian shore."

Through Miss Houghton we came to know and love the plants of field and hedgerow. And it was with fine feeling and sympathy that she led us, also, into the high places of literature. Happy were we who went that primrose way. Her presence was inspiring, uplifting. Always painstaking, always insisting on thorough work and accurate expression. These qualities made her effective as a teacher; she had others which made her loved as a woman.

The motherly Mrs. Clark, with her great good sense and kindly nature, had also a high place in all hearts. It seems, as I remember her, that her brain approached to Huxley's ideal, "a calm, cold, logic engine, trained to spin gossamers, as well as forge the anchors of the mind."

It has been a pleasure to speak of these old familiar faces. And though I now lay down my pen, they will not be forgotten; they have an assured place in my heart—friends of blessed memory. We prepare for the future by an affectionate reverence for what is worthy in the past.

1872-73.

(June 17, 1872—March 29, 1873.)

By the seventh of July, 1872, the Board of Building Commissioners had prepared rooms sufficient for immediate wants, and the school at last found a *home*.

The tax provided for in the first bill proved insufficient to complete the building, and another tax, amounting to $75,000 per year, was levied for the twenty-fourth and twenty-fifth fiscal years, 1873-75. This still did not prove enough, and subsequent appropriations were made of over $3,000, at one time, and $25,000 at another. The building was finally completed in 1876, at a total cost of about $285,000. Though imperfectly planned for school purposes, it was a handsome building, both in architectural design and in detail of finish. Its numerous porticoes, supported by Corinthian pillars, and its handsome entrances, gave exterior grace and beauty, while within, the corridors were wide, the rooms spacious, and the wood work elegantly finished. It is unfortunate that so large an amount of time, money, and skill should have been expended in erecting a building almost entirely of wood. Had it been of more enduring material, it might still have been standing.

As the school increased in size, the need of an additional teacher was strongly felt, and the Board appointed a committee to select a qualified teacher. After considerable correspondence Charles H. Allen, of Wisconsin, well known as an institute lecturer, and for many years connected with Normal Schools, was, on recommendation of the committee, elected as teacher of the natural sciences, music, and drawing. Professor Allen entered upon his duties October 7, 1872.

Since its removal from San Francisco, no training school had been connected with the Normal School. As soon as the school was permanently located, steps were taken to organize this indispensable department of every true Normal School. In November, 1872, Miss Mary J. Titus, a graduate of the Oswego Normal School, was elected Principal of the Training School. The pupils admitted were taken from the public schools of San José, and their number limited to forty. For the first year the value of this department to the Senior Class was entirely in the way of observation, as they were not required to teach.

These necessary additions to the teaching force so increased the expenses of the school that, during this and the succeeding year, a deficiency of over $4,500 was created, which was provided for by the next Legislature.

REMINISCENCES BY MARY E. HENDRIX, CLASS OF MARCH, 1873.

The year 1872 brought some important changes in the Normal School. The beautiful new building that had cost so much time and money, was near enough completion to admit of its being occupied by the school. One room was furnished for the use of the Senior Class, two for the Junior Class, one for the use of the Principal, and one for the Library. A large room in the basement was fitted up for general exercises, and another for the Training School, which was established and placed in the charge of Miss Titus. How pleasant the large roomy building seemed! Up and down the long corridors, and in the unfinished rooms, the pupils could be seen, promenading at recess hours, with books in hand. Not much time could be wasted.

This was Dr. Lucky's last year in the Normal School. He was well liked by his pupils. He was a man of dignified appearance, though he discouraged any display of false dignity. He used to tell us: "The teacher who dares not go out and play with his pupils, for fear of losing his dignity, has *no dignity to lose.*"

One of the studies we enjoyed most was our mental philosophy. Our teacher in this branch was Professor Carlton. He was a fair, slender, nervous man, whose distinguishing characteristic as a teacher was his great earnestness. Whatever his hand found to do he did with his might. His method of recitation was to require the pupil to give the author's opinion, then give his own and illustrate it. The discussions which followed were a source of pleasure and profit.

This was Professor Allen's first year in the school. He seemed to be acquainted with every difficulty that ever beset a teacher in our common schools. Looking forward as we did to the difficulties ahead of us, poetry could not have interested us more than did what he had to say about the practical work of the school-room.

A few weeks before the close of the school, the teachers met in what seemed to us mysterious conclave. We knew at that time it would be decided who would graduate. The pupils were informed privately whether they were successful or not. The anxiety of the class at this time may be imagined. With what bright faces some left the Principal's room!

Contrary to the usual custom, the valedictorian was selected by the teachers. It was thought desirable to choose one who had taken the entire course—gone through the Junior year as well as the Senior. Their choice fell on Miss Delia Snow, of Salt Lake; so to her essay on "The Child" was added the valedictory address. I do not think any one was surprised at the choice, except Miss Snow herself. She well represented the class, both in her ability as a valedictorian and in her success as a teacher. "I was so anxious," she afterward said, "to try the new methods I learned at the Normal School. I took such an interest in my school." I have heard her highly commended by the patrons of the district in which she taught.

Miss Belle Merrit was selected to write the class song for the commencement exercises; she was the youngest in the class, but the selection did us justice. We copied the song from the blackboard, Miss Houghton, our teacher in elocution and rhetoric, calling our attention to its beauties.

The choice of class poet was left to the class. Miss Houghton had said any one in the class could write a poem; so there was no danger of making a mistake. Something was already known of Mr. Chipman's ability as a poet; so he received the vote of the class. He gave us a humorous poem on "Thanksgiving Day."

Now began the drill on our commencement exercises. We were taken, one at a time, into the large, unfinished audience hall to practice. Miss Houghton was an able elocutionist. She seemed to have an ocean of voice at her command. She was appreciative. No beautiful thought, well expressed, ever escaped her notice. The was also an unsparing critic. It was of no use for the girls to lose their tempers. A little temper sometimes came in good play when spirited reading was required.

As preceptress, Miss Houghton was vigilant. We used to think she understood everything. She cautioned the girls against expense and display in the selection of dresses for the graduating exercises. A plain dress of good material, she said, was in better taste. She used to say, "If a **girl** ever wishes to look pretty, it is when she is married, and if you dress your best now, you cannot do better at your wedding." Her advice was generally appreciated and followed.

The graduating class consisted of four young men and sixteen young ladies— **a combination of** fours.

Gay as we felt over our prospects, we could not avoid a solemn feeling, as we met, **for** the last time, in the basement, **for** morning exercises. **As** we looked on the Board for the number of the song selected by Professor Allen, a subdued whisper was heard, "How appropriate!" It was:

> Our Father, through the coming year,
> We know not what shall be;
> But we would leave, without a fear,
> Its ord'ring all to Thee.

1873-74.

(June 18, 1873—March 26, 1874.)

In March, 1873, Dr. Lucky was reëlected as temporary Principal, Professor C. H. Allen as Vice-Principal, and Miss E. W. Houghton and Miss Lucy M. Washburn, a graduate of the Normal School at Fredonia, New York, as assistants, and Miss M. J. Titus as Principal of the Training School. With this Faculty, the school opened its twelfth year June 18, 1873.

At a meeting of the Board of Trustees held August 4, 1873, Professor C. H. Allen was elected permanent Principal, and August ninth, J. H. Braly, who had resigned his office as Trustee, was elected Vice-Principal, and Miss E. W. Houghton was designated Preceptress. Feeling the necessity of the improvement of the school, and its more satisfactory organization, the Board, at the same meeting, appointed a committee consisting of Trustee Cory and the Principal, to present a report upon the condition, wants, and objects of the Normal School. In accordance with this appointment, the following report was presented at the next meeting, October 22, 1873, and was unanimously adopted·

To the Board of Trustees of the State Normal School of California:

GENTLEMEN: Your committee, to whom was referred the matter **of** "The Objects and Wants of the Normal School," beg leave respectfully **to** submit the following report:

The primary object of a Normal School is to fit young persons to enter upon **the work of** teaching, intelligently, and to perform **the work** successfully.

Theoretically, a Normal School should teach only *how* to teach, receiving pupils after they are fully prepared in scholastic attainments, and giving them the necessary instruction in the philosophy of education and methods of teaching.

Practically, it has in all cases, your committee believe, been found necessary to devote much of the time and the labor of the school to preparing pupils in the branches to be taught.

Several causes conspire to make this divergence between the theory and the practice in Normal Schools. Among them are the following:

I. The profession of teaching has, as yet, not become so permanent and remunerative that pupils will take the time, after having acquired sufficient knowledge to obtain certificates, to qualify themselves in methods of teaching, and a school doing only professional work would find itself without pupils.

II. The successful teacher requires more positive, exhaustive, and definite knowledge of the branches he is to teach than is usually given in other schools.

III. It is believed, and perhaps truly, that there is a certain economy in combining the instruction *how* to teach with that which gives **what is** to be taught.

IV. Most persons who desire to fit themselves for teaching, desire at the same time to acquire the knowledge that will fit them for any or all the duties of life.

Whether all this is founded in good philosophy or not, we are obliged to accept it as true, and schools must, to meet the public demand, be organized and conducted accordingly.

It remains, then, to present the plan which will, under the circumstances, best meet the public demand and accomplish the desired end. In connection with this, your committee make the following suggestions:

The school must be manned by a corps of well **qualified instructors.** This involves teachers who, in addition to the thorough and critical knowledge of the branches taught, which is absolutely necessary, shall have devoted time, study, and thought enough to the subject of teaching, so that they have arrived at the natural or normal method of presentation, and who are sufficiently acquainted with the laws of mental growth and development to be able to judge whether their work is accomplishing what they desire. They must also have that somewhat rare power of *selection*, which will enable them to distinguish between essentials and non-essentials, and to work accordingly.

In addition to this, they must have that mental strength and activity which will enable them, when brought into contact with adult and vigorous minds, to lead them instead of being led by them.

If such teachers can be found and secured, the success of your school is certain.

A Normal School, from its very nature, must be progressive. No school, and no teacher in the school, must rest contented upon the laurels already gained, or the point already attained. There is need for constant intercourse with educators the world over. One who would hold and worthily fill his position as a teacher in a Normal School, can do so only by a life of labor.

The course of study and training should provide for two distinct kinds of work. That is, there are certain subjects which teachers are required to *know*, and there are other subjects, which, under existing circumstances, they can only be expected to know *about*. Could our course of study be extended to three, or even four years, we might enlarge the first class of subjects, and diminish the second. That, for the present, seems impracticable.

There must, then, be given a thorough, searching, definite knowledge of the branches which are to be taught in the public schools, and a power to express that knowledge with clearness and precision. Nothing can take the place of this. And especially should this knowledge and power be given in the structure and use of our mother tongue. Language is the teacher's instrument; if he would be successful, he must become the master of it.

Of the second class of subjects—those upon which we may expect only general information--but a *general* knowledge can be given. This knowledge should be accurate, as far as it goes; should give the boundaries and divisions of the subject, and such other information as will enable the pupil to pursue it alone after leaving the school, and, if possible, such a love for study as will give him the inclination so to do.

Many of these so called higher studies have a very important economic value; that is, they are closely connected with the laws of life and health, with the daily avocations of life, and with the protection and development of the resources of our State. The instruction in these should be such as to bring this relation constantly before the pupil, thus compelling him to realize that our schools should prepare children for the practical duties of life.

As many of these studies require for their proper prosecution, illustrative apparatus, the Normal School must have, at as early a time as possible, a complete apparatus.

All of which is respectfully submitted.

BEN. COBY,
CHAS. H. ALLEN,
Committee.

The school had now reached a point where it became almost a necessity to make some provision for pupils from a distance, who, upon examination, were found unqualified for work in Normal Classes. Besides having incurred heavy traveling expenses in coming to the Normal School, these pupils had, in most cases, completed the work of the Grammar Schools in the counties from which they came, and so could gain little by reëntering those schools. It was, therefore, thought best to form a class specially for these, and a Preparatory Class was organized in November, 1873, with Miss Cornelia Walker, formerly of the State Normal School at St. Cloud, Minnesota, as teacher. The special work of this class was a thorough review of the elementary branches in preparation for the work of the Junior Class. A tuition fee was charged of one dollar per week, afterwards reduced to seventy-five cents.

During this year, the Senior Class began regular practice work in the Training School, under the supervision of its Principal, Miss Titus.

Rooms were fitted up to receive specimens in geology and natural history, forming the nucleus of the future Museum.

1874-75.

(June 10, 1874—March 25, 1875.)

By an Act passed March 30, 1874, the laws relating to the Normal School were amended in a few particulars. The new building affording abundant accommodation for all who were likely to apply for admission, the sections providing for competitive examinations of candidates, by County Boards, were repealed. Tuition was no longer required from residents of other States and Territories, but such students were required to sign a declaration of intention to teach, either in California or in the States and Territories where they resided.

The Board of Trustees was authorized, at its discretion, to issue elementary diplomas to those who worthily completed a portion of the course of study, to be prescribed. The State Board of Examination was required to grant second grade State certificates on these elementary diplomas, first grade State certificates on diplomas of graduation, and educational diplomas on past graduate diplomas.

It was distinctly specified that the Trustees should receive no compensation for their services, and no money for traveling expenses.

The State Superintendent was no longer made *ex officio* Secretary of the Board, but the Board was to appoint a Secretary, without salary, and was required to keep a record of its proceedings, open to public inspection. A few other changes and additions were made, of minor importance. Under the new provision, Principal Allen was elected Secretary of the Board.

The school now increased rapidly in numbers, reaching at one time in the year nearly three hundred in the Normal Classes. This necessitated still further additions to the Faculty. Miss Walker was promoted to the Normal Department, her place in the Preparatory Class being filled by Miss Phebe P. Grigsby, and Miss Annie E. Chamberlain, a graduate of the Normal Department of the University of Wisconsin, was elected as assistant in the Junior Classes. Miss Florence Grigsby, a graduate of the class of 1874, was made assistant in the Training School. Notwithstanding these additions, the Principal says in his annual report for 1875:

During the year we have been obliged to keep up four Junior Classes. These have, much of the **time,** numbered forty-five each. The **Senior** Class has numbered about fifty, and of this but one class could be made.

Our instructional force has been quite too small. While **it is as** easy to teach **forty as one, it is** impossible to give to classes of this size the training in expression, **and in** clearness of thought, so desirable in the teacher. From the very nature **of** our work, a Normal School requires a much larger corps of teachers, in proportion to the number of pupils, than **other** schools. The principal work **must be** *training* rather than *teaching.*

Up to this time, the Training School Classes had been made **up** of pupils from the public schools, and the San José Board **of** Education had **paid a certain** sum monthly for each class. **At the** beginning of the second term of **the** school year 1874–75, the Training School **was opened as a tuition school, independent of** the city schools, and soon became nearly self-sustaining.

Work **on the building was** still in **progress.** During the latter **part of the year, class-rooms on the second floor were fitted up for the** better accommodation of the large number in attendance, and the assembly hall, which was at first designed only for public gatherings, was seated, and used for the daily morning assembling of the school.

As no special appropriation for furnishing had yet been made, these expenditures drew heavily upon the current expense fund, **creating a** deficit of **over** $1,000. Referring to this, the annual **report of the Trustees says:**

The school for the coming year will doubtless number more than three hundred, or double the number provided for when the last **appropriation** was made. To meet the increased demand for instruction, **we must increase** the corps of teachers, and unwillingly, on our part, create **a still greater** deficit. The only alternative is to refuse admission to the school **(which, if** pupils are qualified, **we have no** right, under **the law, to do), or to** close the school for a part of the year. We feel assured that we have taken **the** better course, and that the coming Legislature will cheerfully appropriate **a** sufficient amount to meet this deficit, when the circumstances under **which** it has arisen shall be understood.

The appropriation of **$3,000 for** apparatus, and of $500 annually for library, are being expended with great care, purchasing only those articles which will **be of** constant use.

We felt warranted in expending $500 of the apparatus appropriation in the purchase of a very valuable collection of shells, consisting of nearly three **thousand species,** collected and named by the late Dr. Canfield, of Monterey, **to be named the "Canfield Collection."**

1875-76.

(June 15, 1875—March 31, 1876.)

The year 1875-76 was marked by the addition to the Faculty of Professor Henry B. Norton, of the State Normal School at Emporia, Kansas. Professor Norton was elected March 25, 1875, and began his work in the school at the opening of the year, in June. From that time until his death in 1885, he labored tirelessly as teacher and lecturer, both in the school and in Teachers' Institutes throughout the State. A fellow teacher, Miss Houghton, writes thus of his coming:

His skillful handling of all subjects that he taught, his great fund of information, his ready, kindly answers to all questions, made his pupils feel that a new and strong power had been added to the school, while the Faculty, each and all, soon found themselves deferring to his opinions, drawing from his rich store of knowledge, and feeling that he was a man ready to fill any gap, to perform able, generous services here, there, and everywhere.

The growth and progress of the school for the year can best be shown by the following extracts from the annual report of the Principal, in 1876:

The records of the school show a continued and healthful growth. * * * The average attendance for the year has exceeded, by sixty, the highest number enrolled last year, and is more than double the average attendance for the two preceding years, upon which our biennial appropriation was based. We have felt it necessary to raise somewhat the grade of admission, and to drop from the school those whose mental habits convinced the Faculty that they could never make successful teachers. About twenty have thus been dropped, and perhaps an equal number discouraged from entering. Had our effort been simply to make a large school, we might have reported an attendance of more than four hundred; but we have, under your suggestions, striven to have a school composed only of good working members, and of such the school is now chiefly composed. * * *

The Faculty unanimously recommend extending the course to three years, and a provision for graduation at the end of the second year, with an elementary diploma. Teachers will be thus qualified for the great mass of the schools of the State, and it is believed many more will, by this arrangement, remain through the course.

At the beginning of the year one additional teacher was elected, but the growth of the school has left us still very short of help. We have carried through the year five Junior Classes, and these have numbered as high as fifty-six. With such classes no teacher can do really good work. With an opportunity to recite only once in two or three days, even the most earnest pupils will become slack in preparing lessons. The only antidote to this is written recitations. This has been unceasingly applied, but entails such labor upon the teacher as few can endure. I venture the assertion, that the teachers of the Normal School have, for the past year, devoted more time to school work than is required of **laboring** men by the hardest task-masters. Our task-master has been necessity. * * *

We need, and, **to make the school what it** should be, must have, at least two additional teachers, and **confidently indulge** the hope that **our** Legislature, in **its wisdom, will place at** your disposal **an** amount sufficient **to** enable you to meet this demand.

We are using all of the completed portions of the building, and are pressed **for room.** The completion of the building is also a necessity.

The preparatory class and training schools are filling their places well, and **have been** kept full, while many applicants for admission have been **sent** away.

1876-77.

(June 20, 1876—March 31, 1877.)

Beginning with this year the course of study was extended to three years—Junior, Middle, and Senior. For the next four years elementary diplomas were granted to those who completed the work of the Middle year, but as this plan did not prove in all respects satisfactory, the Board, in 1880, decided not to grant elementary diplomas in future.*

In accordance with the reports and recommendations of the Board of Trustees, the Legislature, in March, 1876, increased the appropriation for current expenses to $24,000 per year for the next two years, and made liberal appropriations for library and furniture, besides providing for the deficiency already created. The necessary means being thus provided, two valuable additions were made to the Faculty. In April, 1876, the Board elected as teachers in the Normal Department Professor Ira More, formerly Principal of the State Normal School at St. Cloud, Minnesota, and Miss Helen S. Wright, who had been a teacher in the Normal Schools at Fredonia and at Potsdam, New York.

In the Training Department Miss Mary E. Wilson, of the class of 1875, was elected Assistant in June, 1876, and in November was elected to take the place of Miss Florence Grigsby, who resigned at that time.

EXTRACT FROM REPORT OF PRINCIPAL, MARCH, 1877.

After long and careful deliberation **we have reached the** conclusion that the interests of the school and of the **educational interests of the** State require a change **in** our terms. **We close now about the last of** March. This year one hundred pupils will leave the school **one month before we** close, to attend the March examinations. **This takes away much of interest** and zest from those

---

*The names of students who received elementary diplomas are given after **the** alphabetical list of graduates with full diplomas.

who remain, and those leaving lose the inspiration to go on, always drawn from the closing exercises. Again, we close so late that the graduates, who, of course, cannot leave before April first, will find it too late to engage schools, and will be left without employment when they need it most. If we closed one month earlier, or about two months later, both these difficulties would be in a measure obviated. If we closed two months later, the graduates, after a few weeks' rest, would be ready for the new school year, and we could close on the full tide of attendance. There are many considerations which lead us to conclude that the school year hereafter should begin about the first of August, and close the last of May; and we ask that you so arrange the terms for the next year.

REMINISCENCES BY A MEMBER OF '77.

Happy Normal days of new ways and new associates, and new vistas opening adown the avenues of hope! Return for a joyous while with your golden memories and the glow of the old-time, young impressions fresh upon you. Yet impose not upon me the dignity of class historian; that were better maintained by many another member in a manner pleasingly characteristic; by Miss Salkeld with enlivening diversity; by Mr. Sanborn with an undercurrent of quiet satire; by Miss Snedaker with the boldness of originality; by Miss Royce with painstaking accuracy; by Miss Patterson with modest grace; by Miss Allen with bewitching piquancy and naïveté and a refreshing interspersion of jibe and jest to keep us in a roar; by Miss Sprague with chaste elegance; by sweet Sue Moore with a motherly kindness that would bring us clustering about her feet to listen; or it might acceptably appear with a touch of the poetic fervor shining through Miss Barry's dreamy eyes, or in a setting of the artistic finish characteristic of Kate More's handiwork. Indeed, what a variety of desirable ways are suggested as the individual classmates pass in review before memory's mirror.

Entering for the first time upon the thoroughly systematized work of the Normal course, what a contrast appears between the accustomed mode of routine drill and this, where everything that is done and the way in which it is done have a reason behind them and an object in perspective.

A fitting prelude to the day's work were the devotional exercises, occupying fifteen minutes each morning, when all students and instructors were expected to be present in the assembly hall, either to take part, or to maintain a respectful silence. After a formal registering of class reports by the Vice-Principal, a chapter from the scriptures was read by the Principal, Prof. Charles H. Allen. The words fell sweetly impressive from his lips, the venerable presence of the man harmonizing peculiarly with the situation. Ascending to the reading stand upon the rostrum, the overtasked frame, the flowing beard, white hair, and overhanging brows, the fine, pale features, the penetrating, clear blue eye, even the characteristic, outward swing of the right foot, all combined to form a harmonious whole at once venerable and commanding; a man who wore his honors with a native grace. In general it would be remarked: "This is the right man in the right place;" but here we forget, so at one is he with the school in all its workings, that it could go on without him, the central figure, and we would say, rather: "This is the proper setting for the man." As he descends from the executive chair, he goes crowned with the glory of a work well done, a charge faithfully kept.

After the scriptural reading, grand anthems rolled to the trembling dome, poured forth by three or four hundred voices, led by the musical director, Prof. Z. M. Parvin.

From the assembly hall the classes passed to their various recitation, to receive from their teachers not only instruction, but the characteristic impression which each was inevitably stamping upon his or her pupils.

An almost electric keenness pervaded the atmosphere of Miss Walker's classroom. Maintaining forever a war of wits with her pupils, which kept them on the keen edge of alertness, her method could not fail to arouse the most sluggish intellects to unwonted activity. It acted, indeed, as a wholesome stimulant, a gentle contrast to which lay, not less pleasingly, in the tranquil presence and winning ways of the gentlewomanly Miss Wright, who was elected to the Faculty in March, 1876, succeeding Miss Houghton as Preceptress, upon the resignation of the latter, in March, 1877.

Were I to choose a single word which should most fittingly characterize Miss Houghton, that word—if you will please to accept it in its pureness, entering into the genuine elegance of it—that word should be *thoroughbred*; a woman whose taste was perfect, whose simple presence was a silent educator.

At the same time with Miss Wright, Professor More joined the corps of instructors. He was an iron-clad man with an iron-frame mind; one whose strong personality was not to be fathomed in a day, or a week, or a month; a man likely to be underestimated by immaturity, but liked intensely by those fortunate enough to appreciate him; a man of geometric proportions, physically, mentally, and morally.

Miss Washburn's work throughout was characterized by accuracy and finish. It seems to me that the secret underlying her success was her happy faculty of imparting to her classes a contagion of interest in whatever subject she handled; so that the most persistent drill (and she was persistent) did not become monotonous with her.

Professor Braly's genial face graced the Vice-Principal's chair. Affable, companionable, and thrown by the general duties of that office into contact alike with all the classes, he was a social favorite throughout the school—as with his associates everywhere—and was in demand upon all social occasions.

Foremost among these for pleasurable memory is the reception and banquet given by the Senior Class in honor of the birthday anniversary of our beloved Principal; to which were invited all members of the Board of Instruction and members of the Alumni who chanced to be present, and where wit and merriment sparkled and flowed, while the fair waitresses in dainty muslin caps and aprons with their pink and blue ribbons (a pretty conceit for the occasion) flitted hither and thither dispensing viands—from Yankee baked beans to trifles and delicacies—*ad infinitum*; in-so-much that Professor Norton, when toasts were in order, facetiously remarked upon the *litter-ary* bent of the assemblage. Later in the season, but not less delightful, was the reception given by Professor and Mrs. Allen to the Senior Class in honor of the nuptials of Mrs. Josie Wright Armstrong, a popular member of the class, and, previously, a teacher of experience and ability.

Our Literary Society was of a general character, representing all of the classes. Once, by way of variety, we revived memories of old-fashioned ways by challenging the gentlemen's debating club to an open contest in spelling, Professor Norton, he of blessed memory, the loved and revered of all, teachers and students alike, kindly consenting to preside and "give out the words." The ladies' society dishonored its name of "Work and Win," the "Amphictyons" whipping us right royally. However, we gave, occasionally, delightful public entertainments, when the vast assembly hall was full to overflowing with the *élite* of the city.

Throughout the Senior year we enjoyed the privileges of Professor Allen's lectures upon mental growth and development, and methods of teaching based thereon; with the addition during the last five months of practical work in the Training School, under the supervision of the efficient instructors of that department.

And then we graduated and were happy ever after. Go thou and do likewise.

1877-78.

(August 7, 1877—May 23, 1878.)

The change in the time of opening and closing terms, recommended by the Faculty, was made in 1877, prolonging the summer vacation to August, and making the second term begin in January instead of in November.

Before the opening of the year, Miss Houghton, who had been connected with the school since 1864, sent her resignation to the Board of Trustees on account of failing health. The resignation was accepted by the Board with expressions of regret and of high esteem for Miss Houghton's character and services. They elected Miss Helen S. Wright as her successor in the position of Preceptress.

During the second term, Miss Mary E. B. Norton, a sister of Professor Norton, and for many years a teacher in the Rockford Seminary, Illinois, was elected to a position in the Normal Department, her specialty being botany.

Extracts from Report of Principal, May, 1878.

Contrary to our expectations, the past year has shown a notable increase in the numbers in attendance at the school. We had thought that during last year we had reached the maximum; but, notwithstanding the "hard times," as will be seen, there has been an increase of nearly twenty-five per cent. * * *

We present two classes for graduation. The Senior Class numbers fifty-eight and the Middle Class forty-nine. Of the present Senior Class, fifteen graduated with second grade diplomas last year.

This seems a large number of teachers to be sent out in one year, but will not, we think, oversupply the demand for trained teachers. As Superintendents and District Boards learn the difference between the work of those who have only scholarship to recommend them and those who have, besides this, a definite plan of work and a knowledge of the means to be used in securing the best results, trained teachers will be more and more in demand.

At the beginning of the year, Miss Eliza W Houghton, long connected with the school, and well and favorably known through the State, resigned her position, owing to failing health. We parted with her regretfully, feeling that the school would suffer a great loss by her withdrawal. * * * With the means now placed at the disposal of the Board, the school can, during the next two years, be supplied with teachers so as to reduce the numbers in each class taught, to a maximum of twenty-five. We shall thus be able to do much more satisfactory work, as each pupil can have more opportunity for recitation, and will receive more special training in manner and expression.

REMINISCENCES OF THE CLASS OF '78.

What an inspiration it is to go into Room K and look upon the array of bright faces portrayed in the class pictures! How insignificant our photograph is compared with the fine one '89 has just placed there! Ours is one of the smallest and nearly the oldest in the collection. I wonder if *we* have faded into insignificance like that. Surely photography has advanced since our day; the world has progressed; have we? Perhaps it is our modest example that has suggested this fine display; let us hope that in other directions we have been setting at work forces that are developing great things.

How well I remember the day we went to Santa Clara to sit for this picture! I went with the two Fannies; and just as the artist was showing my negative, which mirrored a smile he had evoked with much labor, one Fanny touched the dripping plate with her index finger. Oh, the wrath of the artist! Oh, the scolding we received! But he atoned for it afterwards by sending us a photograph of all the famous places in Santa Clara. Fanny was our youngest, and we lost trace of her for a long time after graduation; but we found her at last, with a fine looking young husband and "just the dearest baby." The other Fanny was one of the quietest girls in the class, but very sweet and capable. I used to think she was already pluming her wings for Heaven; and in one short year after graduation, the angel with the amaranthine wreath took her home.

The picture reminds us of our fine group of young men, seventeen per cent; can any other class give as good a showing? Mr. Pettit, the mature looking young man at the right, won our warmest admiration when he nursed his room-mate through the small-pox. We were all summoned to the assembly hall one afternoon, and Professor Allen called him to the platform to receive a fine watch, the gift of the school in appreciation of his self-sacrifice. How noble he looked as he gave his word of thanks, adding "I only did my duty!" Henceforth he was a hero in our eyes. We never had a class meeting at which he did not preside, and in our reunions it has always been a pleasant feature to have him in his accustomed place.

There were affinities in our class. We all had our chums. And if two of the most charming girls did monopolize two of the young men, I am sure the rest of us have long since forgiven them. There was one very noticeable trio, Miss Nelson, so dashing and jolly, Miss Chapman, refined and lovable, Miss Raymond, good and faithful. If I remember rightly, they were particularly fond of visiting with Professor More.

He seemed to have an inexhaustible fund of knowledge, but we never could discover when he worked to get it. He did everything so easily, and always had abundance of time to argue and joke with us. It was he who opened our eyes to the wonders of the heavens. Who does not remember gratefully the evenings he gave us with the telescope? Once our class was very suddenly transferred to him for arithmetic. We were very indignant, for our dear Miss Washburn had labored for months to teach us the importance of percentage; and now he swept away our arguments and methods with one ruthless stroke. Afterwards we were told that this was done just to teach us that there is more than one way of doing a thing.

But if any one wished to talk to Professor Norton, the busy man must be stopped in the hall, carrying a bottle under one arm and a coil of tubing on the other. He always met such interruptions with hearty good will. In those days our laboratory work was carried on in a crude way. Each pupil was provided with a square tin pail, converted by Professor Norton's ingenuity into a chemist's water bath, by a movable tin shelf pierced with holes for collecting gases in inverted bottles. The same pail, after the water was turned out, served to hold the rest of our little collection of apparatus. So we received the practical lesson how to make much of little in our own schools.

It was just before our graduation that Miss Norton entered the school. We remember the girlish enthusiasm of those who had never before known any one who had traveled in Europe. In two weeks she put us into a new world of nature and of art.

I never study this picture of ours without thinking of a little treasure box I have. Let us see what its contents will recall. Here is a badge of crape, worn the day we went with our teachers to attend the funeral of Annie Harrigan. We heaped flowers upon her desk at school; and here also are the resolutions we published, Clara Richardson's name heading the committee. This little bunch of pressed violets lay by my plate at the banquet we gave Professor Allen on the golden day that numbered his fifty years. Best of all the feast of good things were the after-dinner speeches from the Faculty—a custom worth reviving by later classes, for this inspiration did much to make us what we are. The influence of that day is a part of my best life; but the only speech I can quote word for word is that of Miss Royce, who said she was the baby of the Faculty, and "children should be seen and not heard." She was assistant in the Preparatory then, and our library, managed by a student and opened but occasionally, was a thing of beauty rather than of utility. I remember taking home but one book during my connection with the school—Darwin's "Origin of Species." It is a constant source of regret that Miss Royce, whose invaluable services have made the Normal library such a power in the school, could not have unfolded these treasures in our day. The next keepsake that appears is a small card of invitation, rosy as our hopes that bright morning, embossed with letters as golden as our memory of that good time—Professor Braly's breakfast party at New Almaden. By nine o'clock, after a delightful ride, we were grouped with our teachers around six blazing camp fires at Hacienda. Each person was provided with a piece of fresh beef, and a long stick upon which to roast it. The recipe had not been included in our study of household science, and some of the inexperienced produced strange contrasts, steaks coal black on one side and lobster red on the other, with a copious seasoning of ashes and cinders. But no amount of inexperience could spoil the delicious coffee, the bread and butter, and the boiled eggs our hostess placed before us. After keen enjoyment of this unique breakfast we spent the remainder of the day climbing the hills, searching for botanical specimens, and visiting together. At night we returned, tendering enthusiastic thanks to the kind Professor whose bounty had made us so happy. How genial he was, always with such warm greetings for all, that each student felt himself the recipient of special favor.

And here is the programme of our Commencement week. We thought we should like a baccalaureate address, so as many as wished went on the last Sunday evening to hear our beloved Professor Norton preach a gospel of development in work, from Phil. 2:12, 13. He taught us that the way of labor is the royal way—God's way; that we must do our duty and leave the rest with God. "Man commenced in a garden, he ends in a mansion; this is a type of growth. Think of Christ the *laborer;* like Him we are to *work.*"

Thus Professor Norton taught us how to labor, Professor Braly taught us to temper our work with the little courtesies that bring sunshine into daily life, while Professor **Allen taught us what to be.** You remember his favorite maxim, "Be what you **would have** your pupils become." He does **not** know how lovingly his "children" think of him, as they try to live out his teachings. Classmates, we are coming into the heat of the **day,** we realize the crisis that is upon the **New West.** As we take up our share of the great day's **toil** with fresh **enthusiasm it** is fitting that we should recall the influences that have fashioned **our lives, and** pay tribute to the hand that has made our Alma **Mater one of the** greatest forces in the true development of this coast. Some day may **he** realize that he has "builded better than he knew."

1878-79.

(August 6, 1878—May 22, 1879.)

No changes of importance were made in the work of the school during this year. Two additions were made to the Faculty. Professor C. W. Childs, of the class of June, 1867, was elected in June, 1878. He had taught successfully ever since his graduation, for six years as Principal of the High School at Suisun City, and had been County Superintendent of Solano County two terms. Professor Childs began his work in the Normal School in August, 1878, his specialties being history and bookkeeping.

Miss Frances L. Webster, of the Normal School at Cedar Falls, Iowa, also came into the school in August, specially as a teacher of reading.

FROM PRINCIPAL'S REPORT, MAY, 1879.

This term closes the most satisfactory year's work that has been accomplished since my connection with the school. With the two additional teachers, elected at the beginning of the year, I have been able to arrange and assign the work in such a way that much more has been accomplished than ever before. Reading and industrial drawing have received especial attention, the result of which will, we hope, be made apparent in the work of our graduates.

The attendance has been somewhat less than that of last year, owing partly to the pressure of "hard times," and, possibly, to the fact that the school is now quite as large as is demanded by the present educational wants of the State. Comparatively more have entered the higher classes, and many, already holding first grade State certificates, have attended the school to improve themselves in the profession of teaching.

REMINISCENCES BY JESSIE WILLIAMSON, CLASS OF MAY, 1879.

How many happy memories cluster round those magic words, Class of '79! We were a happy, care-free set, as memory shows them to me, few of us taking thought for the future and the responsibilities soon to rest upon us as educators of the youth of our land. We were a unique class, in our own estimation, having many distinguishing features that set us apart from ordinary classes. We were of all ages, from the dear little girl who wore short dresses and was the pet of the class, to the step-great-grandmother, if the expression may be used, of thirteen great grandchildren. There were all nationalities and styles, and decidedly more girls than boys. Thos. Edmonds had been a "midshipmite," and was familiarly called the Fiji Islander. He had a turn for poetry, as had also Kate Appleby, Mary Muir, Hattie Haile, and Si Hanscom, and many and various were the songs of the muses served up to us by these interesting members. Then there were the musical ones, Ella Irish, Mary Adams, Charlotte McCleran, Wm. Newcum, and Francis M. Sullivan; Wm. Walter Brown, who always walked the halls with an encyclopedia under each arm, taking in knowledge by absorption; quiet Claude Wakefield, who knew much, but was careful not to tell it if it could be helped; plump little May Crittenden, and Roby Hines, and many others.

We enjoyed the distinction of being the last class to graduate from the old building. Dear old building! Handsomer by far than the new one ever dreamed of being. What if it was not quite so convenient? Does beauty count for naught in this age of art? There were four stately entrances, one from each street. The halls were spacious and finished in handsome woods. The assembly hall, where the school gathered each morning, occupied the entire eastern wing of the building, and was two full stories in height. There was a commodious gallery, and the seats both in it and on the lower floor were in tiers, thus giving a good view from all parts of the house. But the building was a gem without a setting, for at that time the land surrounding it was only an alkali waste.

We might have been known as the class of petitions, for many and various were the written requests made of the Faculty. It seems laughable now, for none of them were ever granted, yet we never hesitated when the spirit moved us to present another. At one time we tired of reading, and a committee consisting of the young men of the class, waited upon the Principal, and requested that we be allowed to discontinue our work in that study We were satisfied on being told that a change would be made at the end of the term. We did not stop to think that it would have been done even if we had not made the request. We were even audacious enough to present a petition requesting the Faculty to graduate one of our number whose name had not been placed upon the list. It is needless to state the answer

We were particularly fortunate in having as our class teacher Professor Braly. No kinder man ever had charge of a class. In spite of our waywardness, by his tact and kindly ways, order and discipline were fully preserved, and perfect harmony reigned between teacher and pupil. We '79ers pity those of later days who have not known our teachers, Professors Braly, More, Norton, and others.

Our chemistry work was done with Professor Norton. We all admired him, for he talked just as steadily and unceasingly while hunting under tables for some missing article or gathering together chemicals in the closet, as while sitting at his desk. Part of the class did experimental work under his guidance, and many laughable incidents occurred. One day Mary Adams was mixing and shaking in a test tube, when to her horror, the Professor announced "Miss Mary now holds in her hand the most deadly explosive known to science." The look on her face convulsed the class and a mighty shout went up.

Geology and astronomy were learned from Professor More. No text-books were used, the instruction being entirely by lecture. No other man ever talked so fast and so steadily as he. By the time a lecture was over, we were worn out and our note books were full.

The terror of the Senior year was the review in grammar and arithmetic conducted by Professor Allen. Boldly would we plunge into a tangle of figures, and after straightening them out to our entire satisfaction hand in our papers for criticism. With fear and trembling did we receive them back again next day only to find zero, zero, zero marked in various places. We were also led through the **mazes of** political economy by Professor **Allen and enjoyed it immensely.**

Now approaches the gala day of the year, Professor Allen's birthday. **Here again** we departed from the usual custom, which was to spread an afternoon feast in honor of the occasion. We determined upon an evening reception. The tables were spread in the library and the large parlors on the opposite side of the hall were thrown open for the reception of our guests. A profusion of flowers, smilax, and evergreens was to be seen everywhere. After the **banquet,** toasts appropriate **to the** occasion were given and then Hattie **Haile,** Mistress of Ceremonies, called **upon** Thomas Edmonds, the poet of the **evening,** who read the **following:**

   Mistress Haile has my thanks, but I hardly agree
   That a man is a poet, who a poet would be.
   I'm a poetical mushroom—here firm as a post,
   For my subject has lent me the power of a host.

   We've assembled this evening with pleasure to share
   In the speech of the wise and the smiles of the fair,
   Though the beauties of both but in a measure display
   How we all do rejoice on our Allen's birthday.

   Here we call him "Our Allen," we hope he'll excuse,
   And we promise his friendship we'll never abuse.
   When we growl at our tasks, our report, our per cent,
   We believe in our heart our benefit's meant.

   Since the days of his youth in a noble career,
   He has well done his part without favor or fear.
   In his own Quaker State, in the East, in the West,
   And especially here, hand in hand with the best.

   Our Minerva, Miss Wright, of poetical art,
   Is not greater in genius than in kindness of heart.
   While Philosopher Braly, so sparkling in jokes
   And philology, reigns a true king of young folks.

   In perception of truth, and in genius to rule,
   Glows Miss Titus, the queen of a wonderful school,
   Where perchance but few others affairs could arrange,
   To well govern and monthly all officers change.

   Misses Washburn and Chamberlain in art so exact,
   Do on every occasion show talent and tact.
   Our great scientist, Norton, true scholar and man,
   Leads us on by example, as a chieftain his clan.

   Here's a point I would raise about Professor of Space,
   For he demonstrates well that each point has its place.
   Now when pupils have troubles, as they have o'er and o'er,
   Why like Oliver Twist, do they cry out for More?

Our Professor C. Childs, **is an artist so free**
When of him we but think it's "Oh, Ho!" and "He! **He!**"
Though we him might appease in angelic strain,
Could we equal Miss Webster or Miss M. McChain.

The name Norton, like Youmans, takes most of its worth
From connection with all the sweet **flowers** of earth.
While are clustered together (like **jewels most** choice,
Or bright birds of a feather) names Wilson **and** Royce.

Misses Walker and Grigsby with Professor **Hamm,**
Well to give them **due** credit, 'twould a folio cram.
To return **to our Allen, our** genial sage,
And his band of instructors illustrate the age.

Now, together they are, and our thanks well can claim,
As they work for our good, quite regardless of fame.
Though humility adds so to Reason's bright light,
That from summit to sea spreads our Faculty's might.

And now friends and classmates, from Mamie to Claude,
We may take as a toast what we all can applaud.
Here wish him of birthdays our number yet more,
And joy ever like this that cries *Allen! Hurrah!*

A short time after this the class was entertained at the house of Professor Allen, and then again at Professor Braly's home. As picnic season approached we became anxious for one more good time together, and a picnic to Blackberry Farm was agreed upon. George Ogden and W. A. Newcum were the Committee of Arrangements and right well did they do their work. We all came home reporting a perfect day as the closing of the social part of our connection with the school. Soon after we received our diplomas, and with mingled feelings of joy and sorrow said that sad word, farewell.

1879–80.

(August 5, 1879—May 20, 1880.)

With the school year 1879–80 came a catastrophe which, in its results, gave the strongest proof of the strength and vitality of the school and of its hold upon the people of the State.

On the morning of Tuesday, February 10, 1880, the Normal School building was totally destroyed by fire. The fire originated in a defective ash chute, and probably had smoldered for hours before it was discovered. When the alarm was given, at two o'clock in the morning, the center of the building and the tower were already in flames, making hopeless the attempt to save any portion of the building; and by five o'clock, the beautiful and costly edifice was a smoldering ruin.

The greater part of the library and a portion of the furniture were saved; but the valuable museum and herbarium, the result of years of collecting and labor, many books of reference, and most of the furniture, valued in all at more than $18,000, were lost. These, with the building, which cost $285,000, make a total loss to the State estimated at nearly $304,000. There were also serious private losses of valuable collections and personal property owned by the Curator of the Museum, the teacher of Botany, and others.

Nothing daunted by this apparently fatal catastrophe, the Executive Committee of the Board of Trustees, with the Principal and a few of the leading citizens, held an informal meeting on the grounds while the fire was still in progress, to devise means for continuing the work of the school. On Tuesday morning the Board of Education of the City of San José promptly tendered the High School building for the use of the Normal School, making arrangements to accommodate the High School classes in other buildings. Of this generous action, through which the school was enabled to continue its work with but one day's interruption, the Trustees, in their annual circular, thus expressed their appreciation: "Too much praise can hardly be awarded to the Board of Education of San José for their action in the matter, to the citizens, in cheerfully acquiescing in their action, and to the teachers and pupils of the city schools, for their ready and cheerful acceptance of a change productive of so much inconvenience to all."

An enthusiastic meeting of citizens was held on the evening of February tenth, and a committee appointed to visit the Legislature, which fortunately was in session at the time, and urge an immediate appropriation to rebuild the lost edifice. April 12, 1880, a bill was approved appropriating $100,000 to erect another State Normal School building at San José. The insurance companies promptly paid to the Trustees the insurance of $50,000 on the old building, and work on the new building was at once begun.

Meanwhile the school, though feeling much the inconvenience of its limited accommodations and loss of apparatus, continued its work uninterrupted.

Extracts from Report of Principal, May, 1880.

During the legislative discussions in reference to the Normal School, two assertions were made upon the floor, which do the school great injustice. As there was no opportunity to answer them there, I beg leave to answer them here.

One assertion was, that the Normal School is a San José, or Santa Clara County, High School; and that it therefore should not be sustained by the State. In answer to this charge I submit the following:

From our records of this year, I find that two hundred and seventy-five pupils have entered the school from outside counties. These are distributed as follows: San Francisco, twenty-seven; San Joaquin, twenty-four; Alameda, fifteen; Monterey, ten; Nevada, eleven; Sonoma and Sutter, each nine; Los Angeles and Stanislaus, each eight; El Dorado and Napa, each seven; Santa Barbara, six; Butte, Sacramento, San Luis Obispo, and Yuba, each five; Amador, Calaveras, Colusa, Mendocino, Placer, and Sierra, each four; Merced, San Benito, San Mateo, Siskiyou, Solano, and Tuolumne, each three; Lassen, Marin, Mariposa, Santa Cruz, and Tulare, each two; Fresno, Humboldt, Kern, Plumas, San Bernardino, San Diego, Shasta, and Yolo, each one. From other States, pupils coming here to qualify themselves to teach in California, sixteen.

It would seem that this should effectually answer the charge that the school is not a *State school*.

We have always declined to receive from San José or Santa Clara County, pupils as free pupils, unless we were satisfied that they were fitting themselves for the work of teaching. The work aimed at has been to supply the schools of the State with trained teachers, without reference to the locality whence they came. No pupils properly qualified have ever been rejected from other counties to make places for pupils from Santa Clara County.

Teachers have been sent from the Normal School to every county in the State but two, and it is more than probable that some have found their way even to those counties. One thing is certain, the influence of the Normal School is felt, and felt for good, in every county in California.

Having examined the catalogues of eastern schools, I am prepared to say that the California State Normal School has had a larger percentage of pupils from the State at large than any other school, save one (Michigan), in the United States.

The second assertion was that the graduates of the school were not as well qualified as many graduates of High Schools; that they could not pass the examination to enter the Junior Class of the University, etc.

The Normal School is not a High School; nor is it a preparatory school for the University. It has for its object the preparation of teachers for the district schools of California. Its course of study and training are all formed with this object only in view. The best graduates of the High Schools in San Francisco, Oakland, Stockton, San José, and other cities of the State, find one year's hard work to complete the reviews, studies, and training required in the Normal School. One third of the time of this year is devoted to the study and practice of teaching. A mere assertion that, after this year's work, they are not as well prepared to teach as those who know a little more Latin or French, or some other more advanced studies, can carry very little weight.

It has never been claimed that all the graduates of the Normal School will become excellent teachers; but the fact is, that the time given to the preparation for the work makes *all* much better teachers, and increases very largely the probabilities of success.

All the graduates are, so far as scholarship is concerned, qualified for their work. Our knowledge of this is based, not on a single examination under peculiar and many times exceptional circumstances, but upon more than a score of examinations, oral and written, continued through months and years. We may possibly err in our judgment, but there is no temptation to lead to erroneous conclusions.

The foregoing are the only serious charges made against the school, and we hope that those who heard and read the charges, will also read the answers.

THE BURNING OF THE NORMAL BUILDING. RUTH GUPPY, CLASS OF MAY, 1880.

In the ebb and flow of daily life, the motley crowd of human beings move on to their appointed destiny, so fashioned by Providence—"that to the future blindness is kindly given." What could encourage the artisan, the tradesman, in his ambitious plans, were he working ever in the shadow of a possible destruction? How could legislators frame laws, vote appropriations, anticipating that in a year or two their labor would be as naught? How could the Normal teachers and pupils of 1880 have moved onward in their chosen way, knowing that in a few hours the fiery demon would, by one sudden stroke, annihilate the work of so many months and years? For on the morning of February tenth, of that memorable year, fire bells rang out the burning of the Normal building.

Firemen appeared, only to realize their inability to combat successfully with the great tongues of flame enveloping the tower and spreading over the roof. The fire started in the second story, and swept in tempestuous haste through the assembly hall, the corridor, and recitation rooms. Attempts were made to force water from the first floor, but the intense heat rendered this futile. The upper windows of the third story were then broken, and water poured in upon the glowing mass which once was the museum. A great crash! and the roof and third floor fell through, giving fresh impetus to the flames already at work in the laboratory and chemistry rooms. Below, men rushed in, secured the records, the most of the library books, and pieces of furniture, and conveyed them to places of safety.

The firemen worked bravely with ladder and hose, but to no avail, for the powerful element moved on, glorying in its strength, and laughing to scorn the strenuous efforts made to arrest its course,

"For the elements still hate,
What mortal hands create."

Sorrowful it was, indeed, to enumerate the losses of those few hours. Miss Norton's herbarium, upon which she had spent so many years of labor, and Mrs. Bush's shell collection of twenty-seven hundred species, neither of which can ever fully be replaced; books, maps, apparatus were, in the most part, all burned.

The loss to the State and to the school was very great; but the sympathy of friends and the hopefulness of Professor Allen expressed in the stirring words, "Though the Normal building is dead, the Normal School still lives," cheered many a despondent one. And with the same spirit the Trustees, in full view of the falling walls, discussed plans for carrying on the school work. They decided to accept the generous offer of the City Board of Education, and make use of the High School building. Accordingly, at the usual hour, on Wednesday morning, the pupils assembled in this place of temporary refuge, thankful there there was to be no interruption in class-room work, yet with anxious inquiry depicted on every countenance. In the grand old anthem sung that morning, and in the remaining exercises, there was a unison and a depth of feeling that left its echo in every heart.

The day following the fire, being the birthday of Professor Allen, the Senior Class, according to custom, were to give a reception in his honor. For days beforehand, busy hands had gathered flowers, and woven wreaths, with which to decorate the Normal library and parlors. Other extensive preparations were in progress, not the least being a huge cake. But

"The best laid schemes o' mice an' men gang aft a-gley."

The question arose as to the disposal of this cake, which, gleaming white and gigantic in proportion, stood a lone monument of defeated plans. The class resolved to raffle it off, and give the proceeds to students who had suffered most loss from the fire. The result was highly satisfactory. By the generosity of the holder of the winning ticket the cake was donated to the class. And shortly after, at a reunion held at the home of Professor Allen, each member had the privilege of testing this triumph of culinary art.

REMINISCENCES BY MARTHA M. KNAPP, CLASS OF MAY, 1880.

We began our work in the building which was consumed by fire in the February preceding our graduation. The feelings aroused by the sight of the conflagration will never be forgotten by those that witnessed the scene. When we met the following morning it seemed as if we were indeed homeless; but the citizens of San José, ever loyal to the interests of the Normal School, generously tendered the use of the High School building, on Santa Clara Street, in which to carry on the work.

The Training Department held its sessions in two small buildings hastily fitted up in the school yard, and was presided over by Misses Titus and Wilson, assisted by Miss Scott. The suggestions and criticisms given by these teachers have been invaluable to us in our work in the public schools.

Room D, where we recited to Professor More in mathematics, is held in pleasant remembrance, though demonstrating the chances of error in finding the first and second figures of the cube root of a number proved a pitfall to some of us. The pleasure experienced by those who gathered around his table and listened to his stories and good humored sarcasm, will long be remembered by the participants. It was through his kindness that we were permitted to view the heavens through the telescope, which had just been added to the school apparatus.

We recall with pleasure Miss Webster's patience and skill in teaching us to read with more expression than we had hitherto used.

Professor Childs assured us that every one could learn to draw, but when the dreaded examination came, and barrels that were shapely were liberally interspersed with those that were otherwise, it is probable that he was convinced that all had not become proficient in that most useful branch. He was good natured, however, gave us credit for our endeavors, and told us how to do better, so that difficulty was safely tided over.

In physiology and school law we were ably instructed by Miss Norton, a lady in the best sense of the word.

Word analysis, so full of interest, as we traced the derivation and change in meaning of our common words, was taught by a man universally respected as a kind friend and a true gentleman—Professor Braly.

Although we did not recite to Miss Washburn, we recognized in her a woman of sterling worth and rare intellectual ability.

Our class was not much given to "outings," but enjoyed them with a keen relish when we could combine profit and pleasure, as we did in the botanical excursion led by our excellent Preceptress, Miss Wright. On that occasion we spent the day at Alma, and returned laden with specimens that more than compensated us for the weariness we felt. As a small sum of money was left after defraying the expenses of that trip, it was decided to invest it in candy. The young ladies agreed to furnish cake, coffee, strawberries, and pure cream, with which to refresh the inner man. It was voted that we meet at the Normal on Saturday, invite the young men of the class, and surprise them with "a spread." Professor More kindly consented to allow us to set the tables in his room. Two of the gentlemen were obliged to be taken into the secret, as their assistance was needed in moving tables. One of the girls, in a fit of absentmindedness, mentioned the expected treat to a third young man, leaving but one to be surprised. Happily, he was equal to the occasion, and everything passed off pleasantly. Dancing was indulged in, and thoroughly enjoyed by every one, although the skill shown by some was criticised by a small boy who was present.

The Middle A Class of 1879 was the last one to whom elementary diplomas were given; and we were particularly elated because Professor More, who had charge of us, stated that we had a higher class average than any of our predecessors. This public acknowledgment of our standing was especially gratifying, as we felt that he never bestowed undeserved commendation.

The thought of the laboratory brings to mind many a lively scene. Strange results brought about by combining chemicals were proclaimed by the inevitable shriek, but no serious accidents occurred. One class-mate, desirous of performing more experiments than she had time to attempt at school, took home some chemicals. During dinner the family were startled by an explosion, and discovered that a fire was the result. Part of the hall carpet and her brother's new overcoat were sacrificed to her zeal.

To Miss Walker our class was largely indebted for help in methods, and visions of frightened Seniors trying to show how they would teach a subject can be called up by each of the sufferers in that trying ordeal.

Many of the Seniors were members of a literary society known as the Philomathean. One meeting, held in the assembly hall of the High School building, is especially remembered. With charade and song, recitation and essay, the evening was pleasantly passed—each successful participant rejoicing in his merited applause—while all were happy in the delightful atmosphere created by youth and good spirits.

We had arranged to honor Professor Allen's birthday by a supper, but the fire that destroyed our beloved Normal prevented the carrying out of our plans. Very pleasant events in our social life were two parties—our worthy Vice-Principal, who evidently knew our weakness for ice cream, and served us generously with a most excellent quality of that article, invited us to one; and Professor Allen gave the other, which was also most heartily enjoyed by all present.

At last came the closing exercises of the year, held in the California Theater, which was filled to overflowing with the friends of the school. The usual number of essays were read, our diplomas were presented by the State Superintendent, F. M. Campbell, and our class of forty-five went forth to its chosen work.

According to established custom, our class planted its tree, and somewhat ambitious were we in its selection, choosing the *Sequoia gigantea*, a genuine Californian.

Although several years have passed, how vividly rises before us a picture of the assembly hall with its rows of earnest faces. It is the beginning of another day, and we have gathered for the simple exercises that precede its work. We listen to beautiful words from the Holy Scripture, join in chant and anthem, and feel the solemn hush of silent prayer. After this, obedient to the tap of the bell, out by each door pass the long files to their appointed places and tasks.

Again we seem to hear the words of counsel so fitly spoken by our honored Principal. Long shall we remember his kindness. May he live to a good old age to enjoy the happiness which attends an earnest, useful life.

How dear to us is the remembrance of him who was an inspiration to every pupil with whom he came in contact! Beloved Professor Norton! No one will ever usurp his place in the hearts of those who knew him.

Many of our classmates are still engaged in teaching; some have become centers of happy homes, and are surrounded by the smiling faces of their own children; while two of our number, Annie E. Osgood and Mary R. Finnie, have learned the wonderful lesson of immortality, which in God's good time we, too, shall understand.

SINCE THE FIRE.

So far in the preparation of this history, the plan has been to present the historical facts and reminiscences of each year in a separate chapter. As space will not permit the continuance of this plan through the remaining years, the history of the period since the fire is given topically, showing, as far as possible, the growth and present status of the school in its various departments.

THE NEW BUILDING.

Work on the building was begun in May, 1880, and prosecuted with such vigor that the school was able to occupy its new quarters for the first time May 2, 1881. Though lacking the beauty of the former structure, the new building has proved far more useful, being well planned, healthful, and in every way better adapted to the wants of a Normal School.

It is worthy of note, as an exceptional experience in the erection of public buildings, that the present Normal School building was completed considerably within the appropriation, the total cost being $148,936 95, enabling the Trustees to return $1,063 05 to the State Treasury. The Board of Trustees to whom this credit is due, was composed as follows: George C. Perkins, Governor; Fred. M. Campell, State Superintendent of Public Instruction; Hon. James Denman, San Francisco; T. Ellard Beans, San José; Dr. Ben. Cory, San José; Hon. C. T. Ryland, San José; A. S. Evans, San José. The officers of the Board were: George C. Perkins, President; C. T. Ryland, Vice-President; Charles H. Allen, Secretary and Executive Agent; C. T. Ryland, T. Ellard Beans, and A. S. Evans, Executive Committee.

The following accurate description of the building, published about the time of its completion, is taken from the San José "Mercury:"

The new edifice is of brick with stone sills and lintels. It covers an area of between four thousand and five thousand superficial feet more than the former building—the enlargement being in the wings. It has a frontage of two hundred and thirty-six feet and five inches, facing the west, with a depth of one hundred and seventy-five feet. It is situated on the site of its predecessor.

The basement contains play-rooms, janitors' rooms, store rooms, rooms for the heating apparatus, engine room, containing the engine for pumping water up to the tanks in the attic, chemistry-room, laboratory, and natural philosophy rooms. The tanks referred to are two in number, having each a capacity of between four thousand and five thousand gallons, one situated over each wing, and directly under the roof. The first story, or main floor, contains eight class rooms, two large training rooms, eight recitation rooms, two cabinet and apparatus rooms, four teachers' rooms, library and reception rooms, preceptress' room, office, three cloak and wash rooms, six flights of stairs to the second story and basement, and twelve-foot corridors extending the whole length and breadth of the building. There are three front entrances to this floor, with Ionic porticoes. The second story contains ten large class rooms, the assembly room, sixty-five by ninety-six feet in area, and twenty-two feet from floor to ceiling; four cloak rooms, eight teachers' rooms, six flights of stairs connecting with the stories above and below, and three balconies in front over the porticoes. The assembly hall is lighted by twenty-two large windows, and besides the ventilation afforded by them, there is a large ventilator in the ceiling, and others in the side walls. The third story occupies only the front portion, sixty-eight feet square, of the front part of the center building. It contains a large museum sixty-five by thirty-four feet, two stairways leading below, and one to the garret and tower. This story is surmounted by an ornate bell tower, twenty-five feet square, rising to a height of one hundred and thirty-five feet above the ground, being twenty feet higher than the dome of the Court House. On the tower is a forty-foot flag-staff, making a distance of one hundred and seventy-five feet from the top of the flag-staff to the ground. The building is supplied with excellent water from an artesian well on the grounds. It is heated by hot water (Harvey's system). The new edifice, although plainer in its exterior than its predecessor, is well adapted to the purposes of the school, being modeled after the most approved Normal School structures in the East, and it has been pronounced by persons who have seen the best school buildings in the East, to be inferior to none on the continent. The walls are firmly bound together to provide against injury by earthquakes, by strong iron straps, built in the brickwork, and extending entirely around the building in one continuous bar four inches wide. The roof is heavy tin. The outside steps and platforms are of granite with sandstone buttresses and trimmings. For thoroughness of work and stability it is second to no building in the State. Its general style of architecture is Ionic. The tower contains a bell weighing three thousand pounds, which cost $1,200. Time is kept by a system of electric clocks extending through all the departments.

This building, so complete in its adaptation to the work for which it is intended, is well furnished with all needed appliances, and leading educators from the East express great surprise at finding a Normal School building so well equipped for its work.

Notwithstanding all these conveniences, the school is rapidly outgrowing its present accommodations. Already the need of more room for the use of the Training Department and the library is urgently felt, and it is quite probable that at no very distant day, the Legislature will be asked to provide for an additional building.

GROUNDS.

When the first Normal School building was erected, the surrounding twenty-six acres, then known as Washington Square, was, as compared with its present condition, an unimproved and dreary waste. Students who climbed to the tower in those days will remember looking down on the network of irregular paths that crossed the square in a multitude of devious ways, each marked out to serve the inclination and convenience of daily foot-travelers; and they will remember, too, the few straggling trees and bushes and, except in the early spring time, the dry intervals between. In place of all this, is now a beautiful park, with green lawns, variegated flower beds, graceful shade trees, and broad walks and driveways.

The first attempt to improve the grounds was made in 1878, when a part of the Tuition Fund was spent in inclosing with a neat fence a portion of the grounds directly surrounding the building, and planting shrubbery and flowers. The shrubbery was largely donated by the public spirited citizens of San José. These were, however, all destroyed by the fire. In February, 1881, the Legislature made an appropriation of $25,000 for improving and fencing the Normal School Square. The Board, after advertising for plans, adopted the plan of R. Ulrich, since well known as the landscape gardener at the Hotel del Monte. Following this plan, the grounds were carefully laid out, the walks and drives graveled, and lawns, flowers, and trees planted. Two additional artesian wells were bored and tanks and pump provided, furnishing an abundant water supply for both building and grounds. All this being completed, enough of the appropriation remained to erect a neat iron fence surrounding the square.

Since that time the greater part of the Tuition Fund, derived entirely from the Training School, has been expended in supporting the grounds. New lawns have, from time to time, been laid out, and additional trees and flowers planted; so that now the grounds are both a delightful place of recreation for the students and an ornament to the City of San José. They also furnish an excellent field of research for the botanical and entomological classes.

LIBRARY.

In no way has the growth in the intellectual life of the school been more clearly indicated than in the increased and increasing use of the library. For several years a student librarian, whose business it was to keep the library open during intermissions, and a short time at the close of the afternoon session, was able to supply all demands for books. With the occupation of the new building came the employment of a special librarian, keeping the library open all day. A marked change was soon visible, due to several causes. The provision in the course of study for a study hour at the school building, for each pupil, opened the door to the increased use of reference books, and gave some added time for general reading. Visiting committees from the State Legislature, seeing both the usefulness of the library and the need of more books, recommended special appropriations, which were cheerfully made. This, in turn, reacted upon both teachers and students, who, finding that more and better books were provided, were induced to make better use of them. Besides these causes, the topical method of study, growing in use and favor, by which the student is given a *subject* to investigate rather than a portion of some particular *book* to master, has necessarily led to the demand for and the use of many books in each subject; while the constant presence of a librarian acquainted with the place and contents of the books, has made their use more extensive. Many students, especially in the higher classes, avail themselves of their study hour for library study, and not unfrequently the library is crowded beyond the point of convenience and comfort. The importance to the student of this familiarity with books can scarcely be overestimated; and its results, as already shown in the increased love for good literature, and the wider culture of the graduates sent out, is highly satisfactory. The library now numbers about thirty-five hundred volumes. By the continued liberal appropriations made by the Legislature new books are added yearly, and the need of more room is constantly evident. This need will, in the near future, lead to the erection of an additional building.

MUSEUM.

The burning of the contents of the old museum was a loss to science, as well as to the State. Chief among its treasures were the specimens in conchology, known as the Canfield collection.

These Dr. Canfield, of Monterey, had been years in collecting from all parts of the world, and it is now next to impossible to obtain many of the species represented in his collection. Of other specialties, there was a large and fine collection of the birds of California, and over three hundred unique specimens of ancient stone implements from Santa Clara County, that cannot be replaced. In the mineral collection was a series of large and interesting specimens of lead, zinc, and fossils from Wisconsin, with agates, alabaster, and many other things contributed by Professor Allen; also, from Mr. O. Sharpe, of Fresno County, a beautiful series of Arizona minerals; and from Mr. Aplin, of Nevada County, a miscellaneous collection of the finest specimens.

Though all these went with the destruction of the building, it is a pleasure to remember the interest displayed in founding a museum, and to note that this interest and liberality have outlived the fire. In the new museum, the names of the same donors are seen, with many others added, telling of the widespread interest in this important educational feature of the Normal School.

Though many treasures were lost that it is difficult, and in some cases impossible, to replace, patience and perseverance, with the kindly remembrance of friends, have furnished the new museum with so many helps to study, that to-day it compares favorably with older and more pretentious collections.

As the room is entered at the north door, the first case to the left shows the few specimens that were reclaimed from the ashes, forming a nucleus for the new museum.

The center of the room is occupied by cases containing specimens in conchology, noticeable among which is a collection of West Coast shells of over three thousand specimens, presented by the well known conchologist, Mr. Henry Hemphill. Another from Miss Jennie R. Bush, contains over fifteen hundred rare California and foreign shells. An interesting feature is the Blaschka glass models of such mollusks as cannot be preserved by ordinary methods.

Other branches of natural history are well illustrated by the twenty cases of minerals, thirty of entomology, two of radiates and crustaceans, one case of silurian fossils, one of California tertiary fossils, and two of native and foreign woods. The aim has been to make the collection instructive and useful, rather than, by making a display, to gratify idle curiosity.

There is not space to name individually all the many benefactors, but the following friends in the East, specialists, deserve honorable mention for their fine contributions when this school had nothing: Professor Riley, United States Entomologist at Washington; Dr. Farlow, cryptogamic botanist, Cambridge, Mass.; George Davenport, botanist, Massachusetts; Frank Collins, a specialist in marine algæ.

To the untiring efforts of Mrs. A. E. Bush, the Curator of the Museum, is mainly due its rapid growth and its excellence. She has spared no pains in establishing exchanges with prominent museums and scientific specialists, in procuring donations, and in collecting, many times devoting her entire vacations to this work. In the satisfactory results she may well feel a personal pride.

HERBARIUM.

By the patient and continuous efforts of Miss Mary E. B. Norton, for many years teacher of botany, an herbarium has been collected, which goes far toward replacing the valuable collection lost at the fire. It numbers several thousand plants, including valuable representative plants from every continent, prominent among them being a set of North American and Pacific Coast ferns. As in the case of the museum, the herbarium has been collected through donations and exchanges. All the plants are carefully classified, labeled, and arranged in special cases.

APPARATUS.

Most of the valuable apparatus lost in the fire has been replaced, and much added, so that the school is, in this respect, well equipped, having all that is needed to illustrate the work taken in mechanics, optics, electricity, and other departments of physics. Besides these, there is a chemical laboratory, provided with all appliances for experimental work by the students. In physics and chemistry the pupils manufacture for themselves much of the apparatus used, the purpose being the better to prepare them for teaching elementary science. The school is well provided with microscopes, which are used individually by students in the study of botany, zoölogy, and physiology.

ADMISSION.

The grade of admission to the Normal classes has from time to time been raised, but, of necessity, very slowly. It has seemed best not to fix it above the point where pupils from country Grammar Schools, who have done reasonably good work, can pass examination for the Junior Class. In 1882 the Principal's report says: "The grade of school is now as high as we can make it and have it possible for the graduates of the High Schools of the State to complete the course in one year. Many of those who attempt it now fail. It may not be considered out of place for the Board to require such pupils to take a year and a half for the work."

In 1884, after the system of granting County Grammar School diplomas became general throughout the State, the Board of Trustees decided to accept these diplomas for admission to the Junior Class, thus establishing a closer connection between the Normal School and the Grammar Schools of the State. Graduates of High Schools also were, by this regulation, admitted to the Junior Class without examination, but were examined if they applied for admission to higher classes. This regulation has continued in force to the present time.

In 1885 the Principal reported:

> We have now had a full year in which to test the gains and losses to be realized from the changes made in our Course of Study, and in the regulations for admission.
>
> We have admitted to the Junior Class thirty-eight on Grammar School diplomas, and fifteen on High School diplomas. Thirteen graduates of High Schools have been admitted to more advanced classes. The pupils admitted on Grammar School diplomas have, as far as possible, been kept in separate classes, to test our grade of admission on examination. The result has satisfied us that it is safe to receive Grammar School diplomas—*not certificates*—from counties where the County Boards give the matter their attention. It also appears that we cannot advance our grade for admission without putting the Normal School out of the reach of the Grammar Schools of the State, as now organized.
>
> The fact that more than half of the graduates of High Schools who present themselves can reach only the Junior Class in the Normal School, shows that much time is wasted in pursuing the so called advanced studies, that might, with greater profit, be devoted to elementary work.

In 1887 the test of admission for those entering on examination was still further raised, as shown by the following extract from the circular for 1887–88:

It is the design to fix the grade of admission at a point where the graduates of the *County* Grammar Schools, who have fairly earned their diplomas, can enter and do the work of the course well in three years. These diplomas are, from year to year, becoming evidence of better scholarship, and the grade of admission to the Normal School has consequently been again advanced. For the coming year, all examined for the Junior Class must show that they can enter the *Advanced* Junior Class. This will give the opportunity for more training work and reviews very desirable to have taken in a Normal School.

The Preparatory Class is discontinued, as we believe the Grammar Schools should now be able to do all the preparatory work.

By a resolution of the Board, adopted May 15, 1883, pupils are admitted only at the beginning of the terms of the schools. The Faculty have, however, power to suspend this rule in cases which, for good and sufficient reasons, they may consider exceptional. *None are, under any circumstances, admitted to the Senior Class after the first examinations each term,* as none are graduated who have not been *one year* in attendance at the school.

The following table shows the number of *new* students admitted each year for the past nine years:

	1880-81	1881-82	1882-83	1883-84	1884-85	1885-86	1886-87	1887-88	1888-89
Number of new pupils admitted	193	197	250	204	173	177	239	166	172
Number of these admitted to Junior Class on Grammar School diplomas					38	44	64	31	41
Number admitted to Junior Class on High School diplomas					15	2	11	9	4
Number of counties of California represented by new pupils		40	46	39	43	34	42	39	40
Number of other States and Territories represented by new pupils		6	6	7	6	3	8	8	12

ATTENDANCE.

As will be seen by reference to the table on page 102, the attendance in the Normal Classes since 1881 has varied from about five hundred to over six hundred.

These fluctuations, with some of their causes, are indicated by the following extracts from reports of the Principal:

From Report of 1882.

It is a notable fact that the attendance is becoming larger in the Advanced Classes, the Middle Classes this year having outnumbered the Junior Classes. This is, in itself, a sign of progress, showing that the school holds its pupils. The number admitted to the Middle and Senior Classes on examination, shows also that the schools of the State are doing better work.

During the last half of the year we have carried on four Junior, four Middle, one Sub-Senior Class, and a Senior Class so large that it has been necessary to make two classes of it in most recitations.

From Report of 1885.

The falling off of attendance during the past two years, and especially during the last year, comes from several causes: First—The grade of admission has been raised nearly 20 per cent, and none admitted from places where Grammar Schools provide for graduation, except upon the Grammar School diploma or an equivalent course. This has worked out the beneficial result of having pupils fit themselves better before applying for admission. Restricting admissions to the first week of the term, save in exceptional cases, has also had its effect. Second—The opening of the Branch School at Los Angeles has drawn the pupils from the southern counties to that school. Third—Your honorable body, on the nineteenth of December, 1883, adopted the following resolution: "*Resolved*, That it is the opinion of the Board of Trustees that the teachers and Principals of the Normal Schools should decline any invitation to attend County Institutes, during the sessions of the schools, except by consent of the Executive Committee or the local committee at Los Angeles."

Accepting this as an indication of the feeling of the Board that our work should be devoted more entirely to the school, I have declined nearly every invitation to attend County Institutes, and our school has been represented in but very few. You, gentlemen, are of course fully aware that the school has been built up and kept up by our making its work known, by coming in contact with people having children to educate, and by stimulating young teachers to try to fit themselves better for their work.

From Report of 1887.

During the present year we have reached the highest number ever enrolled in the school, namely, six hundred and ninety-one in the Normal and Preparatory Departments, and more than eight hundred in the entire school. We have had a larger number of Normal pupils enrolled than any other State Normal School in the United States. The Normal College of New York City, and the Normal School for Girls in Philadelphia, alone outnumber us.

From Report of 1888.

The average enrollment for the year, in the Normal School proper, has been four hundred and ninety. For the instruction of these we have had sixteen regular and two special teachers, aggregating, say, seventeen teachers, or one teacher to a little more than twenty-eight pupils.

It is noticeable that the advanced classes have been relatively larger this year than last. This has been the constant tendency in the school for several years, showing that it holds its pupils, and that a larger number of those who enter remain until they graduate.

The falling off in the Junior Class of from two hundred and ninety to two hundred and five is partly due to the fact that the Board avowed the policy of graduating hereafter but one class each year; and instead of having, as is usual, one hundred and twenty to one hundred and thirty to examine at the opening of the winter term, but about eighty presented themselves.

FROM REPORT OF 1889.

During the year there have been representatives in the school from forty-seven counties in the State. This representation, in a State where the distances traveled are so great, is really surprising, and shows more clearly than any argument that this is a *State* School. True, the representation from Santa Clara County is **34 per cent** of the enrollment, but this is not surprising. This is a large county, and the patronage of **all** such schools is drawn largely from a radius of forty or fifty miles. Many residing in Santa Clara County come from many miles away.

In addition to those enrolled from California, we have had from **Colorado**, 1; **Honolulu**, 2; **Idaho**, **3**; **Illinois**, 1; **Michigan**, 1; **Montana**, 1; **Nebraska**, 1; **Nevada**, 6; **Nova Scotia**, 1; **Oregon**, 1; **Pennsylvania**, 1; **Utah Territory**, 1; **Washington Territory**, 3; **Wisconsin**, 3. These pupils are here, usually, expecting to teach in **California**, and all sign the condition made on entering.

Out of the fifty-two counties of California, the following table shows the number represented by pupils in attendance at the school during each year since 1880:

1880–81.	1881–82.	1882–83.	1883–84.	1884–85.	1885–86.	1886–87.	1887–88.	1888–89.
45	47	49	45	46	45	46	43	47

COURSE OF STUDY.

The changes in course of study made from time to time have been, not so much in the subjects taught as in the relative importance and proportionate length of time given to each subject, and in the place in the course at which it occurs. Beginning, perhaps, with the advent into the school of Professor Norton, more prominence was given to work in Science. The contagion of his enthusiastic love for all scientific study, coming as it did at a time when the study of the sciences was making rapid growth in popularity in the common schools, gave a new interest to observation studies, which the work of the later professors in science has fostered and increased.

It was next felt that to keep pace with the most advanced educational thought of this and other countries, more attention should be devoted to industrial drawing; therefore more time in the course was given to this subject, and a special teacher was employed who, as subsequently reported by the Principal, "is an enthusiast in his work," and "what was one of the weakest points in the course has been made strong." Professional work also demanded more attention, and added time in the Senior Class was devoted to the study of psychology and pedagogy, and more time given to observation and practice in the Training Department.

To make room for this added work, political economy, Kame's Criticism, and a part of the science work were dropped from the Senior year. These changes were incorporated in the Course of Study, as revised in 1884. An important improvement made at the same time was a re-arrangement of recitations, by which each regular pupil was given a study hour at the school, instead of spending the day in unbroken recitations, as previously.

The next important change was made in 1888, when, under the new law, the Boards of Trustees of the several California State Normal Schools, in joint session, adopted a uniform course of study. The radical change then made was in the division of the year into three terms instead of into two, and the forming of new classes in each grade but once a year. This practically admitted new pupils to the school at but one time in the year, and would have resulted, when in full operation, in graduating but one class yearly. A Post Graduate year was also, at this time, added to the course. After this course had been in operation a year, the Boards, at their annual joint meeting, in April, 1889, decided that "The number of terms in the year, the time of opening and closing of terms, the arrangement of vacations, the time of graduation, and the order of succession of studies in the prescribed course, shall be fixed for each school by its local Board of Trustees;" and "that the studies to be pursued and the time to be given to each shall be in accordance with the schedule adopted by the joint Boards for all the California Normal Schools."

Accordingly, the local Board of the school at San José, upon the recommendation of the Faculty, decided to return to the plan of two terms a year, carrying on two sets of classes, and graduating twice a year.

The new course of study in force at the beginning of the school year 1889–90, in the Normal School at San José, is as follows:

COURSE OF INSTRUCTION—1889-90.

	Junior Year.	Middle Year.
PROFESSIONAL	Methods of Study based upon Psychology—Six weeks. Morals and Manners—Four weeks.	Pedagogy and Training School Observation—Ten weeks.
LANGUAGE	Word Analysis, including Spelling—Ten weeks. Sentence Building and Composition—Ten weeks. Number Methods—Five weeks. Geography Methods—Five weeks. Composition and Literary Reading—Twenty weeks.	Language Methods—Four weeks. Rhetoric—Sixteen weeks.
MATHEMATICS	Arithmetic and Number Methods—Ten weeks. Bookkeeping, including Penmanship Methods—Ten weeks. Geometry and Methods—Twenty weeks.	Algebra and Methods—Twenty weeks.
SCIENCE	Botany and Methods—Twenty weeks. Zoölogy and Methods—Fifteen weeks. General Physiology—Five weeks. Human Physiology and Methods—Ten weeks.	Physics and Methods—Twenty weeks.
MISCELLANEOUS	Drawing—Ten weeks. Reading—Ten weeks. Drawing and Methods—Ten weeks. Geography—Ten weeks. History and Methods—Twenty weeks. Drawing—Ten weeks.	Constitution—Five weeks. Reviews—Five weeks.
EXERCISES	Music twice a week. Spelling, with Penmanship, twice a week, from which all who show themselves, upon examination, to be proficient, are to be excused. Delsarie Exercises. General News. Six Lectures in Hygiene.	Music twice a week, once in each section. Manual Training. General News.

	Senior Year.			Post Graduate Year.		
Professional	Pedagogy and Observation in Training School—Ten weeks.	Teaching in Training School—Twenty weeks.		Psychology—Sixteen weeks.	Philosophy of Education—Fourteen weeks.	
		Pedagogy—Ten weeks.	Methods, School Law, and School Governm't—Ten weeks.			
Language	Literature—Ten weeks.	Grammar and Methods—Twenty weeks.		Latin—Twenty weeks.		Latin—Twenty weeks.
Mathematics	Arithmetic and Methods—Twenty weeks.	Geometry and Methods—Ten weeks.		Algebra—Sixteen weeks.	Geometry—Fourteen weeks.	Trigonometry—Ten weeks.
Science	Chemistry and Methods—Twenty weeks.	Physics—Ten weeks.	Physical Geography—Ten weeks.		Geology—Ten weeks.	Astronomy—Ten weeks.
Miscellaneous	Drawing—Ten weeks.			General History—Ten weeks.	Political Economy—Fourteen weeks.	Directed Readings—Ten weeks.
Exercises	Music twice a week. Delsarte and vocalization twice a week. Physical exercise throughout the course.					

TRAINING DEPARTMENT.

From the time of the organization of the Training School in San José, under Miss Titus, this department has been a strong and important feature of the work of the Normal School. Its full recognition as such is indicated in the name by which it has of late years been designated : viz., Training *Department* rather than Training *School*.

With the crowded course of study, it seemed, for many years, impossible to give each member of the Senior Class time for more than two or three weeks of practice teaching, and this was usually attended by the entire loss during that time of recitations in other subjects. But, notwithstanding the shortness of the time, the results of this practice were of great value, and special emphasis has always been laid upon success in teaching as a factor in determining graduation.

As the grade of admission was gradually raised, the course of study more satisfactorily adjusted, and the size of the Senior Classes reduced by graduations twice a year, the time for practice was lengthened. By the course adopted in 1884, it was provided that each member of the Senior Class should spend one recitation each day for three fourths of the Senior Year in the Training Department—the first ten weeks in observation, and the last five months in teaching. This plan has been followed ever since.

During the half term spent in observation, the pupils write out, as regular exercises, criticisms upon the work of pupil teachers and analyses of model lessons given by the regular critic teachers, besides receiving special lectures upon the work they have observed. During the five months of actual practice work, they are required to make special preparation for each recitation, and are under the supervision of the regular critic teachers, who review their work, giving both class lectures and individual criticism. The constant presence of classmates and teachers as observers, cultivates both confidence and independence.

From the one class with which it began, the Training Department has grown until it includes four distinct subdivisions, viz.: Primary, Intermediate, Grammar, and Advanced Grammar. The last was organized after the abolition of the Preparatory Class in 1887.

In the Training Department, an effort is made to keep pace with all the best methods of teaching, and to introduce, as far as practicable, by way of experiment, such new subjects as modern thought suggests the desirability of introducing into the public schools. In harmony with this intention, some parts of the kindergarten system are made use of in connection with primary work, elementary science is taught by observation in the study of specimens, and manual training is given through instruction in industrial drawing, sewing, clay modeling, etc. Of this latter work the Principal, in his last report, says: "To this work the pupils come as to an amusement, and it is therefore a respite from, rather than an addition to, their study tasks. It also tends to the development of special talent—talent that in the near future may become valuable to society."

Besides maps and apparatus, the Training Department has its own library, consisting mainly of well-selected books for children, in history, biography, travel, fiction, etc.

The popularity of this Department is well evidenced by the fact that during the past year it has numbered over two hundred, every seat being taken and many applicants rejected for want of room.

PROFESSIONAL WORK.

In 1884, while the matter of changes in the course of study was under discussion, the Principal, in his report, made the following statement regarding the professional work of the school:

It has been remarked in a meeting of this Board, that if anything justifies the existence of Normal Schools, it is the work they do in giving professional training. At the last meeting of the Board the question was raised whether, in this school, we were sufficiently emphasizing this work. I desire, in this part of my report, to show, not that we are doing too much, for that could hardly be possible, but that it is receiving a large share of our care and attention, and that in amount it far exceeds that given in most Normal Schools.

The professional training may be briefly summed up as follows:

1. From the time the pupil enters the lowest Junior Class until he graduates, his attention is constantly kept fixed upon the fact that he is learning each subject with a view of imparting it to others, and the method of presentation is made a subject of continued observation. As with few exceptions all the faculty are graduates of Normal Schools, and even in the exceptional cases, they are teachers of wide and varied experience, the pupil is, from the beginning, being trained to teach. This continued for three years is, in itself, an amount of training which must be of great value. The philosophy of the work he has not yet culture enough to appreciate, or even understand.

2. During his course, as he advances to riper scholarship, and a greater capacity for grasping the subject, he receives about one hundred and twenty lectures, beginning with an outline of mental philosophy, upon "methods of

teaching, grading, and disciplining a school." These lectures cover not only the philosophy of education, but practical and detailed instruction in the *minutiæ* of teaching. Of these lectures he is required to take copious notes and to rewrite them for future reference. He also takes, during the Senior year, the same number of review lessons upon the subjects taught in the Grammar Schools, and these are a *practical* presentation of methods of teaching. These reviews are given, mainly, without text-books, the pupil taking notes, thus carrying away a voluminous note book of original work, designed to be fitted for his own classes, when he becomes a teacher.

3. He is required to practice in the Training Department until he convinces the critic teachers that he has at least a fair ability in teaching. During this teaching he attends four days a week, a critique upon his own work and the work of his fellow teachers, conducted by the critic teachers, and these sessions, being from one and a half to two hours each, constitute a continued and searching review of his theoretical ideas, as derived from lectures. He also spends some time in observation, during which he is expected to take part in the criticism, thus enabling him to judge of his own work and that of others. This is the regular work in the school, and while I should be exceedingly glad if more time could be given to practice teaching, I feel that if we can increase the time for observation, it will be all, as the school is now organized, that we can do.

The last three classes have each subscribed for and read, with more or less care, a leading educational journal; and all are urged to continue this, and to purchase and study after they leave school, standard educational works.

If it be asked why, after so much professional work, the teachers sent out are not all entirely successful, the answer must be found in the fact that this is a result parallel to that reached by all other professional schools. Of the graduates from law, medical, or theological schools, some fail, many achieve mediocrity, and a few take high rank in their profession. It is not strange, then, that of those preparing for the profession of teaching, a profession requiring more varied acquirements, and greater versatility of thought, some fail in taking that rank which we would desire for them. As a general proposition, our teachers are successful. They are constantly in demand, and of marked failures we very rarely hear. If but few reach the higher ranks of the profession, it may be explained by the fact that the opportunities for such advancement are few, and that the great body of graduates have not yet been long in the field.

In his report for 1886, he adds:

The two classes during the year—one numbering forty-five, in December, and one numbering fifty-three, in May—go out as the first complete result of the changes made in our course of study.

The additional work done in the Training Department has made them, in one sense, experienced teachers. Five months' observation, for which the pupil is held strictly responsible, and five months' actual practice, under judicious and searching criticism, are worth more to the embryo teacher, in the way of experience, than years of practice without supervision.

As we have recommended none for graduation who have not successfully passed this ordeal, we feel confident that these graduates will make excellent teachers.

INDUSTRIAL TRAINING.

Industrial training in the Normal Department has, as yet, too much the character of an experiment to admit of definite conclusions as to its usefulness. In 1887, a work-room was fitted up and provided with tools for the use of pupils. For the first year, the instruction given was entirely by the regular teachers, at such times as could be made convenient for both pupils and teachers. This not proving satisfactory, a skilled mechanic was employed during a part of the past year, to give the necessary instruction. The work has been entirely optional on the part of the students, and the results are quite satisfactory. An exhibit of students' work, made at the close of the term, showed fancy tables, easels, footstools, boxes, and various other articles, of creditable workmanship. The experiment gives a promise which seems to justify its continuance.

GRADUATIONS.

From 1867 to 1883 but one graduating class was sent out yearly. The increasing size of the Senior Class and the demands of the State seeming to call for more frequent graduations, the Principal, in 1882, made the following recommendation:

The matter has been laid before the Faculty, and has been fully discussed, and we unanimously recommend that hereafter two classes be graduated each year—one at the middle of the year, and one at the close. Two very important gains will result from this. First, it will relieve the pressure upon the Senior Class; and second, pupils who fail to reach the required grade in that class at the close of a term, can be graduated regularly with an additional five months' work, whereas it is now necessary for them to wait a whole year before they can be regularly graduated. This change involves somewhat more labor on the part of the Faculty, but we believe the gain will more than compensate for it.

This recommendation was adopted, and in December, 1883, the first " Christmas Class," under the new plan, was graduated. This plan, having been found well adapted to the needs of the school, has been continued to the present time.

It was at first thought that the classes graduated in December would have more difficulty in securing positions to teach than those graduated in the spring. But reports show that, on the contrary, from a half to nearly the whole of each December class have taught before the close of the school year in which they graduated.

In 1884, the Board of Trustees, on recommendation of the Faculty, directed that the honors of salutatorian and valedictorian should no longer be awarded in the school; and in May, 1885, they still further did away with distinction in rank among graduates, by ruling that no figures indicating a grade in scholarship should appear upon diplomas conferred after that date.

As a marked deviation from the general custom of the school, the class of December, 1888, in accordance with their own request, received their diplomas without public graduating exercises. The result was so pleasing, that it is probable this plan will become customary with classes graduated at the middle of the year.

WORK OF GRADUATES.

It is not necessary to dwell at length upon the work of graduates and upon the fact that so large a proportion follow the profession for which the school has prepared them. The "Graduates' Record" and accompanying statistics speak for themselves. It may not, however, be out of place to quote some extracts on this subject from the annual reports of the Principal.

FROM REPORT OF 1884.

The report of the State Superintendent of Public Instruction and records in this office show that about sixty per cent of all the graduates of the school since its beginning in 1862, taught in this State last year. It is greatly to be doubted whether any other school in the country can show so good a record. From the class of 1882, numbering seventy-five, *seventy-one* had taught in the public schools of the State within one year of graduation. From the class of May, 1883, numbering eighty-five, seventy-eight have taught; and many of the class of December, 1883, have already obtained positions.

In 1885, after giving statistics showing that out of the five classes immediately preceding, numbering in all two hundred and fifty-five, two hundred and thirty-nine had already taught, he says:

Of these five classes, nearly ninety-four per cent have taught, to our certain knowledge. Of the sixteen not reported as having taught, two have died, two have been prevented from teaching by death in the family, three have married without teaching, three have engaged in other business or are at home, and five have not been heard from. Some of the latter are doubtless teaching. Of the fifty-one graduated in December, 1884, more than one half are already teaching. We are often asked, "Do your graduates teach?" The above showing gives a most emphatic answer, and speaks volumes for the spirit and usefulness of the school. It sufficiently proves that graduates from the school are in demand. This demand must come because they do satisfactory work. A few of the counties, mostly for local reasons, do not recognize our diplomas as evidence of fitness to teach. Even in these counties, it is not claimed that the graduates are not good teachers. So far as I know, there are now but four counties not granting certificates upon Normal School diplomas. As, however, this is a matter that can be changed at any meeting of a County Board, we cannot know definitely what the usage is. It perhaps should be said, that, while the action of the Boards, in these four counties, in nowise injures the Normal Schools, it can but be an injury to the counties. Each county pays its proportionate amount toward the support of the Normal Schools; but, by refusing to recognize their diplomas, it is, in effect, cut off from any benefit to be derived from their work. For pupils will not be apt to go to a Normal School from a county where its diploma is not recognized; nor will graduates willingly seek employment under a County Board that does not consider the signatures of the Governor of the State, the Superintendent of Public Instruction, and the Trustees and Faculty of a Normal School, a guarantee of qualification quite as good as the signature of the County Board.

FROM REPORT OF 1886.

The question constantly arises, "Where are your graduates to find places? The State is already overcrowded with teachers." This question implies, if it does not assert, that the Normal Schools are sending out too many teachers.

For the surplus of teachers, if such a surplus exists, the Normal Schools are not responsible. The largest classes graduated do not furnish two teachers per year to a county, and this would hardly make good the death rate, to say nothing of marriages and other accidents. There are two other sources which furnish a large number of teachers.

There is a constant influx of teachers from the East, drawn here by our charming climate, or more often by the higher salaries paid here. But the most prolific source is the semi-annual county examination. With from four to twenty teachers licensed at each examination, it is not strange that the ranks are overcrowded.

These candidates are usually prepared for the examination in Grammar or High Schools, and sometimes in so called Normal Classes. Their preparation is likely to be for an *examination* rather than for *teaching*; but being at or near their homes, they secure positions, and often fill them to the satisfaction of the patrons.

Although this state of things may seem to work a temporary evil (by trusting the education of children to untrained teachers), it is an evil that will, in the end, remedy itself, by working out the problem of the "survival of the fittest." People are already beginning to find the difference between trained and untrained teachers; and as this difference becomes more apparent, trained teachers will be more and more in demand.

As I have previously reported to you, our graduates find situations very soon after graduation; and what is still more gratifying, in many cases they make themselves so useful that they continue in the same school from year to year.

OTHER NORMAL SCHOOLS.

In March, 1881, an Act was passed by the Legislature establishing a "Branch State Normal School" in Los Angeles County, the site to be selected and the building erected by the Board of

Trustees of the school at San José. It was further provided that the Branch School should be governed by the same laws and be under the control of the same Trustees, as the San José School. The site selected was the property known as Beaudry Terrace, in the City of Los Angeles.

The school was first opened August 29, 1882. For the first year the Principal of the San José School was the nominal Principal, and the school was conducted by the Vice-Principal, C. J. Flatt. In May, 1883, Prof. Ira More, of the San José Normal School, was elected Principal of the Los Angeles school, which position he still holds.

In March, 1887, the Legislature created a second Branch Normal School for Northern California, to be located and built in the same way as the first.

The same Legislature passed an Act creating a separate Board of Trustees for each Normal School, and otherwise amending the law.

The Normal School for Northern California is located at Chico, Butte County. Its first session will be opened in September, 1889, under the principalship of Professor Pierce.

LAWS RELATING TO THE STATE NORMAL SCHOOLS.

As amended, to take effect July 1, 1887.

354. The Normal Schools at San José and at Los Angeles, and any Normal School established after the first day of January, eighteen hundred and eighty-seven, by the State, shall be known as State Normal Schools, and shall each have a Board of Trustees, constituted as follows: The Governor and State Superintendent of Public Instruction shall be members of each Board, and there shall be five members, whose term of office shall be five years, who shall be appointed by the Governor; *provided*, that the Trustees of the State Normal School in office June thirtieth, eighteen hundred and eighty-seven, shall hold office until the end of the terms for which they were appointed; *provided*, that no appointment made after the approval of this Act shall be for a term of more than five years, and the Trustees in office when this Act takes effect shall become members of the Board of Trustees of the Normal School located nearest to their residences, and the members of any Board of Trustees, when first appointed and organized, shall classify themselves so that the term of one Trustee shall expire annually.

1487. The State Normal Schools have for their objects the education of teachers for the public schools of this State.

1488. The State Normal Schools shall be under the management and control of Boards of Trustees, constituted as provided in section three hundred and fifty-four of the Political Code of the State of California.

1489. The powers and duties of each Board of Trustees are as follows:

First—To elect a Secretary, who shall receive such salary, not to exceed one hundred and fifty dollars per annum, as may be allowed by the Board.

Second—To prescribe rules for their own government, and for the government of the school.

Third—To prescribe rules for the reports of officers and teachers of the school, and for visiting other schools and institutes.

Fourth—To provide for the purchase of school apparatus, furniture, stationery, and text-books for the use of the pupils.

Fifth—To establish and maintain training or model schools, and require the pupils of the Normal School to teach and instruct classes therein.

Sixth—To elect a Principal and other necessary teachers, fix their salaries, and prescribe their duties.

Seventh—To issue diplomas of graduation upon the recommendation of the Faculty of the school.

Eighth—To control and expend all moneys appropriated for the support and maintenance of the school, and all money received from tuition or from donations. In no event shall any moneys appropriated for the support of the school, or received from tuition or donations, be paid or used for compensation or traveling expenses of the Trustees of the school, except when attending the joint meetings provided for by section one thousand four hundred and ninety-two of the Political Code of the State of California, and each Trustee attending such meetings shall receive the same mileage as is allowed by law to members of the Legislature, for not more than two meetings in each school year.

Ninth—To cause a record of all their proceedings to be kept, which shall be open to public inspection at the school.

Tenth—To keep, open to public inspection, an account of receipts and expenditures.

Eleventh—To annually report to the Governor a statement of all their transactions, and of all matters pertaining to the school.

Twelfth—To transmit with such report a copy of the principal teacher's annual report.

Thirteenth—To revoke any diploma by them granted, on receiving satisfactory evidence that the holder thereof is addicted to drunkenness, is guilty of gross immorality, or is reputedly dishonest in his dealings; *provided*, that such person shall have at least thirty days' previous notice of such contemplated action, and shall, if he asks it, be heard in his own defense.

1490. Each Board of Trustees must hold two regular meetings in each year, and may hold special meetings at the call of the Secretary, when directed by the Chairman.

1491. The time and place of regular meetings must be fixed by the by-laws of the Board. The Secretary must give written notice of the time and place of special meetings to each member of the Board.

1492. Joint meetings of the Boards of Trustees of the State Normal Schools shall be held at least once in each school year, alternately, at the different State Normal Schools. The first meeting shall be held at San José, and thereafter at the other Normal Schools in the order of their organization. At such meetings, the Trustees shall have the power, and it shall be their duty:

First—To prescribe a uniform series of text-books for use in the State Normal Schools. The State series of text-books shall be used, when published, in the grades and classes for which they are adapted.

Second—To prescribe a uniform course of study, and time, and standard for graduation from the State Normal Schools.

1494. Every person admitted as a pupil to the Normal School course must be:
First—Of good moral character.
Second—Of sixteen **years of age.**
Third—Of that class of persons who, if of proper age, would be admitted in the public schools of this State without restriction.

1495. Teachers holding State certificates **of** the first or second **grades** may be admitted from the State at large.

1496. Persons resident of another State **may** be admitted upon letters of recommendation from the Governor, or Superintendent of Schools thereof.

1497. Every person making application for admission as a pupil to the Normal School must, at the time of making such application, file with the Principal of the school a declaration **that he** enters the school to fit himself for **teaching,** and that it is his intention to engage in teaching in the public schools of **this** State, or in the State **or Territory where the** applicant resides.

1501. The Principal **of each** State Normal School **must make a detailed** annual report **to the** Board **of** Trustees, with **a catalogue of the pupils, and** such other particulars as the Board may **require or he may think useful.**

1502. He must also **attend County Institutes, and lecture before them on** subjects **relating to public schools and the profession of teaching.**

1503. The Board of Trustees of each State Normal School, upon the recommendation of the Faculty, may issue to those pupils who worthily complete **the full course of** study and training prescribed, **a diploma of graduation. To** each pupil receiving this **diploma, and thereafter teaching successfully in the** public schools of this State for three years, and **to each pupil who worthily** completes the Post Graduate course, the State Board **of Education shall grant** an educational diploma.

1504. The Boards of Trustees, or such Trustees as attend the joint meetings, **shall have** power **to** appoint a Secretary, who shall receive such compensation, **not to** exceed twenty dollars for each joint meeting, as the Trustees present at the meeting may order paid. The Secretary shall keep a full record **of all the** proceedings **of the** joint **meetings of** the Trustees, and shall **notify** the Secretary of each **Board of Trustees of** any **changes made in the course of** study or the text-books to be adopted in the State Normal Schools.

1505. The Superintendent of Public Instruction must visit the school from time to time, inquire into its condition and management, enforce the rules and regulations made by the Board, require such reports as he deems proper from the teachers of the school, and exercise a general supervision over the same.

1507. Each order upon the Controller of State by the Board of Trustees of a State Normal School must be signed by the President of the Board, and countersigned by the Secretary. **Upon presentation of the** order aforesaid, signed and countersigned as aforesaid, the Controller of State must draw his warrant upon the State Treasurer in favor of the Board of Trustees for any moneys, or any part thereof, appropriated and set apart for the support of the Normal School, and the Treasurer must pay such warrants on presentation.

REMINISCENCES SINCE 1880.

Two Episodes in the History of the Class of May, 1882, by One of its Members.

The Hand of Death.

Marching in the ranks of the Senior Class of 1882 might be seen a diminutive personage, scarcely more than three feet in height, whose intelligent face and silvery voice were a pleasing contrast to her dwarfed and somewhat deformed body.

Daily the little feet climbed the stairway, and daily the mind of Bessie Warthen performed with honor the arduous tasks of the first half of the Senior year's work. But the second half opened unfavorably to many, there being much sickness in the city. Measles broke out with violence, and those who had not had this disease lived in daily fear of the contagion. Several Normal pupils became affected, with no serious results; but when her class was told that little Bessie had fallen victim to the dread disease, many feared for her safe recovery. The little form was sorely missed from class-room and hall, and when the news came at last that her heart had stopped its beating because the inflamed lungs gave it no room, grief was universal and a pall seemed hanging over all.

On Saturday, February 26, 1882, her class gathered at her former boarding place, and after listening to words of hope and comfort from her beloved teacher, Professor Norton, they accompanied her remains in mournful procession to the depot, from which her body was sent to her home at Gilroy.

No fears were entertained for the others who were ill, but just eight days after Bessie's death came the news that Flora McFarland, apparently the strongest and healthiest of the whole class, had succumbed to the same disease. What a shock that was. No one knew who next would go, and two other members of the school followed shortly after.

Her remains were interred at San José, as her parents lived too far away for them to be sent home. Funeral services were held in the Methodist Episcopal Church, and though a large concourse of people was present at the church and grave, only two or three of her relatives were able to be among those who accompanied our loved classmate to her grave.

The desks of the departed ones were draped in mourning for thirty days, and floral offerings were daily seen among the crape.

The Monterey Excursion.

The class of 1882 was nearing its graduation. It had been an exceptionally studious and well behaved class, and several of the Faculty had been overheard to say: "Yes; the class of '82 is a representative class; we are proud of our present Seniors."

Of course the pupils were somewhat elated at this, and held their heads high in consequence. But one day, three or four weeks before their school record was finished, a cloud passed over their fair fame, dimming its former luster.

It came about in this wise. The indefatigable railroad company, whose iron bands span the distance between San José and Monterey, was always "getting up" excursions. Plenty of Sunday excursions had passed away without tempting the exploring tendencies of the '82 Seniors, but here was one announced for Monday: "To Monterey and return—reduced rates!"

This was too much. Three or four Seniors read the announcement on Saturday and concluded to go. On Monday morning one of their **number was dispatched to the Normal to spread** the contagion, but as **they feared a negative answer, no** permission of the Faculty was asked. * * * **The large assembly hall was gradually being filled. The** Faculty, all unaware of **the new "departure,"** filed in and took seats on the platform. Our dignified Vice-Principal, **Professor Braly,** came in and took **his seat at the** enrolling desk. At last the hands on the clock above the platform pointed **at** a quarter to nine, and tap went the bell, producing an almost awe-inspiring silence. **The monitors of the Middle** and Junior Classes arose promptly on **their feet, and began the count of their** classes, but a **failure on the** part of the Senior monitor to arise caused the enrolling officer to **notice a total vacancy in the front seats of the Senior Class.** Monitors *pro tem.* were quickly appointed, but never will that class forget the surprised **yet severe and inquiring look which the professor cast** around at the Faculty.

Many of the pupils had become **aware of existing** circumstances, and were breathlessly wondering how the teachers would regard them. The temporary monitors **finished** the count of their classes, **and in** most dignified tones were asked **by the** Professor to report. The mobile features of Miss **Urmy, who had** been **appointed** monitor of Senior A, were gleaming with suppressed mirth as **she answered:** "Present, thirty; absent, all the boys; total, forty." A **general laugh greeted this, and** even Professor Braly smiled as **he saw where the blame was laid.**

Senior B had one boy present, so it could not make a like report. **But throughout** all the classes were reports of Mr. A., Mr. B., or Mr. C.'s being absent, while scarcely a girl had gone.

The boys had their good time on Monday, but as they assembled on Tuesday morning their heads were not quite so erect; and when the mild but grave **words** of Professor Allen showed them the effect of their conduct upon the character of the class and the school, there was not one present but would have **recalled the trip could he have done so.**

Class of May, 1883, by Anna C. Murphy.

It is doubtful whether I can adequately **represent the class of '83,** as I was enrolled among its numbers during only the Senior year.

I had been a country school ma'am, a product of the civilization of the **mountains and the mines.** I was a perfect stranger—a unit of the one hundred and twelve, **but it was not** very long **before we** all coalesced into clubs and coteries, and **began to bind the ties of friendship** that will stretch across the years.

We were divided into two sections, having Miss Wright and Professor Norton, respectively, for class teachers. The latter had charge of our division, **and** taught **also** the rhetoric and literature—the most flexible media through which **one mind can act** upon another: "noblest thought seeking fairest **word."** How gratefully we all look back to that instruction freighted with wisdom **and** serenity far beyond the book's deepest plummet. Such gracious sympathy was ours, such exact help for one's sore or weak spot. Already the dawn of the morning so near was irradiating his uplifted brow, giving him more perfect insight into nature and the hearts of her groping, stumbling children.

The year of '82–'83 was Professor Kleeberger's **first one** with us. Chemistry **was his department.** Many of us did not understand him at first. He seemed **stern, implacable; so** large, and so unchangeable, that trying to influence him was considered about as feasible as trying to pry Jupiter out of his course, or shove Neptune on a little faster. But we grew to find the sweetness under the strength. We found the vein of humor, too, and, in spite of a persistent love of punning—a habit of throwing words together with violence to phonetics and philology—we learned to care very much for him.

Professor Childs labored with us in penmanship and bookkeeping. He had taken the Middle Class through history. Many of his classical jokes are down in our note books, and doing duty in appropriate spots to-day.

Professor More was of mathematics the awful autocrat. He had no patience with originality in geometry, insisted on the barren recital of facts, demanded effete demonstrations and thread-bare conclusions. How the girls did like to flock around his table at intermission. Fancy was free then, and laughter loud. That year was his last, in San José. He had a call to the Normal School at Los Angeles, and generations of girls go on calling him blessed there.

Professor Allen we saw little of, till in the Senior Class. Many who had called him gruff and unsympathetic, recalled the verdict then, as in the method work he reviewed the secret springs of human action, and showed us how close to the great heart of things he was.

The Philomathean Society was in its zenith that year, but a civil war shook it at the last. A dozen irate girls withdrew at one meeting. The young men carried it on for awhile without much of the active feminine element. Then the Faculty took away the charter, and amid muttered words and dark looks at the tyrants in power, the *evening* Philomathean sank into a much-wept grave.

We thought our Commencement a glorious occasion, and our valedictorian, Ida Jones, the fairest that ere the sun shone on. The after years made her only fairer, in face and spirit, although they robbed her of health and strength. Little Kittie Chandler, always the pet of our class, is another to whom time has brought grace and peace and sweetness.

Space forbids individual mention of many others who are dear to all of us. Many I have lost sight of in the rush of growing old. We had one reunion in 1885. Only a few were represented though. In June, 1888, in the parlor of the Palace Hotel, we held an impromptu conclave, *within* the great conclave of the National Convention. Never again till the roll-call on judgment day shall we all assemble as on May 30, 1883.

Five of our number are already waiting quietly on the other side. Early in life and in teaching they laid down book and pencil. One by one we shall join them, for an immortality of advancement, to be graded as our work and discipline here have fitted us, for already eternity's work is begun. Infinity can only multiply it.

CLASS OF DECEMBER, 1883, BY LIZZIE B. CREW (MRS. CANFIELD).

Of all the classes that have graduated from the Normal School ours claims peculiar distinction. It was the first Christmas gift from our dear Alma Mater to this glorious State, and the last class in which honors were granted. Two points, truly, that should make us extraordinarily proficient.

One of the Faculty, Professor Braly, who was our class teacher during two years of our course, left the Normal with us to make his home in Fresno.

While we were Seniors, Professor More went to take charge of a Normal School among the orange groves of Los Angeles, and Professor Kleeberger came to fill his place.

On Commencement day, as is usually the custom, one of the Faculty is appointed to address the graduating class, and we feel much gratified at having had Professor Norton, that dearly loved teacher, appointed to perform this duty. We were the last class that he thus addressed. The class motto, "Onward, the palm awaits you," was taken as his subject. His thrilling words concerning the palms in the world beyond, awaiting those who righteously do their **duty here**, will ever ring in our minds and hearts and **be incentives to** noble work.

The two years spent in the beautiful City of San José and in **the Normal School**, although at times our tasks were difficult, constitute an **epoch in our lives full of** satisfaction and pleasure.

The opening exercises of the school were particularly interesting. At **twenty minutes** before nine all of the school and Faculty assembled in the Normal Hall, where reports were given by the monitors of each class. To get up for the **first** time before **the four hundred** present was a trying position for a new monitor, as the writer can testify. An anthem was then sung by the school and a passage of Scripture **read by our honored** Principal, Professor Allen. The chanting of the Lord's Prayer, which followed, was one of the most impressive things to **which I** have ever listened. It hardly failed to bring tears to the eyes of **one hearing it for the first time, or of one feeling** a little homesick.

From nine to **twelve and one to two-thirty o'clock was devoted to recitations, the classes passing from one room to another, each teacher having his own room.**

Ten-thirty P. M. was the prescribed hour for retiring, so from three o'clock to that time the studying for the next day must be done. If on our reports the **retiring hour was often later than half-past ten, our preceptress, Miss Wright,** would call us into her office and give us one of her characteristic **"quiet talks."**

While we were Seniors, lectures often varied the monotony of **every day** work, and we were particularly blessed by having the talented lecturer, Major Dane, with us frequently during that time.

The well filled library presided over by our faithful friend, Miss Royce, was **a source of** never failing pleasure.

Miss Walker, ever ready to sympathize with the down-hearted, tried to make **us** grammarians, and it is too bad that we who have left the school-room **do not remember more of her excellent** precepts.

Space forbids a mention of every teacher, **but each holds his** own place in **our love and esteem, and the tie** that bound **us in the few short** years of our **intercourse has grown with** our growth and **strengthened with** our strength.

A LEAF FROM OUR CLASS HISTORY. CLASS OF DECEMBER, 1884, BY LOTTIE MATTHIS.

To-day, as **I sit thinking of the past, I can** scarcely realize that more than four years have **elapsed since we, the Christmas** Class of '84, left our Alma Mater, to follow our chosen profession.

Most of us have been so busy that the days have passed almost as quickly as **those** spent in our dear old Normal. We think of those school days **with** pleasure, notwithstanding the many discouragements we encountered **in** toiling up the hill toward that long-sought summit, graduation.

We stumbled often, and sometimes feared falling so **far (below the average) that we should be** compelled to begin **the ascent once more.** But kindly cheer from patient instructors gave us fresh courage, and we pushed on again.

From the first day we were called together in the assembly hall, we felt there was a great work to do, and a great something attainable by each of us.

During **the first week of** examination, and consequent assignment to classes, what strangers we were. Only two familiar rooms, Room K and the assembly hall. There were few familiar faces, and as yet, not even a teacher we could call our own. When the classes were finally arranged, and our programme for Junior work was given us, we realized that the great work was about to begin.

"Room G, Arithmetic."—What that part of the programme signified we learned later, when shingles, carpets, brick houses, and bushel measures were showered upon us mercilessly.

"Room I, Physiology"—An amœba was our first acquaintance in physiology, and Miss Washburn was not long in convincing us that even a bit of protoplasm was not to be despised. Later on in the work, many representatives of the species feline were sacrificed to science. Poor kitty! On one occasion, even a mouse ventured forth to drop a pitying tear. However, some of the young ladies failed to understand the object of its visit, and created such a sensation that mousey retreated in alarm.

"Room E, Bookkeeping."—Under Professor Childs' able instructions we learned the proper use of red ink, day-book, and journal; and when the ten weeks' report reached us, many students learned furthermore that our liabilities far exceeded our resources in the bookkeeping department.

"Room K, Grammar."—We ascertained, with a wonderful degree of accuracy, that there was yet something in connection with personal and relative pronouns which we had failed to find in our previous study of them. "The ribbon was an inch wide," brought several members of the class to grief.

"Room C, Reading."—A full study hour was to be devoted each evening to reading, regardless of the discomfort experienced by nervous landladies, who were startled from their slumbers by such cries as "Fire! fire! fire!" "Sweet California oranges!" "Bring out yer old clo'!"

Last, but not least, came our music hour. Professor Elwood often found his burden hard to bear, for the sopranos would lag along behind the more wide awake altos. "Keep up, stragglers!" pronounced very abruptly, often had the desired effect, in recalling them to consciousness.

Drill in marching occupied an occasional half hour, and not proud were the Junior B's when they received the title of "Crazy Class." Their sorrow gave way to joy a few days later, when one of the more advanced classes marched like a "flock of sheep."

For five months we followed the Junior programme, striving for promotion into the Middle Class. This object attained, we turned our attention to bugs, cotyledons, gravitation, amendments, battles, binary compounds, essays, Anglo-Saxon abstracts, etc.

Dear to the heart of every student is the memory of those green pencil marks which came weekly from the hand of Professor Kleeberger, who presided over chemicals and unknown quantities.

History hour was occasionally enlivened by a debate or a thrilling incident from real life.

Professor Braly labored patiently to impress upon our minds the principles of specific gravity and hydrostatics.

Who does not remember the speeches which were written, committed to memory, and delivered under the directions of Miss Thompson? The criticisms written upon said speeches were worthy of remembrance also.

The name of Professor Norton is dear, so dear to us all. How vividly we recall the many hours spent with that beloved teacher who has since been called to his better home! Not in one subject, but in all things did we receive his able help. How much we owe to him for the example of his pure, noble life!

Besides the class work, many students took an active part in various literary and debating societies of the school. The Philomathean was one of these, and lived long and well.

The Senior year was, to many, the pleasantest part of the Normal work. Many warm friendships had been formed among schoolmates, as well as between teachers and pupils; and the tie which bound the class together grew stronger as we neared our journey's end.

However, there was yet much hard work to be done before graduation. Our struggles with chemical experiments and unknown quantities were not yet ended, and composition, which took so much time, was to be varied now with bits of poetry. Not many of the poems written were published, and, it is thought, few were kept in manuscript form, as all efforts to obtain one for these reminiscences have been in vain.

The word laboratory suggests to our minds visions of broken test tubes, fumes of H Cl, large calico aprons, and fearful explosions.

Daily visits to the museum were made for geology's sake. The trip to Almaden will doubtless be remembered by many of the would-be mineralogists.

Our work in literature and in rhetoric, with Miss Wright as teacher, was usually well prepared, except on days following receptions or "star gazings." The latter generally took place on the Normal grounds, and on one occasion at the uncanny hour of three A. M.

From the beginning of our Normal course much attention had been given to methods in teaching; and our attentive faculties were stimulated by the well known fact that the time would come when we should be given an opportunity for putting theory into practice, as pupil-teachers in the Training Department. The news came at last that Senior A was to go down stairs, and the stoutest heart quaked, for well we knew how much depended upon this test of our ability in school management. Of critics there was no lack, for in each class room was stationed an able body of Senior A's and B's, each individual armed with a pencil and open note book, all ready for an attack upon order, neatness, manner, or discipline. Miss Wilson and Miss Sargent made frequent calls, and seemed to write a great deal in a small note book.

Days had grown into weeks and weeks into months ere our work in that department was declared finished. Joyfully we hastened back to our former class room—Room K—but sadness mingled with our joy when we realized that the work of the Senior year was finished, and that preparations must be made for our departure. Thursday, December eighteenth, was the day chosen for the graduating exercises. On that day we met together as pupils for the last time. When our diplomas were conferred, we felt that we had received our reward for the work completed, but that a much greater work was yet before us, which, if faithfully done, would insure a far richer reward. So we bade farewell to schoolmates, and to those faithful teachers who had guided us so carefully in the past, and went forth, each to take a part in the responsible work of life.

SCHOOL PERIODICALS.

(EDWARD L. SPINKS, Class of June, 1889.)

A history of the school would be incomplete without some mention of its periodicals, their origin, aims, and work. The first attempt at journalism of which there remains any record in the school was made in 1867. In that year appeared a small written sheet, called the "Acorn," interesting to us now chiefly from its being the beginning of what has followed. Only a few numbers remain, but from these may be gained an idea of what the paper was. It consisted of witticisms and poems, and essays on literary, scientific, and educational topics, all in manuscript. It was read monthly before the school society by members of the same. The elegant penmanship, the neatly ornamented covers, and the dainty bows of ribbon show that its importance was appreciated by those having it in charge.

After the disappearance of the "Acorn" there seems to have been no school paper for several years, but on May 20, 1880, the first printed sheet, "The Class Paper," afterwards "The Senior Journal," was given to the world. A complete file, dating from May, 1880, to December, 1885, having been preserved, it appears that the paper, or journal, was a semi-annual publication, and, as the names imply, was devoted to the interests of the Senior Classes. It contained the class and graduating exercises, and served a good purpose in keeping alive a class and school spirit. Its first numbers, each containing four pages, equal to about six quarto pages, were issued in newspaper form. Later supplements were added, and the last issue, December, 1885, appeared as a pamphlet of twelve large octavo pages. Each number was filled with excellent articles, to some of which are attached names that have since become familiar to all members of the school.

But the school was growing; some regular medium of communication, some means of giving expression to school ideas, some tie to unite graduates more closely to each other and to their Alma Mater, was needed; and the best means of supplying this want was a recognized school paper. To these circumstances and conditions, the "Index" owes its existence. But circumstances do not make a paper; work must be done; and though, after the enterprise was well under way, many took an active part, to the energy and perseverance of Messrs. H. F. Clark, L. J. Lathwesen, and H. G. Squier are due the organization and establishment of the paper. Though the matter was agitated during the spring term of 1885, not till August of that year did the Senior Classes come together and take the decisive steps.

Mr. H. F. Clark, Xmas, 1885, was unanimously chosen editor-in-chief, with the Misses Addie C. Spafford, Myra A. Parks, Fannie McKean, and Mary E. Lynch as associates, Mr. Lathwesen as manager, and Mr. Squier as assistant.

The first issue, a little yellow-covered journal containing eight pages of literary matter for the nourishment of Normal minds, and as many more of "ads" for the financial support of the paper, appeared in October, 1885.

Like all new things, the "Index" was subjected to adverse criticism, and received as well its share of commendation. One enthusiastic admirer was heard to remark, "Well, the school now has something to be proud of." Another—not an admirer, said, "Pshaw! it won't survive the Christmas pudding, but will die of the colic before New Year's day." But it lived to become strong and healthy; and, being now the recognized school representative and newspaper, it has, we hope, become a permanent part of the institution.

In December, 1885, the Senior Classes of the Los Angeles Normal were induced to take part in conducting the paper. This department was continued till February, 1888, when the last contributions were received. Since then, all matter for publication has been supplied by our own school, and, we may add, the columns have always been well filled.

At present the "Index" contains twelve quarto pages of reading matter, divided into six departments. The editorial contains short articles of interest to the school and to the teachers; the literary consists of poems, essays, and class exercises; in the educational and scientific are found essays on appropriate subjects, hints to teachers, items of information, and lesson plans from the Training School. "Alumni" is a bureau of personal information for graduates; and "All Sorts," as the name suggests, is a miscellaneous collection of sense and nonsense, wit and wisdom, fact and fancy, intended for amusement.

The paper is under the management of the Senior Classes, the editor-in-chief and half the members of the staff being chosen from the Senior A Class, the business manager, his assistant, and the remaining members of the staff from the Senior B. Reporters for "Alumni" and "All Sorts" work are appointed in all classes, and articles and items for all departments are received from pupils, graduates, and teachers. The paper receives the hearty support of the Faculty, and its literary merits are largely due to the assistance of the teachers of rhetoric and literature. Since the discontinuance of the "Journal," the "Index" has published the class and graduation exercises.

The money for carrying on the paper is supplied by advertising and subscription rates. The present circulation, chiefly among pupils and graduates, is about four hundred. The expense is small, as the officers receive no pay for their services, and nothing but printing and binding is to be paid for.

The "Index" is doing a good work; for it is now firmly established, and, as one friend has said, "The period of experiment is passed, and it has carved for itself a place among the foremost school journals of the land."

The latest venture in school journalism, the "Model Magazine," began its career in September, 1888. It is a semi-monthly sheet written by members of the Model Class, and read before the Model Society. The editor and assistant being chosen anew for each issue, zest is given to the work by inspiring each with a desire to make his number the best. The result is a paper which in matter and execution is a credit to class and teacher. History, science, and literature are discussed, the articles appearing as essays, poems, extracts, biographical sketches, etc., sometimes neatly illustrated by drawings. All the work is done by the pupils. The chief aims are to lead the pupils to become familiar with the important points of our history, to study scientific facts and principles, to learn something of the best authors and their works, to improve in language and composition, and, above all, to cultivate a taste for good reading and an aptitude for investigation.

ATTENDANCE AND GRADUATES.

School Year.	Normal Dep't. Ladies	Normal Dep't. Gentlemen.	Normal Dep't. Total.	Preparatory.	Training Dep't.	Grand Total in School.	Annual Cost Per Capita in Normal Dep't.‡	Number of Graduates. Ladies	Number of Graduates. Gentlemen.	Number of Graduates. Total.	Annual Percentage Graduates Normal Dep't.
1862–63								4		4	
1863–64								18	1	19	
1864–65								19	4	23	
1865–66								25	8	33	
1866–67								27	4	31	
1867–68								37	11	48	
1868–69	180	18	198				$40 00	26	3	29	15%
1869–70*	166	22	188					40	4	44	
1870–71	132	32	164				73 00	17	4	21	13%
1871–72	152	29	181				66 00	13	4	17	9%
1872–73	130	29	159				94 00	16	4	20	13%
1873–74	130	36	166	32	114	312	90 00	28	5	33	20%
1874–75	271	57	328	62	98	488	53 00	36	9	45	14%
1875–76	369	65	434	67	134	635	40 00	30	8	38	9%
1876–77	395	64	459	78	128	665	52 00	36	6	42	9%
1877–78	430	70	500	103	109	712	48 00	48	10	58	12%
1878–79	402	70	472	76	113	661	70 00	36	8	44	9%
1879–80	352	58	410	58	109	577	81 00	41	6	47	11%
1880–81	375	57	432	57	101	590	77 00	32	2	34	8%
1881–82	452	96	548	52	103	703	55 00	62	13	75	14%
1882–83	524	109	633	48	115	796	47 00	79	14	93	15%
1883–84	499	101	600	45	115	760	67 (0	72	16	88	15%
1884–85	450	78	528	38	135	701	76 00	96	13	109	20%
1885–86	425	72	497	56	129	682	76 00	82	18	100	20%
1886–87	544	88	632	59	136	827	60 00	87	11	98	16%
1887–88	526	71	597	†	196	793	65 00	103	18	121	20%
1888–89	507	60	567	†	218	785	68 00	112	17	129	23%
Totals								1,222	221	1,443	

Owing to frequent **changes in Principalship** during the early history of **the school, and the subsequent loss** of records by fire, all the statistics now obtainable with **reference** to attendance during the first six years, give only the number of *new* pupils admitted each year as follows·

Number of new pupils admitted, 1862 31
Number of new pupils admitted, 1863 62
Number of new pupils admitted, 1864 75
Number of new pupils admitted, 1865 83
Number of new pupils admitted, 1866 100
Number of new pupils admitted from January to May 30, 1867 34

Total (ladies, 319; gentlemen, 66) 385

Number **of new pupils** admitted for **school year 1867**–68, about one hundred **and twenty-five. The complete record** for this year is lost.

---

*First half year. The record for the second half of this year is lost.
† Preparatory Class abolished in 1887. The number in the Training Department for the last two years includes the Model Class.
‡ This estimate is made upon appropriations for support *only*, and does not include cost of buildings, or special appropriations for library, furnishing, apparatus, improvement of grounds, etc.

WORK OF GRADUATES.

Class.	Total Number in Class.	No. Known to have Taught since Graduat'n.	No. who have not Taught since Graduation.	No Report as to Teach'g.	Now Teaching in California.	Now Teach'g elsewhere.	Deceased.	Engaged in Mercantile and other Business.	Farmers.	Physicians.	Lawyers.	Editors.	No. held office of Co. Superintendent.	No. since Graduat'd from Higher Institutions.	No. Pursu'd Higher Studies at other Institutions.
May, 1863.	4	3	1	....	1	....	1	....	....	....	....	....	....	....	....
May, 1864.	19	17	1	1	7	....	2	....	....	....	1	....	....	....	....
Dec., 1864.	9	6	1	2	1	....	1	....	....	....	1	....	....	....	....
May, 1865.	14	13	1	....	5	....	1	....	....	....	....	....	....	....	....
Dec., 1865.	11	10	....	1	3	....	2	....	....	....	2	....	....	1	....
June, 1866.	22	21	1	....	8	1	4	1	....	....	1	....	....	1	....
June, 1867.	31	27	1	3	9	....	6	....	....	....	1	....	2	....	....
Nov., 1867.	10	4	....	6	2	....	1	....	....	....	1	....	....	....	....
May, 1868.	38	24	4	10	2	....	6	2	1	2	....	....	1	....	....
May, 1869.	29	28	1	....	7	....	3	....	....	....	....	....	1	....	....
Mar., 1870.	44	40	....	4	10	....	5	1	....	3	....	....	1	1	....
Mar., 1871.	21	19	....	2	5	....	1	2	1	....	....	....	....	....	....
Mar., 1872.	17	17	....	....	5	....	1	....	1	....	1	....	3	....	....
Mar., 1873.	20	19	1	....	7	....	1	1	....	....	1	....	2	....	....
Mar., 1874.	33	26	2	5	5	....	5	1	....	1	....	1	....	....	....
Mar., 1875.	45	40	3	2	13	....	4	2	1	1	....	....	2	1	....
Mar., 1876.	38	37	....	1	9	....	4	3	....	....	....	....	....	1	....
Mar., 1877.	42	42	....	....	14	....	2	2	1	1	....	....	....	....	3
May, 1878.	58	53	2	3	18	2	6	2	1	1	....	....	1	....	....
May, 1879.	44	39	3	2	16	....	2	1	3	1	....	....	1	1	1
Jan., 1880*	2	2	....	....	1	....	....	....	1	....	....	....	....	....	....
May, 1880.	45	41	3	1	16	....	2	1	....	1	....	1	....	1	1
May, 1881.	34	32	2	....	9	3	2	....	1	....	....	....	....	....	2
Jan., 1882*	1	1	....	....	....	....	....	....	....	....	....	....	....	....	....
May, 1882.	74	70	4	....	32	....	2	4	3	1	1	....	1	2	....
Dec., 1882*	8	7	1	....	6	....	....	....	....	....	....	....	....	....	....
May, 1883.	85	81	4	....	43	3	4	2	1	....	....	....	....	....	1
Dec., 1883.	50	50	....	....	19	2	3	1	....	....	....	1	1	....	....
May, 1884.	38	37	1	....	21	1	....	....	....	1	....	1	....	1	5
Dec., 1884.	51	51	....	....	31	2	1	1	2	....	....	....	....	....	1
May, 1885.	58	57	1	....	36	....	3	1	2	....	....	....	....	2	2
Dec., 1885.	45	45	....	....	32	....	....	....	1	....	....	....	....	....	....
May, 1886.	55	50	5	....	30	1	2	1	....	....	....	....	1	1	1
Dec., 1886.	32	30	1	1	20	1	....	1	....	....	....	....	....	....	....
May, 1887.	66	61	4	1	45	....	....	2	....	....	....	....	....	....	1
Dec., 1887.	60	52	5	3	43	1	1	....	....	....	....	....	....	....	2
May, 1888.	61	58	3	....	51	1	....	1	....	....	....	....	....	....	....
Dec., 1888.	58	48	10	....	43	....	....	....	....	....	....	....	....	....	....
Totals..	1,372	1,258	66	48	625	18	78	33	21	12	11	3	16	14	20
Class of June, 1889	71														

* Diplomas granted at this date, but no regular class graduated.

COUNTY REPRESENTATION OF GRADUATES.

The following table gives the number of graduates from each county of California, and from other States and Territories, since the organization of the school:

County	#	County	#
Alameda	95	Sacramento	40
Alpine	0	San Benito	11
Amador	15	San Bernardino	6
Butte	22	San Diego	6
Calaveras	8	San Francisco	216
Colusa	7	San Joaquin	44
Contra Costa	54	San Luis Obispo	3
Del Norte	2	San Mateo	14
El Dorado	18	Santa Barbara	4
Fresno	12	Santa Clara	429
Humboldt	23	Santa Cruz	49
Inyo	1	Shasta	7
Kern	2	Sierra	10
Lake	4	Siskiyou	3
Lassen	4	Solano	30
Los Angeles	10	Sonoma	37
Marin	17	Stanislaus	10
Mariposa	3	Sutter	12
Mendocino	10	Tehama	0
Merced	10	Trinity	2
Modoc	3	Tulare	12
Mono	2	Tuolumne	18
Monterey	14	Ventura	1
Napa	23	Yolo	11
Nevada	38	Yuba	8
Placer	20		
Plumas	1	Total	1,401

State	#	State	#
Arizona	1	Ohio	1
Idaho	1	Oregon	1
Illinois	1	Pennsylvania	1
Iowa	1	Utah	1
Michigan	1	Washington	4
Missouri	3	Wisconsin	2
Nevada	23		
New York	1	Total	42

STATE APPROPRIATIONS.

	Totals.
For the school year 1862–63, support, $3,000; deficiency bill, $1,200	$4,200 00
For the school year 1863–64, support	6,000 00
For the school year 1864–65, support	8,000 00
For the school year 1865–66, support	8,000 00
For the school year 1866–67, support	8,000 00
For the school year 1867–68, support	8,000 00
For the school year 1868–69, support	8,000 00
For the school year 1869–70, support, $8,000; deficiency bill, $1,500	9,500 00
For the school year 1870–71, support, $12,000; library, $500	12,500 00
For the school year 1871–72, support, $12,000; library, $500	12,500 00
For the school year 1872–73, support, $15,000; library, $500	15,500 00
For the school year 1873–74, support, $15,000; library, $500; deficiency bill, $4,512 88	20,012 88
For the school year 1874–75, support, $17,500; library, $500; apparatus, $3,000	21,000 00
For the school year 1875–76, support, $17,500; library, $500; deficiency bill, $5,000	23,000 00
For the school year 1876–77, support, $24,000; library, $500	24,500 00
For the school year 1877–78, support, $24,000; library, $500	24,500 00
For the school year 1878–79, support, $33,300; deficiency bill, $63 17	33,363 17
For the school year 1879–80, support	33,300 00
For the school year 1880–81, support	33,300 00
For the school year 1881–82, support, $30,000; furnishing, $10,000; improving grounds, $25,000	65,000 00
For the school year 1882–83, support	30,000 00
For the school year 1883–84, support	40,000 00
For the school year 1884–85, support	40,000 00
For the school year 1885–86, support, $38,000; library, $500; water supply and improving grounds, $4,000; painting and repairing building, $1,500; museum cases, $500	44,500 00
For the school year 1886–87, support, $38,000; library, $500	38,500 00
For the school year 1887–88, support, $39,000; library, $1,000	40,000 00
For the school year 1888–89, support, $39,000; library, $1,000	40,000 00

Besides State appropriations, the school has an income from tuition fees in the Training Department, which has averaged, for the past ten years, about $3,400 annually.

NOTE.—Appropriations for buildings are given elsewhere in the historical sketch.

MEMBERS OF THE BOARD OF TRUSTEES

FROM THE ORGANIZATION OF THE SCHOOL TO THE PRESENT TIME.

EX OFFICIO MEMBERS.

Governors.

Leland Stanford	May, 1862, to December, 1863.
Frederick F. Low	December, 1863, to December, 1867.
Henry H. Haight	December, 1867, to December, 1871.
Newton Booth	December, 1871, to February, 1875.
Romualdo Pacheco	February, 1875, to December, 1875.
William Irwin	December, 1875, to January, 1880.
George C. Perkins	January, 1880, to January, 1883.
George Stoneman	January, 1883, to January, 1887.
Washington Bartlett	January, 1887, to September, 1887.
R. W. Waterman	September, 1887, to present time.

State Superintendents.

Andrew J. Moulder	May, 1862, to December, 1863.
John Swett	December, 1863, to December, 1867.
Rev. O. P. Fitzgerald	December, 1867, to December, 1871.
Henry M. Bolander	December, 1871, to December, 1875.
Ezra S. Carr	December, 1875, to January, 1880.
Fred. M. Campbell	January, 1880, to January, 1883.
Wm. T. Welcker	January, 1883, to January, 1887.
Ira G. Hoitt	January, 1887, to present time.

Surveyor-General.

J. F. Houghton	May, 1862, to March, 1866.

City Superintendent of Marysville.

Mayor Fowler	May, 1862, to April, 1863.

City Superintendents of Sacramento.

Dr. Gustavus Taylor	May, 1862, to ——, 1864.
Rev. Wm. H. Hill	——, 1864, to March, 1866.

Superintendents of San Francisco.

George Tait	1862, 1863, 1864, 1865.
John C. Pelton	——, 1866, to December, 1867.
James Denman	December, 1867, to April, 1870.

Superintendents of Sacramento County.

Dr. F. W. Hatch	March, 1866, to March, 1868.
Dr. Aug. Trafton	March, 1868, to April, 1870.

Superintendents of Santa Clara County.

Wesley Tonner	March, 1866, and part of 1867.
J. R. Brierly	Part of 1867, to March, 1868.
John H. Braly	March, 1868, to ——, 1869.
N. Furlong	To April, 1870.

Superintendents of San Joaquin County.

Melville Cottle	March, 1866, to ——, 1870.
W. R. Leadbetter	To April, 1870.

Elected Members.

Samuel I. C. Swezey	April, 1866, to April, 1870.
J. M. Sibley	April, 1866, to April, 1870.

Appointed Members.

Henry O. Weller	1870 to 1872.
Andrew J. Moulder	1870 and part of 1871.
C. T. Ryland	1870 to 1881.
James Denman	1870 to present time.
J. H. Braly	1870 to 1873.
B. Bryant, M.D.	Part of 1871 and to 1880.
Ben. Cory, M.D.	1872 to 1882.
T. Ellard Beans	1873 to present time.
A. S. Evans	1880 to 1884.
O. W. Childs	1881 to 1887.
Ralph Lowe	1882 to present time.
Lawrence Archer	1884 to present time.
T. H. Laine	1887 to present time.

BIOGRAPHICAL SKETCHES OF PRINCIPALS.

AHIRA HOLMES.

(Principal from July, 1862, to June, 1865.)

Ahira Holmes, the first Principal of the first Normal School established in California, was born in Plymouth, Massachusetts, in 1823, and received his primary educational training in the public schools of that historical and puritanical town. He entered the State Normal School in Bridgewater, Massachusetts, in 1843, pursuing the studies of the course in that institution until the latter part of 1847, but teaching in the public schools of his native town during the winter months before graduating. After leaving the Normal School, he was appointed to the position of Principal and Deputy Superintendent of the Boston Farm School, a free manual labor institution for boys, located in the suburbs of the city. This position he resigned in a little more than a year thereafter, having been elected Principal of the Milton Center Public Grammar School, in the vicinity of Boston, where he continued to teach until the following year, when he was elected to the Principalship of the Brockton, Massachuetts, High School.

In the early part of 1852, Mr. Holmes came to California, and in the following June received from the Board of Education of San Francisco an appointment as Principal of the Union Street Public School, then designated as the Clarke's Point Public School, just established, the fourth school organized by the City Board, no system of public schools having been provided for by the State Legislature until the previous year. He continued to discharge the duties of Principal of this school during the four subsequent years.

In 1856 Mr. Holmes was elected Principal of the Powell Street Grammar School, afterwards known as the Washington Grammar School, and at the same time received the appointment of Principal of the Free Evening School, the first of the kind opened, under the auspices of the Board of Education, in the city. He continued to perform the duties of Principal of the former school but one term, but was afterwards re-appointed to serve as Principal of the

Union Street Grammar School, which place he filled during two additional years.

In 1861 Mr. Holmes removed to Los Angeles, where he was elected Principal of the only Grammar School then opened in that city. Here he continued one year, when, in June, 1862, he received from the Board of Trustees of the State Normal School an appointment as Principal of that institution. The school was opened in San Francisco in the following July, in accordance with an Act of the State Legislature, approved May second of the same year, and its sessions were continuously held in that city until 1871, when the school was removed to San José.

At the first daily session of the school only six students presented themselves, but during the first part of the semi-annual session there were thirty in attendance, and about this average was maintained during the term. During the three years Mr. Holmes served as Principal of the school there were two hundred and thirty students enrolled and in attendance, of which number forty-four graduated. Many of these graduates have since successfully filled prominent positions in the schools of San Francisco, and other parts of the State.

Mr. Holmes was ably assisted during the last two years of his time of service by Mr. H. P. Carlton and Miss E. W. Houghton, and in the Experimental Department by Misses H. M. Clark and Kate Sullivan.

After resigning his position in the State Normal School, Mr. Holmes was elected Principal of the Mission Grammar School, in San Francisco, and labored in that capacity during two years; then resigning, to engage in another vocation in the city.

He is now living in retirement on a fruit farm in the suburbs of San José.

George W. Minns.

(Principal from June, 1865, to June, 1866.)

George W. Minns was born in the City of Boston in 1813, and received his early education in a private Primary School and in the public Grammar and English High School of that city. He was fitted, under private tuition, for Harvard University, from which he graduated in 1836. For two years he attended the Howard Dane Law School, receiving the degree of LL.B. He then entered the office of the Hon. Rufus Choate, where he remained for two years, and was admitted to practice law in all the Courts of the State.

In 1854 he came to California, via Cape Horn. Through the failure of Page, Bacon & Co., with whom he had been advised to deposit his money, he was left penniless, and learned, as many others have, "that even heavy gold has wings and can fly away as swiftly as paper money."

The succeeding failure of Adams & Co., and of other bankers, caused great business depression, and Mr. Minns, seeing from an advertisement that the City Board of Education intended to establish a High School, with liberal salaries, applied for and was elected to the Professorship of Natural Science. He did not receive his appointment, however, until he had stood a running fire of examination, conducted by members of the Board, and by doctors, lawyers, and ministers, for about three weeks. He accepted this position, as there was very little law business, and he desired to have his family with him; but, he adds, "none of the liberal promises made by the Board were fulfilled."

He was connected with the school about ten years—as long as both sexes attended. On the separation and the establishment of the Girls' High School, he was offered the choice of the Principalships, and chose that of the Boys' High School, being its first Principal. After holding this position one year, he was called to the Principalship of the State Normal School, then in San Francisco. This was done, although at the time the Superintendent of Public Instruction held a letter from Mr. Minns declining to be a candidate. This letter, he informed Mr. Minns, he had "kept in his pocket." Mr. Minns held the Principalship of the Normal School but one year. He returned to Boston, and for nearly fourteen years taught in the east. He was connected with the Eagleswood Military Academy in New Jersey, with Washington University in Missouri, and with the Boston Latin High School. After this he established in Concord, Massachusetts, a private school, in which he fitted young men for Harvard.

At the instance of John Swett, his intimate friend, he was invited to a position in the Girls' High School, of San Francisco, in 1880. Thinking a change of climate might be beneficial to the health of his children, he accepted this position, which he held until 1888.

During the latter part of this time, he was visited by a serious calamity, viz.: a cataract in each eye. An operation was performed, and both crystalline lenses removed. His eyes are now so strong that he can read fine print.

His present residence is in the town bearing the distinguished name of Newton, in the State of Massachusetts.

From Mr. Minns' autobiographical letter the following is taken *verbatim:*

> For five years I was Principal of the City Normal School of San Francisco. I lectured before the *first* State Teachers' Institute held in California, and at various times since. I hold the *first* certificate issued to a teacher by the State Board of Education.
>
> My work in a literary line has been contributions to college magazines, to law reviews, and the preparation of a series of lectures or essays on the most eminent American poets.
>
> I have spent the best part of my life in teaching. The life of the faithful teacher is laborious. It can truly be said that most teachers are overworked and underpaid, and yet there are compensations. The teacher is amply rewarded for all his toils who creates in those under his charge a love of knowledge, who gains their good will, esteem, and affection. Teaching, like the quality of mercy, is twice blessed: "It blesseth him that gives and him that takes." There is a *quid pro quo* of considerable value to be derived, not only from the diversions many and various which recesses and school hours afford, but also from the contemplation of many various and good points of pupils. Their thoughtlessness may lead to many objectionable traits and habits; as, for example, idleness, mischief, disobedience. On the other hand, nearly all of them are open, generous, good natured, very affectionate, forgiving everything in their teachers except partiality and injustice. That teacher is less adorned with graces than are the average of his pupils who cannot say of them, "With all their faults, I love them still."

HENRY P. CARLTON.

(Principal from June, 1866, to July, 1867, and from February to May, 1868.)

Henry P. Carlton was born in Andover, Essex County, Massachusetts. His education, up to the age of twenty, was confined to the district school, which, after the manner of his time and place, was kept open only during the winter months. His work was that of a New England farmer's boy. For five or six winters, beginning with that of his eighteenth year, he taught a district school. He was twenty-one years old when he entered the South Andover High School, where he fitted for the classical course in the Vermont University. On account of his ability as a writer and speaker, he was given, at the close of the sophomore year, the place of honor on the programme of the public exercises of his class. Ill health compelled him to leave college, never to return.

After a six months' sea voyage, he was engaged for several years in an insurance business in Philadelphia.

In 1853 he came "around the Horn" to California, and, in the fall of that year, was made Principal of the North Beach Grammar School. Four years later he was elected Principal of the Powell Street Grammar School. This position he resigned in 1861, to go East. Upon his return, he accepted the offer of a deputyship in the office of John Swett, State Superintendent of Public Instruction, where he remained till October, 1863, when he was elected assistant in the State Normal School, where he labored as Vice-Principal and Principal until March, 1873.

His special work in the school was physiology, natural history, and mental philosophy, applied to teaching. The text-book in the latter study was Russell's work, and the first class completing the course in Normal Training remember well John Swett's expression of delight and surprise at their proficiency. Mr. Carlton's lessons in physiology and his enthusiasm in zoölogical work strongly impressed his pupils. While he was connected with the Normal School he made a collection of nearly all the then known species of land and freshwater shells of the Pacific Coast.

Mr. Carlton exerted a marked influence for good over the growing characters of his pupils. Many of them remember with gratitude his intense interest in their moral welfare, and his anxiety that they should grow in things spiritual as well as in things intellectual.

After leaving the Normal School, he taught a few years in the Boys' High School and some of the Grammar Schools of San Francisco; but the onerous labor of the school-room was too great for his physical condition, and he has not taught for the last ten years. In these years he has done excellent literary work in school journals and other San Francisco papers. He now resides in Oakland. For the last thirty years he has been a teacher in Sabbath schools.

Any just estimate of Mr. Carlton's work must take into account the fact that physical weakness continually oppressed him. Pain and weariness were his almost constant companions. His ideal is so high that he estimates his successful life work a failure. Few have been so useful. His three-score years have been well spent.

GEORGE TAIT.

(Principal from July, 1867, to February, 1868.)

George Tait was born in 1831, in the City of New York, and was reared in the State of Virginia. He received his education at the University of Virginia, then in the most flourishing period of its history. He began his career as a teacher in Virginia, and before he was twenty-one. In 1853, at the age of twenty-two, he came to California, and went into the French Bank at San Francisco, teaching school in the evening. In 1857 he was appointed Principal of the Denman School, and served as such until 1861, when he was elected City Superintendent of Schools. In 1863 he was reëlected. During his term of office he advocated many reforms, particularly in the interest of the primary schools, which he thought should, in regard to the character of their teachers, their buildings, and other appliances of education, rank first in every school department. Next in importance to the judicious selection of teachers, etc., in primary schools, he considered the work of examining, classifying, and promoting pupils. This work was then performed by the Committee on Classification, aided by the Superintendent. Mr. Tait considered this system inadequate, and proposed, in its stead, to commit the task to the grammar masters, under the supervision of the committee, and at the same time to relieve the masters of the charge of any one class, so that they might attend to the general interests of their schools. In his efforts to better the condition of our schools and to raise their standard, he sought inspiration in the wisdom and experience of the leading educators of the East, and in his views on the subject he was supported by the Board of Education.

He also was a warm advocate of religion in the school, and thought the banishment of all religious instruction from the classroom a slur on the morals of the community. Educational authorities differ very much on this important subject, but Mr. Tait insisted strongly upon the excellent moral effect of reading the Scriptures, without comment on the part of the teacher, however. During the years of his incumbency, the practice prevailed in New York and Boston, and was made compulsory by law; and, in fact, prevailed in this State—at least, in the schools of San Francisco, in 1852, but soon after fell into disuse. He also believed in the American system of co-education, but, at the same time, he advised the introduction of the European system into a certain number of schools, in view of the strong prejudice of our foreign element against the former system. He thought this concession necessary in order to extend to the greatest possible number the inestimable benefits of a common school education.

In 1867 he was appointed Principal of the State Normal School, then located in San Francisco. His connection with that institution was, however, very brief, for stress of private business necessitated his resignation in 1868. In that year he moved, with his family, to Oakland, intending to devote himself thenceforth exclusively to his business interests. However, after a short residence in that city, he was prevailed upon by friends to undertake the task of organizing the schools of the young city. His long experience in San Francisco was of the greatest advantage to him in this work. Soon afterwards he became connected with Brayton's College School, and when the College of California became the University of California, he was made one of its professors, and also given charge of the Preparatory Department. He resigned in 1873. With the exception of a term as member of the Board of Education of San Francisco, in 1876–7, his educational career ended here. After this he traveled in Europe for many years. He died suddenly in 1888, at Alameda, California.

Thus, the best years of his life were devoted to the cause of education. He was a natural teacher, and loved his profession. He often remarked that the happiest hours of his life were spent in the school-room. Those who knew him well will testify to his worth, and praise his great services to the State of California. If any man ever exaggerated the advantages of a liberal education, it was Mr. Tait, and in the education of the masses he looked for the solution of the social question.

The character and importance of Mr. Tait's work may be well estimated by reference to the points enumerated in an address by Professor Minns, Principal of the State Normal School, delivered upon the occasion of the presentation of a silver service to Mr. Tait, then about to retire from office, in which he calls attention to the important services rendered by Mr. Tait, and which were as follows:

1. Obtaining from the State Legislature an Act authorizing the transfer of $60,000 from the General Fund to the School Fund. This money was used for building purposes.

2. Improving the finances of the department. Before he was Superintendent there was always a deficit in the School Fund;

during his entire term of office it showed a surplus. Teachers were paid in cash instead of in scrip; and the business of the department was conducted upon a cash basis.

3. Improving the condition of the primary schools, by providing better and healthier accommodations for the children.

4. The revision of the by-laws of the Board, and of the school regulations.

5. The introduction of a graded course of instruction in primary and grammar schools, thereby shortening the course from ten to seven years.

6. Restoring the practice of reading the Bible, without note or comment.

"It was also upon his recommendation," says Mr. Minns, "that Principals were directed to assemble their pupils annually, on the day preceding the birthday of Washington, and to read and explain to them extracts from Washington's farewell address, and to combine therewith such expressions as are likely to kindle in the breasts of the rising generation a holy and inextinguishable love of country."

Dr. William T. Lucky.

(Principal from May, 1868, to August, 1873.)

Dr. William T. Lucky was born in Elizabethtown, Kentucky, April 14, 1821.

When fourteen years of age, with his parents, he removed to Illinois. At the age of sixteen he went to McKendrie College, Lebanon, Illinois. There he entered upon a regular course of study, and remained in the college until he graduated with the honors of his class, in August, 1842. On the same day on which he received his diploma, he was elected professor of mathematics in his *alma mater*, and after teaching two years, his resignation was received with deep regret.

In August, 1844, Dr. Lucky was married to Miss Mary Searritt, and in October following removed to Fayette, Missouri, for the purpose of establishing a first class High School. This was his first individual enterprise, and it seemed a very small beginning, as he opened his school in Fayette with six pupils, and closed on Friday afternoon of the first week with *two*. But Dr. Lucky was of sanguine temperament and full of energy, and his peculiar faculty as an instructor, his rare talent for governing, together with his genial manner, soon filled his school-rooms, and there, with uninterrupted success, he taught for seventeen years. Meantime, under Dr. Lucky's labor and direction, the High School increased, developed, and finely resulted in Howard Female College and Central Male College, both of which are now in a flourishing condition.

In 1847 Dr. Lucky was ordained a regular minister in the Methodist Church, but did not receive special appointments as a pastor. He regarded teaching as his special calling and profession. To become a thorough, useful, Christian educator was a fixed desire and purpose of his life, and he felt that to be vested with the authority of a Christian minister would increase his opportunities for doing good in his chosen field of labor.

Almost in the beginning of the late war, these two colleges, with near three hundred students in attendance, were suspended, and the buildings occupied by soldiers during a greater part of the war. While things were in this unsettled condition, Dr. Lucky was warmly solicited to come to the Pacific Coast and take charge of a Methodist college at Vacaville, in Solano County. He came to California in 1861, accepted the position as President of Pacific Methodist College, in which he remained five years, and through many discouragements was successful in building up a fine school.

From Vacaville Dr. Lucky went to Alameda, with the intention of opening a select seminary for young ladies, but was delayed in his plans for want of suitable buildings. At this time he was elected Principal of the Lincoln High School in San Francisco. After filling this position for one year with marked success, he was elected Principal of the State Normal School, of which he had charge five years—three years in San Francisco and two years after it was removed to San José.

While living in San Francisco, Dr. Lucky became interested in the moral and spiritual welfare of the many prisoners in San Quentin, and volunteered his services as chaplain for two Sabbaths in each month, and for over two years he was faithful to this new post of duty, employing every means possible to cultivate the better principles of their nature and induce them to reform their lives, and become honest men. It was largely the result of his individual effort and labor that a chapel was built when the prison was enlarged, and quite a large library of books was donated by the different churches of the city.

In 1873 Dr. Lucky removed to Los Angeles, and there was appointed Principal of the High School and City Superintendent. In both of these positions he was successful and popular.

In 1876 he made a visit to his many friends in the East. While there he visited the Centennial, attended the National Educational Convention in Baltimore, which convened in July, and a State Convention in St. Louis. He was urged to remain East and accept the Presidency of his *alma mater*, and also warmly solicited to return to Fayette and take charge of one of the colleges he had been instrumental in founding. But, after having been identified with the educational interests of California for fifteen years, he chose to decline the kind offers made him there, and to return to California, to take his place in the ranks and his part in the labor of elevating, improving, and carrying on the grand system of education in this glorious State.

Though Dr. Lucky had a good constitution and seemed in perfect health for many years, yet thirty years of mental labor and continued taxation of brain work, proved too much for even him. He was suddenly stricken down with disease which soon developed into paralysis of the brain, of which he died in San Francisco August 21, 1876.

"Dr. Lucky was a man of no ordinary powers, a man of even balance, a clear thinker, an extraordinary teacher, and an impressive preacher. But few men were more active and energetic than he in whatever he engaged in, and never seemed to tire in his self-imposed task, and but few men have impressed themselves upon more minds than did he. The record of his work is with us, his reward is on high. His life of unselfish labor and usefulness will remain a lasting monument to his memory."

CHARLES H. ALLEN.

(Principal from August, 1873, to July, 1889.)

Charles H. Allen was born in Mansfield, Tioga County, Pennsylvania, February 11, 1828. He received his early education in the common schools, taking one term afterward in Condersport Academy. From here he went to Jamestown, Chautauqua County, New York, with the idea of continuing his education. He was compelled by illness to relinquish his desire for a higher education, a spinal curvature producing such serious nervous disturbance that physicians pronounced it necessary that he should give up all mental labor. Here he entered a workshop, and learned a trade. Being of a strong mechanical turn, he rapidly acquired skill in the various departments, and was soon an expert cutler. His taste for mechanics has followed him all through his life, and a "workshop" has been his principal place of amusement.

From his place in the shop he was unexpectedly called to finish a term of school, the teacher—a former teacher of his—being compelled to resign because of ill health. Mr. Allen taught his first school here, at the early age of fifteen. With no thought of becoming a teacher, he returned to the workshop at the end of the term, and resumed what he thought would be his life work. But it was ordered otherwise. His success in the school-room had been so marked that he was called back to the same school for a longer term, and at a considerable advance in the meager salary paid. During this term of school he read *Abbott's Teacher* and *Page's Theory and Practice of Teaching*, and from these learned that teaching is anything but drudgery. From the reading of these books, followed by "*My School and Schoolmasters*," dates the beginning of his career as a teacher.

Mr. Allen taught in the common schools of western New York for several years, working at his trade during vacations. During this period he attended for one term a Regents, or Normal Class, in the Westfield Academy.

While teaching in Busti, New York, he was, upon the recommendation of the County Superintendent, granted a New York State certificate, a certificate granted only upon great excellence in the art of teaching.

He was now called to the Smethport Academy, in McKean County, Pennsylvania, where he soon became Principal, and began the training of teachers. At this period, also, began his institute work, which has continued all through his life.

His health failing, from overwork, he became a land surveyor for a few years He held the position of surveyor for the German colony which settled upon the tract of land first purchased by Ole Bull for a Danish colony. During this period he regained his health, and, in addition, "picked up" a fair smattering of the German language.

From Germania he was called to Westchester, Pennsylvania, to take the position of Associate Principal of a Normal School. During the long vacation of the Normal School he went to Wisconsin, at the invitation of Chancellor Barnard, to take charge of several Teachers' Institutes. Here he was induced to remain for several months, to complete the work and aid in compiling the proceedings. Chancellor Barnard was compelled to resign his position and give up his work in Wisconsin, upon which event Mr. Allen was elected agent of the Normal School Regents of the State, and given in charge the Institute work and the supervision and examination of the Normal classes, held then in some of the colleges, academies, and high schools. For several years he carried on this work, holding institutes in different parts of the State, and lecturing in almost every hamlet. Tiring of the perpetual strain of this severe labor, he opened a private Normal Class in the Madison High School building. At this time, also, he was made City Superintendent of Schools. The demand for a Normal School was clearly indicated by the patronage extended to this Normal Class, and before the expiration of a year the Regents of the University of Wisconsin invited Mr. Allen to take charge of a Normal Department in the University. He accepted the invitation, and entered the University as a Professor of Normal Instruction. To him belongs the credit of first opening the doors of the University to women. While holding the professorship in the University, Mr. Allen raised a company of students, and went to Memphis as Captain of the company. His company formed a part of the " Hundred day men," of whom so much was said and written. Returning, "honorably discharged," he resumed his work, but was again compelled to give up teaching by failing health. He resigned his position, and spent some months in a general life insurance office in Cincinnati. He was, however, soon called back, and made President of the first Normal School in Wisconsin, at Platteville. Here he organized the Normal School work of the State, and also took charge of the erection of the new building.

A severe attack of bronchitis compelled him again to give up his work, and hoping for the benefits of a change of climate, he went to Portland, Oregon, where he opened and carried on, for eight months, the Bishop Scott Grammar School, as head master. This work was not to his liking. The climate, however, restored his health, and he returned and worked a year as Institute Agent in Wisconsin. While at work in an Institute there, he received his notification of an election as Professor of Natural Science in the Normal School at San José, California. This position he accepted, and in a short time reported for duty. After serving one year as Professor of Natural Science, he was elected, August 4, 1873, Principal **of the School**.

Of Mr. Allen's work in California, both as the head of the Normal **School** and in Institutes, little need be said. His educational ability may be best estimated by a study of the growth of the School, and his method of work, by the extracts from his reports, to be found in the body of this work. That his duties have been various and heavy, no one can doubt. In addition to the labor of Principal, he has had charge of the completion of the old building, the erection of the present building, the improvement of the grounds, and the erection **of** the building at Los Angeles; and the Normal School building at Chico has had also a share of his time and attention.

The wonder is not that, after nearly seventeen years of work in California, his health should give way, but rather, considering **the nature and** amount of work he has accomplished, that it has not given way before.

With an experience that few men have had, Mr. Allen retires to his mountain ranch, to enjoy the evening of a busy life.

This sketch of the life and work of Mr. Allen cannot be more fittingly closed, than by giving in full the official **resolutions unanimously adopted by the** Board of Trustees, on accepting **his resignation:**

Among the customs or rules that a refined civilization has given us, none is imbued with more gravity than that which is **devolved upon** collective bodies, both public and private, of expressing, upon **the death or** retirement of a fellow member or employé, the regard and esteem **in which he is** held, and to which he is entitled by reason of his mental and **moral** worth, and his faithful, valuable, and long-continued services.

This custom is sanctioned by the **most** elevated sentiments that find lodgment in the human breast, and the **outward** expression, while exhibiting the gratification of conscientious duty **in a** worthy personal cause, is yet tinged with the sorrow **and** regret **of a** personal loss.

The Board of Trustees of the State Normal School, at San José, are **called** upon to avail themselves of this custom, to discharge themselves of this **trust.**

We have made it our duty—pleasant in that which affects a knowledge **of the** past, unpleasant in that which looks towards the narrow line dividing the past from the future, **and which shows a vacuum that can never be filled** while old associates hold a place in our **memories—to say for you all what** individually we know you would say, and **much better, for yourselves.**

Professor Charles H. Allen **is about to leave us.** His connection with the **school is soon to be closed. We have been compelled,** sorrowfully, to accept his resignation, on account **of his** continued ill health, a long abstinence from work being imperative. In a word, he asks us for his life; and, as physicians, who are his friends, we are obliged to present the only prescription that will meet his case. And we do this in the sincere and earnest hope that rest and relaxation may bring back the strength he has lost, and that his future days may be long and happy.

For seventeen years he has been connected with the school, sixteen as Principal; seventeen years of faithful, conscientious, laborious work. His influence has been deep, strong, far-reaching. By his teaching, by his management, by his labors on the State Board of Education, by his personal advice and counsel, and by his example, he has shaped the destinies of hundreds of men and women, many of whom are now highly honored by the State, and are the pillars of its present strength, and the hope of its future prosperity. His guidance has ever been in the line of truth and right, as well as purely intellectual application, and the power of his kindly Christian mind has been exerted upon all whose good fate has led them, as seekers for knowledge, within the portals of this grand educational edifice.

California—the whole coast, in fact—owes him a debt of gratitude that can never be repaid.

In view of all these facts, it is meet that this Board should give appropriate and emphatic expression of its sentiments; therefore, be it

Resolved, That in the retirement, on account of ill health, of Professor Charles H. Allen, the State Normal School at San José is deprived of the services of a competent and faithful educator, a wise counselor and friend, a conscientious, painstaking, and talented fellow laborer, and an honest, large hearted, Christain gentleman; that we part with him in unfeigned sorrow and regret, not only on account of personal esteem and regard for his many able qualities, but also by reason of the vast scope, important, and high moral and intellectual character of the work that he has accomplished during his connection with the school, the Board, and the educational affairs of the State generally; that he goes from among us with our best wishes and deepest sympathies, and that the State ought not to forget, as it assuredly never will, one who has done such grand work in her moral and intellectual behalf.

Resolved, That the foregoing preamble and resolutions be spread upon the records of this Board, and that an engrossed copy be prepared under the direction of the Executive Committee, and presented to Professor Allen.

SAN JOSÉ, CALIFORNIA, June 24, 1889.

RALPH LOWE,
T. H. LAINE,
IRA G. HOITT,
Committee on Resolutions.

C. W. CHILDS.

(Principal from July 1, 1889-)

C. W. Childs was born in 1844, in Geneseo, New York; graduated at the Wauwatosa High School, Wisconsin, in 1860, and at the outbreak of the rebellion served for a short time in the army. Subsequently he came to California, and began his life work in teaching a public school at Cold Springs, El Dorado County. Mr. Childs at that time was not of age, yet achieved marked success at the very commencement of his career as a teacher, and as years have rolled on fresh laurels have been added continuously to his pristine success. After teaching several years in California, he entered the State Normal School, and was graduated in 1867.

Finally he took a course in a commercial college in San Francisco, and, thus equipped, returned to his life work. Shortly after finishing his commercial course he assumed the duties of Principal of the High School at Suisun, which position he held for eight years. Here he won a brilliant reputation as a progressive educator, and gained for the school the reputation of being one of the best in the State. By his efforts the school was supplied with efficient apparatus for all necessary purposes, and among other things not especially in the curriculum of a public school, he taught the boys how to set type, both as an accomplishment and for recreation. In acknowledgment of his worth as a teacher and his eminent fitness for the position, he was nominated and elected to the office of County Superintendent of Public Schools of Solano County for two successive terms, almost without opposition. Capable, energetic, and enthusiastic, his administration of the office could not but be a success, and as a sequence of well earned laurels, at the close of his term of office, in 1878, Mr. Childs was elected to the position of teacher in the State Normal School, and in 1886 he was elected Vice-Principal. In June, 1889, he was made Principal. Here has he especially accomplished beneficial results in the interests of education. The State at large feels his influence for good. Popular with the students, possessing the confidence and esteem of his fellow teachers, he has won an enviable reputation. Mr. Childs is an untiring student, and, though not a collegiate, is a fine scholar. He is the author of "Topical Outlines of History," "Topical Outlines of the Constitution," and "The Essentials of Bookkeeping," three exceedingly valuable handbooks for the use of teachers and pupils. In conclusion it may be said: As a teacher, he is progressive; in methods, direct and comprehensive; clear and explicit in explanation of knotty problems, and one who recognized the value of drawing and of Normal training in schools carried to the highest extent. As a man, genial, courteous, affable, not puffed up with conceit, but modest and unassuming. A man among men. His pupils love him, and the teachers of California respect him and acknowledge his worth.

LIST OF TEACHERS.

The names of teachers are given in order, according to the time at which they came into the school. In all cases where it could be obtained, an outline of the preceding and succeeding educational work of each is given. In the case of some of the teachers connected with the school during its early history, these points can not be learned, because of death or removal. A few of those whose addresses are known have failed to respond:

HELEN M. CLARK.—Native of Canada. Graduate of the Toronto Normal School, where she taught several years. Principal of Training School, October, 1862, to May, 1864. Assistant in Training School, September to December, 1865. Taught several years in the San Francisco schools. Afterwards became Mrs. Boyle. Resides in San Francisco.

KATE SULLIVAN.—Assistant in Training School, November, 1862, to May, 1864, Principal of Training School, July, 1864, to June, 1865. Afterwards taught in San Francisco public schools until her death, July 17, 1879. Further particulars cannot be obtained.

MARY R. HARRIS.—Assistant in Normal Department, January, 1864, to February, 1864. Resigned to take a position in San Francisco schools. Further particulars unknown.

MARY D. BODWELL.—Assistant in Normal Department, February, 1864, to May, 1864. Resigned to take a position in Girls' High School, San Francisco. Further particulars unknown.

ELIZA W. HOUGHTON.—Native of Massachusetts. Educated in public schools of Massachusetts and at Mount Holyoke Seminary. Was a pupil of George R. Emerson, in Boston, three years. Taught in Harrisburg Seminary, Pennsylvania, and Providence High School, Rhode Island; in Normal School from July, 1864, to April, 1877, with leave of absence during part of 1869 and part of 1876. Was Preceptress from August, 1873, to April, 1877. Has not taught since. Present address, San José.

MRS. C. H. STOUT.—Principal of the Training School, September, 1865, to fall of 1868. Afterwards became Mrs. Shillaber. Resided in San Francisco several years. Died a year or two ago. Further particulars cannot be obtained.

MRS. MARY L. SWETT.—Native of Connecticut. Educated in Thompson Academy, Connecticut, and San Francisco public schools. Graduated at San Francisco Evening Normal School. Received State educational diploma November, 1865. Vice-Principal of Training School, January, 1866, to June, 1867. Teacher in the Normal School, August, 1867, to December, 1867. Has not taught since. Married to John Swett, May 8, 1862. Has four children. Present address, Martinez, California.

Mrs. C. R. Beale.—Assistant in **Normal Department, July,** 1866, **to June,** 1867. Resigned **to take a position in Girls' High School, San** Francisco. Further particulars **not received.**

Mrs. P. C. Cook.—**Assistant in Training School** part of school year 1867-68.

Mary Heydenfelt.—Assistant **in Training School part of school year** 1867-68.

A. L. Fitzgerald.—Assistant in Normal Department, spring **term,** 1868.

Miss Bush.—Assistant in Normal Department, spring term, 1868.

Mrs. Dorcas Clark.—Educated in Canada. Was a teacher of many years' experience when elected to a position in the California State Normal School. Assistant in Normal Department from May, 1868, to March, 1873. Specialties, mathematics and history. **Has taught** most **of** the time since in Girls' **High** School, San Francisco. **Further particulars** have not been received.

Matilda Lewis.—Graduate **of State Normal School,** Oswego, New York. Principal **of** Training School, **1869 to 1871. Afterwards** became Mrs. Robert W. Jordan, and resided in San Francisco. Died **October 3, 1884.**

Letitia Ryder.—Assistant in Normal Department, 1869.

Mary J. Titus.—Native of New York. Educated in public schools of Wisconsin and Oswego Normal School, New York. Graduated February, 1870. Taught in Ogdensburg, New York, two and a half years; in San José Normal School since November, 1872. Was Principal of Training Department ten years; away on leave of absence one year; teacher in Normal Department since August, 1883. Specialties, mathematics and pedagogy. Preceptress **since** August, 1888.

Lucy M. Washburn.—Native **of** New York. Educated in **New York public schools** and Academy, Normal School at Fredonia, **Vassar College, and Cornell University.** Taught one year in Westfield Academy, New York; one year in Academic Department **of** Normal School, **Fredonia, New York;** two years in Hampton Normal and Agricultural Institute, **Virginia; in Normal** School, San José, from March, 1873, to present time, **with leave of absence of** one year. Specialties, mathematics, physiology, and **zoölogy.**

Cornelia Walker.—Native of New York. **Educated in** New York and Minnesota, in public schools and seminaries, and **in** Normal School at Winona, Minnesota. Taught in city schools of Minnesota four years; in Normal School at St. Cloud, Minnesota, four years; Root's Normal Musical Institute, Chicago, one season; in Normal School, San José, since November, 1873. For the first year, was teacher of Preparatory Class; since November, 1874, in Normal Department. Specialties, grammar, literature, and pedagogy.

J. H. Braly.—Native of Missouri. Educated in public schools and University of Pacific, California, and in Cumberland University, Tennessee, **from** which he graduated in 1859. Taught in public schools of California **six years,** and in private academies five years. Superintendent of Schools **in Santa Clara** County, 1868-69. Was Vice-Principal and **teacher in Normal School,** San José, from **August, 1873, till resignation, December, 1883.** Specialty, natural philosophy. **Married in 1861 to Miss Martha Hughes. Six children,** three living. Present address, San Diego.

Florence Grigsby (Mrs. E. C. Singletary).—Native **of** Wisconsin. Educated **in public** schools of Wisconsin and in California State Normal School, from which she graduated in 1874. Taught in Primary Class of Training Department from June, 1874, to November, 1876. Married January 11, 1877. Two children. Resides in San José.

ANNIE E. CHAMBERLAIN.—Native of Wisconsin. Graduate of Normal Department, University of Wisconsin. Taught in Milwaukee High School several years; in Normal School, San José, from November, 1874, to March, 1879. Specialty, mathematics. Has since taught two years in the Milwaukee Academy, and five years in the High School. Present address, Milwaukee, Wisconsin.

PHEBE P. GRISGBY (Mrs. Jas. T. Hamilton).—Native of Wisconsin. Educated in district schools of Wisconsin and in Platteville Normal School. Graduated in 1871. Taught in Wisconsin public schools three years; in Normal School, San José, from November, 1874, to December, 1885. For nine years of this time was teacher of the Preparatory Class; for the succeeding two years, taught in the Junior Class. Not taught since. Married June 7, 1881. One child. Address, 1013 Scott Street, San Francisco.

HENRY B. NORTON.—Native of New York. Educated in public schools of New York, Wisconsin, and Illinois, Beloit College, Wisconsin, and State Normal University, Illinois. Taught in public schools of Illinois, in Illinois Normal University, and seven years in State Normal School, Emporia, Kansas. Teacher of science in San José Normal School from June, 1875, to June, 1885. Specialties, chemistry, zoölogy, and physical geography. Professor Norton died at his home, in the Santa Cruz Mountains, June 22, 1885, of congestion of the brain.

Resolutions adopted, December 11, 1885, by the Board of Trustees of the Normal School.

Resolved, That by the death of Professor Henry B. Norton, the State Normal Schools have received a deep wound and sustained a great loss. His life and labors were altogether beneficial. He was an excellent teacher, and a constant, industrious, successful student. Whatever he learned by study, investigation, or observation, was freely given to the scholars and utilized to the benefit of his students. His influence upon the common schools and the cause of educating the people, through his services at Teachers' Institutes, was great and good. His coming was welcome; his departure a matter of regret. His career as a citizen was a life pure, useful, without stain. His work and his influence were always healthy and inspiring to good; his life was a lesson.

Resolved, That, as Trustees of the school, where he labored well and successfully, we tender to his widow and bereaved children our sincere condolence, because we, too, are partakers with them in a great and melancholy loss.

IRA MORE.—Native of Maine. Educated at Bridgewater Normal School, Massachusetts (graduated in 1849), and Yale College (graduated in 1855). Taught in Massachusetts public schools six months; Bridgewater Normal School, one year; Chicago Normal School, one year; Illinois Normal University, four years; Principal of Normal School, St. Cloud, Minnesota, seven years; teacher in Normal School, San José, July, 1876, to June, 1883. Specialties, mathematics and physical geography. Since that time has been Principal of State Normal School, Los Angeles, California. Married April 16, 1857, to Miss Lucy C. Drew. Two children living.

HELEN S. WRIGHT.—Native of New York. Educated in public schools and academy, Fredonia, New York, and Boston Art School. Preceptress of Fredonia Academy between five and six years (during this time the school was made a Normal School); Preceptress, Academic Department, Potsdam Normal School, two years; teacher in a seminary in Kentucky, two years; teacher in Normal School, San José, from June, 1876, to June, 1888. Specialties, English language and literature. Preceptress from August, 1877, to June, 1888. Absent during school year 1888–89, on leave of absence, traveling in Europe.

MARY E. WILSON (Mrs. T. C. George).—Native of Wisconsin. Educated in public schools and California State Normal School. Graduated in 1875. Taught one year in public schools of Santa Clara County; critic teacher in Primary Class, Training Department, six years, 1876 to 1882; Principal of Training Department, six years, 1882 to 1888. Married June 7, 1888, to Professor T. C. George, of University of the Pacific. Has since spent a year traveling in Europe. Address, San José.

RUTH ROYCE.—Native of California. Educated in public schools and State Normal School. Graduated in 1877. Taught in Preparatory Class, two years; substitute teacher and assistant in Junior Classes, three years; Librarian since 1881.

MARY E. B. NORTON.—Native of New York. Educated at Rockford Seminary, Illinois, and in Berlin, Germany. Taught two years in public schools of Illinois and Iowa; fifteen years in Rockford Seminary, Illinois; one year, International Academy, Berlin; in Normal School from January, 1878, till resignation, December, 1888. Specialties, botany and geography. Address, San José.

FRANCES L. WEBSTER (Mrs. L. I. Fish).—Native of New York. Educated in New York public schools and State Normal School at Potsdam, from which she graduated in 1875. Taught one term in State Normal School at Leavenworth, Kansas; two years in Iowa State Normal School; in San José Normal School from August, 1878, to March, 1881. Specialties, elocution and composition. Not taught since. Married March 31, 1881. Two children. Address, Martinez, California.

MARGARET K. SCOTT.—Native of Indiana. Educated in California public and State Normal Schools, and in Oxford Female College, Ohio. Taught in public schools of California; in Training Department of San José Normal School, two and a half years, beginning August, 1879. For past six years has been teaching in Los Angeles, as Grammar School Principal. Now Principal of Eighth Street School. Has spent the past year traveling in Europe.

JESSICA G. ALLEN.—Native of New York. Educated in public schools and State Normal Schools, Platteville, Wisconsin, and San José, California. Graduated in 1877. Taught in public schools of California one year; in Junior Class of Normal School, five months—spring term, 1880. Has taught for past four years in Hester School, San José. Married July 20, 1880.

ADDIE MURRAY.—Native of New York. Educated in public and Normal Schools of Minnesota. Graduate of Normal School, Winona, Minnesota. Taught in public schools of Minnesota and California. Was Principal of Model Department of Normal School at St. Cloud, Minnesota, 1874 to 1876. Substitute teacher in San José Normal School, two years, beginning August, 1880. Subjects taught, grammar, arithmetic, and bookkeeping. After leaving the Normal School, was Principal of the New Almaden School one year, and has taught in Los Angeles six years, most of this time as a Grammar School Principal. Is now Principal of Amelia Street Grammar School, Los Angeles.

ELIZA B. BARNES.—Native of Rhode Island. Educated in public schools of Rhode Island. Taught in public schools of Rhode Island, nine years; in public schools of San Francisco, six years; in Normal School, San José, from January, 1881, to resignation, May, 1884. Specialty, drawing. After a prolonged visit in the Eastern States, returned to California, where she is now teaching.

GLORA F. BENNETT.—Native of New York. Educated in district schools of New York and Normal Schools at Brockport and at Geneseo, New York. Taught in district schools of New York, two and a half years; State Normal School at Geneseo, two years; High School in Michigan, one year; seven years in public schools of California; in Normal School since August, 1881. Specialty, English.

LIZZIE P. SARGENT (Mrs. Lizzie P. Wilson).—Native of California. Educated in public schools and Normal School. Graduated in 1875. Taught in public schools of California, six years; in Training Department of Normal School since October, 1881. Was critic teacher in Primary Class, five years; in Grammar Class, one year. Principal of Training Department since September, 1888. Married August 2, 1888.

GEORGE R. KLEEBERGER.—Native of Wisconsin. Educated in public schools of Wisconsin, State Normal School, Platteville, Wisconsin, Yale College, Connecticut. Taught in public schools of Wisconsin as Principal, four years; Connecticut, two years. Teacher of science in Normal School, Whitewater, Wisconsin, three years. Taught in public schools of California as Principal, three and a half years; in Normal School, San José, from February, 1882, to present time. Specialties, chemistry and geology. Married April 19, 1879. Three children, one living.

MARY P. ADAMS.—Native of Wisconsin. Educated in public schools and San José Normal School, from which she graduated May, 1879. Taught one year in public schools; as assistant in Training Department, August, 1882, to March, 1884; as teacher of music and critic teacher in Intermediate Class of Training Department from August, 1887, to present time.

ISABELLA G. OAKLEY.—Graduate of Packer Collegiate Institute, New York. Taught over twenty years, principally in private institutions. Taught in Normal Department, spring term, 1883. Afterwards taught one year in Los Angeles Normal School. When last heard from was teaching in Santa Barbara.

JESSICA B. THOMPSON (Mrs. A. H. Washburn).—Native of Illinois. Educated in public schools of Illinois, San José Normal School, and University of Michigan. Taught in Normal School from August, 1883, to December, 1889. Specialties, literature and language. Married January 22, 1889. Not teaching.

A. H. RANDALL.—Native of Maine. Educated in Maine Wesleyan College and Maine Normal Schools. Principal of Stockton High School, California, from 1867 to 1883. Teacher in Normal School from January, 1884, to present time. Specialties, physics and geometry. Married February, 1869, to Miss Fannie H. Moore.

JENNIE M. HAMMOND.—Graduate of Normal School, 1878. Taught in public schools, six years; assistant and critic teacher in Intermediate Class of Training Department from February, 1884, to May, 1887. Address, San José.

FANNIE M. ESTABROOK.—Native of Illinois. Educated in Illinois State Normal School and National School of Elocution at Philadelphia, and has taught elocution twelve years. Taught reading and elocution in San José Normal School from August, 1884, to present time.

GERHARD SCHOOF.—Native of Hanover, Germany. Graduate of Gymnasium of Clausthal and Military Academy of Hanover. Taught in the San Francisco public schools from March, 1876, to August, 1884; in **Normal** School from August, 1884, to present time. Specialty, drawing. Was Principal of the San José Evening Schools, two terms. Married November 28, 1877. Three children.

MYRTIE C. HUDSON.—Native of Ohio. Educated in public schools, San José Normal School (class of '78), and University of Michigan (class of '85). Taught in public schools of California six and a half years; in Normal School from **January,** 1886, to June, 1889. Specialties, composition and history.

MAMEY MURRAY.—Native of California. Educated in public **schools and in State** Normal School, San José, from which she graduated **December, 1884. Taught** in public school three years; as assistant in Junior Classes **of Normal School,** January to June, 1887. Has spent most of time **since in studying and** teaching music. Address, Auburn.

KATE COZZENS.—Native of California. Educated in public schools and Normal School. Graduated in 1878. Taught in schools of Santa Clara County nine years. Teacher of Model Class, Training Department, since August, 1887.

LAURA BETHELL.—Native of Indiana. Educated in public schools of Indiana, at convent, and in California State Normal School. Graduated December, 1887. Taught language and mathematics in Normal School since January, 1888.

R. S. HOLWAY.—Native of Iowa. Educated in public schools of Iowa. Taught in Iowa five years; in public schools of California as Principal, seven years; in Normal School since January, 1888. **Specialties,** mathematics and physics. Married in 1883.

MARGARET E. SCHALLENBERGER.—Native of California. Educated in public schools and State Normal School, San José, where she graduated in 1880. **Taught** in San José public schools five years; in Normal Department, one **term;** critic teacher in Primary Class of Training Department since January, **1888. Has given special attention** to clay modeling.

VOLNEY RATTAN.—Native of Wisconsin. Educated in public schools and State University of Wisconsin. Taught in public schools **of Wisconsin,** two years; country schools in California, five years; San José **Institute, two** years; Oakland Military Academy, three years; Principal of Santa Cruz schools, one and a half years; teacher of natural science in Girls' High School, San Francisco, thirteen years; teacher in Normal School since January, 1889. Specialties, botany and geography. Married September, 1872. Two children.

NETTIE C. DANIELS.—Native of Michigan. Graduate of University of Michigan. Taught two years **in** State Normal School at Indiana, Pennsylvania. Teacher in Normal School, **San** José, since January, 1889. Specialty, language.

NANNIE C. GILDAY.—Native of Missouri. Educated in public schools and **academy in** Missouri. Taught one year in private school; twelve years in public schools of Kansas City; assistant critic teacher in Training Department, Normal School, since February, 1889. Specialties, music, drawing, and reading.

SPECIAL TEACHERS.

MDLLE. PAROT	Calisthenics—1863-64
HUBERT BURGES	Drawing—1863, **1864, 1869**
W. ELLIOT	Music—1863 **and 1864**
C. J. ROBINSON	Calisthenics—1864
F. K. MITCHELL	Music—1864
E. KNOWLTON	Calisthenics and elocution—1864, 1869
DR. CROSSETTE	Music—1869
MISS HANNAH MILLARD	Drawing—1871–72
OLIVE PARKER	Music—1871–72
Z. M. PARVIN	Music—1876 to May, 1878
MADAME M. A. HAMM	Music—1878–79
MISS M. D. MCCHAIN	Reading—1877–78, 1878–79
MRS. M. F. GUNNING	Drawing—1877–78
PROFESSOR DREW	Penmanship—1877–78
J. H. ELWOOD	Music—1875 and 1880 to present time.
MRS. A. E. BUSH	Curator of Museum—1878 to present time.

ALPHABETICAL LIST OF GRADUATES,

From the First Class, May, 1863, to the Thirty-sixth Class, June, 1889,
Inclusive.

Abbe, Frank B. .... December, 1883.
Abshire, Alfred C. ..... December, 1888.
Adams, Charles C. ..... December, 1885.
Adams, Clara A. .... March, 1870.
Adams, Mary P. .... May, 1879.
Adams, M. Lydia ..... December, 1886.
Addicott, Lily A. ...... December, 1883.
Ahlf, George P. .... May, 1883.
Albee, George B. .... May, 1887.
Albrecht, Annie F. .... May, 1887.
Allen, Carl H. .... December, 1884.
Allen, Hattie E. .... December, 1888.
Allen, Jennie A. .... May, 1887.
Allen, Jessica G. .... March, 1877.
Allen, Kara F. .... June, 1889.
Allison, Arminta E. .... March, 1870.
Allyne, Lucinda N. .... December, 1864.
Alvarez, Adam D. .... May, 1888.
Anderson, Emily .... May, 1888.
Anderson, Eula L. .... May, 1888.
Anderson, Grace L. .... June, 1889.
Anderson, Julia .... March, 1877.
Anderson, Sarah E. .... June, 1867.
Angell, Cora L. .... December, 1887.
Angier, Hattie J. .... May, 1888.
Anglon, Annie E. ..... December, 1888.
Aniser, Emilie .... May, 1878.
Anker, Nana .... December, 1888.
Aplin, Evaline V. .... May, 1882.
Appleby, Kate .... May, 1881.
Aram, Mattie L. .... May, 1878.
Arbogast, Frederick L. .... May, 1888.
Archer, Louise .... May, 1881.
Armstrong, Mrs. Josie R. March, 1877.
Armstrong, Lizzie .... May, 1887.
Arnold, George E. .... May, 1886.
Ashbrook, Martin V. ..... May, 1864.
Ashbrook, Truman P. .... May, 1868.
Ashley, Julia V. .... June, 1867.
Ashley, Osee E. .... May, 1866.
Ashurst, Nellie .... **March, 1872.**

Asmus, Elise M. ...... December, 1884.
Atchison, John B. .... December, 1885.
Atherton, Hattie E. .. December, 1883.
Augustine, Martha ... December, 1883.
Auld, Cecilia M. .... March, 1874.
Avery, Carrie L. .... May, 1887.
Ayer, Edith E. .... May, 1885.
Ayer, Ethel C. .... May, 1887.
Ayers, Tidie .... March, 1876.
Babcock, Dollie C. .... March, 1876.
Bachelder, Ella E. .... May, 1868.
Backus, Hattie E. .... May, 1885.
Bacon, Horace G. ...... December, 1885.
Baggett, Haddie A. ... December, 1888.
Bagnell, Estella M. .... May, 1885.
Bailey, Arline L. .... May, 1888.
Bailey, Henry R. .... May, 1885.
Bailey, Louis C. .... May, 1887.
Bailey, Rebecca .... December, 1888.
Bailey, Walter S. .... May, 1882.
Bailey, William H. .... May, 1885.
Baker, Modena I. .... March, 1877.
Baldwin, Ellen S. .... May, 1864.
Balis, Lola A. .... May, 1882.
Balis, Lutie M. .... May, 1883.
Ball, Hannah M. ...... December, 1888.
Ballou, Alice K. .... May, 1885.
Bankhead, Belle .... May, 1888.
Bankhead, Hugh L. .... May, 1886.
Bankhead, William R. ..... June, 1889.
Banks, Lizzie .... March, 1876.
Bardenwerper, Kate G. .... May, 1879.
Barkley, Lena .... May, 1886.
Barlow, Ada S. .... December, 1887.
Barnes, Emmogene A. ... March, 1875.
Barnes, Eudora A. .... March, 1877.
Barrett, **Lucy A.** .... June, 1889.
Barrett, Maggie G. .... May, 1880.
Barry, Annie S. .... March, 1877.
Barthel, Franklin K. .... June, 1889.
Bass, Mamie .... May, 1886.

List of Graduates—Continued.

Bassett, Mary P.............March, 1876.
Bassham, Minnie C...........May, 1881.
Bateman, Henry.............March, 1875.
Baugh, Florence.........December, 1884.
Beaizley, Alice E. ....May, 1884.
Beal, Charles R............March, 1872.
Beaty, James G..............May, 1883.
Beckman, Mamie T..........May, 1886.
Beckwith, Carrie............May, **1885**.
Beckwith, Kate **B**............**May, 1882**.
Beckwith, A. Rose ....May, 1881.
Beers, Adrianna L...........June, 1867.
Beggs, Ida.............December, 1884.
Beggs, R. Lizzie.............May, 1879.
Bell, Mary ....May, 1869.
Bell, N. Jane.............March, 1871.
Bellew, Katie C. ....June, 1889.
Bellingall, Julia L...........June, 1889.
Benjamin, Julia I..........March, 1871.
Bennett, Addie S.......December, 1884.
Bennett, Clare.........**December, 1887**.
Bennett, Eva...............**May, 1887**.
Bennett, Ida M.............**May, 1880**.
Bennett, Minnie A. ....**March, 1874**.
Benson, Clara A. ......December, 1888.
Bent, Lottie.................May, 1881.
Berger, Lillian........December, 1887.
Berry, Annie M. ....May, 1888.
Berry, Lauren J...........May, 1883.
Bertola, Mariana ....June, 1889.
Betancue, Lizzie C..........May, 1868.
Bethell, Laura.........December, 1887.
Bevans, E. Margaret.......June, 1867.
Beverly, Victoria............May, 1864.
Bickford, Grace ....May, 1887.
Bicknell, Bertha A. ......March, 1870.
Bigsby, **Emma A**............June, **1867**.
Billings, **Ella G.** ....**December, 1883**.
Bird, Belle ....**March, 1877**.
Bird, Maggie M.............**May, 1882**.
Bird, Mary................**March, 1874**.
Black, Anna E......December, **1883**.
Black, James A........December, 1888.
Black, E. May.............March, 1877.
Black, William J. ....May, 1883.
Blackford, May F....December, 1888.
Blackstaff, Mary E. D. ...March, 1874.
Blaine, Corn A..............May, 1883.
Blodget, William O.........May, 1885.
Blythe, Alice..............May, 1878.
Bodley, Julia..............May, **1885**.

Boke, George H........December, **1887**.
Bondshu, Charles F. ....May, **1887**.
Bonnell, Lucy.............May, 1868.
Bonney, Sarah F. ....March, 1876.
Bose, Anna I............. May, 1888.
Botsford, Lucy E. ....December, 1883.
Boulware, Millie R. ....May, 1878.
Bowers, Lillian............May, 1880.
Bowman, Mary S...........May, 1880.
Boyer, Annie B............May, 1878.
Boyle, Sarah J...........March, 1870.
Bradley, Mattie ....**May, 1885**.
Bradshaw, Georgia L..December, **1888**.
Bradshaw, Wm. R....December, **1864**.
Braly, Josephine......December, 1883.
Brauer, Carrie ....May, **1836**.
Braun, Christiana H. ......May, 1882.
Breyfogle, Nellie M. ..December, 1886.
Bride, Laura E. ....May, 1885.
Broadbent, Elijah ....**December, 1864**.
Bromley, Kate I...........May, 1883.
Brooks, Edward R.......March, 1874.
Brown, Ada F...............**May, 1881**.
Brown, F. Alice ....May, 1880.
Brown, Esther A..........June, 1889.
Brown, Floribel C..........May, 1880.
Brown, Julia B...........May, 1868.
Brown, Julia S.. ....December, 1885.
Brown, Mary I. ....March, 1877.
Brown, Samuel A.........March, 1877.
Brown, Susie M...........May, 1887.
Brown, William W.........May, **1879**.
Brownell, Elmer E. .... May, 1884.
Browning, Lizzie M. ..December, 1888.
Browning, Mary E....**December, 1885**.
Bruch, Louis.............March, 1873.
Bruch, Louise L...........May, 1878.
Brunhouse, Fred G. ..December, 1888.
Brunhouse, Mary C.........May, 1883.
Bryant, Annie ....May, 1869.
Buckley, Annie P............May, 1886.
Buckley, Emma S. ....March, 1875.
Buckman, Samuel F........May, 1869.
Burrill, Mary Alice ......March, 1870.
Burston, Selina G..........May, 1878.
Burt, Minnie Clara........March, 1875.
Bush, Jennie R. ......December, 1883.
Bushnell, Emma H........May, 1885.
Butts, Frank A............May, 1884.
Cahill, Josephine.........March, 1873.
Calhoun, Jessie I. ....May, 1884.

132 *Historical Sketch.*

List of Graduates—Continued.

Calhoun, Nannie L. ....May, 1885.	Church, Lillian E.....December, 1887.
Calhoun, Virginia C. ....May, 1884.	Churchill, Clara Belle....March, 1876.
Cameron, Augusta S. ......June, 1865.	Churchill, Jennie.....December, 1887.
Camp, Alice ....December, 1884.	**Cilker,** Jennie A............June, 1889.
Campbell, Amey T. ....June, 1866.	Cilker, Martha E......December, 1887.
Campbell, Anne B........March, 1876.	Clark, Charlotte K........March, **1875.**
Campbell, Cornelia E.......June, 1865.	Clark, **Ida E.**..............**May, 1883.**
Campbell, Grace ....May, 1886.	Clark, **Harry F.**.......**December, 1885.**
Campbell, Ida A...........May, 1888.	Clark, **Hattie** G...........March, 1871.
Campbell, Mrs. Orpah......**May, 1888.**	Clark, James E...........March, **1870.**
Campbell, Ruth G. ....**May, 1869.**	Clark, Lida C. ....December, 1883.
Carey, Mrs. Aimee **L.** ......**May, 1886.**	Clark, Lizzie M. ....May, 1883.
Carey, Elmer E............ May, 1880.	Clark, Mary P............June, 1867.
Carey, Susie D. L. ....May, 1864.	Clark, **Rose** M. ......December, 1887.
Carmichael, M. Emeline....May, 1883.	**Clark, Tillie** M..............May, 1885.
Carothers, Leonora M. ...March, **1870.**	Clarke, Mabel S. .....December, 1887.
Carpenter, Ida M...........May, 1881.	**Clayes,** Lola B. ....December, 1884.
Carpenter, May ....March, 1877.	**Clayes, Madge M.** ....**..May, 1887.**
Carr, Maggie E. ....May, 1885.	**Clayton, Henry A.** ....**May, 1883.**
Carr, Mary C..............June, 1889.	Clayton, Julia ....**May, 1864.**
Carr, Mary E..............March, 1875.	Clayton, Kate J............**June, 1867.**
Carrau, Celina R. ....March, 1871.	**Clift,** Elizabeth B. ....**December, 1888.**
Carroll, Anna ....March, 1873.	Cochrane, Annie......December, 1884.
Carruthers, Isabel........March, 1870.	Cocks, Roxa S. ......November, 1867.
Carswell, Abbie............June, 1866.	Coffman, Alfred B..........May, 1882.
Carswell, Ella W. ....March, 1874.	Coffman, Jennie A. ....May, 1888.
Carver, Lue J..............**May, 1883.**	Coffman, Nelson B. ....May, 1878.
Casey, Joanna T.........**March, 1870.**	Coffman, Pelham H. ....May, 1882.
Casserly, Cillinda **A.**.........**May, 1887.**	**Colby,** Julia C..........**December,** 1888.
Cassin, Bella R. ....May, 1886.	**Colby, Mary A.** ....March, 1870.
Caswell, Annie............May, 1880.	Cole, **Eugene C.** ....May, 1883.
Cathcart, Annie...........May, 1868.	Cole, Marie ....March, 1875.
Cauch, Frank R. ....May, 1885.	Coleman, Ella............May, 1885.
Cauch, Fred L.............May, 1886.	Comstock, Bertha.........May, 1863.
Cearley, Emma S...........May, 1878.	Congdon, Georgietta N. .....Dec., 1884.
Chaloner, Louis B. ....May, 1878.	Conlin, Anne F. ....December, 1885.
Chaloner, Mary L. ....May, 1882.	Conmy, Ellen A..........March, 1871.
Chambaud, Angeline .December, **1883.**	Conn, Frances S. .....December, 1885.
Chambaud, Sarah ....May, 1884.	Conn, Isabella ....May, **1882.**
Chandler, Kittie A.........May, 1883.	Connell, Gertrude........June, **1889.**
Chapin, Thomas L..........May, 1882.	Cook, Anne Edith..........May, **1888.**
Chaplin, Alice M. ....March, 1877.	Cook, Mary A..........December, 1885.
Chapman, Amelia R........May, 1878.	Cooper, William W........May, 1888.
Chapman, E. Mattie ....June, 1867.	Cope, Lizzie ....May, 1868.
Chase, Carrie M.............June, 1867.	**Cormack,** Jessie M........May, 1887.
Chase, Hattie M. ....**May, 1879.**	**Cory,** Ben B. ....December, 1883.
Chew, Mary F..............**May, 1883.**	**Cory,** Hattie ....May, 1886.
Chickering, Belle...........**May, 1884.**	**Cory, Lizzie**............March, 1874.
Childs, Charles W..........June, 1867.	**Cory,** Susie. ....May, 1884.
Chipman, Lemuel J. .....**March,** 1873.	Cosgrave, George ....June, 1889.
Chipman, William T. ....May, 1882.	Cotter, Richard G..........May, 1888.

State Normal School. 133

LIST OF GRADUATES—Continued.

Cottle, Fannie A............ May, 1887.
Cottle, Lizzie C. .... May, 1884.
Cottle, Mary A. .... March, 1871.
Coughlin, Mamie A... December, 1887.
Courter, Henry F. .... March, 1876.
Cowden, Nina .... December, 1887.
Cowie, Anna B. .... March, 1875.
Cox, Livia M............ December, 1885.
Cox, Maggie................... May, 1887.
Coyle, Ida M. .... May, 1888.
Cozzens, Kate .... May, 1878.
Crain, Della.................... May, 1887.
Crew, Lizzie B. .... December, 1883.
Crichton, Florence ... December, 1885.
Crichton, Lottie E........... May, 1880.
Crittenden, Lillian A. ...... May, 1868.
Crittenden, May S........... May, 1879.
Crittenden, Nellie .... May, 1882.
Crofton, Jennie A..... December, 1888.
Cross, Lilian A......... December, 1885.
Crough, Daniel............. March, 1877.
Crowley, Julia A. .... May, 1886.
Crumry, Alice A........... March, 1874.
Cummings, Clara A. .... May, 1864.
Cunningham, Ione M.. December, 1884.
Currah, John M. .... May, 1869.
Currier, Adeline S. .... May, 1878.
Curtis, Mary E........ December, 1883.
Daingerfield, Lida P........ May, 1881.
Daly, Mary R. .... May, 1888.
Danielewicz, Emma........ May, 1888.
Daniels, Celia................ May, 1887.
Daniels, Fannie A........... May, 1878.
Daubenbis, Julia ..... December, 1884.
Davies, Abbie A........... March, 1875.
Davis, Addie A............ March, 1876.
Davis, Amy A............... June, 1889.
Davis, Emma E. .... May, 1880.
Davis, Kate M............... May, 1887.
Davis, Lizzie .... December, 1887.
Davis, Nathaniel W...... March, 1876.
Davis, Rachael M. .... May, 1888.
Davis, Sadie .... December, 1864.
Day, Frances A............... May, 1868.
Day, Frances M........... March, 1874.
Day, Jane O. .... May, 1864.
Day, Mariana .... May, 1882.
Day, Nellie B. .... December, 1887.
Deacon, Lizzie........ December, 1885.
Deal, Effie M..... .... December, 1888.
Deal, Virgia V. .... December, 1887.

De Lamater, G. May.. December, 1887.
De Lamater, Jessie N...... June, 1889.
Denny, Wilhelmina .. December, 1887.
Denton, Josephine .... May, 1886.
De Saisset, Henrietta M. ... May, 1880.
Desimone, Josephine........ May, 1880.
Desmond, Maggie........... May, 1878.
Devine, Katie C....... December, 1888.
Devlin, Kate L........ December, 1887.
De Zaldo, Mary E. .... May, 1884.
Dickey, Emma J............ May, 1885.
Dimon, Ella Jean........... June, 1889.
Dixon, Alfred .... March, 1876.
Dixon, Bessie .... March, 1872.
Dodge, Adelaide L........... May, 1880.
Donnelly, Carrie F.... December, 1884.
Donovan, Julia A............ May, 1885.
Dorn, S. Henrietta .... May, 1878.
Dornberger, Albert L.. December, 1885.
Dornberger, Victor ... December, 1885.
Doud, Nettie........... December, 1865.
Dougherty, Alice H........ June, 1889.
Dowling, Anna H..... December, 1884.
Downey, Kate................ May, 1878.
Downing, Annie...... December, 1884.
Downs, Blanche L........ March, 1877.
Doyle, Carolyn B...... December, 1888.
Doyle, Katie A............... May, 1884.
Doyle, Mary I............. March, 1871.
Doyle, Mary T............... May, 1884.
Dranga, Inanda L........... May, 1882.
Dudley, Lucy J............... May, 1878.
Duncan, Belle............... May, 1883.
Duncan, George F.... December, 1883.
Duncan, Laura .... May, 1883.
Duncan, Lillie......... December, 1884.
Duncan, Luella A. .... May, 1883.
Dunn, Susie M............... May, 1883.
Durham, Melvina I... December, 1888.
Durkee, Annie E. .... May, 1887.
Eames, Roscoe L. .... November, 1867.
Easter, Mary P............... May, 1884.
Easterday, Sarah F.......... May, 1878.
Eastman, Augusta R. .... March, 1870.
Edgerton, Charles L. .... May, 1888.
Edmonds, Thomas.......... May, 1879.
Eley, Zader............ December, 1887.
Ellerhorst, Henrietta T. .... Dec., 1883.
Elliott, D. Carter ..... December, 1887.
Erkson, Louisa A............ May, 1882.
Estabrook, Hattie J........ June, 1867.

10

LIST OF GRADUATES—Continued.

Estabrook, Mary A. H......Dec., 1865.
Estill, Lavinia ....May, 1880.
Evans, Cicero P. ....May, 1883.
Everett, Rose A. ....May, 1880.
Fagg, Bell J...............March, 1875.
Fairchild, Carrie S.........March, 1876.
Fairlee, E. Belle...........May, 1883.
Falconer, Nettie...........May, 1887.
Farley, Cornelia M. ....May, 1882.
Farmer, M. Fannie........March, 1875.
Farnham, Charles E.......March, 1875.
Farnsworth, Julia B......March, 1875.
Farrell, Margaret R. ....May, 1879.
Featherly, Henrietta......June, 1867.
Feely, Frances A. ....May, 1887.
Felker, Allie M. ....May, 1884.
Ferry, Ella A...............May, 1885.
Field, Carrie P. ....December, 1864.
Field, Mabel J.........December, 1886.
Field, Sarah................May, 1868.
Finch, Minnie B..............May, 1887.
Fink, P. Augusta............May, 1863.
Finley, Sallie...............May, 1878.
Finnie, Belle J..............May, 1880.
Finnie, Mary R..............May, 1880.
*Fisher, Augustus W........May, 1884.
Fisk, Annie C. ....May, 1882.
Fisk, Julia A. ....March, 1872.
Fitzwater, M. Cornett. December, 1888.
Fletcher, Annie A........March, 1871.
Flint, Almira T. ....June, 1866.
Foley, Kate J. .... December, 1888.
Foss, William F. F. ......March, 1873.
Fowler, Bessie ....May, 1888.
Fowler, Fannie A..........June, 1889.
Fowzer, Annie R. ....May, 1878.
Franklin, Benjamin H....March, 1876.
Frazier, Annie L......December, 1886.
Freyschlag, Norma ....May, 1884.
Frisbie, Phœbe A........March, 1872.
Frissell, Sarah E......December, 1865.
Fuller, Lena B..............May, 1880.
Gaddis, Anna D............June, 1867.
Gafney, Mamie A. ....June, 1889.
Gage, Marine ....May, 1885.
Gairaud, Josephine A.......May, 1885.
Galindo, Minnie G.........May, 1885.
Galinger, Emily E.....December, 1887.
Gallagher, Addie D. ....May, 1879.
Gallimore, Susie ......December, 1886.
Galloway, Florence ...December, 1885.

Gardner, Carrie M. ...December, 1884.
Gardner, Maggie.........March, 1876.
Gargan, Theresa V.........June, 1889.
Garland, Abbie A........March, 1870.
Garner, Sadie V. ....May, 1888.
Garrison, Gazena A. ....June, 1866.
Gartelman, Kate M..........May, 1883.
Geary, Lawrence J. ....May, 1888.
Gee, Mary A. ....June, 1889.
Geer, Emily F............March, 1871.
George, Laura..............May, 1883.
Germain, Clara............June, 1867.
Gesford, Henry C.........March, 1876.
Gibbons, Anna ....June, 1865.
Gibbons, Bessie E............ May, 1885.
Gibson, Anna A..........March, 1870.
Gibson, Ida M..............May, 1882.
Gibson, Olive E.............May, 1879.
Gillespie, Agnes B..........May, 1888.
Gillespie, Agnes R..........May, 1887.
Gillespie, Cora E...... December, 1886.
Gillespie, Margaret G........May, 1883.
Gillooly, May C. ....December, 1886.
Gilmor, Harriet N.........March, 1875.
Gilmore, Susie M............May, 1883.
Gilmour, Rachel S..........May, 1886.
Gingery, Mandilla ....May, 1887.
Girdner, G. Annie ....December, 1884.
Girvin, Minnie ....December, 1864.
Givens, Lou................May, 1878.
Gleason, Charlotte Z..December, 1887.
Gleason, Isabel S...... December, 1886.
Goble, Lewis...........December, 1885.
Goldsmith, Mary ....May, 1864.
Goodcell, Henry ....March, 1873.
Gordon, George A. ....May, 1884.
Gordon, Georgia A. ....May, 1885.
Gordon, Mary Q............May, 1882.
Gosbey, Stella M............May, 1888.
Gould, Marietta J............May, 1869.
Gove, Lilla B. ....May, 1879.
Gower, Hattie F............May, 1882.
Graebe, Mattie ....December, 1882.
Graffelman, Loleta........March, 1870.
Graham, Frank M...........May, 1885.
Graham, James W....December, 1887.
Graham, Margaret....December, 1885.
Granger, Edith A............May, 1886.
Granicher, Martha ...December, 1882.
Grant, Ellen................May, 1864.
Gray, Albert M.............May, 1886.

* Diploma revoked June 24, 1889.

List of Graduates—Continued.

Name	Date
Gray, Anna L.	June, 1867.
Gray, Ida	December, 1887.
Gray, Minnie	May, 1886.
Gray, Walter	December, 1888.
Green, Ishmael	March, 1877.
Green, Jennie L.	May, 1883.
Green, Katie	March, 1870.
Green, Mary B.	May, 1884.
Green, Nettie A.	May, 1883.
Greene, Ada M.	December, 1885.
Greenwell, Wm. M.	December, 1888.
Greer, Jane E.	December, 1865.
Greer, Mary L.	March, 1870.
Gregory, Clara L.	May, 1882.
Greiersen, Francisca	May, 1885.
Griffin, Eva F.	December, 1888.
Griffin, A. May	May, 1886.
Griffin, Patrick H.	May, 1882.
Griffiths, Emma	May, 1880.
Grigsby, Florence	March, 1874.
Griswold, M. Edith	June, 1889.
Grogan, Annie E.	May, 1869.
Grove, E. Louise	December, 1885.
Grubbs, Oscar H.	December, 1888.
Grubs, Clara M.	May, 1883.
Grummet, Isabel	May, 1886.
Guild, Pacific	March, 1874.
Gummer, Lillie E.	June, 1866.
Guppy, Florence	May, 1887.
Guppy, Ruth	May, 1880.
Haas, Annie E.	March, 1870.
Haile, Mrs. Cornelia	March, 1877.
Haile, Harriet E.	May, 1879.
Hall, Anna	May, 1868.
Hall, Annie J.	December, 1888.
Hall, Bertha M.	May, 1888.
Hall, Fannie	May, 1886.
Hall, Ida L.	May, 1882.
Hall, Ida S.	May, 1882.
Hall, Mary E.	December, 1865.
Hall, Sallie L.	May, 1868.
Hamilton, Agnes S.	May, 1886.
Hamilton, Susie R.	May, 1878.
Hammond, S. Estelle	March, 1874.
Hammond, Hulda A.	March, 1874.
Hammond, Jennie M.	May, 1878.
Hammond, Josiah S.	May, 1868.
Hampton, Sallie B.	May, 1888.
Handly, Sarah C.	December, 1885.
Hanscom, Nathan C.	March, 1875.
Hanscom, Si L.	May, 1879.
Hanson, Margaret A.	December, 1886.
Hanson, Mildred	December, 1884.
Hardman, Deborah W.	March, 1870.
Hardy, George H.	March, 1871.
Harrigan, Josephine	May, 1880.
Harriman, Mary G.	December, 1884.
Harrington, Julia	May, 1883.
Harris, S. Adelaide	December, 1886.
Harris, Dora B.	March, 1873.
Harris, Emily	May, 1884.
Harris, Lillie	May, 1885.
Hart, Mary T.	June, 1867.
Hart, Nellie	May, 1863.
Harte, M. Frances	June, 1889.
Hartman, Kate	May, 1884.
Harvey, Ella M.	June, 1867.
Harvey, Susie H.	December, 1887.
Haskell, Nellie M.	May, 1878.
Hasty, Eva	May, 1884.
Hatch, Lida E. F.	December, 1886.
Hauck, Julia L.	March, 1875.
Hawkins, M. Texana	December, 1888.
Hawxhurst, Theodosia M.	May, 1885.
Hayburn, Annie M.	May, 1869.
Hayes, Gertrude I.	June, 1889.
Hayford, Zilpha	December, 1883.
Hays, Florence M.	May, 1886.
Healey, Mary E.	December, 1887.
Heath, Alice M.	March, 1875.
Heintz, Ella C.	June, 1889.
Henderson, Janet M.	May, 1878.
Henderson, Margaret	Dec., 1887.
Henderson, Margaret P.	May, 1879.
Henderson, Mary A.	May, 1882.
Henderson, Mary J.	March, 1870.
Hendrix, Mary E.	March, 1873.
Heney, Julia	May, 1868.
Henion, Mae E.	May, 1878.
Henn, Carrie M.	March, 1874.
Henning, David F.	March, 1875.
Hennings, Annie C.	December, 1884.
Henry, Agnes G.	May, 1885.
Henry, Cecelia M.	December, 1887.
Henry, Kate	May, 1882.
Henry, Katie L.	December, 1884.
Henry, Maggie R.	May, 1880.
Henry, Nellie	May, 1881.
Herbert, Frank H.	December, 1886.
Herbert, Susie F.	May, 1888.
Herndon, Stella M.	May, 1885.
Herrington, Bertram A.	Dec., 1887.

LIST OF GRADUATES—Continued.

Name	Date		Name	Date
Herrington, Rachel H.	May, 1883.		Hunt, Mattie F.	December, 1882.
Herrmann, Etta E.	December, 1885.		Huntington, Nellie R.	May, 1881.
Herrod, John	May, 1880.		Hunziker, Flora	May, 1886.
Herrod, William	March, 1877.		Hyatt, Minnie M.	May, 1886.
Hetfield, Anne	December, 1884.		Hyde, Mary E.	December, 1888.
Hettz, Lucy D.	December, 1883.		Ingemundsen, I. Manla	May, 1886.
Heydenfelt, Mary G.	June, 1867.		Intermille, Rosina	March, 1875.
Hickman, M. Sue	December, 1888.		Irish, Ella M.	May, 1879.
Higgins, Belle F.	June, 1889.		Irving, Jessie	May, 1885.
Higgins, Eliza F.	December, 1883.		Isbister, Hattie E.	December, 1887.
Hill, Carrie	May, 1882.		Jacks, Fannie R.	May, 1868.
Hillebrant, Lavinia	May, 1882.		Jackson, Ella A.	March, 1874.
Hillman, Evaline C.	May, 1880.		Jackson, Etta H.	December, 1884.
Hilton, Delia C.	May, 1879.		Jackson, Kate M.	May, 1880.
Hilton, Emily H.	March, 1872.		Jaeger, Helena L.	June, 1889.
Hines, Robertine B.	May, 1879.		Jarvis, Ollie	June, 1889.
Hinshaw, Amanda	December, 1887.		Jepsen, Esther E. A.	May, 1887.
Hitchcock, Erastus K.	May, 1882.		Jewell, W. Jerome	March, 1874.
Hite, Fannie M.	May, 1887.		Jewett, Annie S.	May, 1864.
Hixon, George C.	March, 1872.		Jewett, Lizzie B.	May, 1864.
Hobart, Addie K.	May, 1878.		Johnson, Mrs. Edith	May, 1887.
Hobson, Sarah P.	May, 1879.		Johnson, Isabelle	March, 1874.
Hodge, Alice J.	May, 1884.		Johnson, Kate E.	May, 1883.
Hodge, Helen F.	May, 1886.		Johnson, Samuel E.	March, 1874.
Hodges, Charles M.	December, 1883.		Johnston, Lizzie M.	May, 1887.
Holden, M. Genevieve	June, 1889.		Johnston, Marie	May, 1886.
Holland, Sarah E.	May, 1880.		Johnston, I. Petra	December, 1883.
Hollenbeck, Minnie B.	March, 1875.		Joice, Amelia	May, 1868.
Hollingsworth, Thompson	Dec., 1884.		Jones, Absalom T.	May, 1869.
Hollron, Minnie F.	March, 1876.		Jones, Edward W.	May, 1868.
Holmes, Annie M.	June, 1866.		Jones, Frances H.	December, 1886.
Holmes, John M.	May, 1886.		Jones, Ida M.	May, 1883.
Holmes, Mary E.	December, 1886.		Jones, Jennie L.	May, 1888.
Holyer, Mrs. S. E.	December, 1883.		Jones, Lena C.	May, 1886.
Hothersall, George J.	December, 1883.		Jones, Maggie	June, 1889.
Howard, Jennie F.	May, 1880.		Jones, Mary L.	May, 1883.
Howard, Kate F.	May, 1886.		Jones, Nellie R.	March, 1875.
Howard, Maggie	November, 1867.		Jordan, Maggie L.	June, 1865.
Howard, Millie S.	March, 1875.		Jordan, William E.	May, 1882.
Howe, Alvin J.	March, 1870.		Joslin, Alice L.	May, 1887.
Howell, S. Marion	June, 1889.		Joslin, Minnie R.	December, 1887.
Howes, Lucy A.	May, 1886.		Jourden, Annie M.	June, 1865.
Hoyt, M. Jennie	March, 1877.		Judson, Lizzie P.	December, 1883.
Hudson, Myrtie C.	May, 1878.		Julien, Lillian M.	December, 1888.
Huffner, Mary J.	May, 1881.		Jury, John G.	June, 1889.
Hughes, Annie	June, 1889.		Kaufman, M. Winona	May, 1888.
Hughes, John C.	May, 1887.		Keating, Hattie M.	December, 1883.
Humphrey, Alice L.	May, 1879.		Keaton, Lizzie	December, 1885.
Humphrey, Ervin D.	June, 1866.		Keaton, Nellie	May, 1883.
Humphrey, Ida G.	May, 1882.		Keefer, Sallie E.	March, 1874.
Hunt, Byron E.	November, 1867.		Keel, Laura B.	December, 1887.

List of Graduates—Continued.

Keely, Lucy V. .... May, 1888.
Keenan, Lizzie .... May, 1886.
Keller, Lizzie F. .... March, 1877.
Keller, Mollie J. .... June, 1889.
Kelley, Ada V. .... May, 1886.
Kelley, Eulalie .... May, 1882.
Kellogg, Charles M. .... May, 1878.
Kelly, Ella .... December, 1883.
Kelly, James B. .... May, 1881.
Kelly, Mamie C. .... December, 1887.
Kelly, Mary R. .... May, 1878.
Kelsey, Effie J. .... May, 1883.
Kelsey, Lucina H. .... May, 1883.
Kelsey, Mary E. .... May, 1885.
Kelso, Iantha A. .... May, 1878.
Kelsoe, Luella .... March, 1873.
Kennedy, Anna .... December, 1864.
Kennedy, James G. .... June, 1867.
Kennedy, Joseph F. ... December, 1865.
Kennedy, May .... May, 1884.
Kennedy, May E. .... December, 1887.
Kennedy, Rebecca F. .... May, 1886.
Kennedy, Thomas E. .... March, 1872.
Kent, Adah E. .... May, 1879.
Kent, Maggie .... May, 1878.
Ketcham, Ariadne G. ...... March, 1874.
Kimball, Ariadne L. .... May, 1864.
King, Anna A. .... May, 1883.
King, Mrs. Mary A. ...... January, 1880.
King, Mary E. .... March, 1871.
Kingdom, Henrietta E. ..... Dec., 1884.
Kirkwood, William A. .... May, 1882.
Knapp, Martha M. .... May, 1880.
Kneedler, Susie E. .... March, 1874.
Knott, Emily F. A. .... May, 1885.
Knott, Georgie E. .... May, 1883.
Knox, Olive M. .... May, 1887.
Koenig, Theodore T. .... May, 1887.
Kohler, Annie .... December, 1888.
Kooser, Miriam F. ...... December, 1883.
Kottinger, Maggie .... May, 1885.
Kratzer, Lella .... March, 1873.
Krauth, M. Augusta .... May, 1864.
Kuhlitz, Mary L. .... May, 1888.
Kullak, Annie M. .... May, 1885.
Lacy, Flora E. .... May, 1885.
Lacy, Louisa .... May, 1869.
Ladd, M. Alice .... May, 1883.
Ladd, Leoline C. .... June, 1889.
La Grange, Anna .... May, 1868.
Lake, Lulu .... May, 1882.

Lane, Frank M. .... May, 1888.
Larkey, George E. .... May, 1883.
Lasater, Alice M. .... May, 1887.
Lathwesen, Louis J. .... May, 1886.
Lawless, Martha A. ... November, 1867.
Lawrey, Beatrice M. .... May, 1868.
Lawson, Karen M. .... May, 1883.
Lawson, Martin H. .... May, 1886.
Lawton, Susie S. .... May, 1868.
Leahy, Mary A. C. .... March, 1875.
Learned, Ella M. .... May, 1887.
Lee, Carrie E. .... June, 1889.
Lee, Cora A. .... December, 1886.
Leggett, Elizabeth .... May, 1882.
Lehnig, Lydia A. .... May, 1882.
Leimbach, Edith .... May, 1887.
Leimbach, Mabel M. .... May, 1887.
Leland, Anna L. .... June, 1889.
Leonard, Grace E. .... May, 1881.
Leonard, Nettie J. .... May, 1888.
Lewis, Annie H. .... May, 1868.
Lewis, Cloelia M. .... June, 1867.
Lewis, Ella .... May, 1878.
Lewis, Mary .... March, 1875.
Lindberg, Emily U. .... May, 1869.
Litchfield, Sophie E. .... May, 1887.
Little, David F. .... March, 1875.
Little, Mary .... May, 1868.
Littlefield, Nellie A. ...... June, 1865.
Livingston, Maisie V. .... May, 1888.
Locke, Ada .... March, 1876.
Locke, Hattie B. .... June, 1867.
Locke, Ida .... May, 1881.
Locke, Nathaniel H. .... May, 1880.
Locke, Sarah A. J. .... May, 1880.
Locke, William W. .... May, 1885.
Lords, Ella .... May, 1882.
Lorigan, Minnie E. ... December, 1885.
Loucks, Annie .... May, 1878.
Loucks, Lizzie M. ...... December, 1887.
Louttit, J. Alexander .. December, 1865.
Love, M. Lily .... May, 1886.
Low, Fannie .... May, 1883.
Lowden, Maggie .... May, 1886.
Lucy, Addie M. .... June, 1889.
Lynch, Mary E. .... May, 1886.
Lyon, William I. H. .... May, 1878.
Lyons, Fanny S. .... December, 1885.
MacGowan, Kitty C. .... May, 1887.
Machefert, Stella L. .... May, 1888.
Mackay, Minnie L. .... June, 1889.

138   *Historical Sketch.*

LIST OF GRADUATES—Continued.

Mackenzie, Helen C..........May, 1887.
Mackie, Clara A..............May, 1869.
MacKinnon, Lizzie ....June, 1889.
Madden, Ada F...............May, 1888.
Madden, Mary A. L..........May, 1878.
Magoon, William N..........May, 1868.
Maguire, Louise.............March, 1871.
Mahoney, Daniel .....December, 1883.
Mahoney, Lizzie T......December, 1882.
Mails, Louisa A. ....May, 1863.
Maison, Amelia L.... .....May, 1868.
Malloy, Nellie ....May, 1888.
Manchester, Julia A........May, 1886.
Mandeville, Kate............May, 1882.
Mangrum, R. Jennie........June, 1889.
Mann, Jennie S..............May, 1869.
Mansfield, May E..... December, 1886.
Mantz, Robert W. ....May, 1880.
Manuel, Cora J. ....May, 1887.
Marbut, Nora J...........December, 1888.
March, Clara A..............June, 1889.
Markham, Charles E. .....March, 1872.
Martin, Abbie L..... ....May, 1884.
Martin, Bert S................May, 1888.
Martin, Edith J............March, 1874.
Martin, Ella E...............May, 1880.
Martin, Emma T..........June, 1889.
Martin, George W. ....May, 1885.
Martin, Hattie V......December, 1884.
Martin, John W.............May, 1881.
Martin, Julia F............March, 1873.
Martin, Kate..........   ....March, 1875.
Martin, Sarah A....December, 1883.
Marvin, Adella..............March, 1870.
Mason, Wilton M......December, 1887.
Matlock, Nannie T....December, 1888.
Matson, Fannie L............May, 1887.
Matthews, Mary............March, 1870.
Matthis, Lottie J.......December, 1884.
Maxey, Millie F..............May, 1888.
May, Isabel ....March, 1875.
Mayne, Bessie J.......December, 1883.
McAllister, Bessie............May, 1888.
McBride, Henry E. ....December, 1864.
McCabe, Ella............January, 1882.
McCann, Margaret E. .....May, 1879.
McCarthy, Jennie G...December, 1884.
McCarthy, Kate ......December, 1883.
McCauley, Annie F..........May, 1887.
McColgan, Kate F.......... May, 1869.
McCollam, Lizzie...........May, 1868.

McCowan, Blanche.......March, 1877.
McDonald, Mary A.........May, 1880.
McDonnell, Kate..........March, 1876.
McDonnell, Mary A......March, 1875.
McDougall, Alice S. ....May, 1881.
McDougall, Mary S........May, 1881.
McElwee, Kate G. ....December, 1884.
McFarland, S. Ellen ..December, 1888.
McFarland, Flora A........May, 1882.
McGivern, Kate A. ....December, 1884.
McGrath, Thomas J...December, 1884.
McHarry, Mary ....December, 1883.
McIntosh, Margaret E......Dec., 1884.
McJunkin, Alice M..........June, 1889.
McKay, Amelia G..........May, 1887.
McKay, Mabel N.......December, 1886.
McKean, A. Bronson ......June, 1880.
McKean, Annie M........March, 1870.
McKean, Fannie L....December, 1885.
McKean, Lottie..............May, 1868.
McKee, Abbie................May, 1883.
McKenney, Adah M........May, 1888.
McKenzie, Dora C..........May, 1886.
McKenzie, Lizzie A........May, 1880.
McLean, Mary E............May, 1882.
McLellan, M. Grace...December, 1888.
McLeran, Charlotte C. ......May, 1879.
McLeran, Mollie......December, 1885.
McMullan, Susan ....March, 1876.
McMullin, Belle..............May, 1887.
McNaughton, C. D....November, 1867.
McPherson, Florence E.....Dec., 1888.
McPherson, Helen ....May, 1868.
McPhillips, Annie E....January, 1880.
McTigue, Carrie A... .. ....May, 1882.
McWilliams, Jennie A......May, 1887.
Mead, Emmeline R. ......March, 1874.
Meek, Mary E. ....May, 1882.
Megerle, Lisetta ....May, 1878.
Megerle, Louis J. .....December, 1865.
Meily, Albion S..............May, 1884.
Mellen, Carrie M......December, 1886.
Menges, Caroline A......... June, 1865.
Merritt, George W..........May, 1879.
Merritt, Isabel ....March, 1873.
Merritt, Mary............March, 1873.
Mertes, M. Augusta ....May, 1882.
Merwin, E. Belle ....May, 1879.
Metcalf, E. Louesa ....May, 1883.
Metcalf, Mary F. ....June, 1866.
Meyer, Amelia E......December, 1887.

List of Graduates—Continued.

Name	Date
Miles, Ella G.	May, 1884.
Miles, Lula	June, 1889.
Miller, Mrs. Amanda	March, 1874.
Miller, Charles N.	March, 1874.
Miller, Ida P.	May, 1883.
Miller, Lillie J.	May, 1885.
Miller, S. Lizzie	May, 1882.
Miller, Sarah E.	June, 1866.
Millett, Clara B.	May, 1869.
Mills, Charles N.	December, 1884.
Mills, Christenie E.	May, 1882.
Mills, Ella A.	December, 1883.
Mills, Lizzie T.	May, 1881.
Mills, Sophronia	June, 1865.
Miner, Alida	May, 1878.
Mitchell, Katie	March, 1876.
Mize, Albert W.	May, 1883.
Monaghan, Lizzie C.	December, 1885.
Montgomery, Alberta S.	March, 1870.
Montgomery, M. Kate	May, 1884.
Moody, Eva M.	May, 1888.
Mooney, Fannie	December, 1882.
Mooney, Mary T.	December, 1883.
Moore, Alice	May, 1881.
Moore, Lulu L.	March, 1877.
Moore, Matilda M. E.	March, 1871.
Moore, Susie D.	March, 1877.
Moore, Kate	March, 1877.
Morey, Sabia E.	March, 1875.
Morgan, Florence	June, 1865.
Morgan, Lizzie A.	June, 1866.
Morgan, Mary E.	May, 1883.
Morgan, Mary J.	June, 1866.
Morgan, Rose E.	March, 1875.
Morrell, Lizzie M.	May, 1887.
Morrison, Bertha C.	December, 1883.
Morrison, Mattie C.	December, 1887.
Mott, Ellita	December, 1886.
Mott, Mary	May, 1886.
Moulthrop, Mary S.	June, 1866.
Muir, Mary M.	May, 1879.
Mullen, Katie L.	December, 1887.
Mumford, Mrs. Maria E.	March, 1874.
Murch, Clara	May, 1878.
Murch, Lila	March, 1876.
Murdoch, Grace R.	May, 1879.
Murdoch, Maria E.	March, 1874.
Murdock, Ella H.	March, 1873.
Murphy, Anna C.	May, 1883.
Murphy, Anna L.	May, 1886.
Murphy, Annie L.	March, 1874.
Murphy, Ella F.	May, 1881.
Murphy, Isabella M.	March, 1870.
Murphy, Mary S.	December, 1887.
Murray, Frances	December, 1885.
Murray, Mamey	December, 1884.
Murray, Nettie M.	December, 1884.
Murray, William H.	December, 1888.
Mutschlechner, Mary	June, 1889.
Neary, Annie J.	March, 1875.
Neel, Callie F.	December, 1884.
Nelson, Lucy S.	May, 1878.
Neuebaumer, Mary T.	May, 1885.
Newcum, William A.	May, 1879.
Newell, Lizzie A.	June, 1867.
Nicholl, Aggie B.	December, 1885.
Nichols, Edith H.	May, 1887.
Nichols, Emnie H.	June, 1889.
Nichols, Etta E.	December, 1888.
Nichols, Fannie A. E.	June, 1865.
Nichols, Ida C.	May, 1885.
Nicholson, Annie M.	December, 1884.
Northcutt, Carrie A.	May, 1869.
Norton, Mary E.	December, 1884.
Norton, Mary J.	May, 1864.
Oakley, Bonnie	December, 1886.
O'Brien, Catherine	June, 1867.
O'Brien, Frances M.	May, 1878.
O'Brien, Kate C.	May, 1882.
O'Brien, Rosella A.	May, 1882.
O'Connor, Maria E.	December, 1865.
O'Donnell, Margaret M.	June, 1889.
Ogden, George W.	May, 1879.
Ogden, John F.	December, 1885.
Ogilvie, Kittie S.	May, 1883.
O'Hanlon, Fannie	May, 1881.
O'Hara, Katie F.	March, 1876.
O'Hara, Mary L.	May, 1879.
O'Leary, Kate R.	March, 1870.
Olinger, Abner F.	June, 1866.
Oliver, Carrie E.	December, 1886.
O'Neal, Amy E.	May, 1880.
O'Rourke, Maggie	March, 1874.
O'Rourke, Mary J.	May, 1888.
Orr, Annie	December, 1883.
Ortley, Mary L.	May, 1885.
Osborn, Mary M.	May, 1882.
Osgood, Annie E.	May, 1880.
Ostrom, Jennie A.	December, 1887.
Ottmer, F. H.	May, 1882.
Overacker, Allie P.	March, 1887.
Overacker, Kate	December, 1887.

140 *Historical Sketch.*

List of Graduates—Continued.

Overfelt, Bessie ....December, 1883.
Owen, **Julia** ....May, 1883.
Owens, **Effie** ....December, 1888.
Owens, Nellie M. ....June, 1867.
Pacey, Mary L. ....May, 1882.
Page, Nellie ....May, 1885.
Page, Pauline ....December, 1888.
Paine, Sumner F. ....May, 1868.
Palmer, Anna M. ....May, 1868.
Parker, Allura B. ......December, 1888.
Parker, Bessie ....May, 1888.
Parker, Lizzie A. ....May, 1885.
Parker, Olive G. ....May, 1869.
Parker, Phoebe L. ....May, 1881.
Parker, Willis H. ....May, 1887.
Parks, Myra A. ....May, 1886.
Parson, **Agnes** M. ....May, 1884.
Pascoe, Mary J. ....December, 1865.
Pascoe, **William** ....March, 1875.
Patterson, **Alma** ....March, 1877.
Patterson, Laura I. ....May, 1881.
Patterson, Mabel ....June, 1889.
Patterson, Mattie M...December, 1883.
Patton, Charlotte C. ....May, 1888.
Patton, Emma L. ......December, 1888.
Peck, **William** O. ....May, 1886.
Peckham, L. **Carrie** ....May, 1886.
Peckham, Lois A. ....May, 1879.
Peckham, Martha J. ......March, 1872.
Peckham, Mary A. ....March, 1876.
Pelton, Malvina C. ....March, 1871.
Pender, **Agnes** ....May, 1883.
Penniman, Helen N. ......March, 1876.
Pennycook, **Annie** ....May, 1887.
Pepper, Adella ....May, 1869.
Perkins, Madge **H.** ....May, 1884.
Perkins, Mary ....June, 1865.
Perkins, Mary E. .....November, 1867.
Perry, Dora A. ....December, 1884.
Perry, Katie A. ....May, 1878.
Pershin, George S. ....June, 1865.
Petray, **Henry** C. ....May, 1883.
Pettit, **Evan** T. ....May, 1878.
Phelps, Augusta M. ....March, 1872.
Phelps, Belle ....December, 1883.
Phelps, Mattie M. ....December, 1887.
Phillips, Abbie F. .....December, 1886.
Phillips, Leonora E...December, 1888.
Pinkham, Sarah M. ....May, 1887.
Piper, Frances B. ....June, 1866.
Plank, Susanna R. ....March, 1871.

Plumado, Lucy ....December, 1887.
Pollock, Adelaide L...December, 1888.
Pond, C. Lillian ....May, 1878.
Post, Mary H. ....June, 1889.
Pound, Jennie G. .....December, 1887.
Powell, David ....May, 1868.
Powell, Howell ....June, 1867.
Powell, Mattie A. ....June, 1889.
Pratt, Elinor D. ....May, 1886.
Pratt, Mary E. ....May, 1869.
Pratt, Orson M. ....May, 1878.
Pratt, William F. ....May, 1880.
Purdy, Lillian E. ....May, 1888.
Purinton, Edith L. ....May, 1885.
Purinton, Emily N. ....May, 1883.
Purinton, Lillian E. ....June, 1889.
Puter, Lawrence F... December, 1888.
Quinby, Minerva M. ......March, 1877.
Rademacher, Christine....May, 1882.
Ramer, Wilemina ....December, 1884.
Randall, Rosa ....March, 1870.
Raney, Addie M. C. ....May, 1879.
Raney, Oren N. ....May, 1878.
Raney, Sheldon ....March, 1876.
Rasmussen, Anna M. .... Dec., 1886.
Ray, Georgia ....May, 1879.
Raymond, Elissie H. ......May, 1882.
Raymund, Kate ....May, 1878.
Rea, Ianthia ....December, 1882.
Redman, Mollie ....May, 1879.
Redman, Oda ....December, 1888.
Reed, Wallace W. ....May, 1888.
Rees, Josephine D. ....May, 1881.
Remmel, Annie L. ....December, 1888.
Rennie, Lizzie A. .....December, 1884.
Reynolds, Franke B. ....May, 1882.
Reynolds, H. Grace...December, 1886.
Rich, Nellie L. ....March, 1877.
Richards, Cornelia ....May, 1888.
Richards, Lenora A. ....May, 1883.
Richardson, Ada ....May, 1882.
Richardson, Anna M..December, 1886.
Richardson, Clara C. ......May, 1878.
Richardson, Nellie B..December, 1884.
Richmond, Margaret ....May, 1885.
Rickard, Nellie ....May, 1887.
Rickey, Mary H. ....May, 1882.
Ries, Dora B. ....March, 1877.
Riley, Ella ....March, 1877.
Ringo, Mary Enna ....May, 1879.
Rixon, Chattie K. ....March, 1872.

State Normal School. 141

LIST OF GRADUATES—Continued.

Rixon, Hannah M. .... May, 1880.
Rixon, Minnie A. .... May, 1882.
Robb, Meggie L. .... May, 1886.
Robert, Mary C. .... May, 1884.
Roberts, Ella A. .... June, 1867.
Roberts, Lizzie .... March, 1873.
Robertson, Maggie E.. December, 1884.
Robinett, Nellie .... May, 1869.
Rockefellow, Dollie E.. December, 1886.
Rodden, Mary C. .... March, 1876.
Rodgers, **Arthur** .... June, 1866.
Rogers, Lucie A. .... May, 1882.
Roney, Ella E. .... December, 1882.
Roney, Louise G. .... May, 1882.
Rooker, M. Georgia .... May, 1883.
Root, Ellis J. .... March, 1875.
Root, George E. .... March, 1877.
Rose, Anthony .... December, 1888.
Ross, Adeline .... June, 1889.
Rounds, Ida M. .... June, 1889.
Rouse, Marion A. .... May, 1883.
Rowell, Gertie F. .... May, 1888.
Royce, Ruth .... March, 1877.
Rucker, Mary E. .... May, 1878.
Rucker, Susie W. .... May, 1886.
Ruddock, John C. .... March, 1871.
Rumrill, Julia S. .... December, **1885**.
Rumrill, Mary .... June, 1889.
Rumsey, Electra M. ... December, 1884.
Russell, Ella L. .... March, 1871.
Russell, Mary F. .... March, 1876.
Ryan, Sadie C. .... June, 1889.
Said, Ella .... March, 1876.
Salkeld, Libbie .... March, 1877
Sally, Mary E. .... May, 1878.
Sanborn, Allan P. .... March, 1877.
Sanders, Ella I. .... December, 1883.
Sanford, Lella .... December, 1888.
Sargent, **Lizzie** P. .... March, 1875.
Savage, Mary E. .... November, 1867.
Savage, Nellie A. .... March, 1870.
Sawyer, Mrs. **Frances C**... March, 1870.
Sawyer, Philena .... December, 1864.
Schallenberger, Fanny L.. June, 1889.
Schallenberger, Margaret E.. May, 1880.
Schenck, Emma .... March, 1875.
Schilling, Lena B. .... May, 1882.
Schnebly, C. Jean .... May, 1883.
Schoen, Lillie S. .... May, 1882.
Schuck, Kate L. .... May, 1881.
Schultzberg, **Frances** . December, 1888.

Schutte, Daisy C. .... May, **1885**.
Scott, Minnie .... May, 1864.
Scudamore, Lora .... May, 1887
Sears, Marion H. ...... November, 1867
Sears, William A. .... May, 1882.
Seavy, Minnie .... May, 1878.
Sell, Laura F. .... May, 1881.
Selling, Nathalie A. .... March, 1877.
Senter, Kate .... December, 1883.
Senter, Maggie M. .... May, 1880.
Sexton, Kate .... May, 1883.
Sharp, James M. .... March, **1871**.
Sharp, Mabel E. .... May, **1888**.
Sharpe, Nettie C. ...... December, **1885**.
Shaw, Clara E. .... December, 1885.
Shaw, Jeannette .... May, 1882.
Shaw, Sebastian .... March, 1876.
Sheats, Addie .... May, 1882.
Sheats, Arthur R. .... May, 1883.
Shelley, Troy .... May, 1868.
Sherman, Ella I. .... March, **1871**.
Sherman, Fannie A. .... March, 1870.
Sherman, Jennie R. .... June, 1889.
Shine, Nellie .... May, 1884.
Shipley, John C. .... June, 1867.
Shirley, James W. .... March, 1875.
Short, Fannie E. .... May, 1888.
Shuey, Sarah I. .... March, 1870.
Shumate, Albert E. ... December, 1887.
Sickal, Marcus T. .... March, 1871.
Siddons, Kate .... March, 1877.
Simmons, Frances E. .... **May, 1878**.
Simmons, Mary A. .... **May, 1886**.
Simon, Frances .... June, 1866.
Simpson, Cora **A**. .... **May, 1880**.
Sims, M. Kittie .... December, 1887.
Sinclair, Lizzie .... May, 1887.
Sinnott, Delia E. ...... December, 1887.
Sinnott, Grace May .... May, 1880.
Sinnott, Richard J. .... May, 1883.
Slater, Henrietta S. ... November, 1867.
Sledge, Winnie S. ...... December, 1885.
Smith, Edith C. .... May, 1883.
Smith, Flora B. .... December, 1888.
Smith, Flora C. .... June, 1867.
Smith, Grace .... June, 1867.
Smith, Jane .... May, 1864.
Smith, John A. .... May, 1868.
Smith, M. Louise .... May, 1883.
Smith, Maggie E. .... May, 1869.
Smith, Mary .... May, 1868.

List of Graduates—Continued.

Smith, Mary S.	May, 1883.	Stilson, Hattie L.	December, 1885.
Smith, Sara J.	May, 1882.	Stincen, Emma E. C.	March, 1870.
Smoote, Edith S.	December, 1888.	Stirling, Duncan	December, 1886.
Smullen, **Annie** M.	May, 1888.	Stirling, John W.	May, 1883.
Snedaker, Eunice I.	March, 1877.	Stirling, Nellie	May, 1884.
Snell, Mary E.	December, 1887.	Stivers, Charlotte J.	May, 1884.
Snodgrass, David S.	December, 1883.	Stockton, Adelia A.	March, **1875.**
Snook, S. Helen	December, 1885.	Stockton, Alice	**March, 1876.**
Snook, Jennie	May, 1887.	Stockton, Anna M.	**March, 1870.**
Snow, Alice R.	March, 1870.	Stockton, Fanny	May, **1883.**
Snow, Delia R.	March, 1873.	Stockton, William W.	May, **1878.**
Snowden, Florence	May, 1881.	Stoddard, Birdie E.	December, 1884.
Soderstrom, Hilda C.	May, 1887.	**Stokum, Marion**	May, 1868.
Solomon, Esther	May, 1869.	**Stone, Helen** M.	March, 1870.
Solomon, Eve	**May, 1864.**	**Stone,** M. Jeannette	March, **1876.**
Somers, Carrie	December, 1886.	**Stone, Mary** E.	May, 1868.
Somers, **Cora**	May, 1887.	Stowe, Augusta M.	May, 1869.
Soulé, Fannie	June, 1865.	**Stowell, Agnes**	December, **1887.**
Soulé, Maria L.	June, 1866.	Struve, Christine	December, 1886.
Spafford, Adelaide C.	December, **1885.**	**Sullivan, Frances** M.	May, 1879.
Spafford, Helen E.	December, 1887.	**Sullivan, John** W.	May, **1884.**
Spatz, Agnes A.	December, 1884.	**Sullivan, Mary** E.	**June, 1889.**
Spencer, Ella V.	May, 1883.	Summers, Esther	December, 1886.
Spinks, Edward L.	June, 1889.	Sumner, William H.	May, 1883.
Sprague, Josie E.	March, 1877.	Sumner, Etta A.	December, 1887.
Spring, Alida G.	**June, 1889.**	Suñol, Frances A.	May, 1884.
Sprott, Maggie	March, 1870.	Talbot, Annie L.	December, **1882.**
Squier, Heman G.	December, 1885.	Talmadge, Anna M.	December, 1888.
Stackpole, Georgie A.	May, 1869.	**Tarr, Blanche**	**June, 1889.**
Stansbury, Ella E.	May, **1888.**	**Taylor, Annie** L.	May, 1885.
Staples, Elizabeth	**May, 1868.**	**Taylor, George** G.	December, 1888.
Starling, Ella D.	May, 1882.	**Taylor, Leolin**	May, 1882.
Starr, Nellie M.	**March, 1873.**	**Taylor, Mary** A.	March, 1874.
Steane, Gertrude	December, 1887.	**Taylor, Olivia** L.	March, 1873.
Steele, George M.	**June, 1889.**	**Teaford, Nannie** W.	March, 1877.
Stegman, Mattie H.	May, 1869.	**Tebbe,** George A.	May, 1888.
Stenger, Maggie L.	May, 1887.	**Tebbe, William** E.	May, 1887
Stephens, Emma M.	May, 1888.	**Teel,** Mary L.	May, 1881.
Stephens, Mary R.	May, 1883.	Teel, Verona	May, 1881.
Stephens, Virginia P.	March, 1872.	Terry, Eulalia A.	March, **1872.**
Stephenson, Charlotte F.	June, 1866.	Thatcher, Georgia	June, 1889.
Stephenson, Nancy J.	May, 1881.	Theisen, Nettie C.	June, 1889.
Stern, Augusta	May, 1879.	Thomas, Edward E.	**May,** 1882.
Stern, L. May	May, 1883.	Thomas, Ida M.	May, 1885.
Stetson, Emily M.	May, **1888.**	Thomas, Laura L.	June, 1889.
Steves, M. Ada	May, 1879.	Thomas, Mary A.	May, 1869.
Steves, Amy A.	May, 1883.	Thomas, Mary O.	March, 1876.
Stewart, Eliza J.	March, 1877.	Thomasson, Annie E.	May, 1879.
Stewart, Jessie M.	May, 1880.	**Thompson, Anna** C.	May, 1883.
Stewart, Mary J.	May, 1886.	Thompson, Flora C.	May, 1883.
Stilson, Ella M.	May, 1885.	Thompson, Isaac S.	May, 1883.

List of Graduates—Continued.

Thompson, Martha B. . . . . . . May, 1883.
Thompson, M. Ruth . . December, 1885.
Thomson, Gertrude . . December, 1884.
Thrush, Dora . . . . December, 1885.
Thunen, Lizzie . . . . May, 1881.
Thurwachter, Mary E. . . . . Dec., 1887.
Tillotson, Emma . . . . March, 1870.
Tillotson, Henry I . . . . March, 1870.
Tilton, Etta M . . . . March, 1873.
Tinsley, Mary L . . . . June, 1889.
Tolman, Jessie O. . . . . May, 1883.
Tompkins, Claudia M. . . . . . May, 1884.
Towle, H. May . . . . May, 1881.
Toy, Emma M . . . . March, 1875.
Treadway, Addie . . . . May, 1868.
Trimble, Caroline . . . . March, 1876.
Trimble, Mattie M . . . . December, 1884.
Trimble, Mollie F . . . . May, 1879.
Trimingham, Martha A . . . . May, 1885.
Trowbridge, Nelson S. . . . . . June, 1866.
True, Marion E. . . . . . . December, 1885.
Tucker, Lillian E . . . . May, 1888.
Turner, Addie . . . . May, 1879.
Turner, Addie S. . . . . May, 1888.
Turner, Belle J . . . . March, 1875.
Turner, Cynthia M . . . . March, 1870.
Turner, Martha M. . . . December, 1883.
Tuttle, Annabel . . . . . . December, 1886.
Tuttle, Nannie E. . . . . May, 1885.
Tyrrell, Frank G . . . . . . December, 1883.
Tyus, Mary A. . . . . March, 1871.
Urmy, Mabel . . . . May, 1882.
Utter, John F . . . . December, 1883.
Vandervorst, Della . . . December, 1888.
Van Dusen, Marion S. . . . . . . May, 1881.
Van Eaton, Harriet E. . . . . . May, 1881.
Van Heusen, Neelie G. . . . . May, 1887.
Von Dorsten, Emma . . . . . . May, 1887.
Votaw, Emma . . . . May, 1885.
Wade, Margaret . . . . May, 1864.
Wagenseller, Etta M. . . . . March, 1872.
Waggoner, Ida M. . . . . December, 1883.
Wakefield, Claude B . . . . May, 1879.
Wakeman, Angy F . . . . May, 1883.
Wallace, Alma . . . . March, 1872.
Wallace, Lute L. . . . . May, 1887.
Walsh, Mollie E. . . . . May, 1883.
Wambold, Kate C. . . . . May, 1885.
Ward, Grace . . . . May, 1888.
Ward, Ida M. . . . . May, 1880.
Ward, Mary . . . . May, 1868.

Ward, Minnie G . . . . December, 1885.
Warring, Hattie B . . . . May, 1878.
Warring, Nettie C . . . . . December, 1884.
Wash, William A . . . . March, 1874.
Washburn, Dora B. . . . . May, 1883.
Watkins, Delia M . . . . May, 1886.
Watkins, Emma . . . . May, 1882.
Watkins, Florence M . . . . . March, 1875.
Watkins, Kate F . . . . May, 1883.
Watson, Maggie H . . . . May, 1869.
Wear, A. Belle . . . . March, 1876.
Webb, Oliver . . . . December, 1887.
Weck, Bertie . . . . May, 1887.
Weed, Alice . . . . May, 1869.
Weinshank, Regina . . . . May, 1882.
Welch, Henry C. . . . . . December, 1887.
Welch, Maude L. . . . . . December, 1888.
Wells, Alice M . . . . March, 1875.
Wells, Annie L. . . . . December, 1884.
Wemple, Emmet L. . . . . . . March, 1870.
West, Fannie P . . . . May, 1883.
Westfall, Lillian E. . . . . June, 1889.
Wetmore, Edith L . . . . March, 1870.
Whatmore, Amy . . . . May, 1883.
Wheeler, Tenah E. . . . . June, 1889.
Whelan, Ella E. . . . . March, 1876.
Whelan, Maggie L. . . . . December, 1887.
White, Alice M . . . . March, 1876.
White, Elizabeth . . . . June, 1866.
White, Silas A. . . . . June, 1866.
Whiting, Julia M . . . . March, 1874.
Whitmore, Ella L . . . . May, 1869.
Whitney, Anita . . . . May, 1884.
Wible, Annie A . . . . March, 1875.
Wible, Julia F . . . . March, 1875.
Wickham, Nellie T. . . . . May, 1883.
Wignall, Fannie . . . . March, 1872.
Wiley, Maggie L . . . . March, 1877.
Willard, Sadie P. . . . . May, 1888.
Williams, Carrie . . . . May, 1879.
Williams, Cecilia A. . . December, 1883.
Williams, Clara B . . . . March, 1877.
Williams, Emily E. . . . . May, 1887.
Williams, Lillian . . . . . December, 1887.
Williams, Maggie . . . . . December, 1883.
Williams, May E. . . . . May, 1864.
Williams, Nina F. . . . . December, 1884.
Williams, Richard D . . December, 1886.
Williams, Sabrina A. . December, 1865.
Williamson, Jessie . . . . May, 1879.
Wilson, David A . . . . May, 1887.

LIST OF GRADUATES—Continued.

Wilson, Jessie E.	March, 1870.
Wilson, Lewis **B.**	May, 1878.
Wilson, Mary E.	March, 1875.
Wilson, **William** R.	March, 1875.
Wissman, Annie L.	June, 1889.
Witherspoon, Henry E.	May, 1885.
Withington, Augusta S.	March, 1873.
Withrow, Marie	March, 1870.
Wood, E. Alfaretta	May, 1878.
Wood, Alfred A.	May, 1880.
Wood, Flora	December, 1883.
Woodman, Charles A.	May, 1878.
Woodson, Annie	May, 1879.
Woodward, Bessie	May, 1883.
Woodward, N. Zoraide	March, 1874.
Woodworth, Willard D.	May, 1886.
Wooll, Harriet L.	June, 1867.
Workman, Oliver P.	March, 1876.
Wright, Ada E.	June, 1867
Wright, Emily L.	May, 1882.
Wright, Mary A.	May, 1869.
Wristen, Lizzie N.	May, 1883.
Wurtenberg, Marianne	March, 1887.
Wyckoff, Cora K.	May, 1885.
Wyckoff, Nellie	December, 1885.
Wyllie, Hattie I.	**May, 1882.**
Yaney, Elma K.	**May, 1884.**
Yaple, Edith D.	**May, 1885.**
Yates, Jennie	March, 1870.
York, Elizabeth	June, 1866.
Young, M. Frances	December, 1886.
Young, Mary E.	May, 1882.
Youngberg, Mary F.	June, 1865.
Zane, Anna F.	December, 1885.
Zeilian, John J.	December, 1883.

NAMES OF HOLDERS OF ELEMENTARY DIPLOMAS.

(See page 56.)

MIDDLE CLASS—ELEMENTARY DIPLOMAS.

(Graduated March 31, 1877.)

MARIAN ASHLEY.
ELIZA F. AULD.
*ALICE BLYTHE.
ELLIS C. BROWN.
MATTIE E. CHAPPELL.
*NELSON B. COFFMAN.
*ADALINE S. CURRIER.
JACOB DEPPELLER.
LAURA C. GIDDINGS.
ANNIE HARRIGAN.
ARLIE J. JENNISON.
*CHARLES M. KELLOGG.
*IANTHA A. KELSO.
*MARGARET A. KENT.
EMILY McMULLEN
WILLIAM P. MOORE.
*FRANCES O'BRIEN.
*C. LILLIAN POND.
*OREN N. RANEY.
*CLARA C. RICHARDSON.
MABEL SEAVY.
MARY A. SEAVY.
*WILLIAM STOCKTON.
MICHAEL F. SULLIVAN.
ALICE E. THURSTON.
*HATTIE B. WARRING.
MARY WESTPHAL.
*LEWIS WILSON.

(Graduated May 23, 1878.)

MAY ADCOCK.
ANNIE BACON.
*KATIE BARDENWERPER.
*LAURA BETHELL.
ROBERT J. BROWN.
*HATTY M. CHASE.
MATTIE A. COLE.
GEORGE J. COLLIER.
ELLA DONOVAN.
EMMA A. EVERHART.
*LILLA B. GOVE.
NAOMI A. HAYES.
*JOHN HERROD.
*SARAH HOBSON.
KATIE A. HUFFNER.
*ETTA H. JACKSON.
EMMA J. KENDALL.
*ADAH E. KENT.
IDA M. LOVE.
*AIMEE MADAN.
FANNIE M. MARTIN.
*JOHN W. MARTIN.
*ELLA McCABE.
*CHARLOTTE C. McLERAN.
*AUGUSTA M. MERTES.
ALFREDA MORTON.
*MARY M. MUIR.
ANITA MURRAY.
*ELLA F. MURPHY.
ELLEN A. NEWBERRY.
*LOIS A. PECKHAM.
*CHRISTINE RADEMACHER.
*GEORGIA RAY.
IDA E. RHINEHART.
*ENNA M. RINGO.
FLORENCE S. ROYCE.
WILLIAM G. SMITH.
NETTIE E. SPANGENBERG.
*NANCY J. STEPHENSON.
ISABEL SQUIRES.
*AUGUSTA STERN.
*ADA STEVES.
ELLA M. TALLANT.
*MARY L. TEEL.
*ADDIE TURNER.
*IDA M. WARD.
EMMA WEAR.
*JESSIE WILLIAMSON.
*ANNIE WOODSON.

(Graduated January 4, 1879.)

*IDA M. BENNETT.
*EMMA E. DAVIS.
MARY F. FARRELL.
*JULIA HARRINGTON.
LOUISE A. HORNE.
FRANK HUSKEY.
LUCIA JUDKINS.
WILLIAM H. LAWRENCE.
*NATHANIEL H. LOCKE.
*SARAH A. J. LOCKE.
*ELLA E. MARTIN.
*FLORA McCLELLAN.
*H. BURR NEEDHAM.
FRED. W. NOBLE.
*AMY E. O'NEAL.
JOSEPHINE R. PHILLIPS.
MARY E. SMITH.
*MATTIE B. THOMPSON

(Graduated May 22, 1879.)

*KATE APPLEBY.
ANN ASQUITH.
HELEN D. BARIGHT.
*MARY S. BOWMAN.
ANNIE M. BRADY.
FRANCES A. BROWN.
MARY E. BURGER.
*LUCINDA J. CARVER.
*E. ELMER CAREY.
ADELAIDE DALEY.
ALICE R. DORAN.
*LOUISE A. ERKSON.
*LOVINA ESTILL.
*ROSE A. EVERETT.
JENNIE GALLAGHER.
EMILY GILL.
*CLARA L. GREGORY.
*MARGARET R. HENRY.
*JENNIE F. HOWARD.
*M. KATE JACKSON.
*WILLIAM E. JORDAN.
MRS. SARAH KELSEY.
ANNIE M. KENNEDY.
*MARTHA M. KNAPP.
MARGRUIETTA B. LLOYD.
VIRGINIA E. LYNDS.
DEANVER M. LYNDS.
MARY F. McCONNELL.
*LIZZIE A. McKENZIE.
*ANNIE McPHILLIPS.
KATE C. MORRIS.
LUCY E. OWENS.
EMMA C. POWELL.
*WILLIAM F. PRATT.
*MARY H. RICKEY.
MARY A. ROGERS.
*HENRIETTA DeSAISSET.
EMMA SELBY.
*MAGGIE M. SENTER.
MARY E. SENTER.
*CORA A. SIMPSON.
SOPHIE W. SMITHURST.
CORA L. SPEAR.
WALDO S. WATERMAN.
FLORA A. WOODFORD.

(Graduated December 17, 1879.)

SUSIE P. BENSON.
*LUCY M. BOTSFORD.
ANNIE R. BREWSTER.
PAUL J. BRYANT.
*ANGELINA CHAMBAUD.
BIRDIE A. CHESTNUTWOOD.
*LUELLA DUNCAN.
*EVA B. FAIRLEE.
*SARAH E. HOLLAND.
*WILLIAM A. KIRKWOOD.
HOWARD M. LOCKE.
*IDA LOCKE.
*ROBERT W. MANTZ.
P. JENNIE MAYHEW.
*LIZZIE C. MONAGHAN.
*ALICE MOORE.
*HANNAH M. RIXON.
*MARTHA A. STEWART.
MRS. LAURA A. WELLS.

(GRADUATED MAY 20, 1880.)

IDA ALLEN.
FLORENCE APLIN.
*WALTER S. BAILEY.
DELIA BEAUCHAMP.
*ROSA BECKWITH.
*IDA M. CARPENTER.
MARY F. CLAYPOOL.
*A. B. COFFMAN.
*BELLE CONN.
KATE COOLEY.
C. T. COYLE.
*LAURA DUNCAN.
NELLIE FELLOWS.
*ANNIE C. FISK.
HATTIE N. GAPEN.
CARROLL W. GATES.
LUELLA GILLESPIE.
*MARY Q. GORDON.
*NELLIE HENRY
*CARRIE HILL.
*NELLIE R. HUNTINGTON.
MARY JONES.
*ANNA KING.
KATE LATIMER.
*M. H. LAWSON.

CORDELIA B. LEGGETT.
*GRACE E. LEONARD.
OSCAR E. MACK.
EMMA MADDEN.
ALMA MARTIN.
MAGGIE G. MEEHAN.
*MOLLIE MEEK.
*ALBION S. MEILY.
*CHRISTENIE MILLS.
ALICE MORRILL.
THOMAS P. McDONALD.
*MARY S. McDOUGALL.
JULIA E. McLERAN.
*CARRIE McTIGUE.
VIRNETTA OLDHAM.
*FANNIE O'HANLON.
*F. H. OTTMER.
*EMILY PURINTON.
*IANTHA REA.
*CORNELIA RICHARDS.
*LAURA F. SELL.
MILLIE THOMPSON.
SALLIE E. WELLS.
MRS. MARTHA A. WILKINSON.
LUCY WOODSON.

*EMILY WRIGHT.

* Afterwards took the Senior Year and received full diplomas.

GRADUATES' RECORD.

In May, 1883, the Board of Trustees adopted a resolution requiring all graduates, before receiving their diplomas, to sign the following agreement:

> I hereby agree to report to the Principal of the school from which I graduate, at least twice a year for three years after my graduation, and once a year thereafter, so long as I continue in the profession of teaching; and when I shall leave the profession, I will report the fact to him, with the cause therefor. A failure to make such reports may be considered a sufficient cause for the revocation of my diploma.

The graduates since that time, with a few exceptions, have faithfully complied with the conditions of their agreement.

Reports of graduates before this date have been gathered from various sources. Circulars asking for reports were issued in 1886, and sent to all whose addresses were known. Many have responded. Some have kindly sent reports for classmates and others whose history was unknown. Some have failed to respond, and of a few nothing can be learned. The size of the State and the unsettled location of the school during the first few years of its existence have much to do with the incompleteness of the record concerning early graduates. Only such information is published as can be given with a good degree of certainty. This information has been gathered gradually during the past six years. The result, though not so nearly complete as could be wished, is highly satisfactory, and shows, as far as statistics can show, what the school is accomplishing through its graduates. Hearty thanks are here extended to all who have in any way assisted in this important work.

The preparation of this History has shown more forcibly than ever the desirability of keeping on file at the school an accurate account of the work of the graduates, with their addresses. It is hoped, therefore, that the valuable habit of sending reports will not cease with the publication of the History, but that all graduates, whether or not they have previously reported, will send reports, at least annually, of their work and addresses, for reference and future publication. It is of course expected that all members of classes graduated since the obligation to report has been required, will report annually, as pledged.

Each annual catalogue of the school is mailed to all graduates who have reported during the year for which the catalogue is issued.

It should be borne in mind that the time covered by the following "Record" closes with June, 1889, and in many cases, where reports have not lately been received, it closes at an earlier date. Graduates are requested to notify the Principal of the School at once of any errors in the "Record" and of changes in their addresses.

NOTE.—The name of the county represented by each graduate at the time of graduation, is placed opposite his name.

ERRATA AND ADDENDA.

NOTE.—The publication of the History having been delayed longer than was expected, items from reports have been added, as received, up to the time of publication, November, 1889.

PAGE.

171. MARCUS T. SICKAL. Present address, Benicia, Solano County.

172. CHAS. E. MARKHAM. Teaching at Haywards, Alameda County.

186. A. BELLE WEAR. (Mrs. Clement) Present address Livermore, Alameda County.

194. MYRTIE C. HUDSON. (Mrs. Edward Wagner) Present address, Tien-Tsin, China. Married September 6, 1889. Engaged with her husband in missionary work.

198. MARGARET E. MCCANN. (Mrs. H. J. Stafford.) Taught in Temescal two years; in Oakland four years.

216. MARY E. YOUNG. (Mrs. Ed. North) Present address, Newhall, Los Angeles County.

217. JAMES G. BEATY. Taught in Plumas County one year; Butte County two years; Yuba County three years. Teaching in Yuba County.

218. LAURA DUNCAN. Teaching in Honolulu.

226. LIZZIE B. CREW. (Mrs. E. E. Canfield) Present address, Chico, Butte County.

231. LIZZIE C. COTTLE. Taught in Monterey County one year; in Santa Clara County four years. Teaching at Evergreen, Santa Clara County. (OVER)

GRADUATES' RECORD.

In May, 1883, the Board of Trustees adopted a resolution requiring all graduates, before receiving their diplomas, to sign the following agreement

I hereby agree to report to the Principal of the school from which I graduate, at least twice a year for **three** years after my graduation, and once a year thereafter,

PAGE.		
232.	NORMA FREYSCHLAG.	Present address, San Jose.
239.	NETTIE C. WARRING.	Has been teaching in Monterey County for past two years.
241.	TILLIE M. CLARK.	(Mrs. Stephen Smith) Present address, Yuba City. Married November 9, 1889.
261	FANNIE L. MATSON.	Teaching at Sheridan, Placer County.
262.	AMELIA G. MCKAY.	Teaching in Benicia.
265.	NINA COWDEN.	Teaching at Downieville, Sierra County.
265.	LIZZIE DAVIS.	Present address, Golden Gate, Alameda County.
265.	G. MAY DE LAMATER.	Present address, Santa Cruz.
267.	AMELIA E. MEYER.	Present address, College Park, Santa Clara County. Not teaching.
267.	ALBERT E. SHUMATE.	Teaching at New Almaden, Santa Clara County.
272.	ADAH M. MCKENNEY.	Teaching at Los Gatos, Santa Clara County.
274.	HANNAH M. BALL.	Teaching near Tipton, Tulare County.
275.	CAROLYN B. DOYLE.	(Mrs. Irvin Ball)
275.	MELVINA I. DURHAM.	
277.	LAWRENCE F. PUTER.	Studying law in the Michigan University.

Each annual catalogue of the school is mailed to all graduates who have reported during the year for which the catalogue is issued.

It should be borne in mind that the time covered by the following "Record" closes with June, 1889, and in many cases, where reports have not lately been received, it closes at an earlier date. Graduates are requested to notify the Principal of the School at once of any errors in the "Record" and of changes in their addresses.

NOTE.—The name of the county represented by each graduate at the time of graduation, is placed opposite his name.

FIRST CLASS—MAY, 1863.

BERTHA COMSTOCK (Mrs. J. C. Bates) ....San Francisco.
    Present address, 2412 Pine Street, San Francisco.
    Taught in San Mateo County and in San Francisco previous to marriage; not taught since. Married in 1868. Seven children.

P. AUGUSTA FINK (Mrs. T. C. White)............San Francisco.
    Present address, Fresno City.
    Taught in the San Francisco public schools from 1864 until resignation in 1876; for two years was Principal of the Spring Valley Grammar School. Not taught since marriage, November, 1877. One child. Residence, Raisina Vineyard, near Fresno City.

NELLIE HART (Mrs. B. H. Ramsdell) ....San Francisco.
    Present address, Alameda.
    Taught in Santa Clara County two terms, and in San Francisco. Married in 1864. Work suspended several years; has been teaching for the past three years in Alameda. Four children.

LOUISA A. MAILS (deceased) ....San Francisco.
    Did not teach; died soon after graduation.

SECOND CLASS—MAY, 1864.

MARTIN V. ASHBROOK ....Solano County.
    Present address, Fresno City.
    Taught in Contra Costa County and Del Norte County, about seven years in all. Left teaching to study law; now an attorney at law, Fresno City. Married. Two children.

ELLEN S. BALDWIN ....Contra Costa County.
    Present address, 1900 Devisadero Street, San Francisco.
    Has taught in the San Francisco schools since January, 1865. Teaching in Hamilton Grammar School.

VICTORIA BEVERLY (Mrs. Newbury)........Santa Clara County.
    Address in January, 1886, Mountain View.

SUSIE D. L. CAREY (Mrs. S. C. Baker).......Santa Clara County.
    Present address, Pacific Grove, Monterey County.
  Taught in Santa Clara, one year; San José, three years; Los Angeles, two years; Napa, one year; Vallejo, two years; San Francisco, eight years; Placer and Monterey Counties, two years. Teaching at Pacific Grove. Married in 1868 and in 1870. Five children; four living. Has published a book of poems and prose called "Gleanings," and is preparing a book on "Temperance in Public Schools." Holds Business College and Kindergarten diplomas. Has done much work as private teacher outside of public schools, and intends to spend her life in teaching.

CLARA A. CUMMINGS...........................San Francisco.
  Taught. Went to Europe several years ago.

JULIA CLAYTON (Mrs. Sarles)...................San Francisco.
    Present address, 2327 California Street, San Francisco.
  Teaching in the Grant Primary School, San Francisco; has taught in San Francisco eight years. Has two children.

JANE O. DAY (Mrs. Palmer)................Santa Clara County.
    Resided in Oakland when last heard from.
  Taught one year.

ELLEN G. GRANT.............................Nevada County.
    Present address, 414 Larkin Street, San Francisco.
  Has taught in San Francisco since June, 1864; teaching in the Columbia Grammar School.

MARY GOLDSMITH (Mrs. Prag)..................San Francisco.
    Present address, 915 Van Ness Avenue, San Francisco.
  Has taught in San Francisco since June, 1864; teaching in the Girls' High School.

ANNIE S. JEWETT.........................Santa Clara County.
    Present address, 714 Shotwell Street, San Francisco.
  Has taught in San Francisco since November, 1865; teaching in Bartlett Primary School.

LIZZIE B. JEWETT (Mrs. G. W. Towle, Jr.)...Santa Clara County.
    Address in July, 1886, San Rafael.
  Taught.

M. AUGUSTA KRAUTH (Mrs. Morgan).........El Dorado County.
    Present address, Corralitos, Santa Cruz County.
  Taught in Monterey, one year; San Francisco, two years; Santa Cruz County, two years. Not teaching.

ARIADNE L. KIMBALL (Mrs. H. R. Kimball)......San Francisco.
    Present address, Petaluma, Sonoma County.
  Taught a short time as substitute in the San Francisco schools, and seven years in the Protestant Orphan Asylum, San Francisco. Married November 21, 1872; not taught since. Three children.

MARY J. NORTON (deceased) ....San Francisco.
   Taught.

JANE SMITH................................San Francisco.
   Present address, 1413 Post Street, San Francisco.
   Has taught in San Francisco since June, 1864; teaching in Longfellow
Primary School.

MINNIE SCOTT.............................Alameda County.
   Married. Did not teach.

EVE SOLOMON ....San Francisco.
   Taught one year. Married.

MARGARET WADE (deceased)..................San Francisco.
   Taught in San Francisco from June, 1864, until the time of her death,
September 23, 1882. Address of her sister, Miss Nettie Wade, 104 Webster
Street, San Francisco.

MARY E. WILLIAMS ....Marin County.
   Taught.

THIRD CLASS—DECEMBER, 1864.

LUCINDA N. ALLYNE........................San Francisco.
   Present address, unknown.
   Went to Massachusetts.

ELIJAH BROADBENT.........................Sierra County.
   Present address, unknown.
   Taught several years in St. Augustine College, Benicia, in California, and
Nevada. Living in one of the Eastern States.

WILLIAM R. BRADSHAW (deceased) ....Sutter County.
   Taught.

SADIE DAVIS (Mrs. Cornwall) ....San Francisco.
   Present address, San Francisco.
   Taught in San Francisco and in Redwood City.

CARRIE P. FIELD (Mrs. Plunkett)...........Santa Cruz Co.
   Present address, 231 San José Avenue, San Francisco.
   Has taught in San Francisco since April, 1865. Teaching in the Columbia Grammar School.

MINNIE GIRVIN............................San Francisco.
   Married. Did not teach.

ANNA KENNEDY ....San Francisco.
   No report.

HENRY E. MCBRIDE..............................Tulare County.
        Present address, San Luis Obispo.
  Has taught several years. Is now practicing law.

PHILENA SAWYER................................San Francisco.
  Taught. Is married, but present name and address unknown.

FOURTH CLASS—JUNE, 1865.

CORNELIA E. CAMPBELL..........................Sonoma County.
    Present address, **Hubbard House,** 139 Fourth Street, San Francisco.
    Has **taught in San Francisco since** February, 1867. Teaching **in the** South San Francisco School.

AUGUSTA S. CAMERON (Mrs. Bainbridge)..........San Francisco
      Present address, Covelo, Mendocino County.
    Taught in San Francisco two and one half years; Mendocino County, thirteen years. Teaching. **Married January 6,** 1869. Two children. Was **the** first native California graduate, and **probably** the youngest ever **graduated from the school. Has done** much **work outside of the** public schools as teacher in book-keeping, **music, calisthenics, etc.**

ANNA GIBBONS (Mrs. Wm. T. Garratt)............San Francisco.
    Taught in San Francisco from June, 1868, to October, 1882, except one **year's leave of absence.**

MAGGIE L. JORDAN (deceased)..................**San Francisco.**
    Was elected **to a position in San Francisco in June, 1867.** Further history not known.

ANNIE M. JOURDEN (Mrs. James Duffy)...........San Francisco.
      Address in 1886, 1944 California Street, San Francisco.
  Taught.

NELLIE A. LITTLEFIELD.........................San Francisco.
      Present address, **511 Gough** Street, San Francisco.
  Has taught in San Francisco since December, 1865. Teaching in Potrero School.

FLORENCE MORGAN...............................San Francisco.
      Present name and address unknown.
  Married and went East soon after graduation. Did not teach.

CAROLINE A. MENGES............................San Francisco.
     Present address, Norwood House, Los Angeles.
  Taught in San Francisco from December, 1867, to August, 1888.

SOPHRONIA MILLS (Mrs. E. H. Kincaid)....San Joaquin County.
      Present address, Los Angeles.
  Taught in San Joaquin County two years. Married May 1, 1867. **Not taught since.** Seven children.

FANNY A. E. NICHOLS............................San Francisco.
    Taught in San Francisco from July, 1865, to March, 1882. Left the profession on account of ill health.

GEORGE S. PERSHIN..............................Humboldt County.
    Present address unknown.
    Taught in San Francisco. Was afterwards engaged in surveying.

MARY PERKINS ....Placer County.
    Present address, San Francisco.
    Teaching in Spring Valley School, San Francisco.

FANNIE SOULÉ...................................San Francisco.
    Present address, 825 Polk Street, San Francisco.
    Has taught in San Francisco since September, 1865. Teaching in Lincoln Grammar School.

MARY F. YOUNGBERG (Mrs. Elliott Reed).........San Francisco.
    Present address, 279 North San Pedro Street, San José.
    Taught in Willow Glen District, Santa Clara County, five months; in San José, eleven years. Not teaching. Married November 11, 1867. Two children; one living.

FIFTH CLASS—DECEMBER, 1865.

NETTIE DOUD (Mrs. F. B. Wood) ....San Francisco.
    Present address, 2211 Steiner Street, San Francisco.
    Has taught continuously in the San Francisco schools since graduation; is now Principal of the Hermann Street Primary School. Married in 1873.

MARY A. H. ESTABROOK (Mrs. Millington) ......San Francisco.
    Address in 1886, Napa City.
    Taught.

SARAH E. FRISSELL (deceased)..................San Francisco.
    Taught several years. Was married (name unknown), and died in the Eastern States.

JANE E. GREER..................................San Mateo.
    Present address, 1040 Twentieth Street, San Francisco.
    Teaching in Fairmount School; has taught in San Francisco since June, 1868.

MARY E. HALL...................................San Francisco.
    Taught.

JOSEPH F. KENNEDY..............................Contra Costa County.
    Address, unknown.
    Attorney at law. Has taught.

J. ALEXANDER LOUTTIT ....Calaveras County.
    Present address, Stockton, San Joaquin County.
  Taught in Calaveras County, one term; Alameda County, three years; San Joaquin County, **one year**. Left teaching for the profession of law; was City Attorney of Stockton **eight** terms; member of **the** Forty-ninth Congress, U. S. A. Married August 21, 1872. Five children; **is now a widower.** Present occupation, attorney at law.

LOUIS J. MEGERLE (deceased) ....**San** Joaquin **County.**
  Taught eight months in San Joaquin County. Graduated from the University of the Pacific in 1870, and taught in that institution for a **time; left** teaching in 1871 to enter **the** Harvard Law School. Died June **29, 1872,** within two weeks **of graduation.**

MARIA E. O'CONNOR..............................San Francisco.
  Taught in San **Francisco from December, 1865,** to July, 1880. In 1886 was reported as teaching **in a Convent, but address** unknown.

MARY **J.** PASCOE (Mrs. Parolini)...............San Francisco.
    Present address, 37 Post Street, San Francisco.
  Has taught in San Francisco since April, 1866. Teaching in the Garfield Primary School.

SABRINA A. WILLIAMS............................Yuba County.
  Went East soon after graduation.

SIXTH CLASS—JUNE, 1866

ABBIE CARSWELL...............................San Francisco.
  Married. Taught. Name, address, and **history unknown.**

AMEY T. CAMPBELL.....................Contra Costa County.
    Present address, 1220 Jackson Street, San Francisco.
  Taught constantly **since graduation** in the San Francisco schools. Is now Vice-Principal of the **Broadway** Grammar School.

ALMIRA T. FLINT..............................San Francisco.
    Present address, 812 Hyde Street, San Francisco.
  Has taught in San Francisco since June, 1866. Teaching in **Denman** Grammar School.

GAZENA A. GARRISON...........................San Francisco.
  Taught in San Francisco from **April, 1867, to March, 1882.** Teaching in **Marin County.**

LILLIE E. GUMMER (Mrs. **Judge John Hunt**).....San Francisco.
    Present address, San Francisco.
  Taught about five years. Has one child.

ERVIN D. HUMPHREY (deceased) ....San Francisco.
    Was elected to a position in the San Francisco Schools immediately after graduation, and was Principal of the Fairmount, Mission Grammar, and Hayes Valley Grammar Schools successively. In January, 1877, he resigned on account of failing health. In consideration of his faithful services, his resignation was not accepted by the Board of Education, but he was granted an indefinite leave of absence. He went to Ohio in June, 1877. Returned to California in February, 1878, and died March 18, 1878. He left a wife and three sons.

ANNIE M. HOLMES (Mrs. Marcus D. Boruck).....San Francisco.
    Present address, California Street, near Laguna, San Francisco.
    Taught in San Francisco three years. Married April 14, 1869; not taught since. Two children.

MARY J. MORGAN (Mrs. J. Irving Ayers)....Sacramento County.
    Present address, 1758 Taylor Street, West Oakland.
    Taught in San Francisco four and one half years. In 1870 discontinued teaching and married. In 1883, resumed teaching in the Clawson School, Oakland, which position she has held continuously since. Has four children.

LIZZIE A. MORGAN (Mrs. Wentworth T. Crowell), (deceased).
....Sacramento County.
    Taught in San Francisco two years; then married and resigned. After several years, again commenced teaching in Sacramento, where she taught until 1887. After an illness of seven months, died in August, 1887. Left three children, the eldest now a teacher.

SARAH E. MILLER ....San Francisco.
    Present address, 239 Sixteenth Street, San Francisco.
    Has taught in San Francisco continuously since graduation. Teaching in Haight Primary School.

MARY F. METCALF (Mrs. Hugh Davidson).......San Francisco.
    Present address, 611 Haight Street, San Francisco.
    Taught in San Francisco from March, 1868, to October, 1885. Married October 3, 1885.

MARY S. MOULTHROP.........................San Francisco.
    Present address, 1108 Union Street, San Francisco.
    Has taught most of the time since graduation; for the past two years at San Pedro, Los Angeles County, where she is now teaching.

ABNER F. OLINGER..........................San Francisco.
    Present address, Campbellton, Jackson County, Florida.
    Has taught most of the time since graduation: in various counties of California, fourteen years; in Tennessee, three years; in Florida, five years. Teaching in Florida. Married April 16, 1871. Four children.

FRANCES B. PIPER (Mrs. Wm. Hall) ....San Francisco.
    Present address, Stockton.
    Not taught. Married September 18, 1867. Four children; three living.

ARTHUR RODGERS............................San Francisco.
   Present address, Nevada Block, San Francisco.
   Taught in Santa Clara County, three months; San Mateo County, five months; Monterey County, five months; San Benito County, five months. Entered University of California, January, 1870, from which institution he graduated in 1872. Is now practicing law in San Francisco. Is a Regent of the University of California, and has delivered a number of public addresses.

FRANCES SIMON (Mrs. Chas. Leavy).............San Francisco.
   Present address, San Francisco.
   Taught eight years. Has six children.

MARIA L. SOULÉ...............................San Francisco.
   Present address, 516 Van Ness Avenue.
   Teaching in the Denman Grammar School. Has taught in San Francisco since June 1868.

CHARLOTTE F. STEPHENSON (Mrs. Noah F. Flood), (deceased).
   ....Sacramento County.
   Taught. Died December, 1868.

NELSON S. TROWBRIDGE.........................Amador County.
   Present address, Berkeley, Alameda County.
   Taught six months near Lockeford; six months near Vacaville; six months at Michigan Bar. Left teaching January, 1869, for mining and mercantile pursuits. Married May 19, 1869, to Kate J. Clayton, class of 1867. Six children; five living.

ELIZABETH WHITE (Mrs. Scott) ....San Francisco.
   Present address, Portland, Oregon.
   Taught in San Francisco.

SILAS A. WHITE ....San Francisco.
   Present address, 2213 Larkin Street, San Francisco.
   Taught constantly in the public schools of San Francisco since graduation. Principal of Spring Valley Grammar School.

ELIZABETH YORK (Mrs. M. A. De Jough), (deceased)......
   ....San Francisco.
   Taught in San Francisco. Married July 31, 1869. Two children; one living.

SEVENTH CLASS—JUNE, 1867.

JULIA V. ASHLEY (Mrs. Alfred Thurber)....Contra Costa County.
   Present address, Salinas City.
   Taught in Contra Costa County eleven years; has been teaching in Salinas City since January, 1888. Married July 1, 1869. One child.

SARAH E. ANDERSON (deceased) ....San Francisco.
   Taught.

E. MARGARET BEVANS (Mrs. C. Convis) ....San Francisco.
      Present address, New York City.
   Taught four years in San Francisco.

EMMA A. BIGSBY (deceased)....................Sonoma County.
   Taught.

ADRIANNA L. BEERS (Mrs. Maynard)..............San Francisco.
         Present address, 730 Green Street, San Francisco.
   Taught.

CARRIE M. CHASE (Mrs. Wm. S. Murphy), (deceased)......
   ....San Francisco.
      Taught in San Francisco from July, 1868, to March, 1875. Died July 2, 1876. Left one son.

CHAS. W. CHILDS ....El Dorado County.
         Present address, San José.
      Taught in El Dorado County, two years; Suisun City, Solano County, nine years. Was County Superintendent of Solano County two terms. Now Principal of the State Normal School, San José, in which school he has taught since 1878.

E. MATTIE CHAPMAN ....Sonoma County.
   Taught.

KATE J. CLAYTON (Mrs. N. S. Trowbridge) ......San Francisco.
            Present address, Berkeley, Alameda County.
      Taught in Santa Clara County, one year; Amador County, three months; State of Nevada three months. Not teaching. Married May 19, 1869. Six children; five living.

MARY P. CLARK (deceased) ....Amador County.
      Taught in Amador County. Died March 31, 1870. Father's address, W. O. Clark, Drytown, Amador County.

HATTIE J. ESTABROOK (Mrs. W. W. Thompson)__ San Francisco.
      Address in 1886, Napa City. Had taught five years.

HENRIETTA FEATHERLY ....San Francisco.
            Present address, 1107 Mason Street, San Francisco.
      Has taught in San Francisco since July, 1867. Teaching in the Powell Street Primary School.

ANNA D. GADDIS (Mrs. Maxwell).................Yolo County.
         Present address, Woodland, Yolo County.
      Taught in Yolo County until marriage, June 3, 1867. Not teaching. Three children.

CLARA GERMAIN (Mrs. G. S. Potwin)......Contra Costa County.
  Present address, Concord, Contra Costa County.
    Taught ten years in Contra Costa and Alameda Counties. Then married and settled on a farm in Ygnacio Valley, where she resided at last report, April, 1883. Now a widow.

ANNA L. GRAY (Mrs. R. R. Owen) ....San Francisco.
  Present address, Alameda.
    Taught in San Francisco from September, 1867, to October, 1876. Taught in Alameda also. Married June 17, 1884.

MARY T. HART (Mrs. Joseph Austin) (deceased)...El Dorado Co.
    Did not teach. Was for many years musical critic of the *Argonaut*, under the *nom de plume* "**Betsy B.**" Died in San Francisco in 1888.

MARY G. HEYDENFELT (Mrs. Wm. J. Dutton)....San Francisco.
  Present address, corner of California and Devisadero Streets, San Francisco.
    Taught.

ELLA M. HARVEY (Mrs. W. B. Priddy) ....Alameda County.
    Taught in Oakland in the same school seven years, the last year as Principal. Married February 12, 1884. Two children. Her husband is a Methodist minister, and she has, therefore, no permanent address.

JAMES G. KENNEDY........................Santa Clara County.
  Present address, San Francisco.
    Taught in San José several years. Was City Superintendent of San José three terms. In 1885 he moved to San Francisco, where he taught in the city schools, and was afterwards School Inspector two years. Is now Principal of the Cogswell Polytechnic Institute.

CLOELIA M. LEWIS (Mrs. Lewis A. Sage).........San Francisco.
    Address in 1886, Congress Springs, Santa Clara County.
  Taught.

HATTIE B. LOCKE...............................San Francisco.
    No report.

LIZZIE A. NEWELL..............................Sonoma County.
    Taught.

NELLIE M. OWENS...............................San Francisco.
  Present address, 614 Sutter Street, San Francisco.
    Teaching in the Girls' High School. Has taught in San Francisco since July, 1869.

CATHERINE O'BRIEN.............................San Francisco.
  Present address, 319 Oak Street, San Francisco.
    Teaching in the John Swett Grammar School. Taught in San Francisco since September, 1867.

HOWELL POWELL..Sutter County.
    Attorney at law, Sansome Street, San Francisco. Married Miss Mary E. King, class of March, 1871. Three children.

ELLA A. ROBERTS (deceased)................El Dorado County.

FLORA C. SMITH (Mrs. Armstrong) ....Santa Clara County.
                 In 1886 was living in **Arizona**.
    Taught.

GRACE SMITH (Mrs. Preston).......................San Francisco.
        Address in 1885, 1922 Broderick Street, San Francisco.
    Taught in San Francisco **High School.**

JOHN C. SHIPLEY...................................Sonoma County.
        Present address, Healdsburg, Sonoma County.
    Taught constantly since graduation, principally in Sonoma and Mendocino Counties. Married July 16, 1871. Three children. At last report, **1887, was Principal of Healdsburg public schools.**

MRS. ADA E. WRIGHT ....San Francisco.
        Present address, 471 Haight Street, San Francisco.
    Teaching in Eighth Street Primary School. Has taught in San Francisco since February, 1869. Taught in Santa Clara County one year previous.

HARRIET L. WOOLL ....San Francisco.
        Present address, 719 Polk Street, San Francisco.
    Teaching in Spring Valley Primary School. Has taught in San Francisco since September, 1867.

EIGHTH CLASS—NOVEMBER, 1867.

ROXA S. COCKS ....San Francisco.
    At last report was married (name unknown), and living in Washington Territory.

ROSCOE L. EAMES................................Santa Cruz County.
        Present address, 46 O'Farrell Street, San Francisco.
    Taught for two years after graduation in Clayton, Contra Costa County. Engaged **in** bookkeeping and railroading **in** Los Angeles County six years; in bookkeeping **in Oakland four** years; since then has been a stenographer in San Francisco. **Is now Principal of** the Short-Hand Department of Barnard's Business **College and a short-hand** reporter. Is the author of a "Text-Book of Light-Line Short-Hand." Married Christmas, 1874, to Ninetta Wiley.

MAGGIE HOWARD ....San Francisco.
    No report. Married (name unknown).

BYRON E. HUNT ....Solano County.
    Present address, Los Angeles.
  Taught in San Mateo County three years; Alameda County, six months; Sierra County, one year; Placer County, six months; Napa County, five and one half years; Marysville High School, two years. Left teaching in 1881, to practice law. Was a lawyer in Napa City several years. Also filled the office of Justice of the Peace and Police Judge. Is now General Agent for Southern California of the Pacific Endowment League. Married June 1, 1873. Three children.

MARTHA A. LAWLESS............................San Francisco.
  No report. Married (name unknown), and living in San Rafael.

C. D. McNAUGHTON (deceased)................El Dorado County.

MARY E. PERKINS (Mrs. W. A. Mathews) ....Colusa County.
    Present address, Selma, Fresno County.
  Taught. One son.

MARY E. SAVAGE (MRS. McKown)...............San Francisco.
    Present address, 1316 Steiner Street, San Francisco.
  Has taught in San Francisco since March, 1868; teaching in Lincoln Grammar School. Is a widow.

MARION H. SEARS.............................San Francisco.
  No report.

HENRIETTA S. SLATER (Mrs. John A. McIntire)..Sacramento Co.
    Present address, Sacramento.
  Took further work and received a second diploma with Class of May, 1868. Taught one year in San José Institute. Entered High School in Sacramento, and graduated in 1872. Taught two years in public schools of Sacramento. Married in June, 1874. Two children. Not teaching.

NINTH CLASS—MAY, 1868.

TRUMAN P. ASHBROOK (deceased)...............Napa County.
  Taught successfully in Placer, Trinity, and Butte Counties, about ten years. In the fall of 1878 he took the school at Susanville, Lassen County. On the twenty-seventh of December, 1878, while skating alone on Honey Lake, he fell into an air hole and was drowned. Brother's address, M. V. Ashbrook, attorney at law, Fresno City.

ELLA E. BACHELDER (MRS. O. C. Stonder).......San Francisco.
    Present address, San Pablo, Contra Costa County.
  Has not taught. Married in 1872 to Dr. David Goodale, since deceased, and in 1885 to O. C. Stonder. Four children.

LIZZIE C. BETANCUE ....Alameda County.
    Present address, 487 Twenty-sixth Street, Oakland.
    At last report, April, 1883, was teaching in Oakland, where she had taught constantly since graduation, with the exception of a vacation of one and one half years.

LUCY BONNELL (Mrs. Corcoran)....................San Francisco.
    No report.

JULIA B. BROWN (Mrs. Arthur J. Foster)____ El Dorado County.
    Present address, 317 Seventeenth Street, San Francisco.
    Taught twelve years in San Francisco.

ANNIE CATHCART (Mrs. Theller)..................San Francisco.
    Address in 1886, San Francisco.

LIZZIE COPE..San Francisco.
    Present address, Danville, Contra Costa County.
    Taught three months.

LILLIAN A. CRITTENDEN..........................San Francisco.
    No report.

FRANCES A. DAY ....Calaveras County.
    Address in 1886, Mokelumne Hill, Calaveras County.
    Taught sixteen years.

SARAH FIELD (Mrs. Daniel Swett)..........Santa Cruz County.
    Residence, Alameda; mail address, No. 6 Montgomery Avenue, San Francisco.
    Taught in San Francisco seven years. Married September 2, 1875. Not taught since. Two children.

ANNA HALL (Mrs. O. I. Bradley)................San Francisco.
    Address in 1884, Santa Cruz.
    Not taught.

SALLIE L. HALL (Mrs. De Witt Vestal).....Santa Clara County.
    Address in 1886, San José.

JOSIAH S. HAMMOND......................San Joaquin County.
    Present address, Butte City, Montana.
    Taught in San Joaquin County, four years; Yolo County, one year; State of Nevada, eleven months; County Superintendent of Lander County, Nevada, one term. Left teaching in November, 1873, to practice medicine. Now a practicing physician in Butte City. Married December 25, 1867. Six children.

JULIA HENEY (Mrs. John Haynes) ....San Francisco.
    Address in 1886, Tucson, Arizona. Taught in San Francisco from August, 1870, to January, 1880.

FANNIE R. JACKS..Napa County.
    No report.

AMELIA JOICE (Mrs. John E. Cosgriff), (deceased).San Francisco.
    Taught in San Francisco. Married June 26, 1872. Had three children; two now living. Died January 10, 1879.

EDWARD W. JONES..Colusa County.
    At last report, April, 1883, was a merchant in Colusa. Had not taught.

ANNA LA GRANGE (Mrs. C. S. Coleman)........Alameda County.
    Present address, San Leandro, Alameda County.
    Taught two years. Not teaching.

BEATRICE M. LAWREY (Mrs. B. L. Hollenbeck)..Santa Clara Co.
    Present address, Pacific Grove, Monterey County.
    Taught in San José public schools from July, 1868, to November, 1883, except twelve months' leave of absence; in Preparatory Class, State Normal School, from November, 1883, to June, 1887. Not teaching. Married January 31, 1871. Two children.

SUSIE S. LAWTON ....San Francisco.
    No report.

ANNIE H. LEWIS (Mrs. Troy Shelley)..............San Francisco.
    Missionary in Japan.

MARY LITTLE (Mrs. W. E. Price)....................San Francisco.
    Present address, 537 Haight Street, San Francisco.
    Taught in San Francisco from October, 1868, to September, 1888.

WILLIAM N. MAGOON......................................Sonoma County.
    Present address, Stony Point.
    Taught in Sonoma County, six years; and one term each in Colusa, Mendocino, Yuba, Contra Costa, and Monterey Counties—about ten years in all. Since then has engaged in blacksmithing and carriage making. Married April 30, 1884.

AMELIA L. MAISON (Mrs. Thos. Dorland) ..Contra Costa County.
    Address in 1886, San Francisco.

LIZZIE McCOLLAM (Mrs. Geo. Tasheira) ....San Francisco.
    Present address, Sausalito, Marin County.
    Taught two years. Not teaching.

LOTTIE McKEAN (Mrs. A. T. Winn)..............San Francisco.
    Present address, 230 Herman Street, San Francisco.
    Taught in San Francisco from March, 1869, to September, 1880.

HELEN McPHERSON (deceased) ....San Francisco.

SUMNER F. PAINE ....Sutter County.
        Present address, **Meridian, Sutter County.**
    Engaged in farming.

ANNA M. PALMER (**Mrs. C. C. Weisenburger**)....Nevada County.
        Present address, Nevada City.
    Taught about five years in Nevada County. Left school teaching in 1873 to teach music. **Married August 5, 1875.**

DAVID POWELL.................................Sutter County.
        Present address, Marysville, Yuba County.
    Taught in Sutter County, five months; Contra Costa County, twelve months. Left teaching in 1870, to study medicine. Now a practicing physician and surgeon.

TROY SHELLEY..................................Sutter County.
    Missionary in Japan.

JOHN A. SMITH.................................Sonoma County.
        Present address, Point Arena, Mendocino County.
    Has taught most of the time since graduation. Married. Three children.

MARY SMITH...................................San Francisco.
    Taught in San Francisco from August, 1869, to April, 1881.

ELIZABETH STAPLES (**Mrs. Emlin Painter**), (deceased) .....
    ....San Francisco.

MARION STOKUM ....San Francisco.
    No report.

MARY E. STONE (**Mrs. J. M. Caldwell**)...........San **Francisco.**
        Present address, 10 Mission Avenue, San **Francisco.**
    Teaching in Bernal Heights School. Taught in San Francisco since June, 1868.

ADDIE TREADWAY (**Mrs. C. D. Ambrose**), (deceased)...Napa Co.
    Taught three terms in Santa Clara County. Married February 2, 1870. Died November 7, 1879. Daughter's address, Mary L. Ambrose, Ukiah City.

MARY WARD ....Calaveras County.
    Taught in San Francisco from June, 1869, to May, 1875.

TENTH CLASS—MAY, 1869.

MARY BELL ....San Francisco.
    No report.

ANNIE BRYANT (**Mrs. Anderson**) ....Sonoma County.
        Present address, 3044 Sixteenth Street, San Francisco.
    Teaching in **Hayes Valley Primary School.**

SAMUEL F. BUCKMAN_____New York.
    Present address, San Buenaventura.
Has filled the office of County Superintendent.

RUTH G. CAMPBELL _____ San Francisco.
    Present address, 1220 Jackson Street, San Francisco.
 Taught three months **in Napa** County and remainder of the time since graduation in public schools of San Francisco. Now teaching in the Broadway Grammar School.

JOHN M. CURRAGH_____Alameda County.
 No report.

MARIETTA J. GOULD (Mrs. Buzzo)_____Santa Clara County.
    Present address, San José.
 Taught **eleven years in the San José schools.** Not taught since 1884. **Married September 25, 1873. One child.** In 1872–73 was member of County Board of Santa Clara County.

ANNIE E. GROGAN _____El Dorado County.
 No report.

ANNIE M. HAYBURN (Mrs. Ward Brown) _____San Francisco.
    Present address, 342 Grove Street, San Francisco.
 Taught until July, 1882, in San Francisco. Not taught since. Married June 25, 1878. Three children.

ABSALOM T. JONES_____Sonoma County.
 No report.

LOUISA LACEY (Mrs. John Rolls) _____San Francisco.
    Present address, San Rafael.
 Taught four years in San Francisco. **Married** in 1875. Not taught since. Two children.

EMILY U. LINDBERG_____San Francisco.
    Present address, 116 Turk Street, San Francisco.
 Has taught in San Francisco since October, 1874. Teaching in the South Cosmopolitan Grammar School.

CLARA A. MACKIE (deceased) _____San Francisco

JENNIE S. MANN (Mrs. A. L. Mann)_____San Francisco.
    Present address, 2402 Mission Street, San Francisco.
 Principal of Shotwell Street Primary School. **Has taught in San Fran**cisco since October, 1874.

KATE F. MCCOLGAN_____San Francisco.
    Present address, 1809 Ellis Street, San Francisco.
 Teaching in the **South Cosmopolitan Grammar** School. Has taught in San Francisco since June, 1869.

CLARA B. MILLETT (Mrs. W. B. Rankin) .... San Mateo County.
　　Present address, Los Gatos, Santa Clara County.

CARRIE A. NORTHCUTT (Mrs. Angus Boggs) ...... Solano County.
　　No report.

OLIVE G. PARKER .... San Francisco.
　　No report.

ADELLA PEPPER .... Placer County.
　　No report.

MARY E. PRATT (Mrs. A. W. Tate) .... Alameda County.
　　Present address, Corralitos, Santa Cruz County.
　　Taught in Alameda County, three and one half years; Merced County, four years; Contra Costa County, five months. Married December 5, 1877. Two children. Not taught since marriage.

NELLIE ROBINETT (deceased) .... San Francisco.

MAGGIE E. SMITH (Mrs. J. T. McGeoghegan) ...... San Francisco
　　Present address, San José.
　　Taught before marriage.

ESTHER SOLOMON (Mrs. Haber), (deceased) ...... San Francisco.

MATTIE H. STEGMAN .... Mariposa County.
　　At last report was married (name unknown), and living at Pescadero.

AUGUSTA M. STOWE (Mrs. A. M. Crichton) .. Santa Clara County.
　　Present address, 29 San Augustine Street, San José.
　　Taught several years in San José.

MARY A. THOMAS (Mrs. Oscar Dunbar) .... San Francisco.
　　Present address, Astoria, Oregon.
　　Taught in San Francisco from February, 1872, to December, 1879. Taught in Modesto also. One child.

MAGGIE H. WATSON (Mrs. J. H. Currier) .... San Francisco.
　　Present address, 2012 Taylor Street, San Francisco.
　　Taught constantly since graduation in the public schools of San Francisco. Teaching in the Starr King Primary School. Married June 3, 1875

ALICE WEED .... San Francisco.
　　Present address, 1217 Leavenworth Street, San Francisco.
　　Taught six months in San Mateo County, and fourteen years in San Francisco. Teaching in Pacific Heights School.

ELLA L. WHITMORE (Mrs. Wm. Gregory)......Sonoma County.
Present address, Livermore, Alameda County.
Teaching near Livermore. Has taught in Alameda County seventeen years. Married December 24, 1885.

MARY A. WRIGHT (Mrs. Van Schaick) ......Monterey County.
Present address, Gilroy, Santa Clara County.
Taught in Monterey County, one term; in Gilroy, twelve years; now Principal of the Gilroy High School. Married June 6, 1872. One child.

ELEVENTH CLASS—MARCH, 1870.

CLARA A. ADAMS................................San Francisco.
Present address, 1910 Hyde Street, San Francisco.
Teaching in Greenwich Primary School. Has taught in San Francisco sixteen years.

ARMINTA E. ALLISON (Mrs. Wm. White) ....Santa Cruz County.
Present address, 304 Eighteenth Street, San Francisco.
Has substituted in the San Francisco schools at different times, but not taught regularly since graduation. Married April 25, 1870, to Wm. White, a teacher of many years experience. Has two children. Her daughter is a teacher in San Francisco.

BERTHA A. BICKNELL (Mrs. D. P. Fenton) ..Santa Clara County.
Present address, 3624 Sacramento Street, San Francisco.
Taught in Santa Clara County, two years; Solano County, two years; San Francisco, twelve years. Teaching in the Redding Primary School. Was employed as a type-writer two years.

SARAH J. BOYLE................................San Francisco.
Taught in San Francisco from June, 1870, to March, 1889. Not teaching.

MARY ALICE BURRILL (Mrs. N. G. Simonds)......San Francisco.
Present address, 5 Pickman Street, Salem, Massachusetts.
Taught one and one half years in San Francisco. Married September 11, 1873. One child.

JOANNA T. CASEY................................Shasta County.
No report.

LEONORA M. CAROTHERS (Mrs. Barry Baldwin), (deceased).
................................Contra Costa County.

ISABEL CARRUTHERS (Mrs. I. Woodland) ......San Francisco.
Present address, 5 Yerba Buena Street, San Francisco.
Teaching in the Garfield Primary School.

JAMES E. CLARK ....Washington Territory.
No report.

MARY A. COLBY (Mrs. Ramsdell)..............Nevada County.
   In 1887 was teaching in Pasadena. Taught in San Francisco from August, 1870, to July, 1882.

AUGUSTA R. EASTMAN........................San Francisco.
   Taught in San Francisco from January, 1872, to August, 1874.

ABBIE A. GARLAND..........................San Francisco.
   Present address, 215 Powell Street, San Francisco.
   Taught in San Mateo County a year. Has taught in San Francisco since October, 1874. Teaching in the South Cosmopolitan Primary School.

ANNIE A. GIBSON (Mrs. Frank Clayton)........Solano County.
   Present address, 163 Second Street, Portland, Oregon.
   Taught for some time in Solano County. Married May 23, 1872. Four children.

KATIE GREEN...............................San Francisco.
   Taught in San Francisco from August, 1870, to February, 1888.

MARY L. GREER (deceased)..................San Francisco.
   Taught in San Francisco seventeen years. Died May 11, 1888.

LOLETA GRAFFELMAN (Mrs. Winchester)........Alameda County.
   Resides in Oregon. Taught four years.

ANNIE E. HAAS (Mrs. Robert Broad)..........Alameda County.
   Present address, San Francisco.
   Taught one and one half years.

DEBORAH W. HARDMAN (Mrs. C. Ham)...........San Francisco.
   Present address, San Francisco.
   Taught two years.

MARY J. HENDERSON.........................Nevada County.
   Present address, San Francisco.
   Taught four months in Nevada County; seventeen years in San Francisco. Teaching in Noe and Temple Street School.

ALVIN J. HOWE.............................Solano County.
   Present address, Santa Ana, Orange County.
   Physician. Taught two years.

ADELLA MARVIN (Mrs. Clark)................Santa Clara County.
   Present address, St. Paul, Minnesota.

MARY MATTHEWS.............................San Francisco.
   Taught in San Francisco from November, 1871, to November, 1882.

ANNIE M. MCKEAN (Mrs. B. F. Rush)..........Santa Clara County.
   Present address, Suisun, Solano County.
   Taught one year in Santa Clara County. Not teaching. Married June 20, 1876. Four children.

ALBERTA S. MONTGOMERY (Mrs. Ecker) ....Santa Clara County.
Present address, San José.
Taught in San José for seven years after graduation. Married March 17, 1878, and removed to Ohio. One child. Lived in Ohio ten years and then returned to California. Now teaching in San José.

ISABELLA M. MURPHY (Mrs. Miller)............Solano County.
Present address, San Francisco.
Taught four years.

KATE R. O'LEARY..................................San Francisco.
Present address, 2116 Howard Street, San Francisco.
Teaching in the South Cosmopolitan Grammar School. Has taught in San Francisco since May, 1871.

ROSA RANDALL (Mrs. Weir)...................San Francisco.
Present address, Honolulu, H. I.
Taught one year in Contra Costa County before marriage. Three children.

GEORGIE A. STACKPOLE (Mrs. H. Belden).......San Francisco.
Present address, Oakland.

NELLIE A. SAVAGE (deceased)..................San Francisco.
Taught in San Francisco from February, 1872, to November, 1878.

SARAH I. SHUEY.................................Alameda County.
Present address, Lamanda Park, Los Angeles County.
Taught three and one half years in Alameda County after graduation. Took an academic course in the State University, followed by a medical course. Graduated with degree of M.D. in 1878. Has practiced medicine since. Now has charge of a sanitarium in the San Gabriel Valley.

ALICE R. SNOW (Mrs. Geo. Pardee), (deceased)...Santa Cruz Co.
Taught in Watsonville before marriage. Died in Watsonville in 1887. Two children, one living.

MAGGIE SPROTT................................San Francisco.
Present address, 4 Ford Street, San Francisco.
Teaching in Lincoln Evening School. Has taught in San Francisco since March, 1873.

HELEN M. STONE (deceased)...................Alameda County.
Taught eleven years. Died in June, 1882.

EMMA E. C. STINCEN...........................San Francisco.
Present address, 816 Chestnut Street, San Francisco.
Principal of Whittier Primary School. Has taught in San Francisco since September, 1870.

ANNA M. STOCKTON (Mrs. Custer)...........Sacramento County.
Living in Pennsylvania.

FANNIE A. SHERMAN (Mrs. Guppy)........Contra Costa County.
                Present address, Oakland.
   Taught five years.

HENRY I. TILLOTSON ....Solano County
            Present address, Michigan Bluff, Placer County.
   Taught in Alameda County, one and one half years; Contra Costa County, five years. Left the profession in 1875, to engage in a general merchandise business. Since 1886 has been engaged in gold mining.

EMMA TILLOTSON (deceased) ....Solano County.
   Taught one year. Died in 1871.

CYNTHIA M. TURNER (Mrs. P. W. Dooner)..Santa Clara County.
           Present address, 742 S. Fort Street, Los Angeles.
   Taught in Santa Clara County, three years; Calaveras County, five months; San Mateo County, four months. Not teaching. Married May 25, 1876. One child.

EMMET L. WEMPLE................................Sutter County.
           Present address, Antioch, Contra Costa County.
   Taught in Contra Costa County, two years; Sutter County, three months. Entered the Pacific Medical College, May, 1871, and graduated November, 1873. Practiced medicine in Nortonville, Contra Costa County, two years. Since April, 1876, has resided in Antioch and continued in his profession. Married April 15, 1874, to Miss Annie I. Gunn. Has three children. Was Superintendent of Schools in Contra Costa County from November, 1877, to January, 1879.

JESSIE E. WILSON (deceased) ....San Francisco.
   Died November 30, 1872. Her mother's address in 1883, was 13 Ridley Street, San Francisco.

MARIE WITHROW ....Santa Clara County.
           Present address, 925 Pine Street, San Francisco.
   Has devoted her time since graduation to teaching and studying music. Was superintendent of Music in the public schools of San Francisco County several years. Spent a number of years at Munich, Germany, perfecting her musical education. Now teaching music in the Boys' High School, and in the Polytechnic Institute. Has private pupils and classes also.

EDITH L. WETMORE (Mrs. Horswill) ......Contra Costa County.
            Present address, Clayton.
   Is now a widow. Has three children.

JENNIE YATES...................................Sonoma County.
   No report.

TWELFTH CLASS—MARCH, 1871.

N. Jane Bell (Mrs. Sykes)............San Francisco.
    Present address, 13 Dehon Street, San Francisco.
  Teaching in Sanchez Street Primary School. Has taught in San Francisco since August, 1872.

Julia I. Benjamin (Mrs. Owen Moran)............Solano County.
    Present address, Suisun, Solano County.
  Taught from July, 1871, to June, 1876, in Vallejo, Oakland, and San Francisco.

Celina R. Carrau (Mrs. Pechin)............San Francisco.
    Present address, 1778 Green Street, San Francisco.
  Principal of the Greenwich Street Primary School. Has taught in San Francisco since September, 1871.

Ellen A. Conmy (Mrs. John Gordon)............Shasta County.
    Present address, San José.
  Teaching in San José. Taught seventeen years.

Hattie G. Clark (Mrs. Wm. Faull)............Contra Costa County.
    Present address, 2023 Broadway, San Francisco.
  Taught four years in Amador and Contra Costa Counties. Not taught since marriage.

Mary A. Cottle (deceased)............Santa Clara County.
  Taught one year in Santa Clara County. Died soon after.

Mary I. Doyle............San Francisco.
  Taught in San Francisco from July, 1871, to August, 1885. Is married (name unknown), and lives in Mendocino City.

Annie A. Fletcher (Mrs. D. O. Kelley)............Nevada County.
    Present address, Fresno City.
  Taught in San Francisco two years. Married April, 1874. Not taught since. Eight children; seven living. Husband an Episcopal clergyman.

Emily F. Geer (Mrs. R. Cavin)............Sacramento County.
    Present address, Concord, Contra Costa County.

George H. Hardy............Sierra County.
    Present address, Independence, Inyo County.
  Taught three years in Inyo County. Was County Treasurer eight years. Now a clerk and bookkeeper. Married August 13, 1871. Four children.

Mary E. King (Mrs. H. A. Powell)............San Francisco.
    Present address, 921 Myrtle Street, Oakland.
  Taught in San Francisco three years. Not taught since marriage, May 1, 1876. Three children.

MATILDA M. E. MOORE ....San Francisco.
    Present address, 126 Collingwood Street, San Francisco.
    Teaching in Sanchez Street Primary School. Has taught in San Francisco since November, 1872.

LOUISE MAGUIRE (Mrs. John F. Hottel) ....Napa County.
    Present address, Napa City.
    Taught nine years in Napa County, four years of that time in Napa City. Married March 1, 1881. Not taught since. One child.

MALVINA C. PELTON (Mrs. N. I. Wilson)..........San Francisco.
    Present address, 838 Guerrero Street, San Francisco.
    Taught one year in public schools of San Francisco and four years in Zeitska Institute. Married in 1877. Not taught since. Is now a widow. Three children.

SUSANNA R. PLANK (Mrs. Jas. M. Sharp) ....San Francisco.
    Present address, Saticoy, Ventura County.
    Taught in Sonoma County for four years; Ventura County, five months. Not teaching. Married August 6, 1874. Six children.

ELLA L. RUSSELL (Mrs. Clyne)...................San Francisco.
    Present address, Oakland.
    Taught.

JOHN C. RUDDOCK ....Tuolumne County.
    Permanent address, Ukiah, Mendocino County.
    Taught in Sacramento County, six months; Mendocino County, eleven years. Was County Superintendent of Mendocino County three terms. Married February 4, 1880, to Kate Siddons, Class of March, 1877. Two children, one living. His wife died July 24, 1884. Is now Chief Clerk in the office of the Surveyor-General, San Francisco.

ELLA I. SHERMAN (Mrs. George Stone).....Contra Costa County.
    Present address, 169 Tenth Street, Oakland.
    Taught one year in Calaveras County, one year in Napa County, one year in Marin County, four months in Contra Costa County, four months in Oakland. Married July 12, 1875. Not taught since. Three children.

JAMES M. SHARP ....Alameda County.
    Present address, Saticoy, Ventura County.
    Taught in Ventura County three years. Now engaged in farming. Married August 6, 1874, to Susanna R. Plank, of same class. Six children.

MARCUS T. SICKAL ....San Francisco.
    Present address, Benicia, Contra Costa County.
    Taught in Solano County, nine and one half years; Nevada County, one year; Los Angeles, five months. Not taught since 1881 on account of ill health, but intends to teach again. Superintendent of Overfelt Cattle Company, Oregon. Traveling. Married July 3, 1878. Two children.

MARY A. TYUS (Mrs. Williams)............Santa Cruz County.
    Present address, Los Angeles.

THIRTEENTH CLASS—MARCH, 1872.

NELLIE ASHURST ....Colusa County.
  Taught in Colusa County four years; was then married and went to Omaha. Further history unknown. Has been reported **deceased**.

CHARLES R. BEAL..Calaveras County.
  Present address, San Francisco.
  Taught fourteen years in Calaveras County, six years of this time as Principal of San Andreas School. Was Superintendent of Schools in that county eight years. **Edited** a paper at San Andreas ten years. **Not taught** since 1885. Is now **Inspector of** Customs, San Francisco.

BESSIE DIXON..Marin County.
  Present address, 1414 Jackson Street, San Francisco.
  Taught constantly since graduation, **since 1875 in San Francisco.** Teaching in Valencia **Grammar** School.

PHOEBE A. FRISBIE (Mrs. E. L. Bailey)..........Solano County.
  Taught in Vallejo, three years; private school, one year; Monterey County, three months. Not taught since marriage. Married in 1877. In 1885 was living in Battle Mountain, Nevada.

JULIA A. FISK (Mrs. Parker)..................Santa Clara County.
  In 1887 was living in Los Angeles. Not teaching. One child. Has taught.

GEORGE C. HIXON............................Santa Clara County.
  Present address, Santa Barbara.
  Taught in Butte, Monterey, Santa Clara, and Tulare Counties, six years in all. Farming.

EMILY H. HILTON............................Alameda County.
  Present address, 572 Tenth Street, Oakland.
  Taught constantly since graduation, with the exception of one and one half years spent in Europe. Teaching in Oakland.

THOS. E. KENNEDY..........................Santa Clara County
  Present address, 1319½ Broadway, San Francisco.
  Taught in San José several years, to 1885. Practiced law for some time. Now head Inspector of Schools in San Francisco.

CHARLES E. MARKHAM........................Solano County.
  Present address, Oakland, care of Joaquin Miller.
  Taught in San Luis Obispo County, six months; Christian College, Sonoma County, two years; El Dorado County, four years; other places, one and one half years. Was County Superintendent of El Dorado County seven years. Has spent much time in literary work. Has written poems and sketches for prominent magazines, and delivered lectures upon subjects connected with English and American literature. Married. No children. Expects to settle on a fruit farm near Oakland soon.

AUGUSTA M. PHELPS............................Yolo County.
    Present address, **South Hero, Grand Isle County, Vermont.**
    Taught in Contra Costa County, one year; Solano County, five months; Plumas County, three months, Yolo County, three years; Vermont, three months. Was Town Superintendent of Schools in South Hero for a time. Not teaching at present on account of household duties.

MARTHA J. PECKHAM (Mrs. H. F. Pray)____Santa Clara County.
    Present address, Booneville, Mendocino County.
    Taught in Santa Clara County, two years; Napa County, three years; Solano County, nine years; Mendocino County, three years. Teaching. Married March 2, 1879. One child, deceased. Is preparing a work entitled "Lectures to Young Teachers."

CHATTIE K. RIXON (Mrs. Chauncey Gaines) .....San Francisco.
    Present address, Berkeley, Alameda County.
    Taught seven years. Not teaching.

VIRGINIA P. STEPHENS (Mrs. Zumwalt).....Santa Clara County
    Present address, Los Angeles.
    Taught several years in Southern California, then married V. M. P. Zumwalt, of Visalia. Is now a widow, with one child, and is residing in Los Angeles.

EULALIA A. TERRY (Mrs. E. A. Wilson)...._San Joaquin County.
    Present address, 1309 New Broadway Street, Oakland.
    Taught in Sacramento County, one and one half years; in San Francisco, ten years. Is now Principal of the Temescal School, which position she has held for the past four years.

ETTA M. WAGENSELLER (Mrs. John Leininger), (deceased)__
....Sonoma County.
    Taught in Sonoma, Mendocino, Tehama, and Butte Counties. Married September 23, 1875, and resided at Nord, Butte County, where she was active in church and Sunday School work. Her health failed slowly for two years, and in May, 1888, hoping to regain it, she went to Saratoga Springs. There she died June 13, 1888. She was buried at Ukiah, Mendocino County. She left two children.

ALMA WALLACE ....Napa County.
    Present address, Los Angeles.
    Taught in Napa County three years. Since then has taught in Los Angeles.

FANNIE WIGNALL (Mrs. Simon Clasey).....Santa Clara County.
    Present address, Washburn, Blackhawk County, Iowa.
    Taught in San Luis Obispo County, five months; Santa Clara County, one year. Left teaching because of ill health. Married July 18, 1878. Two children.

FOURTEENTH CLASS—MARCH, 1873.

LOUIS BRUCH..................................Santa Clara County.
    Present address, San José.
    Has taught constantly since graduation. Teaching near San José.

JOSEPHINE CAHILL (Mrs. G. E. McStay)....San Joaquin County.
    In 1883 was living in Stockton.

ANNA CARROLL (Mrs. Hawley)..................Placer County.
    Taught in Placer County, five months; San Diego, one year; Santa Barbara County, three years. In 1886 was teaching at Carpenteria. Married in October, 1874. Two children.

LEMUEL J. CHIPMAN..........................Santa Clara County
    Present address, San José.
    Taught in Yuba County, three months; Santa Clara County, three years, the last two as Principal of Schools in San José. Was City Superintendent of San José schools two years. For the past eleven years he has held the office of County Superintendent of Santa Clara County.

WILLIAM F. F. FOSS..............................Yuba County.
    Present address, San José.
    Taught in Yuba County, three years; Santa Clara County, seven years. Now real estate and insurance agent in San José.

HENRY GOODCELL........................San Bernardino County.
    Present address, San Bernardino.
    Taught two years. Was County Superintendent one term. Practicing law. Married Minnie A. Bennett, Class of March, 1874, who died in November, 1886. Three children.

DORA B. HARRIS (Mrs. Rogers)..................San Francisco.
    Present address, Bakersfield, Kern County.
    Taught four years in Vallejo; six years in Kern County. Teaching. Married December 27, 1877 One child.

MARY E. HENDRIX (Mrs. Thompson)......Santa Clara County
    Present address, Cornelius, Washington County, Oregon.
    Taught in Placer County, two years; Monterey County, three years; San Luis Obispo County, two years; Oregon, three years. Teaching. Married June 14, 1874. Husband died in 1880. Three children.

LELLA KRATZER (Mrs. Bacher)............Santa Clara County.
    Present address, Gilroy.
    Taught in Placer County, three months; Plumas County, two years; San Benito County, three years; Santa Clara County, six years. Teaching in Gilroy. Married January 14, 1877. Two children.

Luella Kelsoe (Mrs. Samuel Hirst) .... Sonoma County.
    Present address, Santa Rosa.
    Has taught in Sonoma and Lake Counties constantly since graduation, with the exception of four years. Married July 15, 1886. Not teaching at present, but has not left the profession.

Mary Merritt (Mrs. J. Henry) .... Santa Clara County.
    Present address, St. Cloud House, Sutter Street, San Francisco.
    Taught before marriage. Has six children.

Isabel Merritt (Mrs. Campbell) .... Santa Clara County.
    Present address, Tulare.
    Taught in Napa County, three months; Plumas County, one month; Monterey County, four months; Santa Clara County, four months; Merced County, three months; San Francisco, five years; Tulare County, two years. Teaching. Married June 10, 1881. Three children.

Ella H. Murdock (Mrs. Burnett) .... Santa Clara County
    Present address, Los Angeles.
    Taught in Santa Clara County six years. Has one child.

Julia F. Martin (Mrs. Hornsback) .... Santa Clara County.
    Present address, Los Angeles.
    Taught several years in Gilroy. Teaching in Los Angeles. One child.

Lizzie Roberts (deceased) .... Santa Clara County.
    Taught for a short time.

Delia R. Snow .... Washington Territory.
    Present address, Salt Lake City, Utah Territory.
    Taught in El Dorado County, three months; Placer County, four months; Plumas County, eight months. In 1874 went to Utah, to take a position in a mission school at Salt Lake, in which she taught six months. Then taught in a mission school in southern Utah two and one half years. Not teaching. Left the work partly on account of health and partly because of home duties.

Nellie M. Starr (Mrs. A. J. Hanson) ..... Santa Clara County.
    In 1883 was living in Sacramento.
    Taught before marriage.

Olivia L. Taylor .... San Francisco.
    Present address, 1604 Mission Street, San Francisco.
    Taught in Sacramento County, three months; State of Nevada, over nine years. Not teaching.

Etta M. Tilton .... San Mateo County.
    Present address, San Mateo.
    Taught constantly since graduation; for the past nine years in San Mateo.

AUGUSTA S. WITHINGTON (Mrs. W. H. S. Welch). Amador County.
Present address, 215 South Hill Street, Los Angeles.
Taught in Merced County, one year; Contra Costa County, one year; Amador County, thirteen years. Not teaching. Married October 24, 1883.

FIFTEENTH CLASS—MARCH, 1874.

CECILIA M. AULD .... Santa Clara County.
Present address, Grand View Hotel, Los Angeles.
Taught fourteen years. Teaching in Los Angeles.

MINNIE A. BENNETT (Mrs. Henry Goodcell), (deceased) .... El Dorado County.
Mrs. Goodcell taught very successfully for about eight years. Was teaching what she intended as her last term when she was taken ill with fever. She died in November, 1886, after a month's illness. Her husband was a member of the Class of March, 1873. Three children.

MARY E. D. BLACKSTAFF (Mrs. John McCarthy) ....
Present address, 2213 Polk Street, San Francisco.
Taught in Marin County two years. Not teaching. Married September 16, 1877.

MARY BIRD .... Santa Clara County.
Present address, San José.
Taught three years in Los Angeles; for past ten years as Principal of the Willow Glen School, Santa Clara County.

EDWARD R. BROOKS .... Contra Costa County.
No report.

ELLA W. CARSWELL (Mrs. Wm. Reynolds) .... San Francisco.
Present address, San Francisco.

LIZZIE CORY (Mrs. H. C. LEDYARD) .... Santa Clara County.
Present address, San José.
Taught in San José three years, to 1878. Married in 1879. Not taught since. Two children. Resided in Constantinople, Turkey, for several years. Has lately returned to California.

ALICE A. CRUMRY .... El Dorado County.
No report.

FRANCES M. DAY (deceased) .... San Joaquin County.
Taught five and one half years in San Joaquin County and five months in Calaveras County. Married December 16, 1880. One child. Date of death not reported. Father's address, T. B. Day, Stockton.

FLORENCE GRIGSBY (Mrs. E. C. Singletary)..........Wisconsin.
    Present address, San José.
  Taught two and one half years in Training Department of the Normal School at San José. Married in 1876. Not taught since marriage.

PACIFIC GUILD (Mrs. N. S. Nichols).......Santa Cruz County.
    Present address, Santa Cruz.
  Taught three months in Santa Cruz County. Married November 19, 1874. Not taught since. Two children.

HULDA A. HAMMOND......................Santa Clara County.
    Present address, 777 S. Second Street, San José.
  Taught in Monterey, three years; Dixon, three years; San José, five years. Teaching in San José. Work suspended two years on account of ill health.

S. ESTELLE HAMMOND (Mrs. Greathead)....Santa Clara County.
    Present address, 777 S. Second Street, San José
  Taught in public schools of Santa Clara and San José seven years. Married in 1877. One child. Work suspended after marriage for six years. Left the profession in 1887 for other business. Now engaged in stenography and type-writing. Was for a time an editor of a children's magazine.

CARRIE M. HENN (Mrs. W. J. Landers)....Santa Clara County.
    Present address, San Leandro.
  Taught two years in San José. Married in 1875. Three children.

ELLA A. JACKSON (Mrs. Henry Fisher)............Yolo County.
    Present address, Woodland.
  Taught one year. Married in 1876. Not taught since.

W. JEROME JEWELL (deceased)...................Solano County.
  Went to New York State in 1875, where he taught eleven years. On account of failing health, returned to California in 1886. After a year's rest, began teaching in Pomona, Los Angeles County. Had taught six weeks when he was taken ill with typhoid fever. Died December 4, 1887. Two children; one living. His widow and surviving child reside at Pomona. Mr. Jewell was an earnest Christian man and a teacher of more than ordinary ability.

ISABELLE JOHNSON (Mrs. Curtis Johnson)...Santa Clara County.
    Present address, Rohnerville, Humboldt County.
  Taught in Sonoma and Humboldt Counties. Married in 1878. One child. Not teaching.

SAMUEL E. JOHNSON ....Sutter County.
  No report.

ARIADNE G. KETCHAM (Mrs. L. L. Nattinger)..Humboldt County.
    Present address, San José.
  Taught in El Dorado County, twelve months; Santa Clara County, six years. Not taught since November, 1884. Married February 2, 1879. One child.

SALLIE E. KEEFER (Mrs. John Wade)........El Dorado County.
Present address, 830 Myrtle Street, Oakland.
Taught in El Dorado County, three years; Plumas County, one year; Yuba County, one year; Oakland, one term; Arizona, one year. Married October, 1876. Two children. **Not teaching.**

SUSIE E. KNEEDLER (Mrs. A. P. Logan) ....Santa Clara County.
Present address, San José.
Taught in Solano County, three months; Santa Clara County, three months. Married March 4, 1875. Not taught since. One child.

EDITH J. MARTIN...................................San Bernardino.
Present address, San Bernardino.
Has been teaching in San Bernardino County since graduation.

EMMELINE R. MEAD (Mrs. Leslie A. Jordan).....San Francisco.
Present address, San Diego.
Taught one year in Contra Costa County. Married June 17, 1875. Not taught since. Five children.

CHAS. N. MILLER....................................Santa Clara County.
Present address, corner Thirteenth and Howard Streets, San Francisco. Physician.

MRS. AMANDA MILLER................................Santa Clara County.
Present address, corner Thirteenth and Howard Streets, San Francisco.

MRS. MARIA E. MUMFORD.............................Sacramento County.
Present address, 922 Ninth Street, Sacramento.
Is Principal of a public school in Sacramento. Has taught continuously since graduation.

MARIA E. MURDOCH..................................Santa Clara County.
Present address, Los Angeles.
Taught continuously since graduation. Teaching in Los Angeles.

ANNIE L. MURPHY (deceased).......................Alameda County.
Taught one year.

MAGGIE O'ROURKE...................................San Francisco.
Taught in San Francisco from October, 1876, until August, 1887.

MARY A. TAYLOR (deceased).........................Santa Clara County.
Taught eleven years in Mountain View, Santa Clara County. Was obliged to suspend work in December, 1885, on account of failing health. Died at Mountain View January 16, 1888.

WILLIAM A. WASH...................................Missouri.
Present address, Dallas, Oregon.
Taught in Santa Clara County, five months; Stanislaus County, ten months; Tulare County, three years; Butte County, one year; Washing-

ton Territory, two years; Oregon, one year. Edited a paper at Goldendale, W. T., five years—1881-86. Now editing " Polk County Itemizer," at Dallas. Published a book concerning the late war entitled "Camp, Field, and Prison Life." Married December 24, 1884, to Helen McPheeters. One child.

JULIA M. WHITING (Mrs. E. J. Doering) ....Santa Clara County.
Not taught since graduation. At last report, 1883, was living in Chicago, Illinois. Address, 2330 Indana Avenue.

N. ZORAIDE WOODWARD............................Merced County.
Present address, Merced.
Taught in Alameda County and Merced County constantly since graduation. Teaching in Merced.

SIXTEENTH CLASS—MARCH, 1875.

EMMOGENE A. BARNES (Mrs. Rufus Fiske)..Santa Clara County.
Present address, San Miguel, San Luis Obispo County.
Taught in Santa Clara County, four years; in Marin County, one year. Married May 8, 1879. One child.

HENRY BATEMAN ....Napa County.
Present address, Woodland, Yolo County.
Farmer.

EMMA S. BUCKLEY ....Santa Clara County.
Present address, 65 N. Eighth Street, San José.
Taught continuously since graduation; for the past twelve years in San José.

MINNIE CLARA BURT ....Amador County.
Present address, San José.
Taught continuously since graduation. Teaching in Hester School, San José.

MARY E. CARR (Mrs. J. T. Apperson) ....Solano County.
Present address, Red Bluff, Tehama County.
Taught six years.

CHARLOTTE K. CLARK ....San Francisco.
Present address, 737 Howard Street, San Francisco.
Taught in Napa County, one year; San Francisco, ten years. Teaching in Mission Grammar School.

MARIE COLE..Napa County.
Present address, Haywards, Alameda County.
Taught seven years. Teaching. Graduated from the State University in 1879.

ANNA B. COWIE (Mrs. Denniston)............Tuolumne County.
Present address, 1224 Twenty-first Street, San Francisco.
Taught one year.

ABBIE A. DAVIES **(Mrs.** Hayford)............Santa Clara County.
  Present address, Colfax, Placer County
  Taught in **Contra** Costa and Placer Counties twelve and one half months. Married **October 19,** 1876.

BELLE J. FAGG (Mrs. F. H. Fowler) ....Yuba County.
  Present address, Lincoln, Placer County.
  Taught in Napa County, six and one half months; Yuba County, seven months; San Diego County, five months; Sierra County, **twelve months;** Placer County, three years. At last report, June, 1887, **was teaching at** Bolinas, Marin **County.** Married January 13, 1884. **One child.**

M. FANNIE FARMER **(Mrs. Geo. Bennett).......**Sonoma County.
  Present address, 730 Shotwell Street, San Francisco.

JULIA B. FARNSWORTH ....Santa Clara County.
  Living near San José.
  Not taught.

CHARLES E. FARNHAM ....San Joaquin County.
  Present address, 672 Mission Street, San Francisco.
  Taught one and one half years. **Left teaching to** study medicine. Now practicing medicine and surgery in **San Francisco.** Professor in Cooper Medical College.

HARRIET N. GILMOR (Mrs. W. E. Deering)........Napa County.
  Present address, St. John, Colusa County.
  Taught six years before marriage. Not taught since.

NATHAN C. HANSCOM_____.....San Joaquin County.
  Present address, San Andreas, Calaveras County.
  Taught in San Joaquin County, six months; Stanislaus County, four years; Washington Territory, six months; **Calaveras** County, four years. **Teaching in San Andreas.** For three years was traveling correspondent and editor of newspapers. Married January 24, 1883. One child.

JULIA L. HAUCK.........................Sacramento County.
  Present address, Dresden, Germany.
  Taught in San Benito County, one and **one** half years; San José, five years; Oakland, five **years;** Germany, two years. Teaching in a private school in Dresden.

ALICE M. HEATH.....................Los Angeles County.
  Teaching a private school in Los Angeles County.

DAVID F. HENNING ....Santa Clara County.
  Address, unknown.
  Taught several years in Santa Clara County.

MINNIE B. HOLLENBECK **(deceased)** ....Santa Clara County.
  History unknown.

MILLIE S. HOWARD_____Contra Costa County.
    Present address, Danville, Contra Costa County.
  Taught in Contra Costa County, fourteen months; Plumas County, one month. Not taught since November, 1877, on account of home duties.

ROSINA INTERMILLE (Mrs. Morris Smith)_____Illinois.
    Present address, Susanville, Lassen County.
  Taught in Plumas County, one year; Butte County, six months; Lassen County, one year; Modoc County, one year. Teaching in Modoc County. Married October 22, 1875. Three children.

MILLIE R. JONES (Mrs. G. Ivancovich)_____Marin County.
    Present address, Petaluma, Sonoma County.
  Taught two and one half years before marriage. Not taught since. Eight children; five living.

MARY A. C. LEAHY_____Santa Clara County.
    Present address, San José.
  At last report, May, 1883, was teaching near Watsonville.

MARY LEWIS (Mrs. Bronson)_____Santa Clara County.
    Present address, 1235 Park Avenue, Alameda.
  Taught in Contra Costa County, one year; Santa Clara County, two years. Not taught since June, 1878. Married April 21, 1878. Four children.

DAVID F. LITTLE (deceased) _____Monterey County.
  Taught three years in Monterey. Gave up teaching because of ill health. Died at his home, in Nova Scotia, July, 1884. He did some literary work, mostly political.

KATE MARTIN (Mrs. Lewis Bozeman) _____Santa Clara County.
  In 1886 was living in Montana.

ISABEL MAY (Mrs. W. H. Church)_____Alameda County.
    Present address, 920 Filbert Street, Oakland.
  Taught six years.

MARY A. McDONNELL (Mrs. J. W. Davis)_____State of Nevada.
    Present address, Banning, San Bernardino County.
  Taught six years in Gold Hill, Nevada. Married August 1, 1881. Not taught since. Two children; one living. Husband died January 31, 1889.

SABIA E. MOREY _____San Joaquin County.
    Present address, 1028½ Folsom Street, San Francisco.
  Taught in San Mateo County, five months; Santa Clara County, three months; Marin County, two years; San Francisco, eight years. Teaching in Tehama Primary School.

ROSE E. MORGAN _____Tuolumne County.
    Present address, 1254 Howard Street, San Francisco.
  Taught in Merced County, two months; Tuolumne County, three years; Mendocino County, one month; San Francisco, ten years. Teaching in Peabody Primary School, San Francisco. Held office of County Superintendent in Tuolumne County two years.

ANNIE J. NEARY...... ....Sacramento County.
    Taught constantly since graduation, with exception of one year. Teaching in Sacramento.

WILLIAM PASCOE......................Santa Clara County.
    Present address, College Park.
    Taught in Sonoma County, four months; Santa Clara County, four months; Shasta County, three years; Modoc County, one year; Contra Costa County, one year; Alameda County, four months; Humboldt County, two years. Work suspended four years for other business. Is now in the Auditing Department of Wells & Fargo Express Co., San Francisco. Married July 20, 1880, to Jessica G. Allen, Class of March, 1877.

ELLIS J. ROOT...........................Tuolumne County.
    Present address, Fresno City.
    Taught six years. Since that time has been engaged in mercantile business. Married.

LIZZIE P. SARGENT (Mrs. Lizzie P. Wilson) ....Amador County.
    Present address, San José.
    Taught in Amador County, one year; Oakland, five years; seven years in Normal School, San José. Is now Principal of the Training Department. Married August 2, 1888.

EMMA SCHENCK (Mrs. Fred. Grimes) ....San Francisco.
    Present address, 202 Sixteenth Street, San Francisco.
    Taught in Marin County, two years. Not taught since April, 1877. Married December 25, 1876. Three children.

JAMES W. SHIRLEY (deceased) ....Lake County.
    Was County Superintendent of Lake County in 1878. Died at Lakeport.

ADELIA A. STOCKTON (Mrs. R. B. Stockton) .Santa Clara County.
    Present address, Madera, Fresno County.
    Taught one term in San Luis Obispo County, and one term in San Benito County. Two children.

EMMA M. TOY (Mrs. L. J. Chipman)............San Francisco.
    Present address, San José.
    Taught one year in San José. Married December 7, 1876. Not taught since. One child.

BELLE J. TURNER (deceased) ....Santa Clara County.
    Taught five years. Died in 1880.

FLORENCE M. WATKINS (Mrs. Andrew P. Hill) .Santa Clara County.
    Present address, San José.
    Taught eight years. Not teaching. Two children.

ALICE M. WELLS (Mrs. A. B. Nye) ....Solano County.
    Present address, Oakland, Cal., care "Inquirer."
    Taught nine years in Solano County; one year in Alameda County. Married December, 1886. Not taught since.

ANNIE A. WIBLE..Merced County.
    Present address, Crescent City, Del Norte County.
    Taught in Contra Costa County, one year; Monterey County, six years; San Mateo County, one year; Humboldt County, four years. Not teaching, but expects to resume work soon.

JULIA F. WIBLE (Mrs. Bugbey)...............Tuolumne County.
    Present address, Sacramento.
    Taught until marriage, December, 1879.

MARY E. WILSON (Mrs. T. C. George).......Santa Clara County.
    Present address, San José.
    Taught in public schools of Santa Clara County, one year; in Normal School, San José, twelve years; was Principal of the Training Department six years. Married June 7, 1888. Not teaching.

WILLIAM R. WILSON.......................Santa Clara County.
    Address in 1886, Soquel, Santa Cruz County.
    Had taught nine years.

SEVENTEENTH CLASS—MARCH, 1876.

TIDIE AYRES (deceased)....................San Mateo County.
    Taught two and one half years in Redwood City. Died in October, 1879.

DOLLIE C. BABCOCK (Mrs. Albert Maxson)...Santa Clara County.
    Present address, Milton Junction, Rock County, Wisconsin.
    Taught before marriage.

MARY P. BASSETT (Mrs. O. A. Hale).......Santa Clara County.
    Present address, San José.
    Taught in San José five years. Married in 1881. One child.

LIZZIE BANKS (Mrs. L. B. Sparks)............Nevada County.
    Present address, Michigan Bluff, Placer County.
    Taught four years before marriage. Married in 1880.

SARAH F. BONNEY (Mrs. Milton Henderson)...Alameda County.
    Present address, 615 Tenth Street, Oakland.
    Taught before marriage.

ANNE B. CAMPBELL...........................San Francisco.
    Present address, 1220 Jackson Street, San Francisco.
    Taught in Sonoma, three months; in San Francisco, nine years. Teaching in Washington Grammar School.

CLARA BELLE CHURCHILL..................Santa Clara County.
    Present address, 418 S. Second Street, San José.
    Taught in Santa Clara County, one year; Trinity County, one year; San Benito County, three months; San Luis Obispo County, nine and one half years. Teaching at Paso Robles.

HENRY F. COURTER..............................Monterey County.
Present address, Healdsburg.
Taught in Pioneer District, Santa Clara County, three years; in a private family, eight months; Principal of East San José School one year; taught music one year; Principal of San Yeidro School, Santa Clara County, one year; typesetter and assistant editor in the Pacific Press, Oakland, over a year; Professor of Mathematics in Healdsburg College since August, 1886. Married. No children.

NATHANIEL W DAVIS (deceased) ....Solano County.
Taught several terms. Died in 1883. His widow, Mrs. Alice Davis, lives near Santa Clara.

ADDIE A. DAVIS (Mrs. C. O. Spaulding)....Sacramento County.
Present address, Folsom, Sacramento County.
Taught in El Dorado County, eight and one half years; in Sacramento County, four years. Teaching in Folsom. Married June 10, 1884. One child.

ALFRED DIXON ....Yuba County.
Present address, Michigan Bluff, Placer County.
Taught seven years in Contra Costa County. Is now engaged in mercantile business.

CARRIE S. FAIRCHILD..........................San Mateo County.
Present address, 311 Polk Street, San Francisco.
Taught eleven years. Teaching in Broadway Grammar School.

BENJAMIN H. FRANKLIN ....Santa Clara County.
Present address, Cambria, San Luis Obispo County.
Taught in Cambria, five years. Left teaching September, 1881, to engage in mercantile business. Married June 10, 1876. Three children.

MAGGIE GARDNER (Mrs. O. S. Meeker).....Santa Clara County.
Present address, San José.
Taught in Contra Costa County, three years; Merced County, one year; San José, three years. Has not taught since 1883. Married December 28, 1881.

HENRY C. GESFORD ....Napa County.
Present address, Napa City.
Taught in Napa County until 1880. Then went East and took a law course in Iowa University and Michigan University. Began the practice of law in Napa City, May, 1882. Was Superintendent of Schools in Napa County, 1877-8; State Senator, 1887-8. Married December 3, 1882. One child.

MINNIE F. HOLLRON (Mrs. Gannon)............San Francisco.
Present address, 1755 Ellis Street.
Teaching in Longfellow Primary School. Taught in San Francisco since October, 1877.

ADA LOCKE (Mrs. W. H. Cooke)..............................
Present address, Lockeford, San Joaquin County.
Taught in Marin County, three months; San Joaquin County, sixteen months; Napa County, two months; Tulare County, fourteen months. Married October 30, 1882, to Rev. W. H. Cooke. Two children; one living. In July, 1886, resided in Oakland. Not teaching.

SUSAN MCMULLEN (Mrs. Fred. Runyon)........Alameda County.
Present address, 1059 Poplar Street, Oakland.
Has taught. Two children.

KATIE MITCHELL (Mrs. H. H. West)......Contra Costa County.
Present address, 488 Twenty-third Street, Oakland.
Taught in Lassen County, two years; Contra Costa County, five and one half years. Married January 1, 1884. One child. Went to the Sandwich Islands in December, 1888, on account of her husband's health, and taught there a short time. Returned in March, 1889, because of the death of her husband. Intends to continue teaching.

KATE MCDONALD (Mrs. B. F. Hyde)...........State of Nevada.
Present address, San Bernardino.
Taught in State of Nevada, one year; San Bernardino County, nine years. Married July 14, 1886. Not taught since. One child.

LILA MURCH (Mrs. Kirkpatrick)............San Mateo County.
Present address, Oakland.
Taught two and one half years in Redwood City. Married in 1880. Not teaching.

KATIE F. O'HARA........................Santa Clara County.
Present address, San José.
Taught twelve years. Teaching in San José.

MARY A. PECKHAM (Mrs. G. F. Pillot)......Santa Clara County.
Present address, 85 S. Eleventh Street, San José.
Taught three months in San Mateo County; the remainder of the time since graduation has taught in San José. Married July 3, 1876. One child.

HELEN N. PENNIMAN (Mrs. Geo. Pardee)......Alameda County.
Present address, East Oakland.
Taught ten years in the Grove Street School, Oakland. One child.

SHELDON RANEY...........................San Joaquin County.
Present address, Black Diamond, Contra Costa County
Taught in Fresno County, one year; Santa Cruz County, six years; Contra Costa County, one year. Left teaching in 1884, on account of failing health. Engaged in mercantile business; also Postmaster and Justice of the Peace. Married in 1874. Four children.

MARY C. RODDEN (Mrs. Warfield)............Tuolumne County.
Address in 1886, Oakdale, Stanislaus County.

MARY F. RUSSELL (deceased)............... Alameda County.
    Father's address, Judge J. Russell, Haywards, Alameda County.
    Taught several years. Died April 13, 1886.

ELLA SAID (Mrs. W. E. Houghton)......... Santa Clara County.
    Present address, Bakersfield, Kern County.
    Taught in Solano County, three months; Mono County, three months; Kern County, six years. Not teaching. Married December 25, 1880. One child.

MRS. FRANCES C. SAWYER.................. Santa Clara County.
    Present address, San José.
    Taught constantly since graduation. Teaching in High School, San José.

SEBASTIAN SHAW.......................... Santa Clara County.
    Present address, Los Angeles.
    Taught continuously since graduation: Santa Clara County, five years; Napa County, one year; Merced County, four months; Contra Costa County, one year; Sonoma County, four months; Los Angeles County, four years.

ALICE L. STOCKTON (Mrs. J. A. Boulware)... Santa Clara County.
    Present address, Arroyo Grande, San Luis Obispo County.
    Taught in Santa Clara County, two and one half years. Married December 31, 1878. Not taught since. Four children.

M. JEANNETTE STONE (Mrs. E. A. Bunce)... Contra Costa County.
    Present address, Dougherty Station, Alameda County.
    Taught one year. Not teaching.

MARY O. THOMAS (Mrs. Thomas).......... Los Angeles County.
    Present address, Los Angeles.
    Taught seven years in Los Angeles County.

CAROLINE TRIMBLE (Mrs. Stanley Stephenson) Alameda County.
    Present address, 1846 San José Avenue, Alameda.
    Taught in Placer County, two months; in Alameda County, ten months; Marin County, fourteen months. Married June 28, 1879. Not taught since. Two children.

A. BELLE WEAR (Mrs. Clement)............ Santa Clara County.
    Present address, Haywards, Alameda County.
    Has taught at intervals throughout a period of ten years, about five years in all. **Taught** in Santa Clara, San Luis Obispo, and Alameda Counties. Filled office of Assistant Superintendent of Schools in Oakland for a time. **Married July, 1876. Three children.**

ELLA E. WHELAN (Mrs. Greenman).......... Alameda County.
    Present address, East Oakland.
    Has taught in the Oakland public schools six years. Is teaching in the Durant School. Married July 12, 1878. Is now a widow.

OLIVER P. WORKMAN (deceased) .... Sonoma County.
Taught about one year. Died in 1877.

ALICE M. WHITE (Mrs. David) .... Merced County.
Present address, Sturgeon, Merced County.
Taught in Merced County, nine months; Normal School, San José, one month; Sacramento County, two months. Married May 19, 1877, and moved to Michigan. Did not teach while there. Returned to California in 1888. Since that time has taught one term in Merced County, where she is still teaching.

EIGHTEENTH CLASS—MARCH, 1877.

JESSICA G. ALLEN (Mrs. Wm. Pascoe) ...... Santa Clara County.
Present address, College Park.
Taught in Humboldt County, two months; Plumas County, four months; San Mateo County, five months; Normal School, five months; in Hester School, San José, for past four years. Work suspended four years on account of home duties. Married July 20, 1880.

JULIA ANDERSON .... Santa Clara County.
Present address, Santa Paula, Ventura County.
Has taught in Ventura County eight years since graduation. Work suspended at different times, four years in all, on account of ill health.

MRS. JOSIE R. ARMSTRONG .... Santa Clara County.
Present address, 2002 Pine Street, San Francisco.
Taught one year in San Benito County. Not teaching. Two children one living.

MODENA I. BAKER (Mrs. Tom Scott) .... Alameda County.
Present address, Mission San José, Alameda County.
Taught in Alameda County six years. One child.

EUDORA A. BARNES (Mrs. Crossette) .... Santa Clara County.
Present address, 814 Geary Street, San Francisco.
Taught two years in Santa Clara County; one year in Washington Territory. Now teacher of voice-building and recitation.

ANNIE S. BARRY .... Santa Clara County.
Present address, San José.
Taught in San Joaquin County, five years; Calaveras County, two years; Santa Cruz High School, two years; Santa Clara County, three years. Teaching in Tulare City.

BELLE BIRD .... Santa Clara County.
Present address, 376 Orchard Street, San José.
Taught constantly since graduation in Willow Glen School, San José.

E. MAY BLACK (Mrs. Crandall)_____Santa Clara County.
Present address, 36 Liberty Street, San Francisco.
Taught in Los Gatos, Santa Clara County, three years; Santa Cruz and Monterey Counties, three months. Not teaching. Married June, 1882. Three children.

MARY I. BROWN_____Alameda County.
Present address, Centreville, Alameda County.
Taught in Alameda County, nine years; Los Angeles, one and one half years. Teaching in Centreville.

SAMUEL A. BROWN_____Oregon.
Present address, 169 First Street, Portland, Oregon.
Taught in Napa County, six months; Lake County, six months; Tulare County, six months. Left teaching in August, 1878, to study medicine. Now a practicing physician.

MAY CARPENTER (Mrs. J. E. Ellis)_____Mendocino County.
Present address, Los Gatos.
Taught four years. Not teaching.

ALICE M. CHAPLIN (deceased)_____Mendocino County.
Taught one year. Died in 1881.

DANIEL CROUGH_____Tuolumne County.
Present address, Independence, Inyo County.
Taught in Tuolumne County, seven months; Calaveras County, eight months; Inyo County, seven years. During 1883 and 1884 was Under Sheriff of Inyo County. Married August 5, 1883. One child.

BLANCHE L. DOWNS_____Santa Clara County.
Present address, San Bernardino.
Teaching in San Bernardino. Taught nine years.

ISHMAEL GREEN _____Colusa County.
Present address, San José.
Taught in Sutter County, one year; San Joaquin County, two years; Napa County, one half year; Calaveras County, one half year. Left the profession in 1882. Since that time has engaged in mercantile business.

MRS. CORNELIA HAILE_____Santa Clara County.
Present address, 193 North Fifth Street, San José.
Taught in Lassen County, one year; Placer County, five months; Siskiyou County, one year; Shasta County, one year; Kern County, five months; State of Nevada, three years; Santa Clara County, two years. Teaching in San José. Suspended work three years, 1885-88, on account of ill health.

WILLIAM HERROD_____Nevada County.
Present address, Oakland.
Taught in Nevada County, eight and one half years; State of Nevada, one year; Butte County, one term; Monterey County, two months. Teaching work suspended part of the time, to attend State University and to study short-hand. Now Principal in the Oakland Academy. Married May 29, 1880. Two children.

M. JENNIE HOYT (Mrs. Geo. W. Worthen)....San Mateo County.
   Present address, San José.
   Has taught constantly since graduation, and is still teaching. Married June 7, 1878.

LIZZIE F. KELLER......................San Francisco County
   Present address, Los Angeles.
   Taught in Santa Clara County schools four years; in San José, two and one half years. Is now teaching sixth year in Los Angeles City schools.

BLANCHE McCOWAN (Mrs. John Landis).....Mendocino County.
   Present address, Wheatland, Yuba County.
   Taught in Mendocino County, four and one half years. Married October 16, 1881. Not taught since. One child.

KATE MORE (Mrs. Chas. B. Wells)..........Santa Clara County.
   Present address, Kohala, Hawaii, Hawaiian Islands.
   Taught in Contra Costa County, five months. Left teaching to study art, to which she devoted herself until marriage. Married August 5, 1884. Two children.

LULU L. MOORE.........................San Francisco County.
   Taught in San Benito County, three years; Sandwich Islands, three years. Resigned position in Honolulu April 9, 1886. Since that time has been traveling and studying in Europe. Is teaching private pupils. At present is living at Meran, Austrian Tyrol.

SUSIE D. MOORE (Mrs. Heapy) ....San Francisco County.
   Taught one year in San Francisco and three years in San Benito County. Married in Liverpool in May, 1881, where she resided until the death of her husband in the winter of 1888. Is now with her sister at Meran, Austrian Tyrol. Has one son.

ALLIE P. OVERACKER (Mrs. Geo. Hawkins)....Alameda County.
   Present address, 1409 Twenty-fifth Street, San Francisco.
   Taught one year in Napa County. Left teaching in November, 1878, on account of ill health. Married January 1, 1883. One child.

ALMA PATTERSON........................Santa Clara County.
   Present address, 704 Kerney Avenue, San Diego.
   Taught in Monterey County, one year; Santa Clara County, five years; San Diego County, four years. Work suspended a part of the time on account of sickness. Teaching in San Diego City.

MINERVA M. QUINBY (Mrs. E. A. Kennedy).Santa Clara County.
   Present address, Los Gatos, Santa Clara County.
   Taught three years in Los Gatos. Married December 1, 1880. Not taught since. One child.

NELLIE L. RICH (Mrs. C. L. Neale).........Santa Clara County.
   Present address, 718 Seventeenth Street, Oakland.
   Taught one year. Not teaching.

DORA B. RIES (Mrs. Bernard Faymonville)...San Luis Obispo Co.
    Present address, 2502 Fillmore Street, San Francisco.
    Taught in Alpine County, one year; Fresno City, three years. Married April 19, 1881. Not taught since. Two children.

ELLA RILEY............................Santa Clara County.
    In 1886 was teaching in Eureka, Nevada.

GEORGE E. ROOT (deceased)................Tuolumne County.
    Taught four years in Nevada County; two years at Haywards, Alameda County. Was engaged in other business for two years before his death. Died at La Conner, Washington Territory, October 20, 1884.

RUTH ROYCE..............................Alameda County.
    Present address, San José.
    Taught in Preparatory Class of Normal School, two years; Santa Cruz County, three months; as substitute teacher in Normal School, four years. Librarian of State Normal School, San José, since 1881.

LIBBIE SALKELD (Mrs. M. N. Stone)...........State of Nevada.
    Present address, Virginia City, Nevada.
    Taught three years. Two children.

ALLAN P. SANBORN..........................Solano County.
    Present address, Benicia.
    Taught in Benicia, seven and one half years; near Vacaville, one year; in Sutter County, one half year; Calaveras County, one half year; Contra Costa County, one year; Sonoma County, one half year. Left the profession on account of failing eye-sight. Is engaged in the drug business in Benicia.

NATHALIE A. SELLING...................San Francisco County.
    Present address, 1522 O'Farrell Street, San Francisco.
    Taught constantly since graduation. Teaching in Redding Primary School.

KATE SIDDONS (Mrs. J. C. Ruddock), (deceased)...Mendocino Co.
    Taught in Mendocino County, three years. Was married February 4, 1880, to J. C. Ruddock, Class of March, 1871, and did not teach afterwards. She was taken ill in 1883 with consumption, and died July 24, 1884. Was buried at Ukiah City. She had two children, one living at the time of her death. Mrs. Ruddock was successful as a teacher, and was highly esteemed by a large circle of friends.

EUNICE I. SNEDAKER (Mrs. Judson Rice)...Santa Clara County.
    Present address, San José.
    Taught in Willow Glen, Santa Clara County, two years; Illinois, one year; Contra Costa County, two years; San José, five and one half years. Married October 22, 1887. Not taught since.

JOSIE E. SPRAGUE (Mrs. J. H. Ward) .... San Francisco County.
   Present address, 6 Chilworth Street, Hyde Park, London, England.
   Taught five years in the public schools of Santa Cruz, and three years as a governess in Germany. Not taught since marriage. Married in April, 1885.

ELIZA J. STEWART (Mrs. B. A. Strobridge) .... Alameda County.
   Present address, Haywards.
   Taught eight years in Alameda County.

NANNIE W. TEAFORD .... Santa Clara County.
   Present address, Santa Clara.
   Has taught constantly since graduation in the public schools of Santa Clara.

MAGGIE L. WILEY (Mrs. Edgar Lewis) .... Santa Cruz County.
   Present address, Watsonville.
   Taught four years. Married October 17, 1882. Not taught since.

CLARA B. WILLIAMS .... Santa Clara County.
   Present address, Wrights, Santa Clara County.
   Taught three terms in Santa Clara County. Is now engaged in fruit raising in the Santa Cruz Mountains.

MARIANNE WURTEMBERG (Mrs. M. S. Kohlberg) .. Mendocino Co.
   Present address, 222 Van Ness Avenue, San Francisco.
   Taught in Mendocino County, twelve months. Married February 21, 1886. One child.

NINETEENTH CLASS—MAY, 1878.

EMILIE ANISER .... Napa County.
   Present address, Napa City.
   Taught constantly since graduation in Napa County. Teaching in Napa City for the past seven years.

MATTIE L. ARAM .... Santa Clara County.
   Taught constantly since graduation. In spring of 1888 was teaching in Portland, Oregon.

ALICE BLYTHE (Mrs. Lewis B. Wilson) .... Santa Clara County.
   Present address, San José.
   Taught in Los Angeles County, two and one half months; Santa Cruz County, three months; Santa Clara County, three and one half years, the last fifteen months in San José. Married January 10, 1883. Not taught since. One child.

MILLIE R. BOULWARE (deceased) .... Santa Clara County.
   Taught three months and then gave up the work on account of ill health. Died February 7, 1886.

ANNIE B. BOYER (Mrs. Wm. Cozzens)..........Tulare County.
    Present address, San José.
  Taught five years. Three children.

LOUISE L. BRUCH..........................Santa Clara County.
  Teaching in San José. Taught ten years.

SELINA G. BURSTON ....Sacramento County.
    Present address, 135 S. Hope Street, Los Angeles.
  Taught in El Dorado County, two years; Napa County, four months; Placer County, six months; State of Nevada, six years; Los Angeles, two years. Teaching in Los Angeles.

EMMA S. CEARLEY (Mrs. F. Angelotti) ....Alameda County
    Present address, San Rafael, Marin County.
  Taught six years before marriage. One child (deceased).

LOUIS B. CHALONER........................San Joaquin County.
    Address in 1886, Wallace, Calaveras County.
  Had taught eight years.

AMELIA R. CHAPMAN (Mrs. A. E. Kellogg).....Alameda County.
    Present address, Eighteenth and Mission Streets, San Francisco.
  Taught in San Rafael until marriage, December, 1886. One child.

NELSON B. COFFMAN ....Sonoma County.
    Present address, Healdsburg.
  Taught four years. Now a practicing physician. Married.

KATE COZZENS ....Santa Clara County.
    Present address, San José.
  Taught constantly since graduation in Santa Clara County. Since August, 1887, has taught in the Training Department of the Normal School at San José.

ADELINE S. CURRIER (deceased) ....Sacramento County.
  Taught successfully to the time of her death. Died at Folsom. Date of her death not reported.

FANNIE A. DANIELS (Mrs. Charles D. Stuart) ...Sonoma County.
    Present address, Pacific Grove, Monterey County.
  Taught in Sonoma County, one year; Solano County, four months. Left teaching in November, 1883, on account of home duties. Married August 20, 1885. One child.

MAGGIE DESMOND........................Los Angeles County.
    Present address, Los Angeles.
  Taught in Los Angeles since graduation; for several years in Training Department of the State Normal School.

S. HENRIETTA DORN (Mrs. Housh)..........Santa Cruz County.
  Taught seven years. Married in 1886. Not taught since. Living in Arizona.

State Normal School. 193

KATE DOWNEY (Mrs. R. D. Spedding) ....Nevada County.
    Present address, Sierra City, Sierra County.
  Taught in Nevada, Sierra, and Alameda Counties, nine years in all. Married June 18, 1887. Not taught since.

LUCY J. DUDLEY (Mrs. Campbell)................Solano County.
    Present address, Seattle, Washington Territory.

SARAH F. EASTERDAY (Mrs. T. W. Whitehurst)..Santa Clara Co.
    Present address, Saratoga.
  Taught one and a half years in Monterey County. The remainder of the time since graduation has taught in Santa Clara County; since July, 1882, in primary department of the Saratoga school. Married January 5, 1882.

SALLIE FINLEY................................Sacramento County.
    Present address, Santa Ana, Orange County.
  Taught in Monterey County, six months; Los Angeles County, seven and one half years. Is now spending a year visiting in the Eastern States.

ANNIE R. FOWZER (Mrs. J. H. Clark) ....Mendocino County.
    Present address, Cahto, Mendocino County.

LOU GIVENS (Mrs. C. H. Porter) ....Sonoma County.
    Present address, Biggs, Butte County.
  Taught in San Joaquin County, five months; Merced County, six months; Napa County, one month. Married December 15, 1881. Not taught since. Three children.

SUSIE R. HAMILTON (Mrs. D. C. Agler).....Santa Clara County.
    Present address, Ashland, Oregon.
  Taught in Santa Clara County, two years; Fresno County, one month; San Joaquin County, one month; Placer County, six months; Merced County, two months. Not teaching. Married October 11, 1882. Three children.

JENNIE M. HAMMOND.....................Santa Clara County.
    Present address, 777 S. Second Street, San José.
  Taught in Santa Clara, one year; in Monterey, three years; San José public schools, two years; State Normal School, three and one half years. Teaching. Work suspended a part of the time on account of ill health.

NELLIE M. HASKELL ....San Francisco County.
    Present address, La Cañada, Los Angeles County.
  Taught in Siskiyou County, eight months; Lake County, four months; San Francisco, three years; Los Angeles County, four years. Teaching.

JANET M. HENDERSON....................Nevada County.
    Home address, Grass Valley, Nevada County.
  Taught in Grass Valley, five years; Los Angeles County, five years. Teaching in Los Angeles.

MAE E. HENION (Mrs. J. K. Simms)........Santa Clara County.
     Present address, Stockton.
 Taught three months in San Benito County; seven years in San Joaquin County, the last five in Stockton. Married January 1, 1884.

ADDIE K. HOBART (Mrs. J. F. Halloran).....Sacramento County.
     Present address, Astoria, Oregon.
 Taught in Butte County, two years; State of Nevada, one and one half years. Married January 1, 1882. Not taught since. Two children.

MYRTIE C. HUDSON........................Mendocino County.
     Present address, San José.
 Taught in Amador County, one year; Contra Costa County, two years; Santa Clara County, one year. In 1882 entered Michigan University, from which she graduated in 1885. Taught in State Normal School at San José, from January, 1886, to June, 1889.

CHARLES M. KELLOGG.....................Napa County.
     Present address, Rio Grande.
 Taught several years. Is not teaching on account of ill health.

MARY R. KELLY..........................Contra Costa County.
     Present address, Martinez.
 Taught for three years in Contra Costa County. Suspended work one year on account of ill health. Since then has taught in various places in California.

IANTHA A. KELSO (Mrs. W. R. Cooke).......Stanislaus County.
     Present address, Towles, Placer County.
 Taught in Stanislaus County, four months; Placer County, five and one half years. Not teaching. Married April 14, 1883. Three children; two living.

MAGGIE KENT (Mrs. Albert Dunlap).........San Benito County.
     Present address, Hollister, San Benito County.
 Taught two years in San Benito County. Not teaching. Married April 10, 1881. Three children.

ELLA LEWIS (Mrs. P. J. Hazen)............Stanislaus County.
     Present address, Modesto.
 Taught in Stanislaus County, five years. Married June 16, 1883. Not taught since. One child.

ANNIE LOUCKS...........................Contra Costa County.
     Present address, Pacheco, Contra Costa County
 Taught continuously since graduation at Pacheco.

WILLIAM I. H. LYON......................Sonoma County.
     Present address, Los Angeles.
 Taught in Santa Clara County, three years; Contra Costa County, three years; Solano County, five months; Alameda County, five months. Left the profession December, 1886, on account of ill health. Married December 26, 1888.

MARY A. L. MADDEN (Mrs. W. T. Fitzgerald)....San Francisco.
    Present address, San Francisco.
  Taught in the public schools of San Francisco, nine years. Married in the summer of 1888. Not teaching.

LISETTA MEGERLE ....San Francisco.
    Present address, Alameda.
  Taught in San Joaquin County, six months; Merced County, six months; Sacramento County, six months. Since the summer of 1881 has been teaching in Alameda.

ALIDA MINER (Mrs. E. W. Fogg) ....San Francisco County.
    Present address, Oroville, Butte County.
  Taught until May, 1883, in Alameda and Plumas Counties. Married October 9, 1883. Not taught since. One child.

CLARA MURCH (Mrs. S. T. Ferguson).........San Mateo County.
    Present address, Minneapolis, Minnesota.
  Taught in Redwood City about seven years. Married May 22, 1886.

LUCY S. NELSON (Mrs. Phil. Ruggles) ....Butte County.
    Present address, Rutledge, Oregon.

FRANCES M. O'BRIEN (Mrs. W. J. Freeman).Santa Clara County.
    Present address, San José.
  Taught in Contra Costa County, two months; Santa Clara County, eight years. Teaching in San José, Empire Street School. Married July 20, 1881. One child.

KATIE A. PERRY................................San Benito County.
    Present address, San Felipe, Santa Clara County.
  Taught nine years, most of this time in Monterey and San Benito Counties. At present engaged in stenography.

EVAN T. PETTIT ....Lake County.
    Present address, San José.
  Taught in Contra Costa County, two and one half months; Stanislaus County, three months; Tuolumne County, one and a half years; Santa Clara County, three years; Colusa County, two years. Left the profession of teaching in 1885, to engage in fruit raising.

C. LILLIAN POND (Mrs. C. L. Good) ....Napa County.
    Present address, Colfax, Washington Territory.
  Taught in Napa County, two years. Married January 4, 1881. Not taught since. One child.

ORSON M. PRATT (deceased)................Marin County.
  Died two weeks after graduation.

OREN N. RANEY................................Sonoma County.
    Present address, Los Angeles.
  Taught in Los Angeles County, five years. Since 1883 has engaged in business as searcher of records. Married June 19, 1888, to Miss Cecelia Leffler. One child.

KATE RAYMUND (Mrs. Wm. R. Thompson), (deceased)____Ohio.
Husband's address, Watsonville.
Taught **successfully**. Died February 14, 1884.

CLARA C. RICHARDSON (Mrs. **Clark**)_____Santa Clara County.
Present address, Portland, Oregon.
Taught about nine years in California and Oregon. **Teaching in Portland**. One child.

MARY E. RUCKER (Mrs. Boulware)_____**Santa Clara County**.
Present address, San José.
Taught in Santa Clara County, four years. Left teaching May, **1883**, on account of ill health. Married December 24, 1879.

MARY E. SALLY _____San Benito County
Present address, Hollister.
Taught in San Benito County, four and one half **years**; San Bernardino County, **one half** year; San Diego County, three **years**. Work suspended **two years on** account of sickness. Teaching **at San Jacinto, San Diego** County.

MINNIE SEAVY (Mrs. Fowler) _____San Francisco.
Present address, 804 Jones Street, San Francisco.
Taught in San Joaquin County, two years; Yolo County, six months; San Diego County, six months; Marin County, four years. Married April 13, 1886. Not taught since November, 1886.

FRANCES E. SIMMONS (Mrs. Thad. Rivers), (deceased)_Alameda Co.
Taught one year. Married December, 1879. Did not teach after marriage. Died April 23, 1880.

WILLIAM W. STOCKTON _____Santa Clara County.
Present address, 2223 Post **Street**, San Francisco.
Not taught since graduation. Is an electrical engineer.

HATTIE B. WARRING _____Santa Clara County.
Present address, San José.
Taught in Monterey County, four months; San Luis Obispo County, four months; Ventura County, two years. Not teaching on account of home duties.

LEWIS B. WILSON_____Pennsylvania.
Present address, San José.
Taught in Yuba County, four months; Monterey County, **two years**; **Merced** County, one year; Santa Clara County, four **and one** half years; **part of this** time in night school and business college. Is now Principal of San José High School. Member of County Board of Education. Married January 10, 1883, to Miss Alice Blythe, of the same class. One child.

E. ALFARETTA WOOD _____Monterey County.
Present address, Riverside, San Bernardino County.
Taught in Monterey County, two years; Sonoma County, two years; San Bernardino, six years. Teaching at Riverside.

CHARLES A. WOODMAN..................................Butte County.
    Present address, Chico, Butte County.
  Taught ten years.

TWENTIETH CLASS—MAY, 1879.

MARY P. ADAMS.....................................Santa Clara County.
    Present address, **San José**.
  Taught in Santa Cruz **County, one** year; Santa Clara **County,** three years. Now teaching in Training Department of State Normal School.

KATE G. BARDENWERPER..............................State of Nevada.
    Present address, Carson City, Nevada.
  Is teaching tenth year in the schools of Carson City, Nevada.

R. LIZZIE BEGGS (deceased)........................Santa Clara County.
  Taught **in Santa Clara County, two years**; Stanislaus County, one half year. Attended the State University from May, 1880, to May, 1882. **Died** May 4, 1884.

WILLIAM W. BROWN..................................Napa County.
    Present address, Riley, Grant County, Oregon.
  Taught two years in Fresno and San Luis Obispo Counties. Since 1881 engaged in stock raising.

HATTIE M. CHASE (Mrs. Byron E. DeHart).........Santa Clara Co.
    Present address, 52 S. Spring Street, Los Angeles.
  Taught in San Joaquin County, six months; Santa Clara County, fifteen months. Married October 15, 1882. Not taught since. Two children.

MAY S. CRITTENDEN.................................Santa Clara County.
    Present address, San José.
  Taught first year in Santa Clara County; three years **in Plumas County. Has taught** for past seven years in San José public schools.

THOMAS EDMONDS (deceased).........................San Francisco.
  Taught one term in San Luis Obispo County. Died in 1880.

MARGARET R. FARRELL...............................Marin County.
    Present address, San Rafael.
  Taught most of the time since graduation. Teaching in San Rafael.

ADDIE D. GALLAGHER (Mrs. Morehead)..........San Francisco.
    Present address, San Francisco.
  Taught in San Francisco five years, to January, 1886.

OLIVE E. GIBSON (Mrs. Wm. F. Marshall)...Los Angeles County.
    Present address, Los Angeles.
  Taught five years in Los Angeles. Married in 1885. One child.

LILLA B. GOVE (Mrs. W. H. Marshall) ....San Joaquin County.
    Present address, 41 Eleventh Street, San Francisco.
  Taught five years in San Joaquin County. Married August, 1884. Not taught since. One child.

HARRIET E. HAILE (Mrs. F. P. Gray)..........Solano County.
    Present address, Vacaville, Solano County.
  Taught two years. One child.

SI L. HANSCOM ....Stanislaus County.
    Present address, Modesto, Stanislaus County.
  Taught.

MARGARET P. HENDERSON....................Nevada County.
    Present address, Grass Valley, Nevada County.
  Taught in Nevada County, two and one half years; Alameda County, two and one half years. Not taught since November, 1884, on account of ill health.

DELIA C. HILTON (Mrs. Solomon Rodgers) ....Alameda County.
    Present address, Oakland.

ROBERTINE B. HINES (Mrs. E. S. Hall) ....Ventura County.
    Present address, Ventura.
  Taught in Ventura County, two years. Married September, 1881. Two children. Is not teaching at present, but does not consider that she has left the profession.

SARAH P. HOBSON (Mrs. Martin) ....Santa Clara County.
    Present address, San José.
  Has not taught.

ALICE L. HUMPHREY ....Santa Clara County.
    Present address, San José.
  Taught in Placer County, one year. Is teaching ninth year in San José schools.

ELLA M. IRISH (Mrs. Cox)...............Santa Clara County
    Present address, San José.
  Taught in Monterey County, one term, in San José, two years; in San Luis Obispo County, one year. Not teaching.

ADAH E. KENT (Mrs. Dunlap) ....San Benito County.
    Present address, Hollister.

MARGARET E. MCCANN (Mrs. Henry J. Stafford)..San Francisco.
    Present address, 626 Twenty-third Street, San Francisco.
  Taught in Temescal, Alameda County, five years. Married September 1, 1886. Two children.

CHARLOTTE C. MCLERAN (Mrs. Wm. Easton)....Santa Clara Co.
    Present address, Gilroy.
  Taught four years. Has one child.

GEORGE W. MERRITT..........................Los Angeles County.
                Present address, San Francisco.
    Practicing medicine in San Francisco. **Married.**

E. BELLE MERWIN (Mrs. W. T. Webb) ....Alameda County
            Present address, 626 East Fourteenth Street, Oakland.
    Taught in public schools of Oakland continuously since January, 1880, except a leave of absence for six months. **Teaching.** Married September, 1885. **One child.**

MARY M. MUIR (Mrs. Geo. W. Ogden).....Contra Costa County.
            Present address, Grafton, Yolo County.
    Taught in Contra Costa County, five months; Fresno County, one **year**; Santa Clara County, one year; Amador County, one and one half years. Not taught since December, 1883. Married July 3, **1882.**

GRACE R. MURDOCH........................Santa Clara County.
            Present address, Los Angeles.
    Taught in Los Angeles constantly since graduation.

WM. A. NEWCUM..............................San Francisco.
            Present address, Suisun, Solano County.
    Taught two and one half years. Engaged in mercantile business several years. Now editing a paper at Suisun, Solano County.

GEORGE W. OGDEN..........................Humboldt County.
            Present address, Grafton, Yolo County.
    Taught in Humboldt County, **one** year; Amador County, two years; Marin County, one year. Left teaching because of failing health. Engaged in mining and other business two and one half years. Farming since October, 1885. Married July 3, 1882, to Mary M. Muir, of the same class.

MARY L. O'HARA...........................Santa Clara County.
            Present address, San José.
    Taught in Jefferson School, Santa Clara County, four years; in San José, three years. Teaching in Fourth Ward School, San José.

LOIS A. PECKHAM..........................Santa Clara County.
            Present address, 615 E. Santa Clara Street, San José.
    Taught in Marin County, four **years**; Santa Clara County, five years. Teaching in San José.

ADDIE M. C. RANEY ....Sonoma County.
            Present address, Santa Rosa.
    Taught in Los Angeles **County, one** year; Sonoma County, seven years. Teaching in Santa Rosa.

GEORGIA RAY..............................Sacramento County.
            Present address, Galt.
    Taught nine years.

MOLLIE REDMAN (Mrs. C. A. Oliver)........Santa Cruz County.
Present address, Chico, Butte County.
Taught in Santa Cruz County, three years; Ventura County, two years. Traveled in Europe, two years. Married September 7, 1884. Not teaching.

MARY ENNA RINGO.........................Santa Clara County.
Present address, San José.
Taught in Santa Cruz County, one term; Tulare County, one year; since 1882, in public schools of San José.

AUGUSTA STERN...........................Santa Clara County.
Present address, 372 South Market Street, San José.
Has taught in San José constantly since graduation.

M. ADA STEVES...........................San Joaquin County.
Present address, Hornitos, Mariposa County.
Taught in San Joaquin County, three years; Mariposa County, three years; Fresno County, one and one half years; at Hornitos, Mariposa County, since September, 1887.

FRANCES M. SULLIVAN.....................Santa Clara County.
Home address, 408 South Eighth Street, San José.
Taught in San Benito County, five months; Sierra County, two and one half years; Sutter County, three years; Plumas County, one year. Teaching at Spanish Ranch, Plumas County.

ANNIE E. THOMASSON (Mrs. Clarke)........Santa Clara County.
Present address, Jolon, Monterey County.
Taught three years.

MOLLIE F. TRIMBLE (Mrs. A. K. Whitton)..Santa Clara County.
Present address, San José.
Taught in Santa Clara County, eight and one half years. Left teaching in November, 1887. Married March 22, 1888.

ADDIE TURNER (Mrs. Geo. Shear)..........Butte County.
Present address, Nord, Butte County.
Taught in Butte County about three years. Has left the profession temporarily, and is engaged in farming. Married August 23, 1881.

CLAUDE B. WAKEFIELD.....................El Dorado County.
Present address, Garden Valley.
Taught in El Dorado County, three years; Alameda County, two years. Entered the State University in 1881, and graduated in 1885. Elected County Superintendent of El Dorado County in 1887.

CARRIE WILLIAMS (Mrs. G. W. Hunter).....Humboldt County.
Present address, Eureka, Humboldt County.
Taught two years in Humboldt County. Married January 30, 1881. Not taught since. Two children.

JESSIE WILLIAMSON ....Santa Clara County.
        Present address, 48 S. Sixth Street, San José.
    Taught constantly in **Santa Clara County** since graduation. **Teaching in San José** since 1882.

ANNIE WOODSON (Mrs. Toney)............Santa Clara County.
        Present address, San José.
    Not taught.

DIPLOMAS GRANTED JANUARY 3, 1880.

MRS. MARY A. KING ....Solano County.
        Present address, Nacimiento, San **Luis Obispo County**.
    Taught in Yolo County, one year; in Solano County, four months; in San Luis Obispo County, four years. Work suspended on account **of ill health.** Is now engaged in farming.

ANNA E. MCPHILLIPS......................San Francisco County.
        Present address, 449 Tenth Street, San Francisco.
    Taught in Franklin District, Santa Clara County, five years; San Mateo County, two years. **Teaching in San Mateo County.**

TWENTY-FIRST CLASS—MAY, 1880.

MAGGIE G. BARRETT ....Placer County.
        Present address, **302** Montgomery Street, San Francisco.
    Taught in Nevada County, one half year; Placer County, two and one half years. Left public school teaching in December, 1883, to practice shorthand and type-writing. Is now teaching these subjects **in San Francisco.**

IDA M. BENNETT.........................San Bernardino County.
    In 1886 was teaching in San Bernardino. Had taught six years.

LILLIAN BOWERS..........................Santa Clara County.
        Present address, Garvanza, Los Angeles County.
    Taught five years. Teaching.

MARY S. BOWMAN (Mrs. F. W. Blackmar)..Santa Clara County.
        Present address, San José.
    Has not **taught regularly since** graduation on account of home duties. Substituted and taught private classes about six months. Married June 8, 1885. One child.

F. ALICE BROWN ....Santa Clara County.
        Present address, Bernardo, San Diego County.
    Taught six years in San Diego County.

FLORIBEL C. BROWN .... Alameda County.
      •   Present address, Centreville.
  Taught in Alameda County, seven and one half years; San Bernardino County, one half year. Not teaching at present on account of sickness.

ELMER E. CAREY .... Mariposa County.
    Present address, 1316 California Street, San Francisco.
  Taught in various places in the State for seven years. Now employed as a journalist in San Francisco.

ANNIE L. CASWELL (Mrs. Chas. Schurch) .... San Francisco.
    Present address, 8 Pleasant Street, San Francisco.
  Not taught. Married November 5, 1881. Two children. Husband died September 24, 1885.

LOTTIE E. CRICHTON (Mrs. Dr. Curnow) .... Santa Clara County.
    Present address, San José.
  Taught four and one half years in Santa Clara County before marriage. Not taught since.

EMMA E. DAVIS (Mrs. Holmes) .... Sacramento County.
    Address unknown.
  Taught several years. No definite report.

HENRIETTA M. DE SAISSET .... Santa Clara County.
    Present address, San José.
  Not taught.

JOSEPHINE DESIMONE (Mrs. T. Vock) .... Santa Clara County.
    Present address, San Bernardino.
  Married in 1883. Taught several years in San Bernardino County.

ADELAIDE L. DODGE (Mrs. F. D. Nicol) .... San Francisco.
    Present address, Sonora, Tuolumne County
  Taught one year. Married July, 1883. Not taught since. Two children.

LAVINIA ESTILL .... Lassen County.
    Present address, Bieber.
  Taught one term in Colusa County; one term in Shasta County; four terms in Modoc County; two terms in Lassen County. Teaching in Lassen County.

ROSE A. EVERET .... Santa Barbara County.
    Present address, Santa Barbara.
  At last report had taught six years and was still teaching.

BELLE J. FINNIE .... Nevada County.
    Present address, Grass Valley.
  Taught in Santa Cruz County, five months; Ventura County, four months; as substitute in Grass Valley, four years. Teaching near Grass Valley.

MARY R. FINNIE (deceased)_____Nevada County.
 Taught in Nevada City, five months. Suspended work on account of sickness. Died January 28, 1883.

LENA B. FULLER_____Santa Clara County.
    Present address, San José.
 At last report had taught six years.

EMMA GRIFFITHS_____ Nevada County.
    Home address, Grass Valley.
 Taught in Grass Valley, seven years; Los Angeles, one year. Teaching in Los Angeles.

RUTH GUPPY_____Santa Clara County.
    Present address, San José.
 Taught one year in Santa Clara County. Attended University of Michigan five years, and graduated in 1887. **Not teaching.**

JOSEPHINE HARRIGAN_____San Francisco.
  Present address, 949 Harrison Street, San Francisco.
 Teaching in Mission Primary School. Has taught in San Francisco since September, 1880.

MAGGIE R. HENRY_____San Joaquin County.
    Present address, Fresno.
 Taught eight years in Fresno County since graduation. Not teaching.

JOHN HERROD_____Nevada County.
    Present address, San José.
 Taught in Nevada County, two and one half years; State of Nevada, two years; Amador County, two and one half years; Santa Clara County, one and one half years. Principal of school in East San José.

EVELINE C. HILLMAN (Mrs. T. O. Smith)___Santa Clara County.
    Present address, San José.
 Taught in Humboldt County, five months; in Santa Clara County, **three and one half** years. Engaged several years in studying and teaching music. Married September 27, 1888.

SARAH E. HOLLAND (Mrs. A. B. McNeil)___Santa Clara County.
  Present address, 693 S. Second Street, San José.
 Taught three years in Santa Clara County. Married November 30, 1882. Not taught since. Two children.

JENNIE F. HOWARD (Mrs. Chas. Erkson)_____San Francisco.
    Present address, San José.
 Has taught in San José, eight years. Teaching. Married August 1, 1888.

KATE M. JACKSON (Mrs. Wm. Gapen)_____San Benito County.
  Present address, Bird's Landing, Solano County.
 Taught three and one half years in Oregon; one year at Brentwood, Contra Costa County; one year at Bird's Landing. Not teaching. Married February 2, 1887. One child.

MARTHA M. KNAPP........................Santa Cruz County.
    Present address, Los Angeles.
 Taught in Santa Cruz County, one year; Trinity County, one year; for past six years has been Principal of Training Department in the State Normal School at Los Angeles.

SARAH A. J. LOCKE (Mrs. Wm. T. Smith)...San Joaquin County.
    Present address, Ferndale, Humboldt County.
 Taught in Humboldt County, two years. Not taught since December, 1884. Married December 25, 1882. Three children.

NATHANIEL H. LOCKE......................San Joaquin County.
    Present address, Lockeford.
 Taught in Marin County, two years; San Joaquin County, two years. Was not teaching at last report, 1886. Married December 25, 1884. One child.

ROBERT W. MANTZ........................Santa Clara County.
    Present address, San José.
 Taught in Santa Clara County, three years; Contra Costa County, four months; Alameda County, eleven months; Sierra County, four months. Attended the State University two years, 1882–84. Married January 3, 1889, to Miss Edith Vale.

MARY A. MCDONALD.......................Santa Clara County.
    Present address, San José.
 Taught private class in San José, one year; taught in Sonoma County, one and one half years; since then in Santa Clara County, for past five years in San José.

ELLA E. MARTIN (Mrs. A. Caminetti).........Calaveras County.
    Present address, Jackson, Amador County.
 Taught one year in Calaveras County; four years in Amador County. Not teaching. Married May 29, 1881. Two children.

LIZZIE A. MCKENZIE......................Tuolumne County.
    Present address, Columbia.
 Taught in San Joaquin County, two years; Tuolumne County, six years. Teaching at Columbia.

AMY E. O'NEAL..........................San Joaquin County.
    Present address, Valley Springs, Calaveras County.
 Taught in San Joaquin County, four years; Calaveras County, one and one half years. Work suspended a part of the time because of ill health. Teaching at Valley Springs.

ANNIE E. OSGOOD (deceased) ....Alameda County.
 Did not teach. Died in June, 1881, after a brief illness, at Irvington, Alameda County.

WILLIAM F. PRATT.......................Sutter County
    Present address, San José.
 Taught two years. Now a practicing physician.

HANNAH M. RIXON (Mrs. J. T. Ladd)......San Joaquin County.
                 Present address, Joliet, Illinois.
  Taught one and one half years.

MARGARET E. SCHALLENBERGER .... Santa Clara County
                 Present address, San José.
  Taught in public schools of San José, five years; in Normal School, two years. Now teaching primary class in Training Department of the Normal School.

MAGGIE M. SENTER (Mrs. W. G. Griffith)...Santa Clara County.
                 Present address, Fresno City.
  Taught in Tehama County, five months; Santa Clara County, two years; Fresno County, three and one half years. Married July 29, 1886. Not taught since. Two children.

CORA A. SIMPSON (Mrs. C. P. Van Dyke)......Alameda County.
                 Present address, Haywards.
  Taught two years in Marin County; two years in Alameda County. One child.

GRACE MAY SINNOTT (Mrs. Chas. M. Weber). Santa Clara County.
                 Present address, Coyote.
  Taught six and one half years in Santa Clara County. Married December, 1886.

JESSIE M. STEWART ....Tuolumne County.
                 Present address, East Oakland.
  Teaching in Union Primary School, San Francisco. Taught eight years.

IDA M. WARD (Mrs. I. W. Van Eaton) ......Santa Clara County.
                 Present address, San Jose.
  Taught eight years.

ALFRED A. WOOD............................Sonoma County.
                 Present address, Riverside, San Bernardino County.
  Taught one year. Now a merchant in Riverside.

TWENTY-SECOND CLASS—MAY, 1881.

KATE APPLEBY (Mrs. Goodrich)............Santa Clara County.
                 Present address, San Luis Obispo.
  Taught for a short time before marriage. Not taught since. Three children.

LOUISE ARCHER (Mrs. M. J. Flavin).......Santa Clara County.
                 Present address, 924 Market Street, San Francisco.
  Not taught. Married February 6, 1883. One child.

MINNIE C. BASSHAM ....Santa Clara County.
      Present address, Fresno City.
   Taught in Santa Clara County, one year; Fresno County, six years. Teaching.

A. ROSE BECKWITH ....Santa Clara County.
      Present address, Fresno City.
   Taught in Mendocino County, two months; Contra Costa County, four months; San Benito County, three months; San José, five months; Fresno County, two years and three months. Resigned in the summer of 1886, to go on a trip to the East for eight months. Not taught since, but expects to teach again.

LOTTIE BENT (Mrs. Mathews) ....Contra Costa County.
      Present address, Martinez.
   Taught one year in Contra Costa County. Married May 28, 1884. Not taught since.

ADA F. BROWN ....Santa Clara County.
      Present address, 1519 Scott Street, San Francisco.
   Taught in Shasta County, six months; Santa Clara County, three months; Monterey County, four months; San Luis Obispo County, two and one half years; San Diego, four months. Now studying phonography in San Francisco.

IDA M. CARPENTER ....Napa County.
      Present address, Napa City.
   Taught constantly since graduation, most of the time in Napa City. Is now teaching a class of young ladies in the Government School in Tokyo, Japan.

LIDA P. DAINGERFIELD (Mrs. Theo. B. Wilcox), (deceased) ......
....San Francisco.
   Did not teach after graduation. Was married October 2, 1882, and moved to Portland, Oregon, where she resided until her death. She had one child. Mrs. Wilcox was killed in a railroad accident at Puyallup, December 10, 1888.

NELLIE HENRY ....San Francisco.
      Present address, Los Angeles.
   Taught one and one half years in Contra Costa County; one and one half years in San Fernando, Los Angeles County. For the past four years has taught in Los Angeles County.

MARY J. HUFFNER (Mrs. S. F. Wood) ......Contra Costa County.
      Present address, Escondido, San Diego County.
   Taught in Contra Costa County, two years; San Diego County, three years. Not teaching. Married July 23, 1884. Two children.

NELLIE R. HUNTINGTON (Mrs. F. A. Loring)......San Francisco.
      Present address, 638 Green Street, San Francisco.
   Taught in Siskiyou County, one year; Humboldt County, one year; Mendocino County, one year; Stanislaus County, six months. Not taught since May, 1885. Married September 25, 1883. Two children.

JAMES B. KELLY............................Santa Clara County.
     Present address, San José.
  Taught in Monterey County, six months; Contra Costa County, one year; Placer County, two years; Santa Cruz County, five months; San Luis Obispo County, one year. Married April 22, 1883. One child.

GRACE E. LEONARD (Mrs. W. W. Lowe)....Santa Clara County
     Present address, Camp Verde, Arizona.
  Taught in Tulare County, one year; Monterey County, one year; Los Angeles County, four years. Teaching in Camp Verde.

IDA LOCKE (Mrs. W. H. Pascoe)..........San Joaquin County.
     Present address, Redwood City, San Mateo County.
  Taught in Marin County, four months; San Joaquin County, one year. Left teaching November, 1882, on account of illness in family. Married May 8, 1883. Two children. Husband a Congregational minister.

ALICE S. MCDOUGAL........................Santa Clara County.
  Began teaching at Gilroy Hot Springs ten months after graduation, and has taught constantly in Santa Clara County since that time. Teaching in East San José.

MARY S. MCDOUGAL (Mrs. E. F. Murch)...Santa Clara County.
     Present address, Red Bluff, Tehama County.
  Taught in Tehama County, two months; Santa Clara County, four months. Married March 25, 1882. Not taught since. Two children.

JOHN W. MARTIN..............................Fresno County.
  Taught several years. Is now farming in Fresno County. Married and has children.

LIZZIE T. MILLS.............................Contra Costa County.
     Home address, Martinez.
  Taught in Contra Costa County, two and one half years; Placer County, one year; Alameda County, one year; Marin County, two and one half years; Napa County, one half year. Teaching near Napa City.

ALICE MOORE (Mrs. John Bishop)..........San Francisco.
     Present address, Orange, Massachusetts.
  Taught in San Joaquin County, four months; in Honolulu, one year. Left teaching in December, 1882, to travel in Europe. Married in the summer of 1887.

ELLA F. MURPHY............................Santa Cruz County.
     Present address, Watsonville.
  Taught in Santa Cruz County, two and one half years; Monterey County, two years; San Luis Obispo County, one year. At last report, October, 1886, was teaching in San Luis Obispo County.

FANNIE O'HANLON..........................Santa Clara County.
     Present address, San José.
  Taught in Santa Clara County, four years; Tulare County, three years; Los Angeles, one year. Teaching in Tulare City.

PHOEBE L. PARKER ....San Francisco.
     Present address, San Diego.
  Taught in Mendocino County, four months; Humboldt County, one year; Santa Cruz County, five months; Alameda County, four years. Now teaching second term in San Diego. Work suspended two years on account of ill health.

LAURA I. PATTERSON ....Santa Clara County.
     Present address, San José.
  Taught in Santa Cruz County, one half year; Merced County, one year; Santa Clara County, one year; Fresno County, one and one half years; Lassen County, one half year; San Diego County, two and one half years. Teaching in Fall Brook, San Diego County. Intends to enter a medical college in summer of 1889.

JOSEPHINE D. REES (Mrs. Horace H. Appel), (deceased) ....
.... San Francisco.
  Taught most of the time until her marriage, April 2, 1884. Removed to Tucson, Arizona, where she died November 15, 1884.

KATE L. SCHUCK ....Santa Clara County.
     Present address, Portland, Oregon.
  Taught constantly since graduation. Teaching in Portland.

LAURA F. SELL (Mrs. Samuel Irving).........Tuolumne County.
     Present address, Portland, Oregon.
  Taught three years before marriage. Not teaching. After marriage resided for several years in Sydney, Australia.

FLORENCE SNOWDEN (Mrs. J. E. Ward) .....Santa Clara County.
     Present address, Modesto, Stanislaus County.
  Taught in Stanislaus County, six years. Married February 14, 1887. One child.

NANCY J. STEPHENSON..........................Humboldt County.
     Present address, Rohnerville.
  Taught in Humboldt County, five years. Teaching near Rohnerville.

MARY L. TEEL....................................Alameda County.
     Present address, San Lorenzo.
  Taught seven and one half years, six years of this time in Napa County Teaching at Haywards.

VERONA TEEL....................................Alameda County.
     Present address, San Lorenzo.
  Taught in Colusa County, one year; Los Angeles County, one and one half years; Napa County, one half year; Alameda County, one and one half years; one year in other places. Is teaching in Bieber, Lassen County.

LIZZIE THUNEN..................................Butte County.
     Present address, Cherokee.
  Taught in Butte County, three years. At last report, 1886, was not teaching.

HELEN MAY TOWLE (Mrs. L. E. Baird)..........Solano County.
Present address, Sanger, Fresno County.
Taught three months in Solano County. Married December 25, 1881. Not taught since. Two children.

MARION S. VAN DUSEN.......................Mendocino County.
Present address, Ukiah City.
Taught in Mendocino County, **five and** one half **years. Left teaching** April, 1887, on account of ill health.

HARRIET E. VAN EATON (Mrs. W. S. Bailey)....Santa Clara Co.
Present address, Long Beach, Los Angeles County.
Taught in Hester School, Santa Clara County, five years; in **Los Angeles County, two years. Not teaching.** Married August 29, 1886. **One child.**

DIPLOMA GRANTED JANUARY 21, 1882.

ELLA MCCABE...............................Contra Costa County.
Present address, Brentwood.

TWENTY-THIRD CLASS—MAY, 1882.

EVALINE V. APLIN (Mrs. W. D. Huntington)....Nevada County.
Present address, Oceanside, San Diego County.
Taught in Nevada **County,** one year; Los Angeles County, one year; San Bernardino County, two years. Married June 1, 1886. Not taught since. One child.

WALTER S. BAILEY ....Los Angeles County.
Present address, **Long Beach.**
Taught in Los Angeles County **constantly since graduation. Married** August 29, 1886, to Miss Harriet E. **Van Eaton, Class of May, 1881.** **One child.**

LOLA A. BALIS ....Santa Clara County.
Present address, East San José.
Taught **in Santa Cruz County, one year;** Stanislaus **County, one year. Work suspended from 1884 to 1889, on account of home duties. Teaching in** East San José.

KATE B. BECKWITH ....Santa Clara County.
Taught in Los Angeles County until summer of 1886. Not taught since.

MAGGIE M. BIRD (Mrs. O. M. Keesling).....Santa Clara County.
Present address, San José.
Taught five years. Married August 10, 1887 Not taught since.

CHRISTIANA H. BRAUN (Mrs. Wm. H. Murphy)..Santa Clara Co.
Present address, Antioch, Contra Costa County.
Taught in Santa Clara County, two terms; Monterey County, two terms; Solano County, two terms; Contra Costa County, one term. Married October 2, 1887. Not taught since.

MARY L. CHALONER (Mrs. Frank Belt)......San Joaquin County.
Present address, Hills Ferry, Stanislaus County.
Taught two years.

THOMAS L. CHAPIN..........................Los Angeles County.
Present address, Los Angeles.
Taught three years. Engaged in real estate business.

WILLIAM T. CHIPMAN.........................Santa Clara County.
Present address, San José.
Taught in Santa Clara County, one and one half years; Sierra County, one year; Lassen County, two months. In October, 1884, left profession of teaching, to enter County Clerk's office. Has since taught one term in night school in San José. Has occupied office of Deputy County Superintendent. Married March 30, 1889, to Hattie E. Ogan.

ALFRED B. COFFMAN ....Napa County.
Present address, Red Bluff, Tehama County.
Real estate agent. Not taught.

PELHAM H. COFFMAN..........................Napa County.
Present address, Red Bluff, Tehama County.
Real estate agent. Not taught.

ISABELLA CONN ....Nevada County.
Present address, Los Angeles.
Taught in Fresno County, five years; Los Angeles, two years. Teaching in Los Angeles.

NELLIE CRITTENDEN..........................Santa Clara County.
Home address, San José.
Has taught continuously since graduation in Santa Clara, Merced, and Los Angeles Counties. Is teaching in Pasadena.

MARIANA DAY................................San Francisco.
Present address, Hollister, San Benito County.
Taught in California, two years; a private school in Tonalá, Mexico, one year; returned to California, and taught in Trinity County, one year. Is teaching second term in Fairview District, near Hollister

INANDA L. DRANGA (deceased)...............San Diego County.
Taught in San Diego County until May, 1886, when she gave up teaching on account of failing health. Died at Vallecitas, San Diego County, June 5, 1887, of consumption.

LOUISA A. ERKSON (Mrs. A. O. White) .....Santa Clara County.
    Present address, San José.
  Taught two and one half years in San José. Married in 1884.

CORNELIA M. FARLEY........................Santa Clara County.
    Present address, San José.
  Teaching in High School, San José. **Taught six years.**

ANNIE C. FISK (Mrs. James Gregory)......San Joaquin County.
    Present address, Los Angeles.

IDA M. GIBSON ....Marin County.
    Present address, Bolinas.
  Teaching in Bolinas, where she has taught most of the time since graduation.

MARY Q. GORDON ....Monterey County.
    Present address, Monterey.
  Taught in Monterey continuously since graduation.

HATTIE F. GOWER ....Los Angeles County.
    Present address, Los Angeles.
  Taught in Los Angeles continuously since graduation.

CLARA L. GREGORY (Mrs. J. H. Poor) ......Sacramento County.
    Present address, Penryn, Placer County.
  Taught in State of Nevada, one year; Alameda County, one half year. Married December 24, 1884. Not taught since. One child.

PATRICK H. GRIFFIN........................Tuolumne County.
    Present address, Angel's, Calaveras County.
  Taught in Tuolumne County, four years; Calaveras County, two years. Teaching.

IDA L. HALL................................San Francisco.
    Home address, 627 Nineteenth Street, San Francisco.
  Taught in Tulare County, one year; Los Angeles County, five years. Teaching in Los Angeles.

IDA S. HALL ....Contra Costa County.
    Present address, Alamo.
  Taught continuously in Contra Costa County since graduation. Teaching near Alamo.

MARY A. HENDERSON........................Nevada County.
    Home address, Grass Valley.
  Taught in Nevada City, three years; in Los Angeles, three years. Teaching in Los Angeles.

KATE HENRY................................Contra Costa County.
    Present address, Martinez.
  At last report had taught two years.

CARRIE HILL_____Santa Clara County.
    Teaching in Los Angeles County at last report. Had taught several years.

LAVINIA HILLEBRANT (Mrs. Ammon A. Goff)___Santa Clara Co.
    Present address, Santa Ana, Orange County.
    Taught in Santa Cruz County, five months; Colusa County, five months; Los Angeles County, one year. Married October 8, 1885, and left the profession. Two children; one living. Has contributed frequently to papers and magazines.

ERASTUS K. HITCHCOCK_____State of Nevada.
    Present address, Pacheco, Contra Costa County.
    Taught in Santa Clara County, one year; Santa Barbara County, one year; Alameda County, two and one half years; Los Angeles County, one year; Contra Costa County, one year. Teaching at Pacheco.

IDA G. HUMPHREY_____Santa Clara County.
    Present address, San José.
    Taught in Placer County, one term; one term in Santa Clara County; four years in Alameda County. Has taught in San José since July, 1888.

WILLIAM E. JORDAN_____Fresno County.
    Present address, Kingsburg.
    Taught four years in Fresno County. Now engaged in farming.

EULALIE KELLEY (deceased)_____Santa Clara County.
    Taught one term. Died in August, 1884.

WILLIAM A. KIRKWOOD_____Contra Costa County.
    Present address, Martinez.
    Taught in Contra Costa County, four years. In the fall of 1886 was elected County Superintendent, which office he holds at the present time.

LULU LAKE (Mrs. Preston Menefee)_____San Francisco.
    Present address, San Diego.
    Not taught.

ELIZABETH LEGGETT_____Butte County.
    Present address, Oroville.
    Taught in Sierra County, five months; Butte County, three and one half years. Not taught since November, 1886, and does not expect to teach again.

LYDIA A. LEHNIG (Mrs. R. H. Jamison)_____Alameda County.
    Present address, Agnews, Santa Clara County.
    Taught in San Mateo County, six months; Sacramento County, one year; Santa Clara County, thirteen months; Alameda County, three months. Not teaching. Married September 8, 1886.

ELLA LORDS_____Santa Clara County.
    Present address, Alviso.
    Taught in Monterey County most of the time since graduation. Teaching in Monterey.

KATE MANDEVILLE............................San Francisco.
        Present address, 207 Jones Street, San Francisco.
    Teaching in Clement Grammar School. Has taught in San Francisco since August, 1885. Previous to that time, taught one and one half years in Santa Clara County, and one term in Marin County.

FLORA A. MCFARLAND (Mrs. E. B. Zumwalt).....Santa Clara Co.
        Present address, San José.
    Taught one year before marriage. Married April 8, 1883. One child. Teaching at New Almaden, Santa Clara County.

MARY E. MCLEAN.............................Stanislaus County.
        Present address, Modesto.
    Has taught several years.

CARRIE A. MCTIGUE..........................State of Nevada.
    At last report, 1886, had taught four years in Los Angeles, and was still teaching.

MARY E. MEEK (Mrs. Theo. Daulton).........Alameda County.
        Present address, Seattle, Washington.
    Taught six years in Oakland schools. Married November, 1888.

M. AUGUSTA MERTES (Mrs. J. J. Sheafor).........Placer County.
        Present address, Dunsmuir, Siskiyou County.
    Taught in Placer County, three years; Nevada County, one year. Is now engaged as a bookkeeper. Married April 19, 1887.

S. LIZZIE MILLER (Mrs. Herbert F. Conn)...Santa Clara County.
        Present address, Walla Walla, Washington.
    Taught in Los Angeles County, one and one half years; in Walla Walla, four and one half years. Still teaching. **Married** June 25, 1887.

CHRISTENIE E. MILLS (Mrs. Wm. A. Graves).Santa Clara County.
        Present address, Nicolaus, Sutter County.
    Taught in Sutter County, six months. Married October 3, 1883. Not taught since. One child.

KATE C. O'BRIEN............................San Francisco.
        Home address, 1513 Valencia Street, San Francisco.
    In 1887 was teaching at Markham, Sonoma County. Taught four years.

ROSELLA A. O'BRIEN (Mrs. Barlow).........Santa Clara County.
        Present address, San José.
    Taught **one year.**

MARY M. OSBORN.............................Tulare County.
        Present address, San José.
    Taught in Fresno County, five months; Tulare County, three years. Not teaching at present.

F. H. OTTMER ....Sonoma County.
   Present address, Petrolia, Humboldt County.
  Taught three years in Sonoma County. Left teaching to study medicine. Graduated from Cooper Medical College, November, 1887. Now practicing medicine in Petrolia. Married November, 1888.

MARY L. PACEY ....San Francisco.
  At last report, 1886, had taught three years and was teaching in San Diego County.

CHRISTINE RADEMACHER ....Santa Clara County.
   Present address, San José.
  At last report had taught four years.

ELISSIE H. RAYMOND ....Monterey County.
   Present address, Salinas City.
  Taught in Mariposa County, one year; Monterey County, four years. Teaching at Deep Well, Monterey County. Work suspended a part of the time on account of sickness.

FRANKE B. REYNOLDS......................San Francisco.
   Present address, Kansas City, Iowa.
  Taught one and a half years.

ADA RICHARDSON..........................Sacramento County.
   Home address, 2100 T Street, Sacramento.
  Taught in State of Nevada, one year; Placer County, one year; Santa Clara County, two years; Sacramento County, two years; Ventura County, one year. Teaching in Santa Paula.

MARY H. RICKEY (Mrs. Litner) ....San Diego County.
  Taught three years before marriage. In 1886 was living in Alabama.

MINNIE A. RIXON (Mrs. J. L. Siefkes) .....San Joaquin County.
  Present address, 1132 Kentucky Street, San Francisco.
  Taught one year in San Joaquin County; two years in Alameda County.

LUCIE A. ROGERS ....Santa Clara County.
   Present address, San José.
  Taught four years.

LOUISE G. RONEY ....San Francisco.
   Present address, 1519 Jackson Street, San Francisco.
  Taught in Placer, Del Norte, and Contra Costa Counties five years. Teaching at Paso Robles, San Luis Obispo County.

LENA B. SCHILLING ....Santa Clara County.
   Present address, San José.
  Has taught in San José six years. Teaching in Fourth Ward School.

LILLIE S. SCHOEN........................Santa Clara County.
   Present address, San José.
  Taught continuously in San José since graduation.

WILLIAM A. SEARS......................Santa Clara County.
    Present address, Wrights.
  Taught in Contra Costa County about five years, the last two years as Principal of the Pacheco School. Now has a fruit farm in the Santa Cruz Mountains. Married. One child.

JEANNETTE SHAW.......................Santa Clara County.
    Present address, San José.
  Taught in Santa Clara County continuously since graduation.

ADDIE SHEATS ....Los Angeles County.
    Present address, Tustin City.
  Teaching. Taught six years.

SARA J. SMITH (Mrs. Cunningham).........Santa Clara County.
    Present address, Honolulu, H. I.
  Taught four years.

ELLA D. STARLING......................State of Nevada.
    Present address, Carson City, Nevada.
  Taught six years. Teaching in Carson City.

LEOLIN TAYLOR ....San Bernardino County.
    Present address, San Bernardino.
  Taught in Los Angeles County until May, 1887. Left the profession of teaching to study law. Married October 29, 1886. One child.

EDWARD E. THOMAS......................Santa Clara County.
    Present address, San José.
  Taught in Los Angeles County, three months; Santa Clara County, four and one half years. Left the profession of teaching in June, 1888, to engage in fruit growing.

MABEL URMY............................Stanislaus County.
    Present address, College Park, Santa Clara County.
  Taught in the Hester School, San José, two and one half years; in University of the Pacific, two years. In 1886 suspended work of teaching, to attend the University of the Pacific, from which she graduated in June, 1886.

EMMA WATKINS (Mrs. Henry L. Willey).....Santa Clara County.
    Present address, San José.
  Taught in Santa Clara County continuously seven years; for the past six years in Santa Clara. Married November 13, 1889. Not teaching.

REGINA WEINSHANK......................Los Angeles County.
    Present address, Los Angeles.
  Has taught in Los Angeles County continuously since graduation.

EMILY L. WRIGHT (Mrs. J. G. Bessinger)...Santa Clara County.
    Present address, Lompoc, Santa Barbara County.
  Taught two and one half years in Santa Cruz and Santa Clara Counties. Married February 8, 1885. Not taught since. One child.

HATTIE L. WYLLIE (Mrs. Henry Booksin) ..Santa Clara County.
Present address, San José.
Taught six years. Married October 9, 1888.

MARY E. YOUNG (Mrs. Ed. North) ....Santa Clara County.
Taught about four years, in Monterey and Napa Counties. **Married February 19, 1887.** Not taught since.

DIPLOMAS GRANTED DECEMBER, 1882.

MATTIE GRAEBE........................Santa Clara County.
Present address, San José.
Taught seven years in Santa Clara County; for the past five years in San José.

MARTHA GRANICHER ....Santa Clara County.
Present address, San José.
Taught in Monterey County, four years. **At last report, 1886, was teach**ing in **Pacific** Valley, Monterey County.

MATTIE F. HUNT (Mrs. A. F. Hoehner) ....Sacramento County.
Not taught. Married March 5, 1883. One child.

LIZZIE T. MAHONEY ....Santa Clara County.
Home address, 612 Linden Avenue, San Francisco.
Taught in Mendocino County, three years. At last report, April, **1886, was teaching at Fresno Flats, Fresno County.**

FANNIE MOONEY......................Alameda County.
Present address, 712 Sutter Street, San Francisco.
Taught in Napa County, three **months; Since** August, 1883, in San Francisco. Teaching in South Cosmopolitan Primary School.

IANTHIA REA ....Santa Clara County.
Present address, San José.
At last report, 1885, was teaching second year at Artesia, Los Angeles County

ELLA E. RONEY........................San Francisco.
Home address, 1519 Jackson Street, San Francisco.
Taught in Humboldt County, six months; Del Norte County, two years; San Luis Obispo County, one year; Placer County, one year.

ANNIE L. TALBOT ....Santa Clara County.
Present address, East San José.
Taught in Merced County, five months; Santa Clara County, four years. At last report was teaching in Hall's Valley, Santa Clara County.

TWENTY-FOURTH CLASS—MAY, 1883

GEORGE P. AHLF .... Colusa County.
    Present address, Colusa.
    Not taught. Has engaged in farming since graduation.

LUTIE M. BALIS (deceased) .... Santa Clara County.
    Did not teach. Her health **failed gradually from** the time she graduated until her death, March 15, **1884**. **Address of her** sister, Lola A. Balis, San José.

JAMES G. BEATY .... Yuba County.
    Present address, Oregon House, Yuba County.
    Taught in Plumas County, six months; Butte County, **two years**; Yuba County, two years. Teaching.

LAUREN J. BERRY (Mrs. A. L. Sears) .... Santa Clara County.
    Present address, **Wrights**.
    Taught in Santa Clara County, four years; **Tulare County, two years**. **Married July 3, 1888**. Not teaching.

WILLIAM J. BLACK .... Tuolumne County.
    Taught in the State of Nevada, two years. Justice of the Peace at Lewis several months; also, assayer and bookkeeper for a mining company. At last report, December, 1886, was in a lumber business at San Miguel, Cal.

CORA A. BLAINE .... Santa Clara County.
    Present address, San José.
    Taught in Napa County, three months; Tulare County, two months. Not teaching. Preparing to teach drawing.

KATE I. BROMLEY .... Santa Clara County.
    Present address, **Oroville**, Butte County.
    Taught in Los Angeles County, **one** year; Butte **County, three years**; **Lake County, one year**. Teaching near Upper Lake.

MARY C. BRUNHOUSE .... Santa Clara County.
    Present address, San José.
    Taught in Coulterville, Mariposa County, five **years**; in Bradley, Monterey County, since **August, 1888**.

M. EMELINE CARMICHAEL .... Santa Clara County.
    Present address, San José.
    Taught in Santa Cruz County, one year; San José, five months; Contra Costa County, three and one half years. Teaching in San José.

LUE J. CARVER (Mrs. Jas. E. Conner) ...... Tulare County.
    Present address, Porterville, Tulare County.
    Taught in Kern and Los Angeles Counties three and one half years. **Resigned position in** Los Angeles, November, 1886, on account of failing eyesight. **Not teaching**. Married September 22, 1887.

KITTIE A. CHANDLER............................San Francisco.
  Present address, 213 Duncan Street, San Francisco.
  Taught in El Dorado County, one and one half years; Contra Costa County, one half year; Alameda County, one half year; Marin County, one year. Teaching at Marshall, Marin County.

MARY F. CHEW.............................Santa Clara County.
  Present address, Evergreen, Santa Clara County.
  Taught in Santa Clara County, five years; Monterey County, one half year. Teaching in Monterey County.

IDA E. CLARK.............................San Diego County.
  Present address, 22 Geary Street, San Francisco.
  Taught in Monterey County, five months; Corralitos, Santa Cruz County, two and one half years; Principal of a school in Santa Cruz, one and one half years; taught in San Francisco since spring of 1888. Teaching in Lincoln Grammar School.

LIZZIE M. CLARK.............................Amador County.
  Present address, Ione.
  Taught since graduation near Ione, Amador County.

HENRY A. CLAYTON.........................Santa Clara County.
  Present address, Clayton, Contra Costa County.
  Taught in Santa Barbara County, one year; Contra Costa County, two years. In spring of 1887 was teaching at Clayton.

EUGENE C. COLE.............................Santa Clara County.
  Present address, San José.
  Taught in Monterey County, one year; Stanislaus County, four months.

BELLE DUNCAN.............................Santa Clara County.
  Present address, Salinas City.
  Taught in Sonoma County, two years; Santa Clara County, two and one half years. Has been teaching in Salinas City since November, 1887.

LAURA DUNCAN.............................Santa Clara County.
  Present address, Pasadena, Los Angeles County.
  Did not teach for first year after graduation, because of illness. Taught in Santa Cruz and San Benito Counties, two and one half years; in Pasadena, three years.

LUELLA A. DUNCAN.........................Santa Clara County.
  Present address, Pasadena, Los Angeles County.
  Taught in San Benito and Santa Clara Counties, two years; in Pasadena since 1887.

SUSIE M. DUNN.............................Contra Costa County.
  Present address, 1656 Webster Street, Oakland.
  Taught in Contra Costa County, five years. Teaching at Concord.

CICERO P. EVANS............................Stanislaus County.
   Present address, Carpenteria, Santa Barbara County.
   Taught in Stanislaus County, one year; Guadalupe, Santa Barbara County, two years; in Carpenteria since January, 1887.

E. BELLE FAIRLEE (Mrs. H. B. Spilman)........Sutter County.
   Present address, Pennington.
   Taught two years. Married in fall of 1885. Not taught since.

KATE M. GARTELMAN........................Santa Clara County.
   Present address, Santa Clara.
   Taught in Collins District, Santa Clara County, three years. Not taught since 1886.

LAURA GEORGE (Mrs. Jos. Plunkett).......Santa Clara County.
   Present address, Tuscarora, Nevada.
   Taught three years in Santa Clara County, and two years in Tuscarora. Married December, 1888.

MARGARET G. GILLESPIE ....Santa Clara County.
   Present address, San José.
   Taught in Stanislaus County, two years; in San José, since summer of 1885.

SUSIE M. GILMORE (Mrs. Geo. W. Pierce).....El Dorado County.
   Present address, Davisville, Yolo County.
   Taught in El Dorado County, two years; Fresno County, three years. Married August 15, 1888. Not taught since.

JENNIE L. GREEN...........................Sacramento County.
   Present address, Sacramento.
   Taught in Yolo County, two years. At last report, had not taught since June, 1885.

NETTIE A. GREEN (deceased)...............San Joaquin County.
   Did not teach after graduation, because of failing health. Died April 3, 1884.

CLARA M. GRUBS...........................San Joaquin County.
   Present address, Lockeford.
   Taught two and a half years in Calaveras County; three and a half years in San Joaquin County. Teaching at Lockeford.

JULIA HARRINGTON........................Santa Clara County.
   Present address, Santa Clara.
   Did not teach for first year after graduation, on account of ill health. Taught in Mendocino County, two and one half years; in Santa Clara County, since January, 1887.

RACHEL H. HERRINGTON ....Santa Clara County.
   Present address, Santa Clara.
   Taught in Contra Costa County, one and one half years. Since July, 1885, has taught in the Santa Clara school.

KATE E. JOHNSON............................Yolo County.
Present address, Winters.
Taught in Solano County, one year; Colusa County, four years. Teaching present year at Artesia, Los Angeles County.

IDA M. JONES (deceased) ....Santa Cruz County.
Taught in Colusa County for two months after graduation, and was then obliged to resign because of ill health. Did not teach again until 1886. Then taught one term in Santa Clara County and one year at her home in Laurel, Santa Cruz County. Gave up work again on account of failing health, and died of consumption, at Laurel, May 10, 1889.

MARY L. JONES ....El Dorado County.
Present address, Modesto, Stanislaus County.
Taught in Amador County, one year; El Dorado County, one year; Stanislaus County, four years. Teaching near Modesto.

NELLIE KEATON..............................Santa Clara County.
Present address, San José.
Taught in Monterey County, one and one half years; Santa Clara County, one year; Stanislaus County, one year. Teaching in San José.

EFFIE J. KELSEY (Mrs. J. M. DeWitt)..........Sutter County.
Present address, 216 Jackson Street, San Francisco.
Taught in Santa Clara County, one year. Married September 15, 1884. Not taught since.

LUCINA H. KELSEY (Mrs. G. B. Richardson)...Santa Clara County.
Present address, Lincoln, Placer County.
Taught in Santa Clara County, one and one half years; Placer County, one and one half years; Monterey County, one and one fourth years. Married July 12, 1888. Not teaching.

ANNIE A. KING (Mrs. Charles L. Morrill)...Santa Clara County.
Present address, Oceanside, San Diego County.
Taught in Kern County, two years; Los Angeles County, one year. Left teaching in 1886 on account of sickness. Married June 7, 1887.

GEORGIE E. KNOTT ....Sacramento County.
Present address, Isleton.
At last report, June, 1886, had taught in Sacramento County, three years.

M. ALICE LADD (Mrs. Milton H. Kingsbury)..San Joaquin County.
Present address, 323 Fremont Street, Stockton.
Taught in San Joaquin County, two years. Married in the summer of 1887. Not taught since.

GEORGE E. LARKEY ....Contra Costa County.
Present address, Newhall, Los Angeles County.
Taught three years in Contra Costa County; one year in Los Angeles County. In May, 1887, was teaching at Newhall. Married January 13, 1885, to Miss Mamie A. Bryant.

KAREN M. LAWSON ....Sacramento County.
               Present address, Folsom.
    At last report, December, 1885, had taught three terms in Newcastle, Placer County.

FANNIE LOW (Mrs. Arthur Thatcher) ......Santa Clara County.
               Present address, Kohala, Hawaii, H. I.
    Taught in Santa Clara County, one half year; Kern County, one year; Monterey County, one and a half years. Suspended work in the spring of 1887 on account of ill health. Went to the Sandwich Islands in the summer, where she is now teaching. Married June 24, 1888.

ABBIE MCKEE (Mrs. R. G. Coykendall) ....Santa Clara County.
               Present address, San José.
    Taught two months. Married December 24, 1885. Not teaching.

E. LOUESA METCALF........................San Joaquin County.
               Present address, Lockeford, San Joaquin County.
    Occupied with home duties until fall of 1887. Since then has taught one year in San Diego County, and is teaching the present year in Calaveras County.

IDA P. MILLER (Mrs. J. J. Rice)............Santa Cruz County.
               Present address, Tres Pinos, Monterey County.
    Taught in Santa Cruz and Monterey Counties, four and one half years. Married June 17, 1888. Not teaching.

ALBERT W. MIZE..........................Santa Clara County.
               Address, unknown.
    In May, 1884, had taught one year in Solano County. Reported by a classmate as teaching in Washington Territory.

MARY E MORGAN..........................Santa Clara County.
               Present address, Santa Cruz.
    Taught in a district school in Santa Cruz County, three months; in San Benito County, three months; has taught in Santa Cruz since July, 1884.

ANNA C. MURPHY...........................Placer County.
               Present address, Los Angeles.
    Taught in Colusa, three years; in Los Angeles, two years. Teaching.

KITTIE S. OGILVIE.........................San Francisco.
               Present address, 621 Bush Street, San Francisco.
    Taught in Stanislaus County, one term; Fresno County, two years. Now engaged in type-writing and stenography.

JULIA OWEN (Mrs. George Munson)......Santa Barbara County.
               Present address, San José.
    Taught in Santa Cruz County, one year; Napa County, one year; San Luis Obispo County, two and one half years. Married February 20, 1889. Not teaching.

AGNES PENDER (Mrs. E. W. Conant)........Santa Clara County.
                Present address, San José.
    Taught in Santa Clara County, five years. Married July 2, 1889.

HENRY C. PETRAY............................Sonoma County.
                Present address, Healdsburg.
    Principal of a school in Santa Rosa. Taught one year in **Colusa County**, and five years in Sonoma County. Studying law preparatory to leaving the profession of teaching. Married July 11, 1889, to Miss Annie A. Brooke.

EMILY M. PURINTON (Mrs. H. H. McCloskey)...Merced County.
                Present address, Merced.
    Taught one year in Merced County. Married January 1, 1885. Not taught since. **One child.**

LENORA A. RICHARDS (Mrs. Rich)...........Santa Clara County.
                Present address, San Francisco.
    Taught in Merced County, three months; Stanislaus County, five months; in Del Norte County, one year. In 1885 went to San Francisco, and, while studying stenography, taught in the evening school. For the past two years, has been teaching stenography in the Commercial School, San Francisco. Married July 7, 1888. Expects to teach private pupils after July, 1889.

M. GEORGIA ROOKER (Mrs. Frank T. Green).....State of Nevada.
                Present address, 929 Haight Street, San Francisco.
    Not taught since graduation. Married November 12, 1884. **One child.**

MARION A. ROUSE........................Santa Clara County.
                Home address, Alma.
    Taught in Santa Cruz County, three months; Santa Clara County, two and one half years; Los Angeles County, one year. Teaching in Los Angeles.

C. JEAN SCHNEBLY (Mrs. J. B. Davidson)...Washington Territory.
                Present address, Ellensburg, Washington Territory.
    Taught in Washington **Territory, two and** one half years. Married March 31, 1886.

KATE SEXTON............................Santa Clara County
                Present address, San José.
    Taught in Monterey County, four years; San José, one and **one** half years. Teaching in San José.

ARTHUR R. SHEATS.......................Contra Costa County.
                Present address, San Pablo.
    Taught in Contra Costa County continuously since graduation. Teaching at San Pablo.

RICHARD J. SINNOTT .... Sierra County.
Present address, Gibsonville.
Taught in Sierra County, three years; in Plumas County, one and one half years; in Los Angeles County, one and one half years. Not teaching at present, but expects to teach again soon. Married June 25, 1885. One child.

EDITH C. SMITH .... Sacramento County.
Present address, Folsom.
At last report, July, 1886, had taught in Placer County, six months; Sacramento County, two years. Teaching in Folsom.

M. LOUISE SMITH (Mrs. Frederic S. Cox) .... Santa Cruz County.
Present address, Los Angeles.
Taught three years in Santa Cruz County before marriage. Married August 17, 1886.

MARY S SMITH (Mrs. W. A. Lane) .... Santa Clara County.
Present address, Orland, Colusa County.
Taught in Sacramento County, one year; Napa County, three months; Monterey County, one year; Tehama County, two years. Married March 31, 1889. Not teaching.

ELLA V. SPENCER (Mrs. A. B. Campbell) .... Merced County.
Present address, Smith River, Del Norte County.
Taught in Stanislaus County, one year; Merced County, three months; Del Norte County, three years. Teaching at Smith River.

MARY R. STEPHENS .... Santa Clara County.
Home address, Santa Clara.
Taught in Monterey County, four years. Work suspended one year, 1885, on account of sickness. Teaching near Jolon.

JOHN W. STIRLING .... Monterey County.
Present address, Castroville.
Taught in San Mateo County, one year; Monterey County, two and one half years. Left teaching in spring of 1887. Warehouse keeper for Bank at Castroville.

L. MAY STERN .... Santa Clara County.
Home address, San José.
Taught in Stanislaus County, one year; Alameda County, two years; Merced County, one half year; San Diego County, one year. Work suspended one half year on account of home duties. Teaching at Otay, San Diego County.

AMY A. STEVES (Mrs. Henry Austin) ...... San Joaquin County.
Present address, Stockton.
Taught in San Joaquin County, two years; Mariposa County, three years. Married in the fall of 1888.

FANNY STOCKTON ---------------------------Santa Clara County.
　　　　　　　Present address, San José.
　　Taught in Monterey County, four months; San Benito County, four months; **in San José, three and one half** years. Teaching in San José.

WILLIAM H. SUMNER------------ --------Santa Clara County.
　　　　　　　Present address, San José.
　　Taught in Santa Clara County, three and one half years. Not teaching.

ANNA C. THOMPSON ---------------------Santa Clara County.
　　　　　　　Home address, Santa Clara.
　　Taught in Monterey County, four months; Santa Clara County, **one and one half** years; Stanislaus County, three years.

FLORA C. THOMPSON (Mrs. George Coffee) --Santa Clara County.
　　　　　　Present address, Bakersfield, Kern County.
　　Taught two years in Kern County. Married in April, 1885. Not taught since.

ISAAC S. THOMPSON---------- -------------Santa Clara County.
　　　　　　　Home address, Santa Clara.
　　Taught **six months in Stanislaus County.** In July, 1884, opened school at St. Louis, Sierra County, **where he was** teaching at last report.

MARTHA B. THOMPSON (Mrs. Keeler)-------Santa Clara County.
　　　　　　Present address, Santa Clara.
　　Taught one year in Santa Clara County; five years in Kern **County.** Married in 1889. Not teaching.

JESSIE O. TOLMAN (Mrs. Watkins)---------Santa Cruz County.
　　　　　　Present address, Mineral Park, Arizona.
　　Taught three years in Arizona. Teaching when last heard from.

ANGY F. WAKEMAN ------------------------Alameda County.
　　　　　Present address, 1064 Tenth Avenue, Oakland.
　　Taught in Contra Costa County, one and one half years; Alameda County, two years. At last report was teaching in Franklin School, Oakland.

MOLLIE E. WALSH---------------------------El Dorado County.
　　　　　　　Present address, Placerville.
　　Taught in El Dorado County continuously since graduation. **Teaching.**

DORA B. WASHBURN ----------------------Calaveras County.
　　　　　　Present **address, San Andreas.**
　　At last report, 1886, had taught three years in Calaveras County.

KATE F. WATKINS (deceased)----------------Placer County.
　　Taught in Santa Cruz **two years.** Gave up work on account of failing **health.** Died after a long and painful illness, July 15, 1886.

FANNIE P. WEST (Mrs. W. W. Gillespie)..........Nevada County.
  Present address, San José.
  Taught three years in Nevada City. Married June 30, 1886. Not taught since. Two children.

AMY WHATMORE..............................San Francisco.
  Present address, San Diego.
  Taught in Monterey County, one year; Santa Clara County, two and one half years; San Diego, two years. Teaching in San Diego.

NELLIE T. WICKHAM...........................Napa County.
  Present address, Napa City.
  Taught five years in Napa County. Taking a course in Heald's Business College, San Francisco.

BESSIE WOODWARD (Mrs. T. A. King)......Santa Clara County.
  Present address, San José.
  Taught in San Joaquin County, three years. Married May 4, 1886. Not taught since. Two children, one living.

LIZZIE N. WRISTEN (Mrs. E. H. Bentley)...........Yolo County.
  Present address, Los Angeles.
  Taught in Fresno County, two years. Married May 13, 1885. Not taught since.

TWENTY-FIFTH CLASS—DECEMBER, 1883.

FRANK B. ABBE..............................San Benito County.
  Present address, San Juan.
  Taught continuously since graduation in Aromas District, San Benito County. A part of the time, has been editor of a newspaper.

LILY A. ADDICOTT (Mrs. D. S. Snodgrass), (deceased).Placer Co.
  Address of husband, Selma, Fresno County.
  Taught a private school in Placer County, five months; in public schools of Fresno City from summer of 1884 to fall of 1886. Married October 30, 1886. Did not teach afterward on account of failing health. Died August 3, 1888.

HATTIE E. ATHERTON (Mrs. Hyland E. Barber)....Marin County.
  Present address, Stockton.
  Taught five years in Marin County. Married December 5, 1888. Not teaching.

MARTHA AUGUSTINE...........................Marin County.
  Present address, Normal, Illinois.
  Taught in San Rafael, Marin County, four and one half years. Returned to her former home in Illinois in the summer of 1888, and is now teaching in Normal.

ELLA G. BILLINGS............................Santa Clara County.
    Present address, Santa Clara.
  Taught in Contra Costa County, one term; in San Mateo County, one year. At last report, 1886, was teaching at Woodside, San Mateo County.

ANNA E. BLACK (Mrs. Geo. W. Crawford)....San Benito County.
    Present address, Los Angeles.
  Taught one year in San Benito County, and two years in Santa Clara County. Married August 10, 1887. Not taught since.

LUCY E. BOTSFORD............................Santa Clara County.
    Present address, San José.
  Taught in Fresno County, one year; Santa Clara County, three and one half years. Teaching in Santa Clara County.

JOSEPHINE BRALY (deceased)................Santa Clara County.
  Taught two years—September, 1884, to June, 1886—in Fresno City, and was very successful, especially in primary work. Her special department was music. She was obliged to give up work on account of failing health. Died in Fresno City, May 2, 1887.

JENNIE R. BUSH..............................Santa Clara County.
    Present address, Laribee, Humboldt County.
  Taught in Humboldt County, five years, teaching a private school during vacations of the public school. Also taught music to private pupils, and a part of the time held an evening school. Work suspended since October, 1888, on account of injuries received in a stage accident, while on her way to attend a County Institute.

ANGELINE CHAMBAUD..........................Sonoma County.
    Present address, Santa Rosa.
  Taught in Sonoma County continuously since graduation. Teaching in Santa Rosa.

LIDA C CLARK................................Santa Clara County.
    Present address, East San José.
  Taught in Santa Clara County, four years. Has been teaching in the East San José School, three years.

BEN. B. CORY................................Santa Clara County.
    Present address, Lodi, San Joaquin County.
  Taught in San José and in Lodi, five years in all. Teaching at Lodi.

LIZZIE B. CREW (Mrs. E. E. Canfield)...........Butte County.
  Taught in Chico, nine months. Married February 10, 1886. Not taught since.

MARY E. CURTIS..............................Tulare County.
    Present address, Visalia.
  At last report, 1886, had taught two years in Tulare County. Was not teaching on account of poor health.

GEORGE F. DUNCAN............................Santa Clara County.
　　　　　　　　Present address, Los Angeles.
　　Taught in Santa Barbara County until January, 1887. **Since that time in Los Angeles County.**

HENRIETTA T. ELLERHORST........................San Francisco.
　　　　　Present address, 1931 Pine Street, San **Francisco.**
　　Taught at Brannan Island, Sacramento County, from July, 1884, **to December, 1887. Since January, 1888, has** been teaching near Oakland.

ZILPHA HAYFORD (Mrs. A. J. Storey)............Placer County.
　　　　　Present address, 608 Capp Street, San Francisco.
　　Taught in Placer County, two and one half years. Not taught since **May, 1886.** Married January 20, 1887.

LUCY D. HETTY................................Santa Clara County.
　　　　　　　　Present address, Santa Clara.
　　Taught in Los Angeles County, five months; in Monterey County, fifteen months. Work suspended three terms on account of home duties. For the past two years has been teaching in Santa Clara.

ELIZA F. HIGGINS............................Santa Clara County.
　　　　　　　　Present address, San José.
　　Taught in Marin County, one year. In August, 1885, opened school in Mt. Pleasant District, Santa Clara County, where she was teaching at last report, 1886.

CHARLES M. HODGES..........................San Benito County.
　　At last report, **October, 1886,** was teaching at Paicines, San Benito County. Had taught in that county one and one half years.

MRS. S. E. HOLYER............................Alameda County.
　　　　　　　　Present address, San José.
　　Taught in Santa Clara County, four **months;** Amador County, one year; Fresno County, two years; Tulare County, where she is now teaching, six months. Work suspended a part of the time because of home duties.

GEORGE J. HOTHERSALL........................Nevada County.
　　　　　　　　Present address, Nevada City.
　　Taught three and one half years in Nevada County. Teaching.

I. PETRA JOHNSTON............................San Mateo County.
　　　　　　　　Present address, Half Moon Bay.
　　Taught continuously **since February,** 1885, in public school at Half Moon Bay.

LIZZIE P. JUDSON (Mrs. W. E. Hardy).........San Diego County.
　　　　　　　　Present address, Bernardo.
　　Taught in San Diego County, two years. Work suspended much of the time **on account of** ill health. Not teaching. Married September 11, 1888.

HATTIE M. KEATING . ... .San Joaquin County.
Present address, 266 Rose Street, Stockton.
Taught in Merced County, one year; in Stockton, since August, 1886. Teaching a primary class.

ELLA KELLY .... Yuba County.
Present address, Marysville.
Taught in Sierra County, two years; Yuba County, two years. At last report, 1888, was teaching at Honcut, Yuba County.

MIRIAM F. KOOSER....... .... Santa Cruz County.
Present address, Los Angeles.
Taught in Santa Clara County, three years; in City of Los Angeles since August, 1887.

KATE McCARTHY.......................... Santa Clara County.
Present address, Los Angeles.
Taught in Humboldt County, four and one half years; in City of Los Angeles, one year. Teaching.

MARY McHARRY.......................... Contra Costa County.
Present address, Martinez.
Taught in Fresno County, one term; in Contra Costa County, two years. At last report, 1887, was teaching at Pinole.

DANIEL MAHONEY........................ Nevada County.
Present address, French Corral.
Taught in Fresno County, three years; in Nevada County, one year. Teaching at French Corral.

SARAH A. MARTIN....................... Santa Clara County.
Home address, San José.
At last report, 1884, was teaching in Santa Clara County.

BESSIE J. MAYNE .... Santa Clara County.
Present address, San José.
Was Principal of the public school at Crescent City three years. Since January, 1888, has been teaching in the University of the Pacific, San José. Has taught music at various times when not engaged in public school work.

ELLA A. MILLS (Mrs. John Zielian)......... Santa Clara County.
Present address, Modesto, Stanislaus County.
Taught in Solano County, one year; in Stanislaus County, one year before marriage. Married November 29, 1885. Since that time has taught in Stanislaus County, five months in 1886 and a part of 1888. Not teaching.

MARY T. MOONEY........................ Alameda County.
Present address, North Temescal.
Taught in Monterey County, six months; San Bernardino County, four months; Mendocino County, three months. Since January 12, 1886, has been teaching in the Urban (private) School, 1017 Hyde Street, San Francisco.

BERTHA C. MORRISON (Mrs. B. K. Said)..........Solano County.
        Present address, Bakersfield, Kern County.
    Taught in Solano County, four months; Washington Territory, one month. Not teaching. Married August 12, 1884. One child.

ANNIE ORR............................Santa Clara County.
        Present address, San José.
    Taught in San Luis Obispo County, one year; Contra Costa County, four months; Monterey County, one year; Napa County, one and one half years. Teaching in San Benito County.

BESSIE OVERFELT (Mrs. W. D. Hatch)......Santa Clara County.
        Present address, San José.
    Trught in Monterey County, **three** months; in Santa Clara County, two and one half years. Married December 5, 1886. Two children. **Not taught** since December, 1888, but expects to teach again.

MATTIE M. PATTERSON (Mrs. D. B. Frazee)...Santa Clara County.
        Present address, San Luis Rey, San Diego County.
    Taught in Fresno County, four months; San Diego County, two years. Not taught since May, 1886. Married July 19, 1885. One child.

BELLE PHELPS ....Santa Clara County.
        Present address, San José.
    At last report, December, 1886, had taught one year in Sierra County and two years in Santa Clara County. Was teaching.

ELLA I. SANDERS ....Santa Clara County.
        Present address, San José.
    At last report, 1887, was teaching near Petrolia, Humboldt County. Had previously taught three years in Monterey County.

KATE SENTER............................Santa Clara County.
        Present address, San José.
    Taught in Humboldt County, one year; Marin County, one year; Fresno County, two years. Not teaching at present because of home duties.

DAVID S. SNODGRASS......................Stanislaus County.
        Present address, Selma, Fresno County.
    Taught in Stanislaus County, one term. Was Principal of Fresno City schools from September, 1884, to June, 1887. Resigned to take position as cashier of a bank. Married October 30, 1886, to Miss Lily A. Addicott, of same class.

MARTHA M. TURNER........................San Joaquin County.
        Present address, French Camp.
    Taught in San Joaquin County, one year; in Reno, Nevada, two years. Returned to French Camp in June, 1887, where she has taught since.

FRANK G. TYRRELL ....Humboldt County.
  Taught two years in Humboldt County. Married September 5, 1888, at Harrisonville, Missouri, to Miss Edna B. Scott.

JOHN F. UTTER..........................Mendocino County.
  Present address, Redwood City.
  Taught in Santa Cruz County, one year; San Mateo County, two years. Has held the office of County Superintendent of San Mateo County since January, 1887.

IDA M. WAGGONER (Mrs. Harmon) ....Merced County.
  Present address, San José.
  Taught in Fresno County, one year.

CECILIA A. WILLIAMS.......................Fresno County.
  Present address, Fresno City.
  Taught in Fresno County, four years. Work suspended one year because of sickness. Teaching in Fresno City.

MAGGIE WILLIAMS (Mrs. F. P. Reed), (deceased)..........
  ....Contra Costa County.
  Taught the primary department of the Antioch school from February, 1884, until within a week of her death, April 14, 1887. Married November 6, 1886. Husband's address, Antioch. Mrs. Reed was a very successful teacher, and an active worker in the Sunday School and the W. C. T. U. She was universally beloved and mourned by her acquaintances and friends.

FLORA WOOD (Mrs. Covington) ....San Bernardino County.
  Present address, San Bernardino.
  Taught three years in San Bernardino County.

JOHN J. ZIELIAN ....Tuolumne County.
  Present address, Modesto, Stanislaus County.
  Has taught in Stanislaus County constantly since October, 1884; for the past three years in Modesto. Is Vice-Principal of the Modesto school and a member of the County Board of Education. Married November 29, 1885, to Ella A. Mills, of the same class.

TWENTY-SIXTH CLASS—MAY, 1884.

ALICE E. BEAIZLEY ....Alameda County.
  Present address, Gilbertsville, Otsego County, New York.
  Taught in Napa County, four months. In April, 1885, removed with her family to New York State, where she now resides. At last report was teaching private pupils.

ELMER E. BROWNELL......................Santa Clara County.
  Home address, San José.
  Taught in Contra Costa County, three months; San Luis Obispo County, one year; Alameda County, two and one half years; Santa Clara County, three months. Teaching at Decoto, Alameda County.

FRANK A. BUTTS ....Contra Costa County.
                    Present address, South Vallejo.

    Taught in Plumas County, one year. Principal of the South Vallejo School since July 1, 1888. Married January 2, 1888, to Miss Maude Walcott, a graduate of the State University. His wife died November 26, 1888.

JESSIE I. CALHOUN ....Santa Clara County.
                    Present address, San José.

    Substituted in San Francisco schools for first year after graduation; then as regular teacher four months. In October, 1885, went to Europe, where she made a special study of elocution. After an absence of two years she returned to San José. Is now teaching elocution in the University of the Pacific and to private pupils.

VIRGINIA C. CALHOUN ....Santa Clara County.
                    Present address, San José.

    Has been teaching in the Hester School, San José, continuously since graduation.

SARAH CHAMBAUD ....Sonoma County.
                    Present address, Santa Rosa.

    Taught in Sonoma County, three and a half years. Teaching near Santa Rosa.

BELLE CHICKERING ....San Diego County.
                    Present address, Los Angeles.

    At last report, 1886, had taught two years in Los Angeles County, and was teaching near Santa Monica.

SUSIE CORY ....Santa Clara County.
                    Present address, San José.

    Taught in Fresno County, one year; San José, one year. Resigned in June, 1886, on account of ill health. Has since spent a year in Europe.

LIZZIE C. COTTLE ....Santa Clara County.
                    Present address, San José.

    Taught in Santa Clara County, one and a half years; in Monterey County, one year. At last report was teaching near Salinas City.

MARY E. DE ZALDO ....Santa Clara County.
                    Present address, San Miguel, San Luis Obispo County.

    Taught in Santa Clara County, one half year; Monterey County, one year; San Luis Obispo County, one year. At last report was teaching near San Miguel, where she had taken up a quarter section of land.

MARY T. DOYLE ....Santa Clara County.
                    Present address, San José.

    At last report, 1887, had taught three years in Burnett District, Santa Clara County, and was still teaching.

KATIE A. DOYLE............................Santa Clara County.
　　　　　Present address, Santa Clara.
　　Taught in Monterey County, one year. Since the summer of 1885 has been teaching in the Santa Clara public school.

MARY P. EASTER...........................Santa Clara County.
　　　　Home address, 1718 San Pablo Avenue, Oakland.
　　Has taught three years in Mendocino County. During vacations has studied art.

ALLIE M. FELKER..........................Santa Cruz County.
　　　　　Present address, Santa Cruz.
　　Taught in Santa Cruz County, one year; Monterey County, three years, two years of this time in the Salinas City school; five months in the Kindergarten, San José. Took a kindergarten course in San Francisco in spring of 1889, and received a diploma. Has done much literary work in the way of essays, letters, and poems for newspaper publication.

AUGUSTUS W. FISHER ....Santa Clara County.
　　　　　Present address, unknown.
　　Taught a short time in San Diego and Fresno Counties. Diploma revoked by Board of Trustees of the Normal School, June 24, 1889.

NORMA FREYSCHLAG.......................Santa Clara County.
　　　　　Present address, San Diego.
　　Taught in Kern County, three and one half years; in San Diego County, one year. Was injured by a falling school building during a storm in San Diego, in December, 1888, and has not taught since.

GEORGE A. GORDON.........................Amador County.
　　　　　Present address, Jackson.
　　At last report, 1887, was teaching in Ætna District, Amador County, where he had taught continuously since graduation.

MARY B. GREEN............................Santa Clara County.
　　　　　Present address, Salinas City.
　　Taught in Merced County, three years; in Monterey County, one year. Teaching near Salinas City.

EMILY HARRIS (Mrs. A. J. Gillis) ....Santa Clara County.
　　　　Present address, 732 Folsom Street, San Francisco.
　　Taught four months in Monterey County. Married December 4, 1884. Not taught since. One child.

KATE HARTMAN (Mrs. L. F. Castle)........Santa Clara County.
　　　　Present address, Crook, Crook County, Oregon.
　　Taught one year in Santa Clara County. Married July 15, 1886. Not taught since.

EVA HASTY (Mrs. D. B. North) ....Butte County
　　　　　Present address, Gridley.
　　Taught in Plumas County, five months; Butte County, two years. Married December 19, 1888.

ALICE J. HODGE (Mrs. Fred. A. Gray)......Santa Cruz County.
   Present address, Santa Cruz.
   Taught in Santa Cruz County, five months; Monterey County, one and a half years. Married in 1886.

MAY KENNEDY..................................Yolo County.
   Present address, Capay.
   Taught one year in Stanislaus County; one year in Yolo County; one year in Tulare County.

ABBIE L. MARTIN..............................San Francisco.
   Home address, 2719 Pine Street, San Francisco.
   Taught in Calaveras County, one year; Santa Clara County, three years. Teaching at Gubserville, Santa Clara County.

ELLA G. MILES (Mrs. F. M. Lewis).........Santa Clara County.
   Present address, Fresno City.
   Taught four months in Monterey County; five months in Santa Clara County; two years in Fresno County. Married October 26, 1887. Not taught since.

ALBION S. MEILY..............................Sierra County.
   Home address, Forest City, Sierra County.
   Taught continuously since graduation in Butte County. Teaching at Enterprise.

M. KATE MONTGOMERY.......................Sonoma County.
   Present address, Visalia, Tulare County.
   Taught in Mendocino County, one year; in Petaluma, two years. Work suspended one year on account of ill health. Teaching since October, 1888, near Visalia.

AGNES M. PARSON.............................State of Nevada.
   Present address, Fresno City.
   Taught in San Joaquin County, one year; Santa Cruz County, one year; Kern County, four months. Since September, 1887, has taught in the schools of Fresno City.

MADGE H. PERKINS...........................Santa Cruz County.
   Present address, Santa Barbara.
   Taught in Santa Cruz County, two years; in Santa Barbara, since August, 1887. Work suspended six months to attend business college.

MARY C. ROBERT.............................Santa Cruz County.
   Present address, Watsonville.
   At last report, 1887, was teaching in Watsonville, where she had taught continuously since graduation.

NELLIE SHINE.................................Tuolumne County.
   Home address, Columbia.
   Taught one year in Stanislaus County; three years in Tuolumne County Teaching since summer of 1888 in Los Angeles.

NELLIE STIRLING (Mrs. C. R. Whitcher) ......Monterey County.
Present address, Castroville.
Taught in Monterey County, two years; Salinas City, one year. Married September 21, 1887. Not taught since.

CHARLOTTE J. STIVERS......................Alameda County.
Present address, Irvington.
Taught one year.

JOHN W. SULLIVAN..........................Santa Clara County.
Present address, San Diego.
Taught two years in Sutter County, and one year in Los Angeles County Studied law, and was admitted to the Supreme Court of California while yet teaching. Left the profession of teaching in June, 1887, and is now practicing law in San Diego.

FRANCES A. SUÑOL...........................Alameda County.
Present address, Fruit Vale.
Taught at Suñol Glen, Alameda County, three and one half years. Teaching in Marin County.

CLAUDIA M. TOMPKINS (Mrs. W. A. Stephens)......Yolo County.
Present address, Madison.
Taught at Madison, two and one half years. Married January 12, 1887. Not taught since.

ANITA WHITNEY..............................Alameda County.
Home address, 1076 Fourteenth Street, Oakland.
Not taught. Has spent time since graduation in study. Is attending Wellesley College, Massachusetts, and expects to graduate in June, 1889.

ELMA K. YANEY..............................Inyo County.
Present address, Bishop Creek.
Taught continuously since graduation in Inyo County.

TWENTY-SEVENTH CLASS—DECEMBER, 1884.

CARL H. ALLEN.............................Santa Clara County
Present address, Wrights.
Taught in the State of Nevada, one term; in Fresno County, one term. Now engaged in fruit raising in the Santa Cruz Mountains.

ELISE M. ASMUS............................San Francisco.
Present address, 917 Polk Street, San Francisco.
Taught one term.

FLORENCE BAUGH (Mrs. C. H. Betts).........San Diego County.
Present address, Bradley, Monterey County.
Taught two and one half years in Monterey County. Suspended work in May, 1887, on account of ill health. Married December 7, 1885.

IDA BEGGS......................................Santa Clara County.
    Present address, Los Gatos.
  Taught in Fresno County from graduation until November, 1888. Since that time has been teaching in Los Gatos.

ADDIE S. BENNETT (Mrs. E. S. Pinney)...........Tulare County.
    Present address, Tulare.
  Taught one year in Tulare County, then left the work permanently on account of ill health.

ALICE CAMP.....................................Santa Clara County.
    Present address, San José.
  Taught at Pacific Mills, Santa Cruz County, one and one half years; in Santa Clara County, two years; in Felton, Santa Cruz County, one year.

LOLA B. CLAYES.................................San Francisco.
    Present address, Stockton.
  Taught in Stanislaus County, two years. Since September, 1886, has taught constantly, both summer and winter, in Calaveras County. Summer school at Big Trees.

ANNIE COCHRANE.................................Mono County.
    Present address, Bodie.
  Taught three years in Mono County. In December, 1887, was teaching at Bodie.

GEORGIETTA N. CONGDON (Mrs. Fred. Bailey).....Santa Clara Co.
    Present address, Port Townsend, Washington Territory.
  Taught in Santa Barbara County, four months; Sierra County, six months; Los Angeles County, four months. Prevented from teaching a greater length of time by sickness in the family. Married January 10, 1889. Not teaching.

IONE M. CUNNINGHAM.............................Santa Cruz County.
    Present address, Soquel.
  At last report, 1887, was teaching in Summit District, Santa Cruz Mountains, where she had taught one and one half years.

JULIA DAUBENBIS................................Santa Cruz County.
    Present address, Soquel.
  Taught continuously in Santa Cruz County since graduation; for the past three years in Branciforte School.

CARRIE F. DONNELLY.............................San Francisco.
    Present address, 318 Oak Street, San Francisco.
  Taught four months in San Benito County, in spring of 1885. Work suspended from that time until September, 1888. Since then has been teaching in New Almaden, Santa Clara County.

ANNA H. DOWLING................................Nevada County.
    Present address, Moore's Flat.
  Taught one and a half years in a private school at Grass Valley. At last report, 1887, was teaching first year in public schools, at Iowa Hill, Placer County.

ANNIE DOWNING (deceased)................Monterey County.
Taught **four** months in spring of 1885, in Monterey County. Was prevented by sickness from further work. Died at her home in Salinas City, November 2, 1886.

LILLIE DUNCAN.............................Santa Clara County.
Present address, Los Angeles.
Taught in San Benito County, one and one half years. In August, 1886, began teaching at Norwalk, Los Angeles County, where she was teaching at last report, May, 1887.

CARRIE M. GARDNER (Mrs. W. H. Peake) ....Butte County.
Present address, Corning, Tehama County.
Taught in the Chico School from October, 1885, to May, 1887. Married May 11, 1887. **Not teaching.**

G. ANNIE GIRDNER (Mrs. Geo. A. Pratt)....**Santa Clara County.**
Present address, Challenge Mill, Yuba County.
Taught one term in Sacramento County; two years at Orland, Colusa County; one year in Marysville; one term in Yuba County. Teaching second term at Challenge Mill. **Married February 20, 1889.**

MILDRED HANSON.........................Santa Clara County.
Home address, San José.
Taught in Tulare County, one year; San Luis Obispo County, two years; Washington Territory, one year. Now teaching in Waitsburg, Washington Territory. To return to California soon.

MARY G. HARRIMAN......................Santa Clara County.
Present address, Dutch Flat, Placer County.
At last report had taught one year in Placer County. Was not teaching.

ANNIE C. HENNINGS ....Alameda County.
Present address, 1652 Fourteenth Street, West Oakland.
Taught in **Alameda** County constantly since graduation. Teaching in Oakland.

KATIE L. HENRY ....San Joaquin County
Present address, Stockton.
Taught two years in **Fresno** County. Not teaching.

ANNE HETFIELD (Mrs. Hasty)..............Humboldt County.
Present address, Eureka.
Taught in Humboldt County, two years. Married March 5, **1887.** One child. Work suspended after marriage two years. Teaching in Humboldt County.

THOMPSON HOLLINGSWORTH................. Santa Cruz County.
Present address, Jolon, Monterey County.
Taught three months in Santa Cruz County. **Suspended** work in June, 1885, to take up land in Monterey County. Now farming, but expects to teach again. Married April 26, 1887.

ETTA H. JACKSON................................Santa Clara County.
    Present address, Alameda.
  Since July, 1885, has taught continuously in the public schools of Alameda.

HENRIETTA E. KINGDON..............................Sierra County.
    Present address, Scales.
  Taught in Scales three years, to December, 1887. Is now taking a course in the Cooper Medical College, San Francisco. Teaching private school at Scales during vacation.

HATTIE V. MARTIN................................Santa Clara County.
    Present address, 2719 Pine Street, San Francisco.
  Taught in Sacramento County, one year. Since the summer of 1886 has been teaching in San Francisco, Pacific Heights School.

LOTTIE J. MATTHIS...............................Monterey County.
    Present address, San Miguel, San Luis Obispo County.
  Taught in Monterey County, three years; in Franklin School near San José, one year. Not teaching at present.

JENNIE G. MCCARTHY..............................Santa Clara County.
    Present address, Los Angeles.
  Taught three years in Humboldt County. Now teaching in Los Angeles.

KATE G. MCELWEE..................................San Francisco.
    Present address, Auburn, Placer County.
  Taught in El Dorado County, one year; Placer County, three years. Teaching at Auburn.

KATE A. MCGIVERN.................................San Francisco.
    Present address, 381 Dolores Street, San Francisco.
  At last report, 1886, had taught one year in Del Norte County.

THOMAS J. MCGRATH................................Sierra County.
    Present address, St. Louis.
  Taught three years in Sierra County. During 1886 was bookkeeping and clerking. Teaching at Goodyear Bar. Is President of the Board of Education of Sierra County.

MARGARET E. MCINTOSH.............................State of Nevada.
    Present address, Reno.
  Taught in Boca, Nevada County, one year. At last report, 1886, was to teach the same school again.

CHARLES N. MILLS.................................Santa Clara County.
    Present address, Eureka Mills, Plumas County.
  Taught in Sierra County, one year; Plumas County, one and one half years; Sutter County, one half year. In 1887 was teaching at Eureka Mills.

MAMEY MURRAY..................................Placer County
   Present address, Auburn.
   Taught in Sierra County, one year; Placer and Sacramento Counties, twelve months; Normal School, San José, five months; Salinas City, one month; Placer County, six months. Has given much attention to music, and is now teaching music pupils in Auburn.

NETTIE M. MURRAY..............................Placer County.
   Present address, Auburn.
   Taught four years. At last report was teaching.

CALLIE F. NEEL (Mrs. J. W. Thomas).....Santa Clara County.
   Present address, Gilroy.
   Taught in a joint district of Santa Clara and San Benito Counties, two and one half years.

ANNIE M. NICHOLSON...........................Fresno County.
   Present address, Madera.
   Taught in Santa Cruz County, one term. Since September, 1885, has taught in the school at Madera. Is now Principal.

MARY E. NORTON................................Marin County.
   Present address, San Rafael.
   Has taught three years in the San Rafael schools. Previous to that taught one year in a country school in Marin County.

DORA A. PERRY..................................Solano County.
   Present address, Suisun.
   Taught in Solano County, one year; in Los Angeles County, one and one half years. In 1887 was teaching in Los Angeles.

WILEMINA RAMER.............................Santa Clara County.
   Present address, Santa Cruz.
   Taught at Dougherty's Mill, Santa Cruz County, three years. Since that time has been teaching in the Santa Cruz schools.

LIZZIE A. RENNIE..............................Santa Cruz County.
   Present address, Yuba City.
   Taught in Solano County, two years; in Sutter County, two years. Teaching in Yuba City.

NELLIE B. RICHARDSON (Mrs. Walt. S. Huyck)..Santa Clara Co.
   Present address, San Diego.
   Taught in Merced County, two years; Santa Barbara County, one term. Work suspended one year because of sickness. Married in November, 1887, and has not taught since.

MAGGIE E. ROBERTSON.......................Santa Clara County.
   Home address, 44 Whitney Street, San José.
   Has taught continuously in Monterey County since graduation; for the past three years at Paraiso Springs.

ELECTRA M. RUMSEY (Mrs. A. C. Sherwood)........Yolo County.
Present address, San Diego.
Taught in San Mateo County, three months; in San Diego County, one year. Has also taught private pupils. At last report was not teaching.

AGNES A. SPATZ.. San Francisco.
Present address, Alameda.
Taught in Alameda County since graduation. Teaching in Alameda.

BIRDIE E. STODDARD.................................... San Francisco.
Present address, 426 Sutter Street, San Francisco.
Taught four months in Sonoma County. Since January, 1886, has been teaching in San Francisco, Potrero School.

GERTRUDE THOMSON (Mrs. Epperly).............San Francisco.
Present address, Avenales, San Luis Obispo County.
Was prevented from teaching for two and one half years after graduation by sickness. Has been teaching since August, 1887, in San Luis Obispo County.

MATTIE M. TRIMBLE........................ Santa Clara County.
Present address, San José.
Has taught one and one half years in Santa Clara County. Teaching in Orchard District.

NETTIE C. WARRING........................Santa Clara County.
Home address, San José.
Taught in Monterey County, one term. Since October, 1885, in Ventura County. At last report, 1887, was teaching at Saticoy.

ANNIE L. WELLS............................Santa Clara County.
Home address, San José.
Taught in Monterey County, one year. At last report, 1886, was teaching in Sierra County.

NINA F. WILLIAMS(Mrs. Harry Van Valkenburgh).Santa Clara Co.
Present address, Cholame, San Luis Obispo County.
Taught during 1885 in Monterey and San Benito Counties. Spent two years attending the Art School in San Francisco. In 1887-88 taught one year in San Luis Obispo County. Married November 14, 1888.

TWENTY-EIGHTH CLASS—MAY, 1885.

EDITH E. AYER............................Santa Clara County.
Present address, Milpitas.
Has taught continuously in the Milpitas school since graduation.

HATTIE E. BACKUS........................San Benito County
Present address, Hollister.
At last report, 1887, was teaching at Cienga, San Benito County. Had taught in that county two years.

ESTELLA M. BAGNELL.........................Santa Clara County.
              Present address, Madera, Fresno County
    Taught one year in Santa Clara County; three and a half years in Fresno County; since 1887 at Madera.

HENRY R. BAILEY...............................Marin County.
              Present address, Tomales.
    Taught one year in Lake County. Spent two years in dairy-farming. At last report, August, 1887, was teaching the Tomales school. Member of County Board of Education. Married. One child.

WILLIAM H. BAILEY (deceased) ....Marin County.
    Taught one **year**; then engaged in farming. Died in San Francisco, October 3, 1889.

ALICE K. BALLOU ....Santa Clara County.
              Home address, San José.
    Taught one term in Santa Clara County. Is now taking a course in **the** Boston Conservatory of Music. To return to California in summer of **1889.**

CARRIE BECKWITH............................**Humboldt County.**
              Home address, Hydesville.
    Taught three years at Table Bluff, Humboldt County. Teaching in Washington Grammar School, San Francisco, since August, 1888.

WILLIAM O. BLODGET..........................Shasta County.
              Present address, Millville.
    Taught one year in Butte County, and two and one half years in **Shasta County. Much** of the time has taught twelve months in **the year, alternating summer and winter schools.**

JULIA BODLEY ....Santa Clara County.
              Present address, San José.
    Taught one and one fourth years in Santa Clara County after graduation. Since that time has been engaged in the office of the City Clerk, San José.

MATTIE BRADLEY.............................Nevada County.
              Present address, Nevada City.
    Taught in North Bloomfield, one year; since August 30, 1886, in **the** Primary School, Nevada City.

LAURA E. BRIDE (Mrs. Wm. H. Powers).........San Francisco.
              Present address, San Francisco.
    Taught three years in the schools of San Francisco. Married February 19, 1889.

EMMA H. BUSHNELL...........................Santa Clara County.
              Present address, Waynesburg, Pennsylvania.
    Taught four months **in Solano County.** In September, 1886, removed, with her family, to Pennsylvania. Since then has spent her time in study **at the Waynesburg College.**

NANNIE L. CALHOUN ....Sonoma County.
    Present address, Windsor.
Has taught continuously near Windsor since graduation.

MAGGIE E. CARR ....Humboldt County.
    Present address, Rohnerville.
Taught constantly in Humboldt County since graduation.

FRANK R. CAUCH................................Santa Barbara County.
    Present address, Selma, Fresno County.
Taught in Modoc County, three years—a part of this time twelve months in the year. Since September, 1888, has taught at Selma. Member of Board of Education in Modoc County. Married November 11, 1887, to Miss Lydia V. Addicott.

TILLIE M. CLARK ....Santa Clara County.
    Home address, San José.
Teaching near Yuba City, Sutter County, third year in the same school.

ELLA COLEMAN (deceased)........................Santa Cruz County.
Taught six months in Monterey County. Gave up work on account of sickness. Died June 10, 1886.

EMMA J. DICKEY ....Humboldt County.
    Present address, Eureka.
Has taught in Humboldt County continuously since graduation. Teaching in Eureka.

JULIA A. DONOVAN ....Sacramento County.
    Present address, Folsom.
In 1887 was teaching at Grizzly Flat. Had taught two years in El Dorado County.

ELLA A. FERRY ....Alameda County.
    Present address, 1317 Jackson Street, Oakland.
In 1887 was teaching in the Oakland schools.

MARINE GAGE (deceased).........................Sacramento County.
Taught in Galt two years and six months. Died June 3, 1888. His death, from quick consumption, occurred six weeks after he closed his school. Mr. Gage was a noble man and an earnest teacher. His work received the highest praise from those who knew him best.

JOSEPHINE A. GAIRAUD (Mrs. D. T. Bateman)...Santa Clara Co.
    Present address, Mountain View.
Has taught continuously since graduation at Mountain View, Santa Clara County.

MINNIE G. GALINDO.............................Alameda County.
    Present address, Mission San José.
Taught one year in Sunol, and since then has taught in Mission San José.

BESSIE E. GIBBONS..............................Alameda County.
Present address, West End, Alameda.
Substituted four months in San Leandro; taught one year in Napa County; one year in Monterey County. Since January, 1888, in Alameda County.

GEORGIA A. GORDON..............................Monterey County.
Present address, Monterey.
At last report, 1887, was teaching in Monterey County. Had taught one year.

FRANK M. GRAHAM..............................Kern County
Present address, San José.
Taught in Merced County, two years; Butte County, six months; Santa Clara County, one year. Teaching at Berryessa, near San José.

FRANCISCO GREIERSEN..............................Stanislaus County.
Present address, Oakdale.
Taught in Stanislaus County, one year; in Fresno County, three months. Work suspended much of the time since graduation because of sickness. Not teaching at present.

LILLIE HARRIS..............................Alameda County.
Present address, Pleasanton.
Has taught continuously in Pleasanton, since March, 1886.

THEODOSIA M. HAWXHURST (Mrs. Frederick E. Glass)......
..............................Contra Costa County.
Present address, Antioch.
Taught three years in Contra Costa County. Married December 19, 1888. Not teaching.

AGNES G. HENRY..............................San Joaquin County.
Present address, 253 Fremont Street, Stockton.
Taught two years in Fresno County. Not teaching.

STELLA M. HERNDON..............................Santa Clara County.
Present address, San José.
Teaching at Saratoga. Has taught in Santa Clara County three and one half years.

JESSIE IRVING..............................Alameda County.
Present address, 711 Fifth Street, Oakland.
In 1887 was teaching in Oakland, where she had taught one term.

MARY E. KELSEY (Mrs. L. M. Damewood)..Santa Clara County.
Present address, Royal, Lane County, Oregon.
Taught in Placer County, three months; in Oregon, three years; in Porterville, Tulare County, one term. Teaching in Royal. Was married in Oregon January 22, 1887.

EMILY F. A. KNOTT..................................Marin County.
        Present address, 609 Post Street, San Francisco.
    Taught two years in Sonoma County. Has not taught since the spring of 1887, because of home duties.

MAGGIE KOTTINGER ....Santa Clara County
        Present address, San José.
    Did not teach, except a short time in a private family, until August, 1887; then taught one year in Santa Clara County. Now teaching in Merced County, near Snelling.

ANNIE M. KULLAK ....Santa Clara County.
        Home address, San José.
    Taught two years in the Santa Cruz Mountains, near Wrights; one year in San Luis Obispo County; since July, 1888, at Moss Landing, Monterey County.

FLORA E. LACY............................Santa Cruz County.
        Present address, San Diego.
    Has taught since March, 1886, in San Diego and Santa Cruz Counties.

WILLIAM W. LOCKE......................San Joaquin County.
        Home address, Lockeford.
    Taught about two years in San Joaquin County. Is now at Exeter, New Hampshire, preparing for college.

GEORGE W. MARTIN (deceased) ....Shasta County.
    Mr. Martin was taken ill with lung trouble during the second term of the Senior year, and was obliged to leave school before the close of the term. The disease developed rapidly in spite of all attempts to check it. He died at his home in Millville, Shasta County, October 8, 1885.

LILLIE J. MILLER ....Santa Clara County.
        Present address, New Almaden.
    Has taught continuously since graduation in the primary grade of the New Almaden school.

MARY T. NEUEBAUMER......................Tuolumne County.
        Present address, Columbia.
    Was prevented by sickness from teaching for several months after graduation. Since August, 1886, has taught in Placer County. At last report, was teaching at Newcastle.

IDA C. NICHOLS.............................Sonoma County.
        Present address, Freestone.
    Since graduation has taught two and one half years in Sonoma County. Has spent the remainder of the time pursuing higher studies. Teaching at Glen Ellen, Sonoma County.

MARY L. ORTLEY (Mrs. F. A. Wilcox)......Santa Clara County.
        Present address, Santa Clara.
    Taught in Santa Clara County, one year. Married June 13, 1886. Not taught since.

NELLIE PAGE..............................Santa Clara County.
                Present address, Mountain View.
    Taught one year in Mariposa County. Since summer of 1886 has taught at **Mountain View**.

LIZZIE A. PARKER..........................Alameda County.
                Present address, Berkeley.
    Has taught continuously since graduation in the **Prescott School**, Oakland.

EDITH L. PURINTON (Mrs. Elsworth G. Sharon)..Santa Clara Co.
                Present address, San José.
    Taught in **Merced** County, two years. Not **taught since May, 1888**. Married April **7, 1889**.

MARGARET RICHMOND.........................Humboldt County.
    At last report, 1887, was teaching at Ferndale, Humboldt County. Had taught two years.

DAISY C. SCHUTTE (Mrs. Robert I. Lillie)........San Francisco.
                Present address, **Honolulu, Hawaiian** Islands.
    Taught one term in Los Angeles **County, and** one **year in Humboldt** County. Gave up work because of failing health, and went to the Sandwich Islands, where she was married July 14, 1887.

ELLA M. STILSON..........................San Mateo County.
                Home address, San José.
    Did not teach for first year after graduation. Has since taught **one year in Monterey County,** and one and a half years in Contra **Costa County. Teaching.**

ANNIE L. TAYLOR (Mrs. **Heman G. Squier**)........San Francisco.
                Present address, Gibsonville, Sierra County.
    Taught about two years in Sutter County. Married May 19, 1887. Not taught since.

IDA M. THOMAS............................Santa Clara County.
                Present address, San José.
    Teaching at Evergreen. Has taught in Santa Clara County constantly since August, 1885.

MARTHA A. TRIMINGHAM....................Alameda County.
                Present address, Suñol Glen.
    Taught three years in the Suñol Glen school. In September, 1888, opened school in Daneville, Placer County.

NANNIE E. TUTTLE.........................Santa Cruz County.
                Present address, Watsonville.
    Taught one year. At last report was not teaching, because of ill health.

EMMA VOTAW (Mrs. John Barry)............Amador County.
                Present address, San José.
    Taught one year in Amador County. Not taught since marriage.

KATE C. WAMBOLD ....Sonoma County.
        Home address, Cloverdale.
    Taught two years in San Simeon, San Luis Obispo County, to May, 1887; in San Luis Obispo, one and one half years; in Mendocino County, one term. Has suspended work to take the Post Graduate course in the Normal School at Los Angeles.

HENRY E. WITHERSPOON ....Arizona Territory.
        Present address, Etna, Siskiyou County
    Taught private pupils in San José until October, 1886. Since that time has taught in Siskiyou County; for more than a year past at Etna. Has written on mining and geology for a mining paper.

CORA K. WYCKOFF..............................Alameda County.
        Home address, 1512 Ninth Street, Oakland.
    Taught five months in Monterey County. In April, 1886, resigned, and went to the Sandwich Islands. Since May, 1886, has been teaching in the East Maui Seminary, Makawao, Maui.

EDITH D. YAPLE (Mrs. Jas. S. Moulton).....San Joaquin County.
        Present address, Ripon.
    Taught two years near Ripon. Married July 31, 1887. Since that time has taught in the school at Linden, of which her husband is Principal.

TWENTY-NINTH CLASS—DECEMBER, 1885.

CHARLES C. ADAMS.............................San Joaquin County.
        Present address, Lathrop.
    Taught in San Joaquin County continuously since graduation. Teaching at Lathrop.

JOHN B. ATCHISON ....Butte County.
        Present address, Oroville.
    In December, 1887, was teaching his first school, at Forest City, Sierra County. Previous to this was engaged in printing.

HORACE G. BACON ....San Benito County
    In December, 1886, had been Principal of the school in Alamo, Contra Costa County, one year.

JULIA S. BROWN (Mrs. Joshua Downs)........Santa Clara County.
        Present address, San José.
    Taught in Solano County, one term, of three and one half months. Married November 11, 1886. Not taught since.

MARY E. BROWNING.............................Amador County.
        Present address, Ione.
    Taught one year in Monterey County; two years in Fresno County. Work suspended several months because of sickness. Not teaching at present.

HARRY F. CLARK ....Sutter County.
    Present address, Saticoy, Ventura County.
   Taught in Sutter and Yuba Counties, one year; was Principal of the school at Brentwood, Contra Costa County, two years. Left the profession in November, 1888, and is now farming. Married July 27, 1887, to Miss **Aggie** B. Nicholl, of **the same class.** One child.

ANNE F. CONLIN ....Nevada County.
    Present address, Grass Valley.
   In July, 1887, had taught one year in the Grass Valley schools, and expected to continue.

FRANCES S. CONN ....Nevada County.
    Present address, **Fresno City, Fresno** County.
   Taught two **years in the primary department at North San Juan,** to April, 1888. **Is teaching in Central Colony, near Fresno City.**

MARY A. COOK ....State of Nevada.
    Present address, Los Angeles.
   Taught in Santa Clara County, one and one half years. Has taught in Amelia Street School, Los Angeles, since October, **1887.**

LIVIA M. COX (Mrs. Frank Glass) ....Contra Costa County.
    Present address, Martinez.
   Taught the same school, near San Ramon, Contra Costa County, for two years, to November, 1887. Married December 28, 1887. One child. Not teaching.

FLORENCE CRICHTON ....Santa Clara County.
    Present address, San José.
   Taught two years in Sierra County and one year in Santa Clara County. **Not teaching at present.**

LILIAN A. CROSS ....Placer County.
    Present address, **Roseville.**
   Taught first half year in Sacramento County; second half year in Humboldt County. **In** January, 1887, was teaching a joint district of Sacramento and Placer Counties, near **Antelope.**

LIZZIE DEACON ....San Francisco.
    Present address, 811 Twentieth Street, San Francisco.
   In April, 1887, had been teaching one month in Sierra District, Santa Clara County; first school.

ALBERT L. DORNBERGER ....Santa Clara County.
    Present address, Mayfield.
   Taught a private **school in Stanislaus County one year.** Since July, 1887, has been Principal of the Mayfield **school.**

VICTOR DORNBERGER ....Santa Clara County
    Present address, Mayfield.
   Taught music in **San** Francisco for several months. Since July, 1887, **has** taught in the Mayfield school.

FLORENCE GALLOWAY........................... Sonoma County.
  Present address, Valley Ford.
    Taught in Humboldt County, two years; Sonoma County, one year. Teaching in Sonoma County.

LEWIS GOBLE................................. Humboldt County.
  Present address, Ferndale.
    Taught two and one half years in Humboldt County. Now teaching at Laws, Inyo County.

MARGARET GRAHAM (Mrs. Joseph Hood).......... Kern County.
  Present address, San José.
    Taught six months in the State of Nevada, and one year in San José. Married June 21, 1887. One child.

ADA M. GREENE............................... San Joaquin County
  Present address, San José.
    Taught one month in Monterey County; one year in Santa Clara County. Teaching at Berryessa.

E. LOUISE GROVE............................. San Francisco.
  Present address, 546 Elm Street, Oakland.
    Taught for one year, from July, 1886, in Alameda County. At last report, February, 1888, was teaching in Los Angeles.

SARAH C. HANDLY............................. Santa Clara County.
  Present address, San José.
    In September, 1886, began teaching at Benton, Mono County. At last report was teaching the same school.

ETTA E. HERRMANN............................ Santa Clara County.
  Present address, San José.
    At last report was teaching in Santa Clara County. Had taught in that county five months, and in Sacramento County one term.

LIZZIE KEATON............................... Santa Clara County.
  Present address, San José.
    Taught two and one half months in Stanislaus County; two years in Monterey County. Since July, 1888, has been teaching at Mountain View, Santa Clara County.

MINNIE E. LORIGAN........................... Santa Clara County.
  Present address, Santa Clara.
    Taught one year at Felton, Santa Cruz County. Is now teaching in Santa Clara.

FANNY S. LYONS.............................. Sacramento County.
  Present address, Folsom.
    At last report, 1887, had taught one year in Sacramento County.

FANNY L. MCKEAN ....Santa Cruz County.
Home address, San José.
Taught in Santa Cruz County, one year; in San Bernardino County, one year; in Monterey County, four months. Teaching near Weimer, Placer County.

MOLLIE MCLERAN..........................Santa Clara County.
Taught three years in Alviso, Santa Clara County; part of this time as Principal. Is now teaching at Trinity Center, Trinity County.

LIZZIE C. MONAGHAN ....Santa Clara County.
Present address, San José.
Since graduation has taught continuously in the Hester School, San José.

FRANCES MURRAY ....Alameda County.
Taught in Marin County, five months; in Oakland, one year. At last report, was teaching in Darwin, Inyo County.

AGGIE B. NICHOLL (Mrs. H. F. Clark)......Contra Costa County.
Present address, Saticoy, Ventura County.
Taught one term in Contra Costa County. Married July 27, 1887. One child.

JOHN F. OGDEN ....Santa Clara County.
Present address, San José.
Has taught since spring of 1887 in same school near Yuba City, Sutter County.

JULIA RUMRILL ....Contra Costa County.
Present address, San Pablo.
Has taught continuously since graduation in San Pablo.

NETTIE C. SHARPE ....State of Nevada.
Home address, Gold Hill.
Has taught since October, 1886, in Nevada. Is teaching second year at Washoe City.

CLARA E. SHAW.........................Santa Clara County.
In August, 1886, had just opened **her first school** near Erie, San Benito County. No report since.

WINNIE S. SLEDGE ....Fresno County.
Present address, Madera.
Taught three months in a country district in Fresno County directly after graduating. Since November, 1886, **has** taught in the Fresno City schools.

S. HELEN SNOOK.........................Alameda County.
Present address, **1678** Taylor Street, Oakland.
Since January, 1886, has taught continuously in the Oakland schools.

ADELAIDE C. SPAFFORD..........................Alameda County.
           Present address, 2315 Sutter Street, San Francisco.

Taught one term at Alma, Santa Clara County; two years in the Eureka Academy, Eureka, Humboldt County. **Teaching** near San Luis Obispo.

HEMAN G. SQUIER..............................Sierra County
           Present address, Gibsonville, Sierra County.

Has taught continuously since July, 1886, one term in Sutter County, and the remainder of the time in Plumas County. Now teaching at Quincy, Plumas County. Married May 19, 1887, to Annie L. Taylor, Class of May, 1885.

HATTIE L. STILSON............................San Mateo County.
           Home address, San José.

Has taught two years in San Diego County and one year in Contra Costa County. Teaching near Wildomar, San Diego County.

M. RUTH THOMPSON..........................Santa Clara County.
           Present address, Santa Clara.

Has taught since April, 1886, in Santa Clara County. Is now teaching in Santa Clara.

DORA THRUSH................................San Joaquin County.
           Present address, Stockton.

Taught one term in Fresno County in 1887; one year in San Joaquin County. Teaching in Stockton.

MARION E. TRUE (Mrs. W. H. Edwards)........Lassen County.
           Present address, Los Angeles.

Taught two years in Lassen County. Married in June, 1888, and left the profession of teaching.

MINNIE G. WARD..............................Butte County.
           Present address, Oroville.

Spent some months after graduation in studying music. In January, 1888, had taught one term in Butte County, and expected to teach the same school again.

NELLIE WYCKOFF..............................Alameda County.
           Home address, 1512 Ninth Street, Oakland.

Taught two and one half years in Monterey County. Since September, 1888, near Woodland, Yolo County.

ANNA F. ZANE................................Humboldt County.
           Present address, Eureka.

Since summer of 1886 has taught continuously in the Eureka schools. Previous to that taught one term near Hydesville.

THIRTIETH CLASS—MAY, 1886.

GEORGE E. ARNOLD............................Santa Clara County.
    Present address, Milpitas.
    Has taught two years at Loyalton, Sierra County. Teaching.

OSEE E. ASHLEY..............................Santa Clara County.
    Present address, Milpitas.
    Last report, May, 1887, had taught one year at Milpitas.

HUGH L. BANKHEAD ....Placer County.
    Present address, Pino.
    Is teaching third year in Tehama County, at Paskenta. Has also taught six months at St. Louis, Sierra County.

LENA BARKLEY................................Butte County.
    Present address, Chico.
    Taught two years in Butte County.

MAMIE BASS..................................Alameda County.
    Present address, Pleasanton.
    Taught in Alameda County, two years. Teaching near Livermore.

MAMIE T. BECKMAN............................Nevada County.
    Present address, Nevada City.
    At last report, 1887, had taught one year in Nevada County, and was to continue.

CARRIE BRAUER (Mrs. Frederick W. Plapp)......San Francisco.
    Taught two years in primary grades in Anaheim, and one year in Los Angeles. Married August, 1889, in San Francisco.

ANNIE P. BUCKLEY............................Placer County.
    Home address, San José.
    Taught in Stanislaus County, one year; Placer County, one year Teaching since September, 1888, near Paskenta, Tehama County.

GRACE CAMPBELL ....Alameda County.
    Home address, Oakland.
    Has taught at Livermore, Alameda County, continuously since graduation.

BELLA R. CASSIN ....Santa Cruz County.
    Present address, Watsonville.
    Has taught in Santa Cruz County continuously since graduation.

FRED. L. CAUCH..............................Santa Barbara County.
    Taught from January, 1887, to May, 1888, in Carpenteria, Santa Barbara County. Has left the profession of teaching, and gone East, to take a two years' course in a dental college.

HATTIE CORY............................Santa Clara County.
Present address, San José.
Taught one term in Contra Costa County, and one term in Santa Clara County. In 1887–88 took a year's course of study in Mills' Seminary, and graduated. Not teaching at present.

JULIA A. CROWLEY........................State of Nevada.
Present address, Virginia City.
Has taught since September, 1887, as Assistant Principal in the Virginia City High School.

JOSEPHINE DENTON........................Nevada County.
Present address, San José.
Has taught continuously since graduation in the San José Fourth Ward School.

RACHEL S. GILMOUR.......................Humboldt County.
Present address, Eureka.
Taught three years in Humboldt County. Teaching near Eureka.

EDITH A. GRANGER (Mrs. Elmer E. Chase)....Alameda County.
Present address, San José.
Taught at Alvarado, Alameda County, until marriage. Married April 19, 1888.

ALBERT M. GRAY..........................Tulare County.
Present address, San José.
Taught one and one half years in Evergreen, Santa Clara County; one year in the San José day schools; two terms in the evening school, where he is now teaching. Is engaged as a life insurance agent.

MINNIE GRAY............................Tulare County.
Present address, San José.
Taught in Tulare County, two years; Santa Clara County, one year. Teaching in Santa Clara County.

A. MAY GRIFFIN.........................Contra Costa County.
Present address, Martinez.
Taught one year at Riverside, San Bernardino County. Since July, 1887, has taught near Martinez.

ISABEL GRUMMET.........................Butte County.
Home address, Oroville.
Is teaching her third term at Oregon City, Butte County.

FANNIE HALL............................Alameda County.
In October, 1887, was teaching in Santa Ana; second year in Los Angeles County.

AGNES S. HAMILTON......................Alameda County.
At last report was teaching second year at Richland, Sacramento County.

FLORENCE M. HAYS..............................Shasta County.
     Present address, Burney Valley.
  Is teaching second year in Shasta County. Suspended work one year on account of home duties and other business.

HELEN F. HODGE (Mrs. C. R. Arnold)......Santa Cruz County.
    Present address, Hueneme, Ventura County.
  Taught in Santa Cruz County, one year; in Ventura County, one year. Married April 4, 1889. Not teaching.

JOHN M. HOLMES (deceased)...................Fresno County.
  Taught two years in Fresno County. Died in Fresno City, September 2, 1889, after an illness of eight weeks.

KATE F. HOWARD............................Contra Costa County.
    Present address, Walnut Creek.
  Taught two years in Contra Costa County. Teaching.

LUCY A. HOWES...............................Santa Clara County.
    Present address, San José.
  In August, 1887, had closed one year's work in Los Angeles County, and expected to teach in Santa Clara County.

FLORA HUNZIKER (Mrs. E. A. Cooley).........Sonoma County.
    Present address, Cloverdale.
  Taught two years in the Cloverdale school, until marriage. Not teaching.

I. MANLA INGEMUNDSEN..........................Napa County.
    Present address, Napa City.
  Has taught in Napa County continuously since graduation; since July, 1888, in Napa City.

MARIE JOHNSTON.............................Humboldt County.
    Present address, Eureka.
  Taught in Humboldt County, two years. At last report was not teaching.

LENA C. JONES.............................Contra Costa County.
    Present address, Walnut Creek.
  At last report was to open third year of work at Walnut Creek.

LIZZIE KEENAN................................Nevada County.
    Present address, Nevada City.
  Has taught three years in Pleasant Valley, Nevada County. Teaching.

ADA V. KELLEY.............................Santa Cruz County.
    Present address, Watsonville.
  Taught one year in Santa Cruz County.

REBECCA F. KENNEDY............................Amador County.
    Present address, Ione.
  Taught one and one half years in Amador County; three months in Los Angeles County.

Louis J. Lathwesen......................Santa Clara County.
                Present address, San José.
   Taught one term in Fresno County. Has not taught since except **three months** in the City Night School, San José. For two years past **has been** engaged in McNeil Brothers' Printing House, San José.

Martin H. Lawson.........................Santa Clara County.
             Present address, Bradley, **Monterey County**.
   Has not taught since graduation. Is Station Agent at Bradley.

M. Lily Love............................Santa Clara County.
               Present address, Los Gatos.
   Has taught in the Los Gatos school continuously since graduation.

Maggie Lowden...........................Alameda County.
           Present address, 971 Center Street, Oakland.
   Taught one year in Alameda County. Not teaching.

Mary E. Lynch (Mrs. Wm. R. Rhinehart)........Yuba County.
           Present address, Gridley, Butte County.
   Taught two years in Sutter County, and one year in Butte County. Married June 5, 1889, and left the profession.

Julia A. Manchester.......................Merced County.
               Present address, Merced.
   At last report had taught one year in Merced County.

Dora C. McKenzie (deceased)................Marin County.
   Taught in San Rafael, Marin County, five months, beginning in January, 1887. Gave up work because of illness. Died in San Rafael November 7, 1887. Resolutions of respect to her memory were adopted by her fellow teachers and published in the San Rafael papers.

Mary Mott..............................Sacramento County.
   At last report, August, 1887, was teaching near Ferndale, Humboldt County. Had previously taught one year near Roseville, Placer County.

Anna L. Murphy........................Contra Costa County.
              Present address, Brentwood.
   In December, 1887, had taught one and a half years in the same school near Brentwood.

Myra A. Parks............................Lassen County.
              Present address, Janesville.
   Has taught one and one half years near Janesville, Lassen County. Since January, 1887, has held the office of County Superintendent of Lassen County. On account of the duties attending this office, her teaching work has been suspended part of the time.

William O. Peck...........................Sierra County.
               Present address, Loyalton.
   At last report, 1887, had been engaged in mining business since graduation and had not taught.

L. CARRIE PECKHAM..............................Santa Clara County.
     Present address, San José.
 Has not taught since graduation.

ELINOR D. PRATT................................Humboldt County.
     Present address, Eureka.
 Has taught in Humboldt County continuously since graduation; for the past two and one half years in Eureka. Teaching in Eureka.

MEGGIE L. ROBB................................Santa Clara County.
     Present address, San José.
 Taught in Monterey County, one year. Since August, 1887, has taught in the San José schools.

SUSIE W. RUCKER..............................Santa Clara County.
     Present address, San José.
 Taught one year in Hamilton District, Santa Clara County. Since summer of 1887 has taught in the Hester School, San José.

MARY A. SIMMONS (deceased)..............Humboldt County.
 Taught near Arcata, Humboldt County, one year. Her health, which was poor during her Senior year, failed rapidly, and she died of consumption, September 13, 1887. Miss Simmons was a faithful, conscientious teacher, much beloved by her pupils. Resolutions of respect to her memory were passed by her fellow teachers, at the Humboldt County Institute held in October, 1887.

MARY J. STEWART.............................Santa Clara County.
     Present address, Alma.
 Is teaching in Lexington District, near Alma, where she has taught continuously since graduation.

DELIA M. WATKINS (Mrs. Campbell)..........Amador County.
 Taught one year in Amador County; six months in Los Angeles. Married in summer of 1888. Not teaching.

WILLARD D. WOODWORTH.....................Sutter County.
     Present address, Yuba City.
 Has taught three years in Central District, near Yuba City.

Members of Earlier Classes who made up conditions and received their Diplomas with the Class of May, 1886.

MRS. AIMEE L. CAREY (*nee* Madan), 1878-79....Santa Clara Co.
   Present address, 1316 California Street, San Francisco.
 Has not taught since graduation.

MINNIE M. HYATT (Mrs. Henry J. Barton), 1884-85..........
....San Francisco.
     Present address, San Francisco.
 Has not taught since graduation. Married June 5, 1889.

THIRTY-FIRST CLASS—DECEMBER, 1886.

M. LYDIA ADAMS............................State of Nevada.
    Home address, Genoa, Nevada.
 At last report, January, 1888, had been teaching four months near Woodfords, Alpine County. First school.

NELLIE M. BREYFOGLE.......................Fresno County.
    Present address, Madera.
 Has taught since September, 1887, in the Primary Department of the Madera School.

MABEL J. FIELD............................Santa Clara County.
    Present address, San José.
 Has not taught since graduation.

ANNIE L. FRAZIER..........................Santa Cruz County.
    Present address, Watsonville.
 Taught continuously in Santa Cruz County since graduation. Teaching in the Primary Department of the Watsonville school.

SUSIE GALLIMORE...........................Santa Clara County.
    Present address, San José.
 Teaching in San José. Has taught two years in Santa Clara County, and seven weeks in San Mateo County.

CORA E. GILLESPIE.........................Santa Clara County.
    Present address, San José.
 Taught three months in Sacramento County in 1887, and three and one half months in Santa Clara County in 1888. Work suspended because of ill health.

MAY C. GILLOOLY...........................State of Nevada.
    Present address, Virginia City, Nevada.
 In October, 1887, had opened first school in Fresno County. No report since.

ISABEL S. GLEASON.........................Alameda County.
    Present address, San Leandro.
 Taught two years near San Leandro. Since than has substituted in the Oakland schools.

MARGARET A. HANSON........................Santa Clara County.
    Present address, San José.
 Taught one term in Santa Clara County, and one term in Santa Cruz County. Teaching at Woodside, San Mateo County.

S. ADELAIDE HARRIS........................State of Nevada.
    Present address, Reno, Nevada.
 In October, 1887, had taught in Reno since graduation.

LIDA E. F. HATCH ....San Francisco.
                          Present address, Salinas City
    Has taught the Graves School, near Salinas City, continuously since graduation.

FRANK H. HERBERT ....Santa Clara County.
                     Present address, Santa Barbara.
    Taught one term in Monterey County in spring of 1887; then left the profession to become a bookkeeper. Now with Southern Mill and Warehouse Company, Santa Barbara.

MARY E. HOLMES ....State of Nevada.
                    Present address, Gold Hill, Nevada.
    Taught one year in Alameda County, and one year at Gold Hill, Nevada. Teaching as Vice-Principal of High School.

FRANCES H. JONES ....Colusa County.
                      Present address, Colusa.
    Has taught two years near Colusa.

CORA A. LEE ....Santa Clara County.
                      Present address, San José.
    Taught five months in Monterey County in 1887, and five months in Alameda County in 1888. Teaching in San Luis Obispo County.

MAY E. MANSFIELD ....Tuolumne County.
                    Present address, Columbia.
    Has taught two years in Tuolumne County. Teaching in Columbia. Member of Board of Education.

MABEL N. McKAY ....Santa Clara County.
                    Present address, Newcastle, Placer County.
    Has taught the same school near Newcastle since September, 1887.

CARRIE M. MELLEN ....Alameda County.
               Present address, 932 Fourteenth Street, Oakland.
    At last report, April, 1888, was teaching near Ventura. Had previously taught one term in Monterey County.

ELLITA MOTT ....Sacramento County.
    In July, 1888, opened first school near Elk River, Humboldt County. No report since.

BONNIE OAKLEY ....Sacramento County.
                    Present address, Folsom.
    No report since graduation.

CARRIE E. OLIVER ....Santa Cruz County.
                    Present address, Soquel.
    In October, 1887, was teaching near Soquel, where she had taught continuously since graduation.

ABBIE F. PHILLIPS ....Trinity County.
                Home address, Lewiston.
    Taught three months at Pacific Grove, Monterey County; private class at Lewiston, one year. Since July, 1888, has been teaching near Cayucos, San Luis Obispo County.

ANNA M. RASMUSSEN.... .Modoc County.
                Present address, Fort Bidwell.
    At last report had taught one year in Modoc County, and expected to continue teaching.

ANNA M. RICHARDSON......................Alameda County.
                Present address, 535 Laurel Street, Oakland.
    Taught one and one half years in Monterey County; one year in Oakland. Teaching in Grant School, Oakland.

CARRIE SOMERS................................Placer County.
                Present address, Newcastle.
    Has taught in the Primary Department of the Auburn school since October, 1887.

DUNCAN STIRLING ....Monterey County.
                Present address, Castroville.
    Taught one year in Los Angeles County, beginning in July, 1887. Since November, 1888, has been teaching at Meridian, Sutter County.

CHRISTINE STRUVE........................Santa Cruz County.
                Present address, Watsonville.
    Has taught in Monterey County since graduation. Teaching near Salinas City.

ESTHER SUMMERS ....Santa Clara County.
                Present address, San José.
    Taught one year in Del Norte County. Teaching near San José since July, 1888.

ANNABEL TUTTLE (Mrs. W. R. Radcliff).....Santa Cruz County.
                Present address, Watsonville.
    Taught one and one half years in Los Angeles; one year in Watsonville. Married September 12, 1889. Not teaching.

RICHARD D. WILLIAMS....................Contra Costa County.
                Post Office address, Pleasanton, Alameda County.
    Has been teaching since March, 1887, at his home in Contra Costa County, nine miles from Pleasanton.

M. FRANCES YOUNG ....Santa Cruz County.
                Present address, Laurel, Santa Cruz County.
    Taught one year near Watsonville, Santa Cruz County, and one year near Laurel. Teaching.

Member of Class of 1884-85, who made up Conditions and Received Her Diploma with Class of December, 1886.

H. GRACE REYNOLDS..Lake County.
      Present address, Upper Lake.
 Taught in Lake County since January, 1887. Teaching at Clover Creek.

THIRTY-SECOND CLASS—MAY, 1887.

GEORGE B. ALBEE..Humboldt County.
      Present address, Eureka.
 Taught five months in Trinity County; three and one half months in El Dorado County; one and one half months in Humboldt County; one year in Sierra County. **Teaching at Sierra City.**

ANNIE F. ALBRECHT..San Francisco.
   Present address, 1917 Green Street, San Francisco.
 Is teaching second year in San Diego County, at Escondido.

JENNIE A. ALLEN..Alameda County.
     Present address, San Lorenzo.
 Is teaching second year at Pomo, Mendocino County.

LIZZIE ARMSTRONG..Mono County.
   Present address, Coronado, San Diego County.
 Taught one term in San Luis Obispo County, and two years **at Coronado. Teaching.**

CARRIE L. AVERY..Contra Costa County.
     Present address, San José.
 Taught one year and a half near Madrone, Santa Clara County. Teaching near Salinas City.

ETHEL C. AYER..Santa Clara County.
     Present address, Milpitas.
 Taught one term at Cupertino, Santa Clara County.

LOUIS C. BAILEY..Marin County.
   Present address, Freestone, Sonoma County.
 Taught one year in Lake County. Not teaching.

EVA BENNETT..Santa Clara County.
     Present address, San José.
 Taught three months at Alviso. Since December, 1887, has taught in the Santa Clara Street School, San José.

GRACE BICKFORD..Colusa County.
     Present address, Elk Creek.
 Teaching second year near Elk Creek, Colusa County.

CHARLES F. BONDSHU............................Mariposa County.
    Present address, Crescent City, Del Norte County
    Has taught in Del Norte County since August, 1887. Is Principal of the Crescent City School and a member of the Board of Education.

SUSIE M. BROWN (Mrs. G. H. Anderson).....Santa Clara County.
    Present address, San José.
    Taught one year in Monterey County before marriage. Married January 19, 1889. Not teaching.

CILLINDA A. CASSERLY ....Sierra County.
    Present address, Goodyear's Bar.
    Has taught one year in Sierra County. Did not teach for first year after graduation, because of ill health.

MADGE M. CLAYES ....San Francisco.
    Present address, Stockton.
    Taught first year, to May, 1888, in Butte County; three months in San Luis Obispo County. Teaching near Stockton.

JESSIE M. CORMACK............................Santa Cruz County.
    Present address, Edna, San Luis Obispo County.
    Teaching in San Luis Obispo County.

FANNIE A. COTTLE............................Santa Clara County.
    Present address, San José.
    Taught one year in Merced County. Not teaching.

MAGGIE COX ....Santa Cruz County.
    Present address, Watsonville.
    Is teaching second year in the Lindley school, near Watsonville.

DELLA CRAIN...................................Butte County.
    Present address, Gridley.
    Teaching second year near Gridley, Butte County.

CELIA DANIELS ....Modoc County.
    Present address, Lake City.
    Taught one year in Concord, Contra Costa County; one term at Lake City. Teaching in Modoc County.

KATE M. DAVIS ....Alameda County.
    Present address, Livermore.
    Taught two years in the Livermore school.

ANNIE E. DURKEE ....Alameda County.
    Present address, Warm Springs.
    Has taught continuously since graduation in the Primary Department of the Warm Springs school.

NETTIE FALCONER............................Santa Clara County.
    Present address, San José.
    Teaching second year in Mariposa County. Address, Lewis.

FRANCES A. FEELY ....Santa Clara County.
    Present address, Patchin.
 Taught one year in Sacramento County; one term in Napa County. Has not taught since November, 1888, on account of ill health.

MINNIE B. FINCH ....Sacramento County.
    Present address, Natoma.
 At last report, October, 1887, was teaching in Natoma, Sacramento County.

AGNES R. GILLESPIE ....Utah Territory.
    Present address, Park City, Utah Territory.
 Has taught continuously since graduation in Park City.

MANDILLA GINGERY ....Humboldt County.
    Present address, San José.
 Taught one year in Humboldt County and two terms in Sonoma County. Teaching near Fort Ross, Sonoma County.

FLORENCE GUPPY ....Santa Clara County.
    Present address, San José.
 Has devoted her time since graduation to the study of music.

FANNIE M. HITE (Mrs. Sanford Scott) ....Santa Clara County.
    Present address, Chiles, Napa County.
 Taught one term at Emmet, San Benito County; one year at Chiles, Napa County. Married December 13, 1888. Expects to continue teaching.

JOHN C. HUGHES ....Missouri.
    Present address, Sierra City, Sierra County.
 Has not taught since graduation on account of other business.

ESTHER E. A. JEPSEN ....Napa County.
    Present address, Napa City.
 At last report, August, 1887, was teaching in the primary grade of the Napa City school.

MRS. EDITH JOHNSON ....Merced County.
    Present address, Santa Cruz.
 Teaching in Fresno County; first school since graduation.

LIZZIE M. JOHNSTON ....Alameda County.
    Present address, 404 Sixteenth Street, East Oakland.
 Taught one year in Fresno County. Is teaching second term in Hunter District, near Vallejo.

ALICE L. JOSLIN ....Contra Costa County.
    Present address, Antioch.
 Substituted four months in Contra Costa County, and five weeks in Calistoga, Napa County; taught at San Ramon, Contra Costa County, one year.

OLIVE M. KNOX............................Santa Clara County.
     Present address, San José.
 Taught one term in Monterey County. Since January, 1888, has taught in the Hester School, **San José.**

THEODORE T. KOENIG.......................**Santa Clara County.**
     Present address, San José.
 Taught in **Santa Clara County, three months;** at Hopetown, Merced County, one year; as **Principal of school at Fort** Bidwell, **Modoc** County, one term. Attending **Cooper Medical College, San** Francisco.

ALICE M. LASATER.........................Washington Territory.
     Present address, Walla Walla.
 Taught two years in Humboldt County. Teaching near Table Bluff.

ELLA M. LEARNED..........................San Joaquin County.
     Present address, Stockton.
 Taught one and one half years in San Benito County; **five months in San Joaquin** County. Teaching.

EDITH LEIMBACH...........................Sacramento County.
     Present address, **Sacramento.**
 Has taught one year in Sacramento **County.**

MABEL M. LEIMBACH........................Sacramento County.
     Present address, Sacramento.
 Teaching second **year at** Michigan Bar, Sacramento County.

SOPHIE E. LITCHFIELD.....................Sonoma County.
     Present address, Sebastopol.
 At last report, October, 1887, was Principal of the school at Sebastopol.

KITTY C. MACGOWAN........................San Francisco.
     Present address, 131 Post Street, San Francisco.
 Has taught one year in Humboldt County, and is teaching **near Arcata.** **Work suspended one** term, spent in Honolulu.

HELEN C. MACKENZIE.......................San Francisco.
     Present address, San Diego.
 Has **taught** continuously **in** San Diego **since August, 1887.**

CARA J. MANUEL...........................Calaveras County.
     Present address, Murphy's.
 No report since **graduation.**

FANNIE L. MATSON.........................Iowa.
     Present address, San José.
 Is the inventor of a language and number frame for use in schools. Upon the preparation and introduction of this she has spent her time **since** graduation, and **therefore has not taught regularly.**

ANNIE F. McCAULEY..........................Contra Costa County.
     Present address, Danville.
  Teaching second year near Antioch, Contra Costa County.

AMELIA G. McKAY............................Santa Clara County.
     Present address, San Diego.
  Taught one year in Placer County; since spring of 1888 has taught in San Diego County.

BELLE McMULLIN..............................Stanislaus County.
     Present address, Modesto.
  Has taught since January, 1888, near Modesto.

JENNIE A. McWILLIAMS........................Solano County.
     Present address, Vallejo.
  Taught three months in San Diego, and one term in Solano County.

LIZZIE M. MORRELL (Mrs. H. D. Norton)......Santa Clara County.
     Present address, Wrights.
  Taught one year in Ventura County. Married September 19, 1888. Not taught since.

EDITH H. NICHOLS............................Santa Clara County.
     Present address, Pacific Grove, Monterey County.
  Taught one year in Monterey County, near Soledad. Teaching.

WILLIS H. PARKER............................Santa Cruz County.
     Present address, Lompoc, Santa Barbara County.
  Taught in Santa Barbara County, four months; in Los Angeles County, one and one half years. Teaching at McPherson, Los Angeles County.

ANNIE PENNYCOOK.............................Solano County.
     Present address, Vallejo.
  Has taught continuously since graduation in Vallejo.

SARAH M. PINKHAM............................San Mateo County.
     Present address, Pescadero.
  Taught one year in Monterey County.

NELLIE RICKARD..............................Santa Clara County.
     Present address, Los Gatos.
  Taught fall term of 1887 in Monterey County. Since January, 1888, has taught in Santa Clara County. Teaching in Los Gatos.

LORA SCUDAMORE..............................Lake County.
     Present address, Lakeport.
  Has taught continuously in Lake County since graduation.

LIZZIE SINCLAIR.............................Alameda County.
     Present address, Warm Springs.
  Teaching since September, 1888, near Salmon Falls, El Dorado County

JENNIE SNOOK (Mrs. O. M. Tupper)............Alameda County.
      Present address, San José.
  Taught in Santa Clara County, two months; in Alameda County, eight months. Married October 17, 1888. Not teaching.

HILDA C. SODERSTROM.........................Santa Clara County.
      Present address, San José.
  Taught one year in Santa Clara County. Teaching, since August, 1888, in San Luis Obispo.

CORA SOMERS...................................Placer County.
      Present address, Newcastle.
  Is teaching second year in Placer County.

MAGGIE L. STENGER............................Nevada County.
      Present address, Nevada City.
  Has taught in Nevada County continuously since graduation.

WILLIAM E. TEBBE..............................Butte County.
      Present address, Yankee Hill.
  Taught one year in Butte County; one year in Siskiyou County. Teaching at Etna, Siskiyou County.

NEELIE G. VAN HEUSEN..........................Butte County.
      Present address, Chico.
  Taught during fall term of 1887 near Oroville. Spent several months in the Eastern States. Has been teaching since September, 1888, in Chico.

EMMA VON DORSTEN..............................Santa Clara County.
      Present address, San José.
  Teaching second year in Primary Department of Hamilton District, Santa Clara County.

LUTE L. WALLACE (Mrs. J. W. Carpenter)....Stanislaus County.
      Present address, Ceres.
  Has taught two terms near Ceres.

BERTIE WECK...................................San Francisco.
      Present address, 2107 Howard Street, San Francisco.
  Taught in Fresno County, six months; in the Fruit Vale school, Alameda County, one term. Teaching in Monterey County.

EMILY E. WILLIAMS.............................Santa Clara County.
      Present address, San José.
  Has taught continuously since graduation in Midway District, Santa Clara County.

DAVID A. WILSON...............................Butte County.
      Present address, Cherokee.
  At last report, October, 1887, was Principal of the school at Cherokee.

THIRTY-THIRD CLASS—DECEMBER, 1887

CORA L. ANGELL............................State of Nevada.
    Home address, Silver City.
 Taught one term at Aurora, Nevada; one term at Silver City. Teaching in Reno.

ADA S. BARLOW ....Santa Clara County.
    Present address, Mayfield.
 Has taught since graduation near Mountain View, Santa Clara County. Now teaching in Mountain View.

CLARA BENNETT ....Santa Clara County.
 No report since graduation.

LILLIAN BERGER............................Alameda County.
    Present address, 1454 Tenth Avenue, Oakland.
 Taught near Germantown, Colusa County, one year.

LAURA BETHELL............................Santa Clara County.
    Present address, San José.
 Has taught in the State Normal School, San José, since January, 1888.

GEORGE H. BOKE ....Butte County.
    Present address, Nelson.
 Taught two months in Modoc County. Has been Principal of the school at Newcastle, Placer County, since September, 1888.

LILLIAN E. CHURCH ....Santa Clara County.
    Present address, San José.
 Teaching in San Benito County since August, 1888.

JENNIE CHURCHILL............................Santa Clara County.
    Present address, San José.
 Teaching in Santa Clara County, since March, 1888.

MARTHA E. CILKER ....Santa Clara County.
    Present address, Los Gatos.
 Taught five months in Santa Clara County; since September, 1888, in Fresno County.

ROSE M. CLARK............................Sacramento County.
    Present address, Sacramento.
 Teaching at Franklin, Sacramento County.

MABEL S. CLARKE ....Alameda County.
    Present address, Niles.
 Has taught one year in San Luis Obispo County.

MAMIE A. COUGHLIN............................State of Nevada.
    Present address, Gold Hill.
 Taught three terms near Altamont, Alameda County. Now teaching at Bishop, Cal.

NINA COWDEN..Sierra County.
                        Present address, San José.
    Taught four months in Tulare County; seven months in San Diego County. Not teaching.

LIZZIE DAVIS...Santa Clara County.
                        Present address, San José.
    Taught one year at Jolon, Monterey County. Not teaching because of ill health.

NELLIE B. DAY..Nevada County.
                        Present address, Spokane Falls, Washington.
    Teaching since September, 1888, at Spokane Falls.

VIRGIA V. DEAL...San Francisco.
                        Present address, 2007 Bush Street, San Francisco.
    Teaching in Monterey since October, 1888.

G. MAY DE LAMATER...Santa Cruz County.
                        Present address, San José.
    Teaching in Santa Cruz since February.

WILHELMINA DENNY...Santa Clara County.
                        Present address, San José.
    Taught for a short time in Fresno County. Work suspended several months on account of sickness. Teaching in Monterey County.

KATE L. DEVLIN...Humboldt County.
                        Present address, Arcata.
    Has taught one year in Humboldt County.

ZADER ELEY...Fresno County.
                        Present address, Herndon.
    Has taught in Fresno County continuously since graduation.

D. CARTER ELLIOTT..Michigan.
                        Present address, San Francisco.
    Has not taught since graduation. Is attending Dental Department of University of California.

EMILY E. GALINGER..Humboldt County.
                        Present address, Arcata.
    Has taught in Humboldt County one and one half years. Teaching.

CHARLOTTE Z. GLEASON.....................................Alameda County.
                        Present address, San Leandro.
    Taught one year in Alameda County. Teaching.

JAMES W. GRAHAM..Tulare County.
                        Present address, Yokohl.
    Teaching near Yokohl since September, 1888.

IDA GRAY -- Yuba County.
              Present address, Marysville.
    Taught **one term in Sutter County;** one year near Marysville. Teaching near Nicolaus, **Sutter County.**

SUSIE H. HARVEY ----------------------------- Alameda County.
              Present address, Alvarado.
    Has taught in Alvarado school since January, 1888.

MARY E. HEALEY ------------------------------ Santa Clara County.
              Present address, San José.
    Has taught in Hall's Valley, Santa Clara County, since January, **1888.**

MARGARET HENDERSON ------------------- Humboldt County.
              Home address, Eureka.
    Teaching third term near Newark, Alameda County.

CECELIA M. HENRY --------------------------- Contra Costa County.
              Present address, Alamo.
    Has taught continuously since graduation in Contra Costa County.

BERTRAM A. HERRINGTON ---------------- Santa **Clara** County.
              Present address, San Miguel, San Luis Obispo County.
    Taught one year. Is now a lawyer and real estate agent in San Miguel.

AMANDA HINSHAW ----------------------------- Sonoma County.
              Present address, Sebastopol.
    Is teaching third term since graduation in Pleasant Hill District, **Sonoma County. Taught the** same school for three years before **entering the Normal School.**

HATTIE E. ISBISTER ---------------------------- Nevada County.
              Present address, Sweetland.
    Taught one year in Placer County. Teaching.

MINNIE R. JOSLIN ------------------------------- Contra Costa County.
              Present address, **Antioch.**
    Has not taught since graduation.

LAURA B. KEEL (Mrs. Martin F. Hauck) ---- Santa Cruz County.
              Present address, San José.
    Taught four months in Alviso, Santa Clara County, and **three weeks in** the Normal School as substitute. Married April, 1889.

MAMIE C. KELLY ------------------------------- Santa Clara County.
              Present address, San José.
    Has taught near Fresno City continuously since graduation.

MAY E. KENNEDY ------------------------------ San Francisco.
              Present address, 110 Haight Street, **San Francisco.**
    Elected to the substitute class in the **San** Francisco School Department in August, **1888.**

LIZZIE M. LOUCKS............................Contra Costa County.
    Present address, Pacheco.
  Has taught one and one half years near Pacheco.

WILTON M. MASON............................San Joaquin County.
    Home address, Lockeford.
  Taught in **Fresno County, one term;** since July, 1888, near Galt, Sacramento County.

AMELIA E. MEYER............................Nevada County.
    Present address, Cape Town, Humboldt County.
  Has taught one year in Fresno County. Is teaching at Cape Town.

MATTIE C. MORRISON............................Santa Clara County.
    Present address, San José.
  Teaching third term near Los Gatos, Santa Clara County.

KATIE L. MULLEN............................Plumas County.
    Present address, La Porte.
  Teaching at La Porte since **February, 1888.**

MARY S. MURPHY............................Placer County.
    Present address, Iowa Hill.
  Taught in Placer County, one term. Since January, 1889, has taught in Los Angeles.

JENNIE A. OSTROM (deceased)............................Amador County.
  Taught three months in Amador County. She was obliged to give up her work on account of sickness. An attack of brain fever, lasting for many weeks, was followed by quick consumption, which caused her death December 1, 1888.

KATE OVERACKER............................Alameda County.
    Present address, **Centerville.**
  Has spent her time since graduation in study. Entered the Cooper Medical College, San Francisco, in January, **1889.**

MATTIE M. PHELPS............................Yolo County.
    Present address, Red Bluff, Tehama County.
  Taught **four months** in Placer County; one **year** in Sutter County. Teaching in Colusa County.

LUCY PLUMADO............................El Dorado County.
    Present address, **Placerville.**
  Taught one year at Smith's Flat, El Dorado **County. Teaching.**

JENNIE G. POUND............................San Francisco.
    Present address, **Fowler,** Fresno County.
  Has taught at Fowler since February, 1888.

ALBERT E. SHUMATE............................Missouri.
    Present address, San José.
  Not taught since graduation.

M. KITTIE SIMS (Mrs. T. M. Stark)........San Joaquin County.
   · Present address, 322 First Street, Portland, **Oregon**.
  Married January 18, 1888. Since September, 1888, has been **teaching in**
the Primary Department of the school at Sellwood, **Oregon**.

DELIA E. SINNOTT........................Santa Clara County.
      Present address, San José.
  No report.

MARY E. SNELL.............................Shasta County.
      Present address, Cayton.
  Taught continuously since graduation in Shasta and Modoc Counties.
Teaching at Cayton.

HELEN E. SPAFFORD........................San Francisco.
    Present address, 2315 Sutter Street, San Francisco.
  On account of home duties did not teach for a **year** and a half after
graduation. Teaching near Cambria, San **Luis** Obispo County.

GERTRUDE STEANE........................Alameda County.
      Present address, Pleasanton.
  Has **taught in Alameda County** since March, **1888**. Teaching at Sunol
Glen.

AGNES STOWELL...........................Marin County.
      Present address, San Rafael.
  Taught four months in San Luis Obispo County. Has been teaching in
San Rafael since **July**, 1888.

MARY E. THURWACHTER..................Santa Cruz County.
      Present address, Watsonville.
  On account of ill **health, did not teach until July, 1888. Since that time**
has taught near Watsonville.

OLIVER WEBB ....Santa Clara County.
    Present address, National City, San Diego County.
  Taught three terms at National City. Teaching in Siskiyou County

HENRY C. WELCH........................Santa Clara County.
      Present address, San José.
  Taught four months in Santa Barbara County and four months as Principal of school at Templeton, San Luis Obispo County. Not **teaching** at
present.

MAGGIE L. WHELAN ....Alameda County.
      Present address, San Leandro.
  Substituted one term in Oakland schools, **and** taught one term in Mendocino County.

LILLIAN WILLIAMS......................Santa Clara County.
      Present address, San José.
  Has taught one year at Santa Paula, Ventura **County**.

Member of the Class of May, 1885, who made up Conditions and received her Diploma December, 1887.

ETTA A. SUMNER (Mrs. A. Kinnear) ....Santa Clara County.
        Present address, San José.
  Not taught since graduation. Married October 30, 1888.

THIRTY-FOURTH CLASS—MAY, 1888.

ADAM D. ALVAREZ........................Contra Costa County.
        Present address, Pinole.
  Taught one term in Fresno County.

EULA L. ANDERSON.......................Santa Clara County.
        Present address, San José.
  Teaching near San José.

EMILY ANDERSON ....San Francisco.
      Present address, **2661 Howard** Street, San Francisco.
  Has not **taught** since graduation.

HATTIE J. ANGIER ....Alameda County.
      Present address, Del Mar, San Diego County.
  Taught one year in Del Mar. **Teaching in San Diego.**

FREDERICK L. ARBOGAST....................Nevada County.
        Present address, Nevada City.
  Teaching since July, 1888, at Liberty Hill, Nevada County.

ARLINE L. BAILEY ....San Francisco.
      Present address, 226 Fair **Oaks** Street, San Francisco.
  Taught one term at Iowa Hill, Placer County. Teaching **at Pomona, Los Angeles County.**

BELLE BANKHEAD............................Placer County.
        Present address, Pino.
  Teaching since September, 1888, in Placer County.

ANNIE M. BERRY............................State of Nevada.
        Present address, Dayton, Nevada.
  Taught one year **at Wabuska,** Nevada. Teaching **at Dayton.**

ANNA I. BOSE..............................Santa Clara County.
        Present address, San José.
  Taught one year in Pioneer District, Santa Clara County. Now Principal of Berryessa School.

MRS. ORPAH CAMPBELL ....Santa Clara County.
        Present address, San José.
  Taught two months in California. Spent some time **studying music. Teaching in the Sandwich Islands.**

IDA A. CAMPBELL................................Solano County.
        Present address, Vallejo.
    Teaching **since** September, 1888, in Solano County.

JENNIE A. COFFMAN..............................Santa Clara County.
        Present address, San José.
    Has not taught since graduation.

ANNIE EDITH COOK...............................Santa Clara County.
    Teaching since graduation near Lidell, Napa County

WILLIAM W. COOPER..............................Alameda County.
        Present address, Haywards.
    Taught one **term in Fresno** County. Is now Principal in Alviso District, Alameda County.

RICHARD G. COTTER..............................Santa Clara County.
        Present address, San **José.**
    Taught one year in Fresno County. Teaching **in San Benito County.**

IDA M. COYLE...................................**Santa Clara County.**
        Present address, San José.
    Teaching since graduation in Fresno County.

MARY R. DALY...................................Sacramento County.
        Present address, Antelope.
    Taught one year near Antelope. Teaching.

EMMA DANIELEWICZ...............................Amador County.
        Present address, Sutter Creek.
    Teaching since **November, 1888, at Middle Fork, Amador** County.

RACHAEL M. DAVIS...............................Santa Clara County.
        Present address, Golden Gate, Alameda County.
    Teaching since July, 1888, in Bay District School, Alameda County.

CHARLES L. EDGERTON............................Del Norte County.
        Present address, Smith River.
    Teaching since July, 1888, near Crescent City.

BESSIE FOWLER..................................Sonoma County.
        Present address, Cloverdale.
    Teaching since August, 1888, in the Primary Department of the Cloverdale school.

SADIE V. GARNER................................San Benito County.
        Present address, Hollister.
    Has taught in **Bartlett District, San Benito County,** continuously since graduation.

LAWRENCE J. GEARY..............................Contra Costa County.
        Present address, Walnut Creek.
    Teaching second **term in Alamo** District, near Walnut Creek.

AGNES B. GILLESPIE........................Santa Clara County.
   Present address, San José.
  Teaching since October, 1888, at Easton, Fresno County.

STELLA M. GOSBEY (Mrs. B. D. Merchant)....Monterey County.
   Present address, Oakland.
  Taught one term in Soledad, Monterey County. Married April 24, 1889.

BERTHA M. HALL...........................Santa Clara County.
   Present address, Santa Clara.
  Teaching since graduation in Placer County.

SALLIE B. HAMPTON ....San Joaquin County.
   Present address, Spokane Falls, Washington.
  Has been prevented from teaching by illness. Expects to teach soon.

SUSIE F. HERBERT ....Santa Clara County.
   Present address, San José.
  Teaching second term in Chualar Cañon, Monterey County.

L. JENNIE JONES ....Solano County.
   Present address, Vallejo.
  Taught one year in Fresno County.

M. WINONA KAUFMAN ....Santa Clara County.
   Present address, San José.
  Taught one year in Placer County. Teaching near San Miguel.

LUCY V. KEELY............................State of Nevada.
   Present address, Virginia City, Nevada.
  Taught four months in Placer County; four months in State of Nevada. Teaching at Columbus.

MARY L. KUHLITZ ....Santa Cruz County.
   Present address, Watsonville.
  Taught four months in Monterey County. Resigned in January, 1889, on account of poor health, and is not teaching.

FRANK M. LANE............................Fresno County.
   Present address, Fresno City.
  Teaching since September, 1888, at Watts' Valley, Fresno County.

NETTIE J. LEONARD ....San Francisco.
   Present address, 819 Howard Street, San Francisco.
  Taught one year near Pleyto, Monterey County.

MALSIE V. LIVINGSTON....................San Francisco.
   Present address, San José.
  Taught one year in Jackson District, Santa Clara County. Teaching at Turlock.

Stella L. Machepert..................................Santa Clara County.
Present address, San José.
Taught four months in Santa Cruz County, in the fall of 1888. Not taught since, on account of sickness.

Ada F. Madden.......................................Idaho Territory.
Present address, Caldwell, Idaho.
Taught one year in Idaho, near Boise City.

Nellie Malloy......................................Santa Clara County.
Present address, San José.
Teaching in Lockwood school, Alameda County, since graduation.

Bert S. Martin.....................................El Dorado County.
Present address, Georgetown.
Teaching since graduation at Georgetown.

Millie F. Maxey....................................Santa Clara County.
Present address, San José.
Taught one year in Laguna District, Santa Clara County. Teaching in Berryessa school.

Bessie McAllister..................................Marin County.
Present address, San Rafael.
Taught one term near Roseville, Placer County. Teaching at Lakeview, Oregon.

Adah M. McKenney...................................State of Nevada.
Present address, San José.
Teaching second term in Santa Cruz County.

Eva M. Moody.......................................Santa Clara County.
Present address, San José.
Teaching second term in Vineland District, Santa Clara County.

Mary J. O'Rourke...................................Santa Clara County.
Present address, San José.
Teaching since August, 1888, in Mount Pleasant District, Santa Clara County.

Bessie Parker (Mrs. W. I. McCall)...................Modoc County.
Present address, Selma, Fresno County.
Taught one term at Selma, Fresno County. Gave up work on account of sickness. Married October 31, 1889.

Charlotte C. Patton................................San Francisco.
Present address, 6 Bond Street, San Francisco.
Teaching second term near Petaluma, Sonoma County.

Lillian E. Purdy...................................San Francisco.
Present address, 2114 Steiner Street, San Francisco.
Teaching second term at Big Trees, Calaveras County.

WALLACE W. REED..............................Santa Clara County.
                    Present address, San José.
    Taught six weeks and resigned because of sickness. Is now an express messenger for Wells, Fargo & Co.

CORNELIA RICHARDS..............................San Luis Obispo County
                    Present address, Cambria.
    Taught one term in San Luis Obispo County, and one term in Mono County. Teaching in Mono County.

GERTIE F. ROWELL..............................Fresno County.
                    Present address, Easton.
    Teaching since September, 1888, near Easton.

MABEL E. SHARP..............................Fresno County.
                    Present address, Madera.
    Taught one year at Firebaugh, Fresno County.

FANNIE E. SHORT..............................Nevada County.
                    Present address, Boca.
    Taught four months in Lassen County in fall of 1888. Since that time has taught in the Primary Department of the school at Reno, Nevada.

ANNIE M. SMULLEN..............................Tuolumne County.
                    Present address, Sonora.
    Taught one year in Tuolumne County.

ELLA E. STANSBURY..............................Napa County.
                    Present address, Napa City.
    Has taught in Napa County continuously since graduation.

EMMA M. STEPHENS..............................Santa Clara County.
                    Present address, San José.
    Taught one year in San Luis Obispo County. Teaching in Santa Clara County.

EMILY M. STETSON..............................Santa Cruz County.
                    Present address, Laurel.
    Taught one year in Contra Costa County, near Livermore. Teaching.

GEORGE A. TEBBE..............................Butte County.
                    Present address, Yankee Hill.
    Teaching since September, 1888, at Fort Jones, Siskiyou County.

LILLIE TUCKER..............................Del Norte County.
                    Present address, Crescent City.
    Teaching second term near Crescent City, Del Norte County.

ADDIE S. TURNER..............................San Joaquin County.
                    Present address, French Camp.
    Teaching since September, 1888, in Monterey County, near Jolon.

GRACE WARD............................Santa Clara County.
  Present address, San José.
  Teaching at Roseville, Placer County.

SADIE P. WILLARD ....Alameda County.
  Present address, 122 Eleventh Street, Oakland.
  Taught in Napa County, five months. Is substituting in the Oakland schools.

THIRTY-FIFTH CLASS—DECEMBER, 1888.

ALFRED C. ABSHIRE ....Sonoma County.
  Present address, Cloverdale.
  Teaching in Timber Cove District, Sonoma County.

HATTIE E. ALLEN......................Santa Clara County.
  Present address, San José.
  Taught one term at Bell's Station, Santa Clara County. Teaching near Madrone.

ANNIE E. ANGLON ....San Francisco.
  Home address, 629 Eddy Street, San Francisco.
  Teaching at Pino, Placer County.

NANA ANKER..........................San Francisco.
  Present address, Cloverdale, Sonoma County.
  Teaching near Adelaida, San Luis Obispo County, since March, 1889.

HADDIE A. BAGGETT...................Siskiyou County.
  Present address, Yreka.
  Teaching in Siskiyou County since March, 1889.

REBECCA BAILEY ....Alameda County.
  Present address, Livermore, Alameda County.
  Teaching at Livermore since January, 1889.

HANNAH M. BALL ....Tulare County.
  Present address, Woodville.

CLARE A. BENSON....................Santa Clara County.
  Present address, New Almaden.
  Taught one term in Santa Clara County. Teaching.

JAMES A. BLACK.....................Nevada County.
  Present address, Nevada City.
  Taught four months in Contra Costa County. Teaching at Mount Eden, Alameda County.

MAY F. BLACKFORD ....Santa Clara County.
  Present address, San José.
  Teaching second term in Monterey County.

GEORGIA L. BRADSHAW ....Santa Clara County.
                Present address, Milpitas.
    Taught four months in San Antonio Valley.

LIZZIE M. BROWNING..........................Amador County.
                Present address, Ione.
    Teaching in Placer County.

FRED. G. BRUNHOUSE.........................Santa Clara County.
                Present address, San José.
    Taught four months in San Joaquin County. Teaching in Mariposa County.

ELIZABETH B. CLIFT ....Alameda County.
                Present address, 1547 San Pablo Avenue.

JULIA C. COLBY ....Solano County.
                Present address, Benicia.

JENNIE A. CROFTON..........................Sacramento County.
                Present address, Los Gatos, Santa Clara County.
    Taught five months in Fresno County.

KATIE C. DEVINE ....Santa Clara County.
                Present address, San José.
    Teaching in the Franklin school, near San José.

EFFIE M. DEAL..............................Santa Clara County.
                Present address, San José.
    Teaching near Evergreen, Santa Clara County, since February, 1889.

CAROLYN B. DOYLE (Mrs. Irwin A. Ball) ....Lassen County.
                Present address, San José.
    Taught one term in Lassen County. Married July 3, 1889.

MELVINA J. DURHAM ....Contra Costa County.
                Present address, Pacheco.
    Teaching near Brentwood, Contra Costa County.

M. CORNETT FITZWATER ....San Luis Obispo County.
                Present address, San Luis Obispo.
    Teaching in San Luis Obispo County.

KATE J. FOLEY ....Santa Clara County.
                Present address, San José.
    Teaching second term in Monterey County.

WALTER GRAY ....Butte County.
                Present address, Chico.
    Taught four months at Lompoc, Santa Barbara County.

WILLIAM M. GREENWELL......................Butte County.
                Present address, Hansonville, Yuba County.
    Teaching at Mendocino City.

EVA F. GRIFFIN..............................Contra Costa County.
     Present address, Martinez.
  Teaching in Contra Costa County, near Martinez.

OSCAR H. GRUBBS...........................San Joaquin County.
     Present address, Lockeford.
  Taught one term near Oleta, Amador County. Teaching in Greenwood, El Dorado County.

ANNIE J. HALL (Mrs. Andrew D. Van Arsdell)..Santa Clara Co.
   Present address, Paso Robles, San Luis Obispo County.
  Not taught since graduation. Married April 18, 1889.

M. TEXANA HAWKINS..........................Fresno County.
     Present address, Fresno City.
  Taught one month in Fresno County and resigned on account of sickness.

M. SUE HICKMAN.............................Santa Clara County.
     Present address, San José.
  Teaching in San Luis Obispo County, near Paso Robles.

MARY E. HYDE...............................Santa Clara County.
     Present address, Santa Clara.
  Taught one term in San Luis Obispo County.

LILLIAN M. JULIEN..........................Siskiyou County.
     Present address, Yreka.
  Teaching in Siskiyou County.

ANNIE KOHLER...............................Napa County.
     Present address, St. Helena.
  Teaching since graduation at Independence, Inyo County.

NORA J. MARBUT.............................Santa Clara County.
     Present address, San José.
  Teaching near Adelaida, San Luis Obispo County.

NANNIE T. MATLOCK..........................Shasta County.
     Present address, San José.
  Teaching in Creston, San Luis Obispo County.

S. ELLEN McFARLAND.........................Alameda County.
   Present address, 559 Simpson Avenue, Oakland.
  Taught at Mission San José, Alameda County, one term. Teaching at Mount Eden.

M. GRACE McLELLAN..........................San Mateo County.
     Present address, San Mateo.
  Not taught since graduation.

FLORENCE E. McPHERSON......................Santa Clara County.
     Present address, San José.
  Teaching in San José.

WILLIAM H. MURRAY ....San Joaquin County.
   Present address, Lockeford.

ETTA E. NICHOLS ....Nevada County.
   Present address, Grass Valley.
 Teaching second term near Cambria, San Luis Obispo County.

EFFIE OWENS..............................Sacramento County.
   Present address, San José.
 Teaching in Kern County since January, 1889.

PAULINE M. PAGE..........................Santa Clara County.
   Present address, San José.
 Taught one term in Fresno County.

ALLURA B. PARKER ....Santa Clara County.
   Present address, Monterey.
 Teaching in Monterey since January, 1889.

EMMA L. PATTON..............................Monterey County.
   Present address, Natividad.
 Taught one term at Natividad.

LEONORA E. PHILLIPS..........................Merced County.
   Present address, Central Point.
 Teaching in Merced County.

ADELAIDE L. POLLOCK ....San Francisco.
   Present address, Seattle, Washington.
 Teaching at Seattle.

LAWRENCE F. PUTER..........................Humboldt County.
   Present address, Eureka.
 Teaching in Eureka.

ODA REDMAN..............................Santa Cruz County.
   Present address, Watsonville.
 Teaching in Santa Cruz County.

ANNIE L. REMMEL............................Alameda County.
   Present address, Alameda.
 Teaching in Contra Costa County.

DOLLIE E. ROCKEFELLOW....................Contra Costa County.
   Present address, 326 Larkin Street, San Francisco.
 Teaching Lockwood school, Alameda County, since February, 1889.

ANTHONY ROSE.............................Alameda County.
   Present address, Newark.
 Teaching at Newark.

LELLA SANFORD............................Contra Costa County.
    Present address, Martinez.
  Taught in Contra Costa County one term. Teaching.

J. FRANCES SCHULTZBERG ....Santa Clara County.
    Present address, San José.
  Taught five months in Aurora, Nevada.

FLORA B. SMITH...........................Santa Cruz County.
    Present address, Santa Cruz.
  Teaching in San Luis Obispo County.

EDITH S. SMOOTE..........................Sacramento County.
    Present address, Elk Grove.
  Taught one term in Fresno County. Teaching.

ANNA M. TALMADGE.........................Sacramento County.
    Present address, Courtland.
  Not taught since graduation.

GEORGE G. TAYLOR ....Butte County.
  Present address, 53 Flood Building, San Francisco.
  Taught a few weeks as **substitute.** Is now agent for the Educational Company, San Francisco.

DELLA VANDERVORST ....Santa Clara County.
    Present address, San José.
  Teaching in Fresno County.

MAUDE L. WELCH ....Santa Clara County.
    Present address, San José.
  Teaching in Santa Clara County.

THIRTY-SIXTH CLASS—JUNE, 1889.

NOTE.—The names **starred are** the names of those who are known to have **engaged in** teaching before the time when this History goes to print.

KARA F. ALLEN ....Santa Clara County.
    Present address, Santa Clara.

*GRACE L. ANDERSON.......................Santa Clara County.
    Present address, San José.

*WILLIAM R. BANKHEAD ....Placer County.
    Present address, Pino.

*LUCY A. BARRETT ....Placer County.
    Present address, Roseville.

*Franklin K. Barthel _____ Santa Clara County.
  Present address, San José.

Katie C. Bellew_____ Santa Clara County.
  Present address, Milpitas.

*Julia L. Bellingall _____ Santa Clara County.
  Present address, San José.

*Mariana Bertola _____ Contra Costa County.
  Present address, Martinez.

*Esther A. Brown _____ Santa Clara County.
  Present address, San José.

*Mary C. Carr _____ Santa Clara County.
  Present address, San José.

*Jennie A. Cilker_____ Santa Clara County.
  Present address, Los Gatos.

*Gertrude Connell _____ San Bernardino County.
  Present address, Riverside.

*George Cosgrave _____ Calaveras County.
  Present address, Angels Camp.

*Amy A. Davis_____ Santa Clara County.
  Present address, San José.

Jessie N. De Lamater _____ Santa Cruz County.
  Present address, Santa Cruz.

*Ella Jean Dimon _____ El Dorado County.
  Present address, Placerville.

Alice H. Dougherty _____ Alameda County.
  Present address, Livermore.

*Fannie A. Fowler_____ Santa Clara County.
  Present address, Santa Clara.

*Mamie A. Gafney _____ Santa Clara County.
  Present address, San José.

*Theresa V. Gargan _____ San Mateo County.
  Present address, Halfmoon Bay

*Mary A. Gee _____ Solano County.
  Present address, Vallejo.

M. EDITH GRISWOLD..............................Santa Clara County.
    Present address, San José.

*M. FRANCES HARTE..............................Santa Clara County.
    Present address, San José.

*GERTRUDE I. HAYES..............................Alameda County.
    Present address, Livermore.

ELLA C. HEINTZ..............................**Sacramento County.**
    Present address, Sacramento.

*BELLE F. HIGGINS..............................Napa County.
    Present address, Napa City.

*M. GENEVIEVE HOLDEN..............................Napa County.
    Present address, Napa City.

S. MARION HOWELL..............................**Santa Clara County.**
    Present address, San José.

*ANNIE HUGHES..............................Nevada County.
    Present address, Nevada City.

HELENA L. JAEGER..............................Santa Clara County.
    Present address, San José.

*OLLIE JARVIS..............................**Alameda County.**
    Present address, Newark.

*MAGGIE JONES..............................**Santa Clara County.**
    Present address, San José.

*JOHN G. JURY..............................Santa Clara County.
    Present address, San José.

*MOLLIE J. KELLER..............................Nevada County.
    Present address, Nevada City.

LEOLINE C. LADD..............................Santa Clara County.
    Present address, Gilroy.

CARRIE E. LEE..............................Santa Clara **County.**
    Present address, San José.

*ANNA L. LELAND..............................Siskiyou County.
    Present address, Dunsmuir.

*ADDIE M. LUCY..............................Solano County.
    Present address, Vallejo.

*Minnie L. Mackay ....Santa Clara County.
               Present address, San José.

*Lizzie MacKinnon ....Alameda County.
               Present address, Oakland.

*R. Jennie Mangrum ....Santa Clara County.
               Present address, San José.

*Clara A. March ....Yolo County.
               Present address, Yolo.

*Emma T. Martin ....San Francisco County.
               Present address, San Francisco.

*Alice M. McJunkin ....Santa Clara County.
               Present address, San José.

*A. Bronson McKean...................Santa Clara County
               Present address, San José.

Lulu Miles ....Santa Clara County.
               Present address, San José.

*Mary Mutschlechner......................Sonoma County.
               Present address, Cloverdale.

*Emnie H. Nichols ....Monterey County.
               Present address, Pacific Grove.

*Margaret M. O'Donnell.....................Nevada County.
               Present address, Nevada City.

*Mabel Patterson ....Santa Clara County.
               Present address, San José.

*Mary H. Post ....Santa Clara County.
               Present address, Santa Clara.

*Mattie A. Powell ....Yolo County.
               Present address, Yolo.

*Lilian E. Purinton....................Santa Clara County.
               Present address, San José.

*Adeline Ross...........................Alameda County.
               Present address, Newark.

Ida M. Rounds...........................Solano County.
               Present address, Vallejo.

*Mary Rumrill..................................Contra Costa County.
        Present address, San Pablo.

*Sadie C. Ryan..................................Alameda County.
        Present address, Oakland.

*Fannie R. Schallenberger..............Santa Clara County.
        Present address, San José.

Jennie R. Sherman............................State of Nevada.
        Present address, Reno.

*Edward D. Spinks..............................Merced County.
        Present address, Athlone.

*Alida G. Spring............................Sacramento County.
        Present address, Elk Grove.

*George M. Steele......................San Luis Obispo County.
        Present address, San Miguel.

*Mary E. Sullivan..........................Santa Clara County.
        Present address, San José.

*Blanche Tarr....................................Amador County.
        Present address, Volcano.

*Georgia Thatcher.........................Mendocino County.
        Present address, Hopland.

*Nettie C. Theisen............................El Dorado County.
        Present address, Placerville.

*Laura L. Thomas..........................Santa Clara County.
        Present address, San José.

*Mary L. Tinsley................................Trinity County.
        Present address, Weaverville.

*Lilian E. Westfall........................Monterey County.
        Present address, Pacific Grove.

*Tenah E. Wheeler......................San Francisco County.
        Present address, San Francisco.

*Annie L. Wissman........................Santa Clara County.
        Present address, San José.

PROSPECTUS OF STATE NORMAL SCHOOL AT SAN JOSE, FOR 1889-90.

CALENDAR FOR 1889-90.

FIRST TERM.

Entrance examinations, August 30 and 31, 1889.
Term opens September 3, 1889, and closes January 31, 1890.
Holiday vacation, December 21, 1889, to January 6, 1890, both inclusive.

SECOND TERM.

Entrance examination, February 3, 1890.
Term opens February 4, 1890; closes June 27, 1890.
Mid-term vacation, April 12 to April 21, 1890, both inclusive.
Alumni Association and reunion, Friday evening, June 27, 1890.

FACULTY.

C. W. CHILDS..............................Principal and Teacher of Pedagogy.
GEORGE R. KLEEBERGER...
..................Vice-Principal and Teacher of Chemistry and Geology.
Mrs. LIZZIE P. WILSON..
...............Principal of Training Department and Critic Teacher.
MARY J. TITUS.....................Preceptress and Teacher of Pedagogy.
A. H. RANDALL...Physics and Mathematics.
R. S. HOLWAY..Physics and Mathematics.
VOLNEY RATTAN.................... ....Botany and Geography.
LUCY M. WASHBURN................................Physiology and Zoölogy.
CORNELIA WALKER.........Literature, Pedagogy, Grammar, and Reading.
GLORA F. BENNETT....................Literature, Grammar, and Reading.
NETTIE C. DANIELS..........................Grammar and Word Analysis.
Mrs. J. N. HUGHES..................................History and Botany.
LAURA BETHELL................ ....Mathematics and Grammar.
GERHARD SCHOOF...Drawing.
FANNIE M. ESTABROOK...Reading.
J. H. ELWOOD..Teacher of Music.
RUTH ROYCE ....Librarian.
KATE COZZENS...........................Teacher in Training Department.
MAMIE P. ADAMS..........................Teacher in Training Department.
MARGARET E. SCHALLENBERGER....Teacher in Training Department.
NANNIE C. GILDAY ... .Teacher in Training Department.
JOHN P. NAAS.........................Instructor in Manual Training.
Mrs. A. E. BUSH ....Curator of Museum.

www.ingramcontent.com/pod-product-compliance
Lightning Source LLC
Chambersburg PA
CBHW032104220426
43664CB00008B/1124